THE TREES
OF
NORTH AMERICA
Alan Mitchell
Illustrated by David More

THUNDER BAY
P·R·E·S·S
San Diego, California

THUNDER BAY
P · R · E · S · S

Thunder Bay Press
An imprint of the Advantage Publishers Group
5880 Oberlin Drive, San Diego, CA 92121-4794
www.thunderbaybooks.com

First edition published in USA in 1987 by
Collins and Brown Limited
64 Brewery Road, London N7 9NT
This revised edition published in 2002

A member of **Chrysalis** Books plc

ISBN 1-57145-877-8

Library of Congress Cataloging-in-Publication Data available upon request.

Printed in Singapore

1 2 3 4 5 06 05 04 03 02

Designer: Julian Holland
Illustrations: David More
Line drawings: Nicholas Hall

KEY TO ABBREVIATIONS OF STATES

Alabama	AL	Maine	ME	Ohio	OH
Alaska	AK	Manitoba	MB	Oklahoma	OK
Alberta	AB	Maryland	MD	Ontario	ON
Arizona	AZ	Massachusetts	MA	Oregon	OR
Arkansas	AR	Michigan	MI	Pennsylvania	PA
British Columbia	BC	Minnesota	MN	Province of Quebec	PQ
California	CA	Mississippi	MS	Puerto Rico	PR
Colorado	CO	Missouri	MO	Rhode Island	RI
Connecticut	CT	Montana	MT	Saskatchewan	SK
Delaware	DE	Nebraska	NE	South Carolina	SC
District of Columbia	DC	Nevada	NV	South Dakota	SD
Florida	FL	New Brunswick	NB	Tennessee	TN
Georgia	GA	Newfoundland	NF	Texas	TX
Hawaii	HI	New Hampshire	NH	Utah	UT
Idaho	ID	New Jersey	NJ	Vermont	VT
Illinois	IL	New Mexico	NM	Virginia	VA
Indiana	IN	New York	NY	Washington	WA
Iowa	IA	North Carolina	NC	West Virginia	WV
Kansas	KS	North Dakota	ND	Wisconsin	WI
Kentucky	KY	Northwest Territories	NWT	Wyoming	WY
Louisiana	LA	Nova Scotia	NS		

Islands belonging to the U.S.

American Samoa	AS
Caroline Island	TT
Guam	GU
Mariana Islands	TT
Marshall Islands	TT

CONTENTS

Introduction

North America has an enormous wealth of tree species from all the temperate parts of the world. The trees chosen for this book include all the common and frequently seen trees and a wide selection of uncommon, rare and extremely rare kinds. The very rare trees are chosen on the basis of particular interest or beauty and those in which one specimen is prominent or likely to be easily found in a major tree collection. All the important cultivars grown long enough to be of reasonable size are included.

Nearly 500 species are illustrated together with 250 varieties. Trees are shown in typical landscapes along with much crucial detail of bark, flowers, fruit and shoots which assist in the identification of even uncommon variants and rare species.

The text compliments David More's detailed drawings—it does not enlarge on the shapes or colors shown in the plates; instead it covers in great detail the origin, history, distribution and growth. Where a seasonal color of leaf or fruit is not shown, it will, if of value for identification, be mentioned, and similarly the dimensions of leaves and fruit may be given. The main emphasis is on the introduction, location and size of some of the best specimens, together with features of particular interest in botany and growth. Up-to-date dimensions of many giant and rare specimens are included.

Names are given without a capital initial when referring to a group like oaks, eucalyptus or maples and with capital initials for the first word of species, as Sessile oak and Blue gum and for one-word species like Katsura and Medlar.

Finally, a practical reference section gives invaluable advice on the choice and cultivation of trees. It also contains maps showing where tree species are most likely to be found in their natural environment.

BROADLEAVED TREES

Black and other Willows

The Willows form the largest group of woody plants native to North America with at least 90 species and 50 hybrids and 300–400 worldwide. They also raise the most problems, after the thorns, as to which are full species, which are varieties or hybrids and which are too shrubby to warrant inclusion in a book on trees. In this book, only well marked species will be included and only those which can exceed 30ft on a single stem are regarded as trees. Willow species are all dioecious, that is each tree is either wholly male or wholly female. This rule is broken only in a few hybrid weeping willows. The flower catkins open in most species well before the leaves unfold, but an exception is the Shining willow in which they open well after the tree is in full leaf. The seeds bear a tuft of fluffy white hairs and are carried far in the wind. All the tree-form willows grow very fast even if for only a few years in the smaller species, and some can grow to 80ft in 15 years. Most of the large-growing species can be raised easily from cuttings. For rapid growth into sturdy plants, these must be cut back to the ground at the start of the second season, and a single shoot selected from the two or three which may grow up. The willows are in the same family as the poplars but while all poplars are wind-pollinated, the willows are pollinated by insects and the flowers secrete nectar to attract them. Many are good, early bee-plants. In the *National Register of Big Trees*, 1978 edition, 11 out of the 18 species growing in the eastern states have champion trees in Michigan and 10 of the 14 in the west are in Oregon. However, this probably owes more to the presence of a champion-hunter than favourable growth conditions.

BLACK WILLOW (1), *Salix nigra* is generally the biggest and most frequently seen willow from NB, south of the Great Lakes to WI south to TX and northern FL. In a form sometimes distinguished as Goodding willow with rather smaller, duller leaves, it extends through UT and NV to northern CA. Along the coastal plain from VA to AL and MS and particularly around Dismal Swamp, VA, the Black willow is abundant in roadside swamps standing behind the fringing belt of the lower, yellow-green Coastal Plain willow, its dark-barked stems visible through the light foliage of this smaller willow and its open crown towering above it. In such places and by riversides in TX, AR and OK it is commonly 50ft and more tall and has been reported to have reached 120ft. Only the introduced White and (very rare) Crack willows can also exceed 100ft but the Peachleaf is locally about as big as the ordinary countryside Black. The bark of young Black willows has coarse, overlapping plates of pink-gray. On older trees the dark bark comes away in strips. Single stems are less seen than groups of three or four sprouting from a common base. The leaves are 4–6in long and the longer ones are often curved, more green and less glaucous gray beneath than in the Peachleaf.

PEACHLEAF WILLOW (2), *Salix amygdaloides*, also called the Almond willow, is native over an extensive area in the middle of the sub-continent from MI to AB, and eastern OR, CO and OH with outliers along the St. Lawrence River to the southeastern corner of PQ and into TX. It is common beside creeks in the Prairie States and is the biggest growing willow to the west of them. Its bark can be nearly as dark as that of the Black willow, but is often gray-brown, sometimes tinged red. The leaf, narrowing to its apex, is glaucous, gray-green beneath. Again, single stems are unusual and two to three often spring from the same base.

PACIFIC WILLOW (3), *Salix lasiandra* grows from central AK to southern CA and east to SK and the Black Hills, SD and can be a tree of over 60ft or low and bushy.

SANDBAR WILLOW (4), *Salix exigua* ranges almost everywhere in several scarcely distinguishable forms, from mid AK and PQ to LA and is shrubby in most parts.

BONPLAND WILLOW (5), *Salix bonplandiana* seldom achieves 30ft, growing by streams from UT and NV through CA into AZ. Its 6–7in long leaves are silvered beneath.

EUROPEAN WHITE WILLOW (6), *Salix alba*, naturalised here and there over a wide area from ON to GA, is seen as a big tree mostly in parks. The tall crown is pointed until height growth ceases and the small, 3in leaves hang in unusually dense masses. They are distinctively blue-gray. An enormous tree, over 100ft tall and 21ft round the trunk, is (or has been) on the campus at Smith College, Northampton MA.

bark   bark   **5 Bonpland willow**   **2 Peachleaf willow**

3 Pacific willow   **4 Sandbar willow**

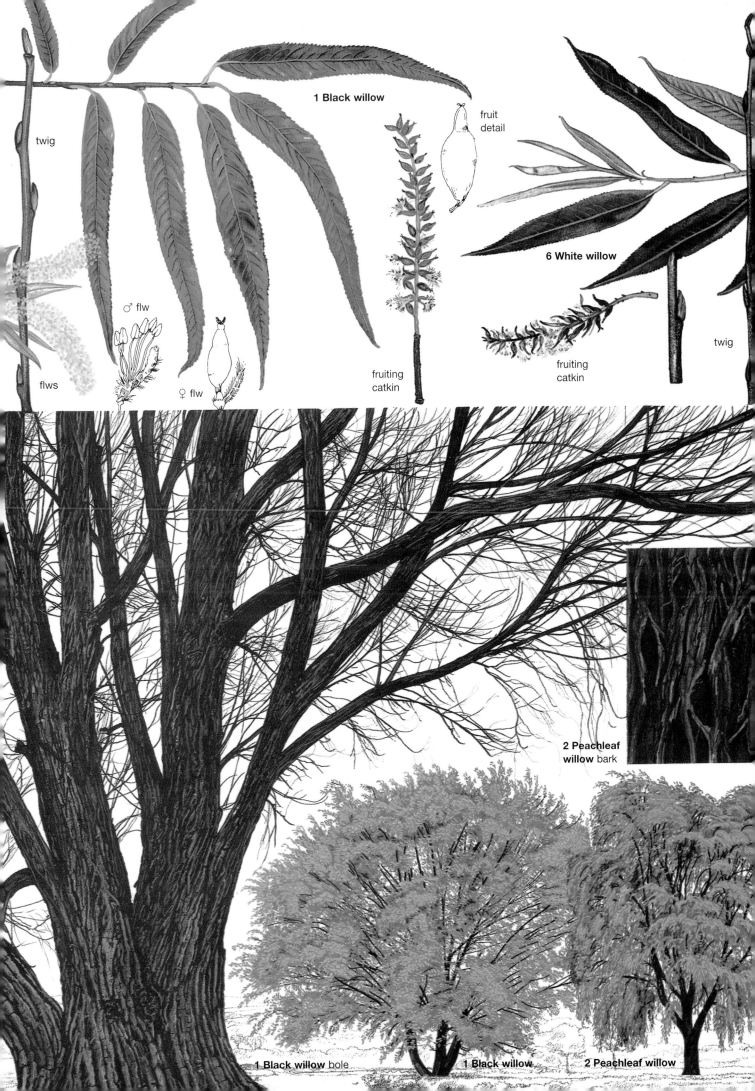

1 Black willow

twig

flws

♂ flw

♀ flw

fruit
detail

fruiting
catkin

6 White willow

twig

fruiting
catkin

**2 Peachleaf
willow** bark

1 **Black willow** bole

1 **Black willow**

2 **Peachleaf willow**

Weeping and other Willows

SHINING WILLOW (1), *Salix lucida* earns the name with its highly glossy shoot and good shining leaves. It is a very hardy, tough tree growing about as far north as any, from Labrador across northern ON, and MB and eastern SK to the Black Hills, SD, northern IA through OH and PA to NJ with small outliers in WV, VA, MD and DE.

COASTAL PLAIN WILLOW (2), *Salix caroliniana* is a bushy plant across the great expanse of the Coastal Plain from VA to TX where the roads are like low causeways with a ditch or swamp each side. From Dismal Swamp, VA to the Delta, LA this is often the main component of the scrub nearest the ditch, in a broad band in front of the much taller Black willows. In the summer it is a distinctive yellow-green with slender leaves slightly curved, to nearly 4in long, somewhat blue-gray beneath and on hairy, ½in stalks. The tree grows beyond the Coastal Plain up the Mississippi Valley into OK, KS and MO and east to southern PA.

MACKENZIE WILLOW, *Salix mackenzieana* grows in the west in roadside ditches and swamps from Yukon to Vancouver Island, BC and WA to the Sierra Nevada, CA and inland to SK, WY and UT. It has shorter, broader leaves than the Coastal plain willow and is outstanding for the reddish new shoots, which turn shining yellow and then the next year shine out orange in the winter and spring. It is notable by Togwatee Pass to Lander, WY; Livingstone-Missoula, MT; around Cour d'Alene, ID and in the Okanagan Valley, BC. A smaller form with yellow leaves is in small gardens from MT to BC.

BABYLON WILLOW (3), *Salix babylonica* is the Weeping willow of the southern states, a Chinese tree taken along trade-routes to the Levant in ancient times. American nurseries acquired plants thus adapted to hot climates and more tender than the Chinese trees. The shoots are pale yellow-green turning olive-brown by winter and hang in slightly longer, more slender and darker-leafed sprays than in the hardy hybrid, and the trees are usually female only. This is the preferred weeping willow where it can be grown, from Philadelphia, PA and Washington, DC where it is common, along the Coastal Plain to TX and north to KS and MO. It is scarce in the west but is seen in Blanding, UT, Las Vegas, NV, Flagstaff, AZ and at Victorville, CA.

The **Ringleaf willow, 'Crispa' ('Annularis')** is a smaller, slender tree hardly weeping at all but with pale grayish green leaves curled close to the shoot and showing whitish undersides. It is grown in the Arnold Arboretum and at Smith College, Northampton, MA; in Brooklyn Botanic Garden, NY and in the Dawes, Holden and Mount Airy Arboreta in OH. In the west, it is 5ft 6in round in Denny Blaine Park, Seattle, 40ft x 7ft in Point Defiance Park, Tacoma, WA, and 40ft x 6ft in the Strybing Arboretum, CA.

GOLDEN WEEPING WILLOW (4), *Salix × chrysocoma* is probably of French origin. Its shoots become bright yellow as spring approaches; it leafs out early, stays green late into the fall, has softly fine-haired leaf undersides, and is largely male but often has some female flowers. In general it is a larger tree and taller than the Babylon, brighter, fresher green in leaf. It is very common in and around towns and by farmhouses across southern Canada and the northern USA with big trees in OH and particularly in MI. Here one in the Beal Garfield Gardens, East Lansing was 88ft x 12ft 8in in 1978 and one in Hidden Garden, Tappen was 88ft x 12ft 6in. Big trees are also frequent in Upper NY where in Washington Park, Albany one is 75ft x 11ft and ON where one in Ottawa Botanic Garden was 62ft x 12ft in 1976. This tree is common in CO and frequent in WY and MT, common in ID but small and not thriving. It improves greatly as one crosses into BC where there are many big trees. One in Penticton was 87ft x 13ft 1in in 1977 and there are many on Vancouver Island and around Vancouver City and into WA.

DRAGON'S CLAW WILLOW (5), *Salix matsudana* 'Tortuosa' is a cultivar of the Babylon willow, if the Pekin Willow, *S. matsudana* is the same as *S. babylonica* as is now thought probable. It grows very fast from cuttings and these are made from the youngest, most curly shoots, but as the stem thickens it straightens out the curves. It leafs out early and stays green late, often into December. It is grown in small numbers from ON to AL and IN in the east but in the west only from WA north into BC and commonly around Seattle – about three trees per mile in some suburbs. In Queen Victoria Park, Niagara Falls it was 52ft x 6ft and at the School of Horticulture there it was 66ft x 8ft 4in in 1976. Smith College, Northampton, MA had one 56ft x 9ft 1in and 50ft trees are at Mohonk Mountain, the Bailey Arboretum and Planting Fields, NY. At the Holden Arboretum, OH it was 52ft x 8ft 8in and others are in the Dawes, Spring Grove Cemetery, Cincinnati and in Jacksontown. In AL it is in Bellingrath Garden and in IL at the Morton Arboretum.

BASKET WILLOW (6), *Salix viminalis* is a European osier grown in swampy places and cut to the ground annually to yield flexible shoots for making baskets. It is naturalised from PQ to New England.

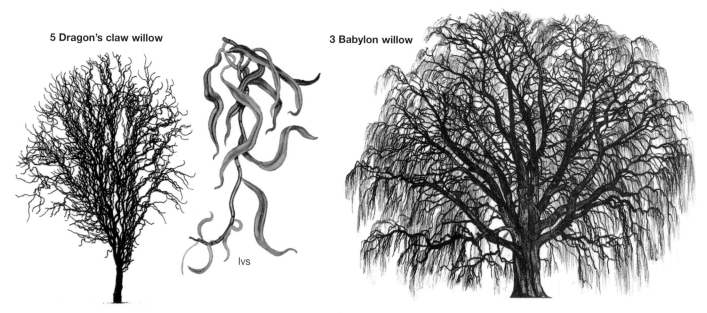

5 Dragon's claw willow

lvs

3 Babylon willow

3 Babylon willow

6 Basket willow

5 Dragon's claw willow

twig

♂ flws

4 Golden weeping willow

2 Coastal plain willow

4 Golden weeping willow spring

fruit

1 Shining willow

6 Basket willow

4 Golden weeping willow summer

Aspens and White poplars

The poplars on this page belong to one of the four groups into which the genus *Populus* is divided, the White poplars. This includes the aspens, White and Gray poplars. They have a different sort of bark from that of the other groups, young shoots and branches being very smooth, gray or green, soon developing lines of small, diamond-shaped black pits. Then the bark becomes paler and at maturity it is partly or wholly white, often very strikingly so in the American aspens; in large, pitted areas among roughened black areas in the White poplars. The White poplars are Old World species distinguished from the aspens by their new shoots and leaves emerging covered in short, dense, white woolly hair which remains through the season on the underside of the leaves and to some degree on the shoots. In the White poplars, the shape of the leaf differs much according to the vigor of the shoot bearing it and a strong young shoot will have some quite deeply lobed leaves. Aspens have finely or coarsely toothed leaves of the same shape on all the shoots. The leaf-stalk on White poplars is not markedly flattened, but those of the aspens are very much flattened, a feature which is the cause of the leaves fluttering in the lightest breeze.

Both White poplars and aspens grow numerous and often widespread suckers from their root-systems, the most usual means of their local spread. Unlike the other groups of poplars, this group is generally difficult to raise from cuttings, except the White poplar itself, and the trees are best increased either by lifting rooted suckers or by sowing seed. This must be fresh, just ripened seed and sown at once, when it will germinate within a day or two. The catkin scales in this group are fringed with long white or pale brown hairs which give the opening flowers a fluffy appearance. The flowers enlarge very early in the year, becoming brownish purple or gray somewhat curved catkins and await a warmer spell when spring really starts, before expanding fully and shedding pollen. Pollination is entirely by wind, so the flowers open while the trees are still leafless. All in this group can display bright yellow colors in the fall, but the aspens are brighter and more reliable than the others.

QUAKING ASPEN (1), *Populus tremuloides* is also called the Trembling aspen, the Golden aspen or Golden trembling aspen, Mountain aspen and Trembling poplar. The pre-occupation with quaking and trembling comes from the way that even the smallest breeze will make the leaves flutter, often audibly, caused by the slender leaf-stalks being strongly flattened. The tree has a remarkably extensive range, across the north of the continent in a broad belt from NF to DE in the east, to the coast of AK and near the coast of BC in the west, and southwards through most of the ranges of the Rocky Mountains. Although it does not grow south of a line from VA to KS it has the widest distribution of any tree in North America. Roadside thickets of remarkable density are familiar features in many areas like Lake Champlain, VT to Montreal and London to Toronto, ON regions; from Madison to Minneapolis WI–MN; by the Icefield Parkway, AB; Butte to Missoula, MT; the Grand Tetons National Park, WY and, with notably brilliantly white bark, in the Poudra River valley and Cameron Pass, CO and in the mountains north of Flagstaff, AZ. These stands become a spectacular brilliant gold in the fall.

BIGTOOTH ASPEN (2), *Populus grandidentata* is restricted to the east, from NS to NC, west to just inside ND and southward to MO. It is more scattered in woodland than in big thickets but is common by roadsides in the middle parts of its range, notably in DE, PA and WI. Its foliage is more luxuriant than that of the Quaking aspen, with firm, substantial bright green leaves. These are commonly 3 x 3in but can be 6 x 5in.

WHITE POPLAR (3), *Populus alba* is an Old World tree introduced a long time ago. It ranges from North Africa through southern Europe to Central Asia and the Himalayas. It does not grow large but tends to lean and bend and to have a short life, but its way of suckering and replacing itself makes this unimportant in its usual role, which is as part of a shelterbelt since it can thrive and spread on poor, sandy soils and withstand exposure well. It is very local from Montreal, PQ and in ME and south to LA and eastern TX but is much more frequent as the outer part of shelterbelts in MN, ND and in the Prairie States. This tree is, however, easily mistaken for the Gray poplar, which is more common in most areas, a little less bright white beneath the leaf and a much sturdier tree. **Bolle's poplar** or **Pyramidal white (4)** was brought from the Turkmen region of the southern USSR after 1876 and is widely planted, perhaps in more than one form, for the bark of young trees is very much whiter in some trees than in others. It is scarce in the east, although growing at the school of Horticulture, Niagara Falls, ON; in Annapolis, MD; at Youngstown, PA and there are several in Athens, GA. It is common in the Prairie States, along the Eastern Rockies through MN, WY and CO to NM and frequent in the Pacific West. One in the Butchart Garden, Vancouver I. is the biggest seen, 125ft x 10ft 6in in 1976. A notably fine planting is throughout Ely, NV where one of those along Main Street was 104ft x 10ft 7in in 1982.

GRAY POPLAR (5), *Populus canescens* is a hybrid between the White poplar and the European aspen and is a far bigger, more vigorous tree than either. It is used much as the White poplar and mistaken for it, but is much more common than that tree on the Coastal Plain and is the 'White poplar' seen in New Orleans and generally from SC to AK. It is also frequent in the west in small gardens from CO to MT. There is a big tree by the Capitol at Helena.

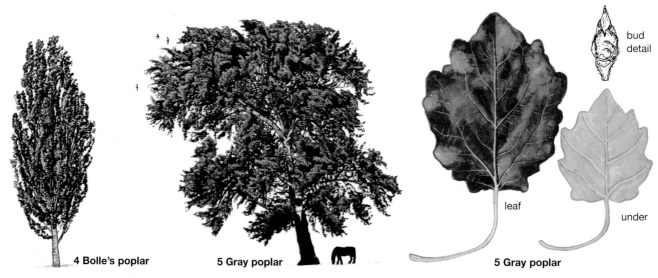

4 Bolle's poplar   5 Gray poplar   leaf   bud detail   under   5 Gray poplar

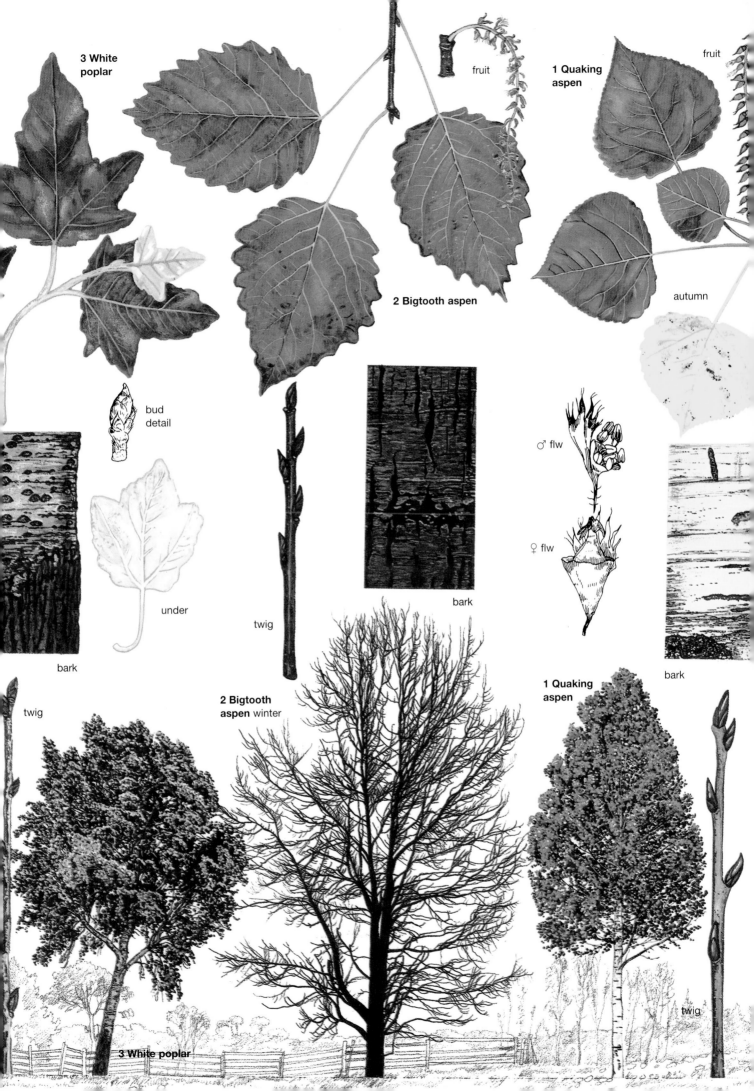

3 White poplar

fruit

1 Quaking aspen

fruit

2 Bigtooth aspen

autumn

bud detail

under

twig

bark

♂ flw

♀ flw

bark

bark

twig

2 Bigtooth aspen winter

1 Quaking aspen

twig

3 White poplar

twig

Cottonwoods and Lombardy poplar

The poplars here are in the Black poplar group, the largest group in the genus and the one within which there is the most hybridisation. The chief differences between the Black poplars and the White poplar–Aspen group are that the Blacks have leaves always green beneath, often paler but of similar shade to the upper side, and have minutely thickened, translucent margins; the catkin-scales lack the long-haired margin; the male catkins are bright or deep red, and the bark begins at an early age to fissure into woody ridges. They also live longer and grow bigger trunks, and with very few exceptions, they are easily raised from cuttings.

EASTERN COTTONWOOD (1), *Populus deltoides* is the cottonwood general in several forms across the United States east of the Rocky Mountains. It has been divided by different botanists into many more minor species or forms and is also known as the Southern cottonwood, Carolina poplar and Necklace poplar in various parts but here only the readily distinguishable form, the Plains cottonwood, is shown and described separately. The Eastern cottonwood grows wild the length of the Hudson Valley to around Montreal, PQ, but was almost absent from the coast from PA to NC originally. It is now planted commonly in that and in many other areas in which it is not native, as far north as Winnipeg, MB. It is a fine tree with a good straight bole and young trees are columnar to a domed top while old ones are broad and heavily branched. The crowns are luxuriant in leaf and rich green, most noticeably in the south-east from SC to eastern TX where the leaves tend to be much bigger than in the north. In Canada and New England they are, on old trees, 3–4in both ways, but in GA they can be found twice this size, with stalks 6in long, and on sprouts the leaves can be 8 x 10in. As far north as the Queen Victoria Park, Niagara Falls, ON a tree is over 120ft tall; in Central Park, New York the biggest in 1976 was 92ft x 13ft; a splendid specimen at the Holden Arboretum, Mentor, OH was then 143ft x 13ft but a most majestic tree 115ft x 21ft stands by the Mississippi at Lillydale near St Paul, MN.

PLAINS COTTONWOOD (2) (var. *occidentalis*) can be regarded as a closely allied but separate species and given the name *Populus sargentii* and is distinct in crown, bark and leaf as well as having a range to the west of the Eastern cottonwood, but is now more generally regarded as a geographical form of that tree. It occurs by riversides in dry, prairie country from southern SK to NM and has been planted in AZ around Tuba City, Flagstaff and Tucson. Within range, it is commonly planted as a shade tree at roadside pull-outs from ND to NE and it is the common poplar by creeks and roadsides in NM, notably by Rt 104, in Santa Fe, Albuquerque and Gallup and through western CO into southern UT. The leaf is distinctive in its long, untoothed 'drip-tip' and the tree in its pale, ridged bark and downswept outer branches bearing big brushes of upcurved shoots. In October the whole crown turns bright gold.

NARROWLEAF COTTONWOOD (3), *Populus angustifolia* grows by streams between 5,000 and 10,000ft up in the mountains of the Eastern Rockies from the southern extremes of AB and SK to the Mexican border. It is most abundant in CO, as by Rt 14 over the Cameron Pass from Rustic to Walden, in WY and by Rt 89 to Livingstone, MT and stands out in winter and spring with bright ashen gray branches and pinkish-white shoots. The leaves are 3–4in long on a slender stalk.

LOMBARDY POPLAR (4), *Populus nigra* 'Italica' is an erect-growing male form of the European Black poplar spread by cuttings around the Po Valley in northern Italy and brought to Britain in 1758. The original tree, in Essex, stands today, broken into two stems but sprouting well. From there it was spread rapidly over Europe and was soon planted in all parts of North America. It can be seen in every state of the United States and all across southern Canada but in some regions it has not been a great success and is prone to pests and disease. This is very marked in MD and eastern PA, in AK and OK, and in MT and ID, but worst in TX. On the other hand, it thrives exceptionally and achieves large sizes around Ottawa, ON and in most of southern BC although the adjacent part of east WA is an area of near-failure. The biggest noted is in Point Defiance Park, Tacoma, WA, 132ft x 8ft. One area notably lacking in specimens is from mid-AZ to near San Diego, CA. This is largely semi-desert but so are many other areas in which fine trees tower from the towns along watercourses, as in the Owens Valley and the Mojave Desert at Yermo and Bailey Road. There are fine trees in Santa Fe, NM and in CA one on the campus at Berkeley is 125ft x 12ft. In these hot areas the Lombardy poplars turn into towers of bright gold in the fall. At Carson City, NV one near the Capitol is 90ft x 11ft. In the east, it is only in the high Alleghenies that this poplar is missing from large areas.

4 Lombardy poplar bole

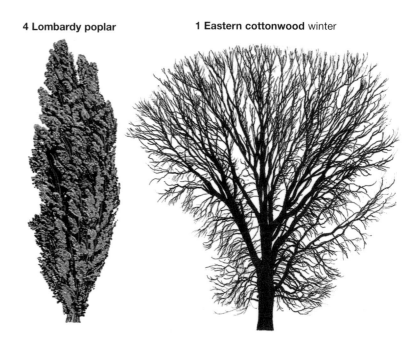

4 Lombardy poplar

1 Eastern cottonwood winter

fruit

1 Eastern cottonwood

4 Lombardy poplar

3 Narrowleaf cottonwood

1 Eastern cottonwood twig

2 Plains cottonwood

3 Narrowleaf cottonwood

1 Eastern cottonwood

1 Eastern cottonwood bole

Balsam and other Poplars

The Balsam poplars are found in North America and eastern Asia. The leaves of balsam poplars open before those of other groups, and have stalks round in section and without glands. In most species they are of mixed sizes; those opening first and near the base of the short, spur-like shoots and long leading shoots are small. Those towards the tips are borne larger and larger as the season and growth progress. On lateral spurs making little extension, the small and big are closely mixed and on the long leading shoot of a vigorous tree the size increases steadily to the top. The leaves are rounded at the base, or taper to the stalk and are not truncate. The underside is pale and whitish. Early growth is very rapid, and some species grow numerous suckers from their root-system.

BALSAM POPLAR (1), *Populus balsamifera*, formerly *P. tacamahaca*, ranges extraordinarily widely east–west from the length of the Labrador coast to northwest AK and is along the northern limit of tree growth all the way. It extends southwards across only the tip of BC and south in AB almost to the border of the USA which it enters fully in ND and WI but there are outliers on many mountains in ID, WY and CO, then curves closely round Lake Michigan to New England with some areas in WV. It has a smoothly rounded shoot and generally smaller leaf, less white beneath than the similar Black cottonwood, and much more open, less leafy crown. Its suckering abilities are superior to any poplar except the aspen and white poplar. In the more thickly wooded southern parts of its range this tree is prominent only in New England and ON but further north it becomes dominant broadleaf over large tracts and in AB from prairie to Rocky Mountain passes in the fall its clear bright yellow is the main constituent of the season's colors.

BLACK COTTONWOOD (2), *Populus trichocarpa* takes over abruptly from the Balsam poplar westward through the Rocky Mountain passes. This change is notably sharp in the Kicking Horse Pass from AB to BC where the traveller suddenly sees that the big-leaf poplars are darker, more leafy and more white on the leaf underside. It is easily the biggest broadleaf in the west. Mature trees have many nearly upright, long upper branches opening slightly to make a narrow, ragged dome. Lower branches are of mixed sizes, curving out level from among a tangle of dead snags. The leaves are leathery, somewhat oily, and vary on the same shoot from 4–8in and on new growth to 10–12in with the 1–2in stalk often stained crimson. The shoot is at first shining yellow with narrow ridges below each leaf, becoming smooth and red-brown. The range is

from AK on Kodiak Island and the Kenai Peninsula on the coast to the OR/CA boundary and in the Sierra Nevada to the southern mountains, while inland it follows the eastern crest of the Rocky Mountains through BC and beyond into ND and SD, MT and ID and on scattered tops in NV, UT and WY. It is the only balsam except the Narrowleaf over this area, except in ID and MT where it is common beside Rt 200 and 202 Missoula to Ross Creek and from Cour d'Alene to BC where the Balsam is scarce. It is abundant and large on Vancouver Island.

BALM-OF-GILEAD POPLAR (3), *Populus candicans* is probably a hybrid or selection of Balsam poplar. It is unknown in the wild and is thought to have been raised by early settlers. Also called Ontario poplar, it is always female and spreads by suckering. It has a more open crown, broader, more heart-shaped leaves than Balsam poplar with downy stalks and shoots. The **'Aurora' (4)** form was first sold after 1920 in Cornwall, England and although prone to disease, its foliage makes a striking splash in midsummer.

SIMON POPLAR (5), *Populus simonii* is a balsam from northeastern Asia with markedly angled shoots and very early into leaf. It is a very hardy, slender-shooted elegantly foliaged tree useful for amenity where winters are severe. The upright form **'Fastigiata'** was sent to America in 1913 and is seen as often as the type. The leaf stalk of the Simon poplar is very short but variable and the diamond-shaped leaf is distinctive.

PALMER COTTONWOOD (6) is a black poplar, as is shown by the flattened leafstalk and glands at its top end as well as the green underside to the leaf, which is thin and has an entire apex like the Plains cottonwood. It is often regarded as a regional form of the Eastern cottonwood not deserving of a separate botanical name. It is confined to the Chisos and nearby mountains in the Big Bend region of west TX.

CHINESE NECKLACE POPLAR (7), *Populus lasiocarpa* has heart-shaped leaves up to 15 x 8in on 8in pink or red, flattened stalks. It has dark gray, shaggy and peeling bark and a broad crown of few level branches. It is usually grafted and most of the trees are derived from one or two raised from the original seed from Wilson in 1900. One of these had the remarkable feature of bearing catkins with male flowers on the outer half and female on the inner. In collections the few trees seen are mostly like this but occasionally fully male or female trees may be found.

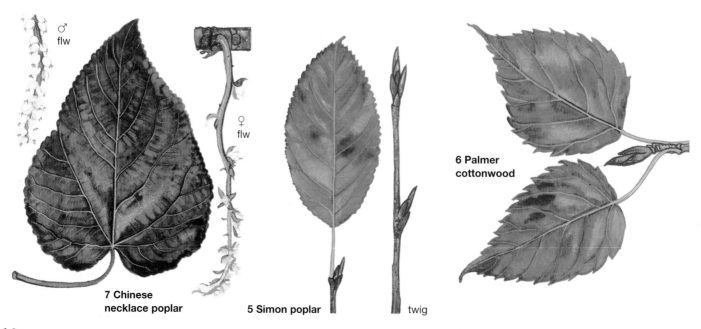

♂ flw

♀ flw

6 Palmer cottonwood

7 Chinese necklace poplar

5 Simon poplar

twig

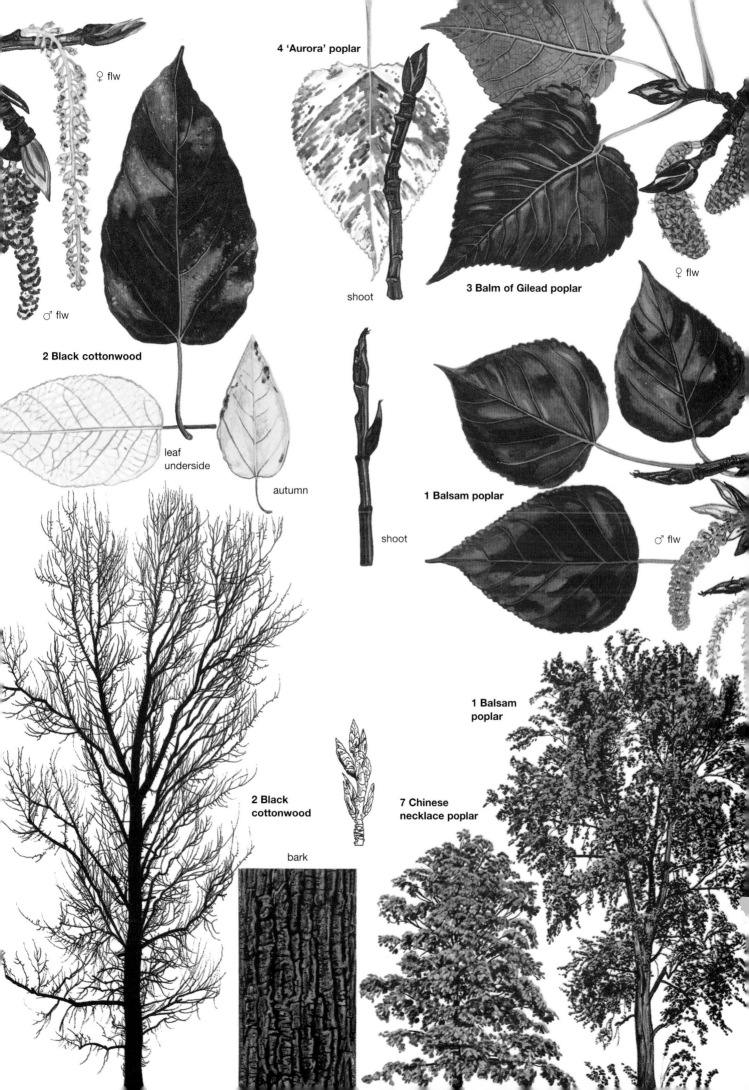

♀ flw

4 'Aurora' poplar

♂ flw

2 Black cottonwood

shoot

3 Balm of Gilead poplar

♀ flw

leaf underside

autumn

shoot

1 Balsam poplar

♂ flw

1 Balsam poplar

2 Black cottonwood

7 Chinese necklace poplar

bark

Cottonwoods and Italian poplar

The fourth Section into which the genus *Populus* is divided has no common language name, unlike the White, Black and Balsam Sections. This is because it has no members in Europe and only one far from prominent or well known in America, and it was not until the flora of Interior China was explored after 1900 that it was found to be a group of more than one rather odd species. Although very different in most ways from the White poplars, this fourth group has foliage which emerges from the bud well covered in dense white hairs. In this it resembles the White poplars, whose botanical Section name is *Leuce*, meaning 'white' in Greek. Hence this new Section is called *Leucoides* from 'leucos' white, and '-*ides*', the same as. (Identical is from the same root but should mean 'absolutely the same as', not only 'resembling'.) The Black poplars are *Aegiros* Section and the Balsams are *Tacamahaca* from a Canadian Indian name.

SWAMP COTTONWOOD (1), *Populus heterophylla* from the lowlands around the Appalachian Mountains is the American member of the *Leucoides* Section. It is known in CT and on Long Island, NY but its main populations are on the Coastal Plain to northwest FL and eastern LA and along the Mississippi and Ohio rivers to IN and MI. Although widespread it is local and rare in most parts of its range and found only on the edges of flooding river-bottom swamps. It is at its best and most numerous in the middle Mississippi Valley and lower Ohio Valley. It may be overlooked as its large, hanging leaves make it rather unlike a cottonwood. They are about 8 x 7in and, a feature of this group, tend to be all of the same size regardless of their position on the shoot, in contrast to the not dissimilar balsam poplars in which there is great variation in size on the same shoot. The bark is soon rough and shaggy with the ends of long, thick, reddish brown plates projecting. The shoots are very stout and after shedding the thick hairy coating, become shiny gray or pale orange, and bear bright red-brown somewhat resinous buds.

FREMONT COTTONWOOD (2), *Populus fremontii* is a western counterpart of the Eastern cottonwood with the Plains cottonwood an intermediate between them. Like the Eastern it has been divided into several geographical forms at one time regarded as separate species but now only as varieties. The Fremont cottonwood replaces the Eastern in CO, UT, NV, NM, AZ and CA, but in these predominantly dry areas it is neither as numerous nor as luxuriant as that tree. Nor is it always certain that the big cottonwoods here and there in parks and squares and obviously planted are Fremont rather than Eastern since native American trees are so widely planted outside their natural ranges and the two differ only in details of foliage. The leaves of Fremont are not as big as the larger-leafed forms of the Eastern, nor so densely held. They are relatively broader and, more positively, they lack the two little green glands on the stalk near the blade. There are good trees in Carson City, NV, near the Capitol, to over 100ft x 10ft. In Sutter Park, Sacramento, CA, there is a splendid old hulk with sprouts to 60ft but notable for its girth of 25ft. However, the Champion, measured in 1970 near Patagonia, AZ, girthed 34ft 10in.

BLACK ITALIAN POPLAR (3), *Populus* × *canadensis* 'Serotina' is a male selection from a number of hybrids which arose in Europe soon after the introduction of the Eastern cottonwood to Europe a little after 1700. It probably originated in France around 1750 and was taken to America not long after. It shows great hybrid vigor and in England it can be 70ft x 7ft in twenty years and 150ft x 20ft in little over 100 years, but survives not much beyond that, breaking up as the winds tear out the heavy branches. It is presumably for this vigor in regions of cool summers that it has been planted in some of the northeastern states of the USA and in southeastern Canada, for otherwise it has no advantages over the native Eastern cottonwood unless it be that it is assuredly a male tree and will not spread cotton-wool seeds everywhere in summer while the native tree may be of either sex. The Black Italian has a distinctive crown of incurved branches making a cup shape on a good clean stem. Its leaves mostly lack the little glands on the stalk of the cottonwood and unfold much later and orange-brown. In full leaf it is a slightly gray-green. At the Ottawa Botanic Garden there are two trees, the larger 105ft x 12ft in 1975, and in Montreal Botanic Garden one was then 90ft x 11ft. There are big trees by Lake Shore Drive and in nearby suburbs of Chicago, IL. In 1876 the **Golden poplar (4), 'Serotina Aurea'** was marketed in Belgium. It is scarce in North America but is prominent in summer wherever it is grown. It grows less rapidly than 'Serotina' itself and has a more dense crown.

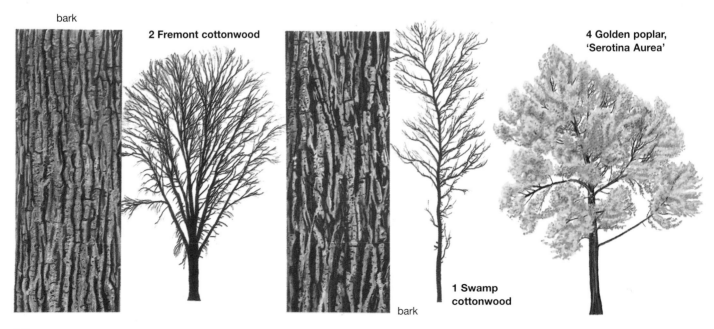

bark

2 Fremont cottonwood

4 Golden poplar, 'Serotina Aurea'

1 Swamp cottonwood

bark

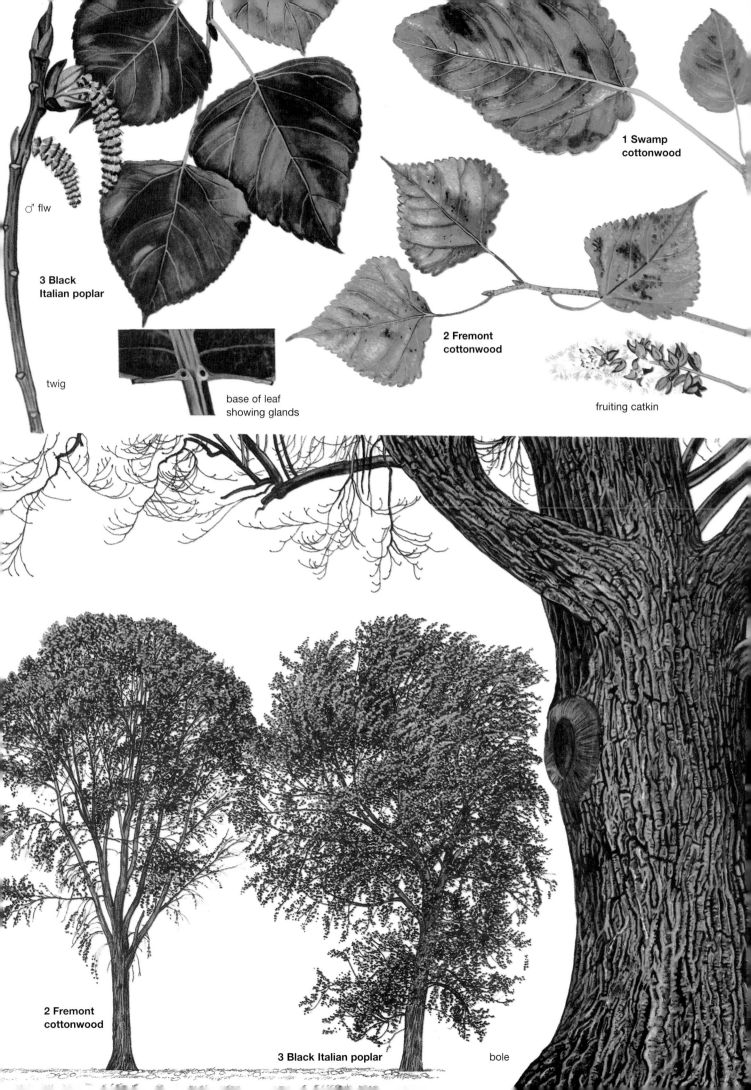

♂ flw

3 Black
Italian poplar

twig

base of leaf
showing glands

1 Swamp
cottonwood

2 Fremont
cottonwood

fruiting catkin

2 Fremont
cottonwood

3 Black Italian poplar

bole

Walnuts

The Walnuts are about 20 species found in the southwestern, central and eastern parts of the USA, Central America and into the Andes, and from southeastern Europe across Asia to Japan. Six species occur in the USA but only two of them have extensive ranges, both in the eastern half of the country. They are in the same Family as the hickories but whereas the walnuts and the wingnuts, also in that Family, have chambered pith, the hickories do not. This feature can be seen when a shoot is sliced obliquely. Being stout, it has a large core of pith which is easily seen to be made up of hollows separated by transverse plates, about 20 to the inch. The timber of walnuts is fine-grained, hard and takes a high polish, which together with its fine figure and resistance to woodworm conferred by the small vessels makes it valuable for quality furniture. In addition, it is remarkably stable once seasoned and worked and this, with the other features, makes it ideal for gun-stocks where even slight warping could make the barrel and the sights out of true. The European, 'English' or Persian walnut was the species first exploited for these qualities, but the American Black walnut was found to be at least as good and to be available in much superior, straight lengths.

BLACK WALNUT (1), *Juglans nigra* is a fine, handsome tree ranging from the southern Hudson Valley and south ON to IA and eastern TX. It did not spread into SC, the east of GA or to LA and the Lower Mississippi and has been little planted there, but its northern range has been extended and there are trees on Westmount, Montreal, PQ and in Ottawa Botanic Garden, ON, as well as by the Legislative Building in Winnipeg, MB. It has been widely planted in the west and the Champion Tree in 1975 was 132ft x 22ft in northern CA. It is frequent in parks and town gardens in MT, ID, WA, where Wenatchee has some 85ft x 10ft near the town centre, and around Vancouver and Victoria, BC it is present but less frequent, as it is in OR. There are a few in NM in Albuquerque and Santa Fe and in Denver, CO. Within the range, one in Queen Victoria Park, Niagara Falls, ON is 85ft x 12ft and one at Hagley Mills PA is 110ft x 10ft. At the Bailey Arboretum, Locust Valley, Long Island, NY, an old tree is 75ft x 18ft. One at the Philbrook Art Center, Tulsa, OK, is over 80ft x 10ft. Over much of its southeastern range it may be with the Pecan, which has been planted in orchards and gardens, and which it resembles in shape, stature and in the big leaf with numerous leaflets, but fortunately the Pecan bark grows paler, whiter and more flaky with age and the bark of the Black walnut grows more ridged and darker brown, often becoming black.

BUTTERNUT (2), *Juglans cinerea* ranges from Quebec, PQ, and NB to MN but scarcely south of TN and MO. Like the Black walnut, it is common in the forests along the Skyline and Blue Ridge Drives in the Alleghenies, as scattered single trees, and both show up in the fall as they shed their leaflets early while the leafstalks remain on the trees. It has been planted in Winnipeg, MB and in the west where it is frequent in southern interior BC and in WA. The leaf is up to 2ft long with dense soft hairs on the stalk and on the pale underside.

SOUTHERN CALIFORNIA WALNUT (3), *Juglans californica* is confined as a native tree to streamsides in southern CA near the coast from Santa Barbara and on the lower San Bernardino Mountains. Its leaf is only 9in long and it is shrubby or with a short trunk.

NORTHERN CALIFORNIA WALNUT (4), *Juglans hindsii* is local in central CA near the coast from the lower Sacramento to the Napa Valley, but has been spread eastwards; it grows in Kings Canyon National Park.

ARIZONA WALNUT (5), *Juglans major* is wild in AZ and the adjacent parts of NM and TX. It can be seen in Oak Creek Canyon south of Flagstaff and above Jerome, and, planted, in Phoenix.

JAPANESE WALNUT (6), *Juglans ailantifolia* is a tough, broad-crowned tree with big, 2–3ft leaves on stalks covered in slightly sticky hairs, and abruptly tipped leaflets. It is sometimes seen in parks in southern Canada, both east and west, and in New England and WA. A good tree stands in Shelburne Falls, MA.

MANCHURIAN WALNUT (7), *Juglans mandschurica* is very like the Japanese walnut but its leaflets taper more gradually to their tips. It is a very leafy, slightly gray-green in summer. A fine specimen is in Assiniboine Park English Garden in Winnipeg, MB and one in Highland Park, Rochester, NY is 85ft tall, but there are many more in BC especially around Vernon.

ENGLISH WALNUT (8), *Juglans regia* maybe native to China only or may range to Asia Minor, but certainly not to England. It is the only walnut with entire leaf-margins. It is infrequent in the east from MA to OH and in the west from southern BC to NM but locally common in orchards in the Okanagan Valley, BC and in the Central Valley, CA. There is one at the 'oldest house' in Santa Fe, NM.

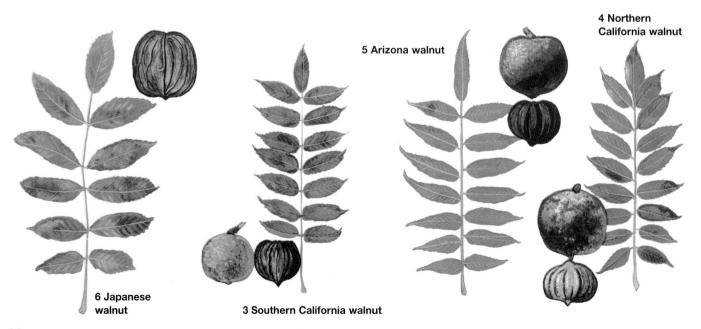

5 Arizona walnut

4 Northern California walnut

6 Japanese walnut

3 Southern California walnut

♀ flw

8 English walnut

♂ catkins

fruit with husk

7 Manchurian walnut

sliced twig to show chambered pith

1 Black walnut leaf

2 Butternut   nut

1 Black walnut bark

8 English walnut 23m

1 Black walnut 30m

Pecan, Hickories and Wingnuts

The Hickories are a small group with 11 species in the eastern USA, another in Mexico and one or two in South China. They are in the Walnut Family and have similar pinnate leaves and large fruit but differ from the walnuts and wingnuts in having shoots with solid pith and male flower catkins branched into three parts and the fruit in four segments. Their timber is very tough, elastic and shock-resistant and is used in the best quality axe handles, baseball bats and other sports goods and tools. They are not easy trees to raise as this must be done from seed which must be fresh as it does not store, and it transplants very badly so is best sown in the final position or in pots and moved out at the beginning of their first summer.

PECAN (1), *Carya illinoensis* makes the finest tree of all the hickories as well as the most splendid bright pink nuts. It was native in the Mississippi Valley from IN and IL to TX, MS and LA but has been planted widely across the eastern USA. It is found now north to Washington, DC and all down the Coastal Plain where, in the south there are many orchards, to Pensacola, FL. It is also planted occasionally in the west. The slender yellow-haired bud of the pecan is like only that of the Bitternut which is very different in bark and leaf.

BITTERNUT HICKORY (2), *Carya cordiformis* is distinguished by its slender scaly bright golden bud, gray to brown bark finely networked in ridges and its terminal leaflet tapering to the almost stalkless base. It is native and usually common in woods almost everywhere east of the line from mid-MN to east TX as far north as MA and the St. Lawrence Valley to beyond Montreal, PQ. It is not much seen on the Coastal Plain nor is it planted noticeably anywhere beyond its range. In valleys in the Great Smoky Mountains of TN there are some trees 120ft x 10ft but elsewhere it is rarely more than about 80ft.

SHAGBARK HICKORY (3), *Carya ovata* has almost the exact range of the Bitternut except that it does not spread out from the foothills on to the Coastal Plain. The shoot is stout, green at first then deep purple-brown and often has a ring of brown hairs at the nodes. The 5-parted leaf has the terminal leaflet much the biggest, to 14 x 8in on a 1–2in stalk. The whole leaf is over 2ft long and its stalk has a swollen hairy base.

SHELLBARK HICKORY (4), *Carya laciniosa* has bark as shaggy as the Shagbark but nearly always has a 7-parted leaf, even bigger, to 2½ft long and the terminal leaflet has a slender stalk barely ½in long. It has a more restricted range largely from OH to MO.

MOCKERNUT HICKORY (5), *Carya tomentosa* has a smooth gray bark when young and is still rather smoothly ridged when old. The shoot and leafstalk are covered in hard dense, short hairs and the terminal leaflet has a slender 1⅛in stalk. A crushed leaf has the scent of paint, soap or mown grass. It has much the same range as the Bitternut, but is common on Long Island NY where the twisting hanging shoots and heavy hanging leaves are noticeable.

PIGNUT HICKORY (6), *Carya glabra* also has a smooth bark becoming ridged, gray and purplish, but it has a small, usually 5-parted leaf 6–10in long and without hairs. Its range is very like that of the Bitternut. In Highland Park, NY and Winterthur, DE there are trees 115ft tall.

NUTMEG HICKORY (7), *Carya myristiciformis*, is a local southern species from SC along the plains to OK with leaflets silvery white beneath, and with brilliant golden-bronze fall colors. The bark is dark red-brown and scaly.

SAND HICKORY (8), *Carya pallida* also has leaflets silvered beneath but slender-pointed, and its bark is dark brown, short intertwined ridges. It ranges from NJ around the Coastal Plain and up the Mississippi to IN. In Auburn Arboretum, GA one is 75ft x 6ft.

CAUCASIAN WINGNUT (9), *Pterocarya fraxinifolia* is a hugely suckering vigorous tree in a few gardens in the northern USA and southern Canada, like the Brooklyn Botanic Garden and Planting Fields, NY and by the Niagara Falls where two are over 80ft tall. The fruit, little nuts in 1in rounded wings, are strung down 18in catkins, densely on the lower half and are very conspicuous from summer to late fall.

CHINESE WINGNUT (10), *Pterocarya stenoptera* is similar but has rather smaller leaves with the main stalk broadly winged with toothed flanges and the fruit turn pink in summer. There are 80ft trees in the Morris Arboretum, PA and at Brooklyn Botanic Garden, NY. When seed of this species was sent to the Arnold Arboretum, MA from France in 1879, the trees raised turned out to be hybrids between that and the Caucasian wingnut.

HYBRID WINGNUT (11), *Pterocarya × rehderiana* has even greater vigor than its parents and a grooved, slightly flanged leafstalk. The original trees in the Arnold Arboretum were 85ft x 10ft and 95ft x 8ft in 1975. There are now trees in other botanic gardens.

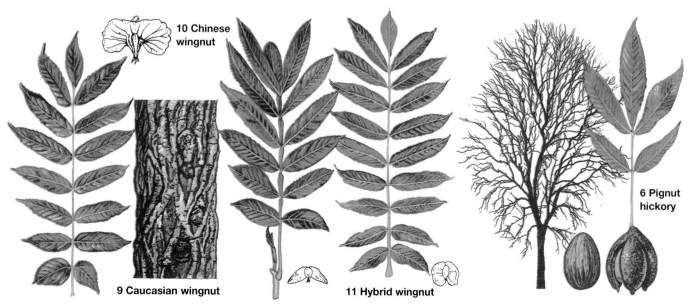

10 Chinese wingnut

9 Caucasian wingnut

11 Hybrid wingnut

6 Pignut hickory

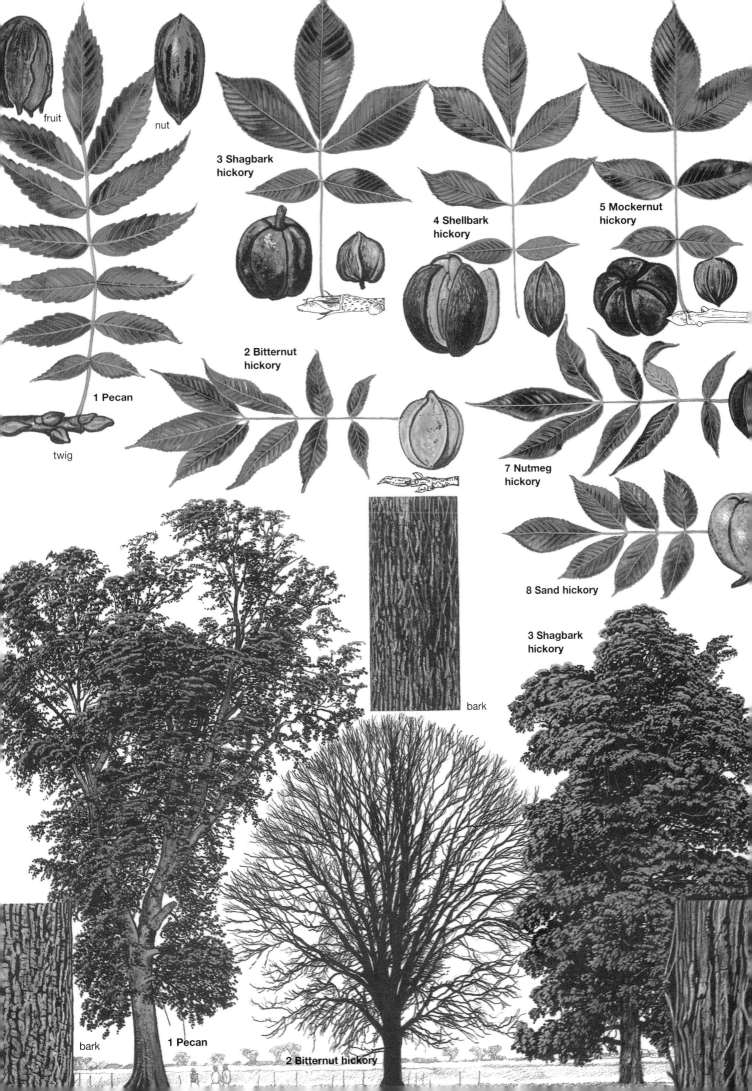

fruit

nut

3 Shagbark hickory

4 Shellbark hickory

5 Mockernut hickory

1 Pecan

twig

2 Bitternut hickory

7 Nutmeg hickory

8 Sand hickory

bark

3 Shagbark hickory

bark

1 Pecan

2 Bitternut hickory

Paper, Silver and other Birches

The birches are a group of about 50 species which grow round the northern circumpolar plains and to the south from FL and Spain to China. Many are only shrubs and 7 are trees native to North America. Hybrids among them are frequent in the wild and in botanic collections. The bark of most species includes a white pigment, betulin, in varying amounts even within single species with wide ranges, and it rolls, peels or curls off in most species. Birches grow rapidly in their early years, being pioneer trees, seeding on to open ground and unable to establish under any appreciable shade of other trees or of their own kind. They are short-lived and may die back and decay then fall to pieces when 60–100 years old. The timber of the larger growing birches is very tough and logs big enough to be spun and peeled yield the sheets used in plywood. Most birches will strike roots as cuttings but this is seldom done except to propagate selected trees, since seed is copiously produced and, sown reasonably fresh, very fertile.

PAPER BIRCH (1), *Betula papyrifera* extends from Labrador and VA in the east to Yukon, western AK, WA and MT in the west, south to NE and OH. In this great range five varieties are usually recognised with minor but consistent differences from the typical form. The English names given to them, Western, Northwestern, Alaskan, Kenai and Mountain, indicate where they were first described but to some extent they overlap and confuse the issue; Western paper birch, for example typically in WA, MT and ID ranges across to Labrador, and the type form extends into WY and CO. Hence they are treated here as one big variable species. The alternative name, Canoe birch, is more interesting than the official name, Paper birch. This birch is one of those with new shoots roughened by numerous small warts, and with hairy, 1in, stout leafstalks. In New England, NY and ON the bark is pure dull whitewash white with small black dots and patches while in some forms it is variably red-brown to gray. In the same region and into OH and PA most trees are damaged by the Bronze birch borer and have lost the main stem above 6–8ft and grow big, upturned lower branches.

WATER BIRCH (2), *Betula occidentalis* is a shrubby little tree also known as the Red, Black or Spring birch, prominent by streams in much of the interior Rocky Mountains and notably so at Mammoth Hot Springs, north WY and from Helena to Missoula, MT, also by Independence Creek and other valleys on the eastern flanks of the Sierra Nevada, CA and around Denver, CO. It is a bush with arching stems with dark brown, sometimes bright orange-brown bark and shiny bright green leaves.

GRAY BIRCH (3), *Betula populifolia* has very white bark with black 'Chinaman moustaches' where branches arose, and long-tailed leaves and warty yellow shoots turning red-brown. It grows from NS and NB through New England and NY where it is a very common roadside and garden tree to OH and PA where it is local in mountains and in a few places along the Alleghenies to NC. It has been planted in the Morton Arboretum, IL, at Racine, WI and in Waterworks Park, Des Moines, IA.

EUROPEAN SILVER BIRCH (4), *Betula pendula* has long been planted all across North America, from south PQ to southern CA but not south of PA, IN and MO in the east except in MD and DE. It is common in towns and gardens from IL to PA and ON. In the west, it is common in BC, especially around Victoria and in WA, ID and MT, in southern UT and in CO also around Santa Fe, NM, Flagstaff, AZ and Tustin and Arcadia, Los Angeles, CA. It is a warty shooted birch with a white bark distinguished from native birches by black, diamond-shaped patches on the bark and by living up to its name *'pendula.'* The outer crown is fine shoots hanging in tails from rising branches. It is more strikingly pendulous in the form **'Tristis' (5)** in which dense shoot systems, dark purple in winter hang from more level branches. The **Cutleaf** or **Swedish birch (6)**, **'Dalecarlica'** was found north of Stockholm, Sweden in 1767 and has been very widely planted as grafts from the old tree which was blown over in 1887. This has whiter, less marked bark than the Silver birch, deeply cut leaves and a narrower, long-pendulous crown. It is frequent in towns from Montreal, PQ and Winnipeg, MB south only to Washington DC but in the Prairie States it is very common and also in MT, WY, ID, through southern BC, notably on Vancouver I, and through WA. The form **'Gracilis'**, with more deeply cut leaves, may often be the one seen. The **Fastigiate birch (7)**, **'Fastigiata'** is found in some collections from ON to DE and around the cities of Vancouver, Seattle and San Francisco, CA. **Young's weeping birch (8)**, **'Youngii'** arose in a nursery in Surrey, England and is a mophead grafted on a leg of Silver birch and usually only 10–15ft tall. It is growing in Ottawa city and Botanic Garden, ON; by Lake Shore Boulevard, Toronto; in Ithaca NY and in Olympia, WA.

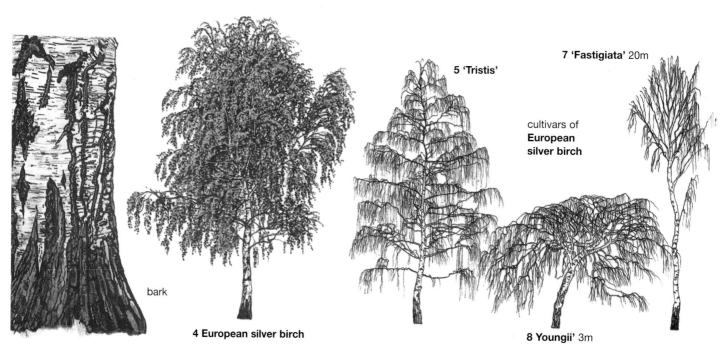

bark

4 European silver birch

5 'Tristis'

7 'Fastigiata' 20m

cultivars of **European silver birch**

8 Youngii' 3m

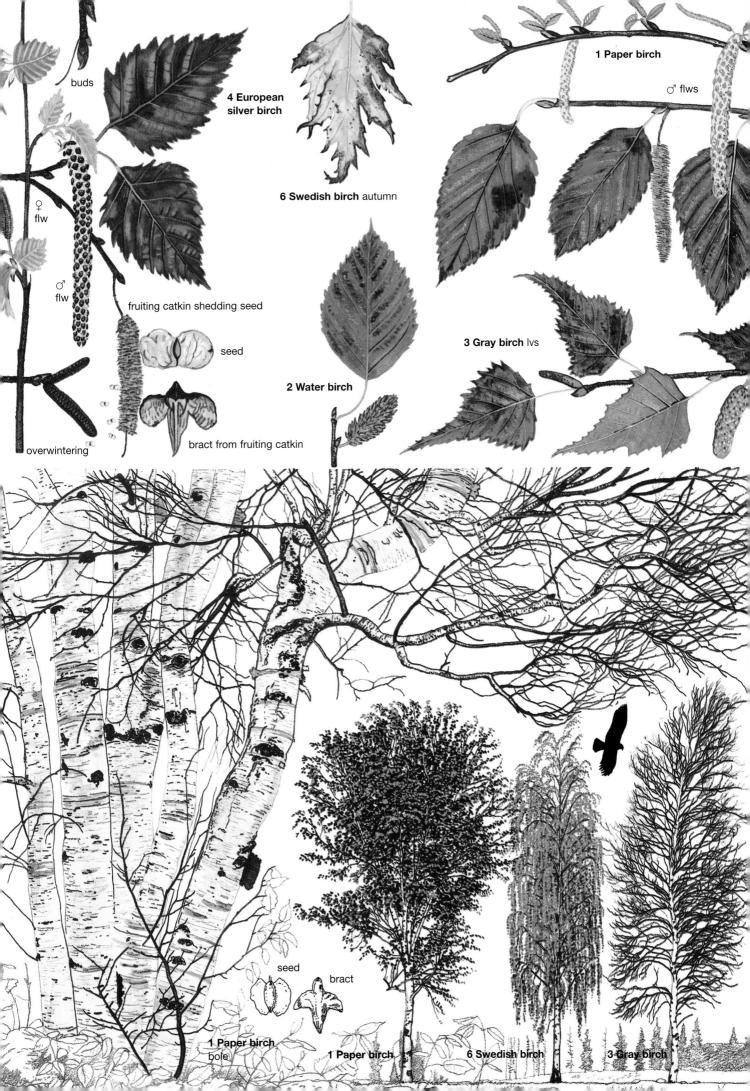

buds

4 European silver birch

♀ flw

♂ flw

fruiting catkin shedding seed

seed

overwintering

bract from fruiting catkin

6 Swedish birch autumn

2 Water birch

1 Paper birch

♂ flws

3 Gray birch lvs

seed

bract

1 Paper birch
bole

1 Paper birch

6 Swedish birch

3 Gray birch

Yellow, Sweet and other Birches

The birches are of exceptional value to those in regions of cool summers and severe winters who are making new plantings. Land for new planting is usually open and exposed and the young tree brought in from the shelter of nursery beds has to grow its new foliage in unaccustomed exposure from a root-system likely to be damaged and reduced by transplanting. This poor outlook is made much worse by the absurd practice of planting trees grossly oversized for the operation. The tree then has much more crown and usually much more truncated roots. Garden trees should be no more than 2–3ft tall at planting. Any need for a stake shows an oversize tree has been bought and it will never grow as fast or well as a small one. Only a few trees, the pioneers, pines, larches, some willow and birches establish happily in an exposed site, while most trees, particularly beeches, oaks and many large-leafed decorative trees, need something near to woodland surroundings in which to flourish and they struggle for years when set in the open without side-shelter. The Silver, Gray and perhaps the Paper birches can be had in quantity cheaply. They will grow rapidly and give vital shelter to other trees and can then be cut out, or, if left, they interfere little with the others, having narrow and light crowns, and being short-lived, will die out when the others become large. The fine tracery of shoots of the birches has a moderating effect on radiation frosts which can be damaging in early fall and late spring, so they are valuable high shelter for tender shrubs.

RIVER BIRCH or **BLACK BIRCH (1)**, *Betula nigra* has a broadly U-shaped natural distribution with the Eastern arm ending in a patch in MA and CT and the western arm threading itself up the upper reaches of the Mississippi into WI and MN. The main body of the U sweeps from MO to TX and round the Alleghenies up to NY and in the middle is a large patch in KY, TN and WV. Where the range runs along the Gulf Coast near Tallahassee, FL this is the most southerly birch in the world. From here to LA it is in a region of hot, wet summers and warm winters, so plants from this area are very differently adapted from those in MN or CT and there should be sources of seed to suit a very wide range of climates. But apart from specimen trees in Montreal Botanic Garden, PQ and in the University of Washington Arboretum, Seattle, WA and a few in Waterworks Park, Des Moines, IA, this tree is not planted beyond its range. The French Market in New Orleans, LA can be only a few miles south of once native woods. The River birch lives up to its name particularly in TX, AR and OK where it is most seen along creek-sides and also in other parts as along US 50 in OH and WV and on the Coastal Plain. This is less obvious where tree cover is general and not confined to river bottoms. This is the only birch with leaves bearing lobes and with silvered undersides but both features vary in intensity. Young trees, often sprouts from a common stump, have pinkish or pale coffee-brown bark with orange-gray to dark brown rough scales. Old trees can have dark purple-gray bark with orange fissures or be blackish red with small scales.

YELLOW BIRCH (2), *Betula alleghaniensis* shares several distinctive features with the Sweet birch. They both have quite large, flat, many-veined leaves sparsely set; hemispheric crowns of rather even-sized radiating branches; abundant fruit standing erect, and give a strong scent of oil of wintergreen if their shoots are skinned and warmed. They differ in their bark and in minor details of their leaves. The Yellow birch bark is pale gray-brown with a yellow-brown tinge, flaking and peeling horizontally with tight and loose rolls. Its leaf is 3–6in long with 12–15 pairs of veins. The upper scores for these are only a little above those of the Sweet birch, but all the same, when the leaves of both are on the floor of woods, mixed, as in PA and VA, those of the Yellow birch stand out as bigger, flatter and broader. The Yellow birch occurs from NF and NB and ND through WI and MI to PA and along the mountains just into GA. It is common up to over 5800ft along the Skyline and Blue Ridge Drives in VA and NC. It has been planted in a few parks in the west, like Beacon Hill Park, Victoria, BC and Point Defiance Park, Tacoma, WA where a very big tree was 75ft x 8ft 4in in 1975.

SWEET BIRCH or **CHERRY BIRCH (3)**, *Betula lenta* has smoky gray-black to dark red bark with purplish flakes and the teeth at the ends of the veins on its leaves project as short whiskers. Its crown is less open than in the Yellow birch. Both trees turn brilliant gold rather briefly in the fall. Sweet birch is more southerly and easterly than Yellow birch, from ME to AL south of Lakes Erie and Ontario and not west of mid-OH. Fairly big trees are common in parks and gardens within its range, to 100ft x 11ft at Longwood Gardens, PA, 50ft x 9ft at Vanderbilt Mansion, Hyde Park, NY and 62ft x 9ft at the Tyler Arboretum, Lima, PA but it seems not to have been planted outside the range.

BLUELEAF BIRCH or **BLUE BIRCH (4)**, *Betula coerulea-grandis* is considered to be a hybrid between the Gray and the Paper birches. It is found from NS to VT and ME, has warty shoots and white bark rarely flaking and does not exceed 35ft.

3 Sweet birch summer

winter

new bark

old bark

♀ flws

fruiting catkins

1 River birch

♂ flw

seed enlarged

3 Sweet birch

bract & seed

2 Yellow birch

winter catkins

4 Blueleaf birch

seed enlarged

bark

1 River birch bole

1 River birch

autumn

2 Yellow birch

Alders

The Alders are about 30 trees and shrubs of northern temperate parts with one species extending down the Andes to Peru. Ten are native to North America of which five or so can be trees rather than shrubs. Alders are rarely more than 70–80ft tall anywhere, although a Caucasian species is known to over 130ft. Alders are in the Birch Family and two of the features which distinguish them as a group are highly unusual. The fruit not only resembles a small cone, but ripens into a hard, woody structure even more like one and may remain on the tree long after it has shed the seeds. Secondly, the roots grow nodules that house nitrifying bacteria which take nitrogen from the air. This enables the tree to grow well on newly bared or made-up soils which are often very short of nitrates that a plant can use. As the alder leaves fall each year and decay, they enrich the soil enabling other trees to colonise it. European, Gray and Red alders are planted on quarry spoils, the banks of newly cut roads and similar places for this purpose. Most of the alders grow for preference on the banks of running water or lakes receiving a good flow of water. They extend thick, dark red systems of roots into the water, useful in stabilising the banks. These roots acquire oxygen from the water, and so stagnant pools with little or no available oxygen are not colonised. Bottomlands liable to periodic flooding are suitable as the floodwater is aerated. Growing so closely associated with water, alders yield wood which, not surprisingly, is durable in water, and, a more scarce quality, when alternately wet and dry. It has been used in canal lock and bank construction. It is hard and dense and makes the best charcoal for gunpowder.

SPECKLED ALDER, *Alnus rugosa* has been regarded as the extension into North America of the Gray alder of Northern Europe but unlike that fine tree this is hardly more than a shrub. It ranges from NF to AK and south to BC, ND and NJ.

MOUNTAIN ALDER, *Alnus tenuifolia* ranges from central AK broadly through the Rocky Mountains to central CA and to NM. The buds are bright red and the bark is scaly, bright red-brown.

WHITE ALDER (1), *Alnus rhombifolia* may be 100ft tall with long, slender branches, drooping at the tips, and is found by running water in the Rocky Mountains in the USA only, from ID and MT to southern CA.

The bark of young trees is pale and dark gray and smooth ageing to dark brown, scaly plates.

SITKA ALDER (2), *Alnus sinuata* is usually shrubby and grows from central AK and Yukon to northern CA and has blue-gray bark.

RED ALDER or **OREGON ALDER (3)**, *Alnus rubra* is the most prominent broadleaf tree in many parts of its long, narrow range close to the coast from AK to southern CA, and the only alder in America likely to attract the attention of travellers. It does this by growing in tight groups by roadsides in the Coast Mountain and Cascade valleys like Quaking aspen, although less crowded, but with bark almost as shining white, particularly in OR and CA. Its large leaf, to 6 x 4in, has the extreme margin sharply turned down and the fruit is the biggest of any alder, to over 1in long. It has small outliers in the mountains of north ID but seems not to be planted anywhere. Yet in cultivation in Britain it grows with great vigor with annual shoots for several years of 4–5ft. Like all the other alders, this has no fall color beyond the leaf fading to gray or black before being shed.

ITALIAN ALDER (4), *Alnus cordata* grows very rapidly into a shapely, tall tree on any normal soil and is now widely used by roads in Britain but is very rare in America. It has handsome, usually glossy, heart-shaped leaves with little tufts of straight orange hairs on the midrib beneath. There are three trees in Rose Court, Ghiardelli's, San Francisco, CA.

EUROPEAN ALDER (5), *Alnus glutinosa* is stated to have been introduced as late as 1866, but nevertheless it is naturalised, having escaped from plantings, from NF and PQ to PA and IL although seldom seen in the countryside. It is grown in some arboreta, for example, the Holden and Secrest in OH, the New York Botanic Gardens and the George Landis Arboretum near Schenectady, NY, and in Monument Park, Canton, OH. There are two big trees in Superior Avenue, Cleveland, OH. The **Cutleaf alder, 'Laciniata'** with triangular lobes grows to the same sizes as the type tree and is in the Biel Garfield Garden, East Lansing, MI. The **Imperial alder, 'Imperialis'** with deeply cut leaves remains a small tree, seldom bigger than the one in Queen Victoria Park, Niagara Falls, ON which was 40ft x 3ft 2in in 1975.

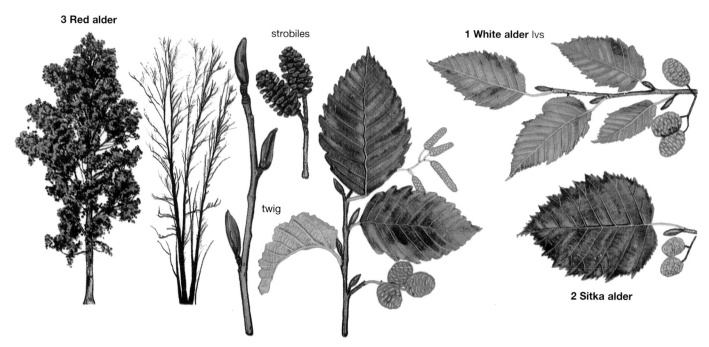

3 Red alder

strobiles

twig

1 White alder lvs

2 Sitka alder

♀ flws

♂ catkins

immature fruit in summer

5 European alder

♂ catkin

Green alder

♂ catkin

4 Italian alder

opened fruit in winter

♀ flws

Gray alder

flws fruit

♂ catkins

Gray alder 20m

4 Italian alder 27m

5 European alder 25m

5 European alder

Hornbeams and Hazels

Hornbeams and hop-hornbeams are small to moderately large trees related to the alders and birches and now given their own Family, *Carpinaceae*. The hop-hornbeams, like the alders and birches, have their male catkins exposed and partly extended during the winter, but the hornbeams have theirs in small ovoid buds which open in mid-spring. There are 42 members of this family, 8 of them hop-hornbeams in which the nut is enclosed in a bladder and 34 hornbeams with the nuts in pairs on a leafy bract. Both groups range from eastern Asia across Europe and have a few species in North America. The hornbeams, with just one North American species, have leaves with numerous, prominent, straight veins, parallel from midrib to marginal teeth, and botanists have used the term 'carpinifolia' or hornbeam-leafed to describe some other species quite unrelated, like an elm and a maple, which show this feature.

The timber, found in reasonably large sizes only in the European hornbeam, is extraordinarily strong and hard. It is often described as 'bony', and the name 'hornbeam' is from the Anglo-Saxon for 'hard wood' or 'tree'. It is so hard that woodworkers prefer not to work with it as it blunts their tools. However, this quality was of extreme value before cast-iron was available for use in cog-wheels in wind and water mills. Here the teeth mesh when turning slowly but with great force and only hornbeam wood is hard and strong enough to do this without rapid wear. It was also used for the centers of cartwheels where great stresses must be borne with holes through the center and radially. It is still used for the action and hammers in some pianos and as the center of butchers' chopping blocks. These have outer parts of beech or maple which wear away faster than the hornbeam center, which thus preserves the raised middle required.

AMERICAN HORNBEAM (1), *Carpinus caroliniana* is also called the Blue beech and Water beech as well as Ironwood. It has an odd distribution. From ME and PQ to MN south to TX and east to the coast all the way to northern FL is normal enough, but it is common again across the big gap to southern Mexico, Guatemala and Honduras. In the USA it is locally common near the extremes of its range as in northwestern MA, southern IN and in the Chicot National Forest, LA. It is little planted in parks or gardens and one in Highland Park, Rochester, NY 30ft x 4ft with two stems is about as far towards achieving tree status as it goes. Hence the European hornbeam is much more often planted. However, the American species has more elegant foliage and is far superior in its orange crimson and purple fall colors. There are hedges of it in State Point Park, Pittsburgh, PA. Trees show the smooth, silvery gray bark on stems fluted into rounded ridges typical of all hornbeams.

EUROPEAN HORNBEAM (2), *Carpinus betulus* was introduced before 1800 and has been planted in rather a few parks and gardens from southern ON to MI and PA but not noticeably in the west. It is a larger tree than the American, with larger, shinier but duller, coarser foliage and leafs out green, not orange-red. In the fall it turns yellow and dull orange. Its stem being often bigger is more deeply fluted and eccentric. The form **Pyramidal hornbeam (3) 'Fastigiata'** is much more widely planted both in the east and the west and its regular egg-shaped, densely branched crown is often seen in parks and streets as far south as Washington DC and west to St. Louis, MO and particularly in OH. It is frequent also in southern BC from Penticton to Victoria and in WA. In Seattle, the streets around 3rd Street are planted with it, and it is seen in Salem, OR. There is a splendid avenue 45ft tall in the School of Horticulture garden, Niagara Falls, ON.

EASTERN HOP-HORNBEAM (4), *Ostrya virginiana* has almost exactly the same range as the hornbeam even as far as the outlier in Central America but also has another in the Black Hills, SD. It is wild on Mount Royal, Montreal and planted in the streets of the city. It is 60ft tall in some parks in MA. The leaf, 3 x 2in, is distinctive in that the teeth at the ends of the 12 pairs of veins project beyond those between them, with short whisker tips. The fall colors are pale orange and purple. The bark, cream-gray in young trees, striped buff, becomes with age dark brown and purple, shredding finely.

KNOWLTON HOP-HORNBEAM (5), *Ostrya knowltonii* is a version with smaller, 2in, more round-tipped leaves and smaller fruit, found in the canyons of UT, AZ, NM and western TX.

CORKSCREW HAZEL (6), *Corylus avellana* 'Contorta' is sometimes seen in the west, as in the Van Dusen Botanic Garden, Vancouver; the Butchart Garden Vancouver I. and Beacon Hill Park, BC and in the Denver Botanic Garden, CO.

TURKISH HAZEL (7), *Corylus colurna* grows into a fine, sturdy, leafy and very vigorous tree, excellent in cities. It can be 90ft tall in Britain but has not yet been planted in America long enough to exceed 60ft. There is one of this height in the School of Horticulture garden at Niagara Falls, ON, and another in the Bailey Arboretum, Long Island, NY with others 40–50ft tall in the botanic gardens at Montreal, PQ; Ottawa, ON; the Morton Arboretum, IL and smaller trees in the Van Dusen Botanic Garden, Vancouver, BC.

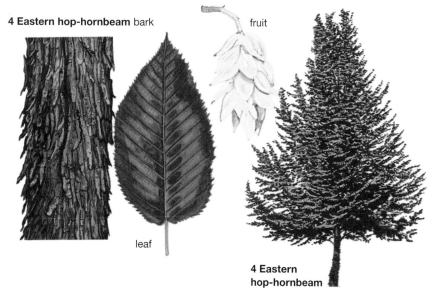

4 Eastern hop-hornbeam bark

fruit

leaf

4 Eastern hop-hornbeam

2 European hornbeam bark

2 European hornbeam autumn leaf

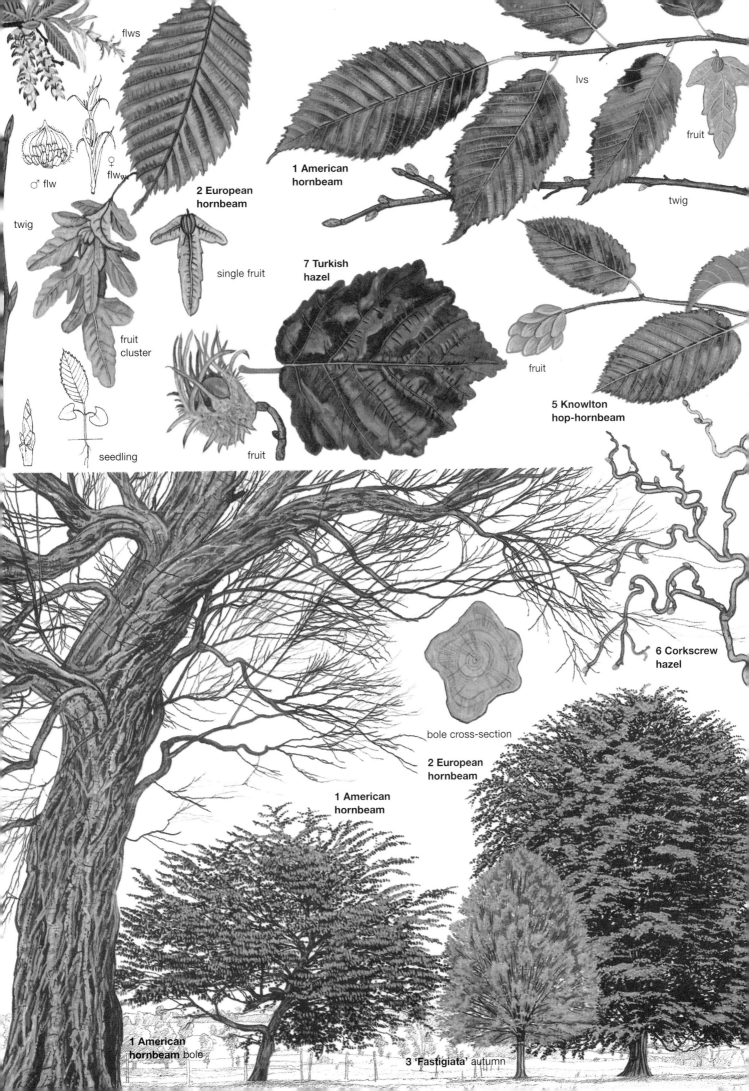

flws

♂ flw

♀ flw

twig

fruit cluster

seedling

2 European hornbeam

single fruit

7 Turkish hazel

fruit

1 American hornbeam

lvs

fruit

twig

5 Knowlton hop-hornbeam

fruit

6 Corkscrew hazel

bole cross-section

2 European hornbeam

1 American hornbeam

1 American hornbeam bole

3 'Fastigiata' autumn

Beeches

The beeches are about 10 species with one in North America, two in Europe and the rest in eastern Asia. They are mostly big or medium sized trees, often important for timber, and are in the same family as the oaks and chestnuts. They are distinct from the others by their male flowers being in clustered heads on slender stalks, not on long catkins, and the females one to two on short, stout stalks. The bark is generally smooth, pale gray, often silvery, and their buds slender and acutely pointed. The fruit is a woody, four-lobed involucre with hard, blunt short spines, enclosing three angular nuts.

AMERICAN BEECH (1), *Fagus grandifolia* is the only beech which can spread by suckers which grow around the base of the trunk. It does this most in the more northerly parts of its range and very seldom in the south. It is a much more elegant and attractive tree than the European beech. Its bark is many shades paler gray and more silvery and its leaves are shining rich green, slender-tipped ellipses with well marked and regular yellow veins in 13–16 pairs. In winter it stands out with retained lower leaves bleached almost white. Normally the leaves are 4in long, sometimes nearer 6in, but a marked variant has small, 3in leaves, thick, leathery and darker green. This is seen in the southeastern part of the range and has sometimes been called var. *caroliniana*. The species has a wide range, from NS to north of Lake Huron and the south of Lake Superior, and, sweeping round east of IL to eastern MO, AR and TX but scarcely enters FL. It is common in woodlands almost throughout, and notably from Montreal, PQ to Ottawa, Toronto and London, ON and from Philadelphia, PA on the plains and Piedmont to Atlanta, GA and ascends to 5600ft at Wesner Bald and the Blue Ridge Drive in NC. It is in many parks from Portland, ME to Milwaukee, WI often as remnant forest but also planted. There are occasional plantings in the far west, in the University of Washington Campus and in the Arboretum; in Cornwall Park, Bellingham and there are two in a city park in Olympia, all in WA.

EUROPEAN BEECH (2), *Fagus sylvatica* grows from England to the Caucasus Mountains and will have been among the first trees brought across to America, more for the known quality of its timber or as a reminder of home than for its decorative qualities. It is a coarser, darker tree, with darker gray bark on the trunk and upper branches not so silvery as in the American beech. Its leaves reach 4 x 3in and are a beautifully fresh green at first but soon become dark. There are only six to seven pairs of veins, less regular and prominent, and the margins are wavy and only obscurely toothed. It is common only in Newport RI in streets and yards, and in Manchester, NH, Beverley and Pride's Crossing, MA but it grows best in the Hudson Valley where it is less frequent in general but is in all the big gardens and parks. Elsewhere it is frequent in eastern OH but scarce or absent beyond a few in ON, MI, PA, DE and DC. In the west it is common in and around Vancouver, Victoria, BC, and rare further south.

The **Dawyck beech** or **Fastigiate beech (3)** is named from the Scottish estate on which it was found in 1860. It is seen in towns and parks from ON to WI, OH and PA, but no further south, and in Vancouver streets; Lincoln Street, Spokane, in Wenatchee, WA and at the County Courthouse, Salt Lake City, UT. In Arnold Arboretum, MA it was 92ft x 6ft in 1975; and noted in Auburn Cemetery nearby; in Hidden Garden, Tappen, MI, at King of Prussia; Mill Creek Park, Youngstown and most parks in OH.

The **Copper** or **Purple beech (4)**, 'Purpurea' was first noted near Zurich, Switzerland, in 1680. The name covers all the seedlings which arise and have variously muddy brownish black purple foliage and disfigure so many garden landscapes. A few superior forms are grafted and include '**Swat Magret**' from Germany in 1895. Large trees are frequent from ME to WI to MD and MO, notably large in the Hudson Valley, NY and in PA. In Marquand Park, Princeton, NJ it is 100ft x 18ft; at University House, Rochester it is 100ft x 16ft, at Lyndhurst Garden, NY it is 85ft x 16ft. There are far too many around Odessa and Annapolis, MD, Leesburg and Rondhill, VA and Racine WI. It is common in Vancouver, Victoria and Sidney, BC and south by Blame and Bellingham in WA to Olympia and Tacoma and is grown in Salt Lake City, UT, Denver and Loveland, CO.

The **Weeping beech (5)**, '**Pendula**' is also biggest in the Hudson Valley and frequent in parks from ON and MA, common from Middletown to Newport, RI, and frequent through PA and MI to WI but in BC and WA it is more confined to the large parks and botanic gardens.

Fernleaf beech (6), '**Aspleniifolia**' has the same distribution, commonest again in RI, MA, NY, PA and OH but more seen in south ON. At Lyndhurst Garden one is 62ft x 13ft. This tree is a graft chimaera with internal tissue of ordinary beech, and damage from hail or wind results in shoots with leaves grading from ordinary beech to fully cut or strap-shaped, and many only slightly lobed. Out of leaf it is known by its fine shoots and some sprouts of them on the trunk.

4 Copper beech 'River's Purple'

2 European beech autumn

5 Weeping beech

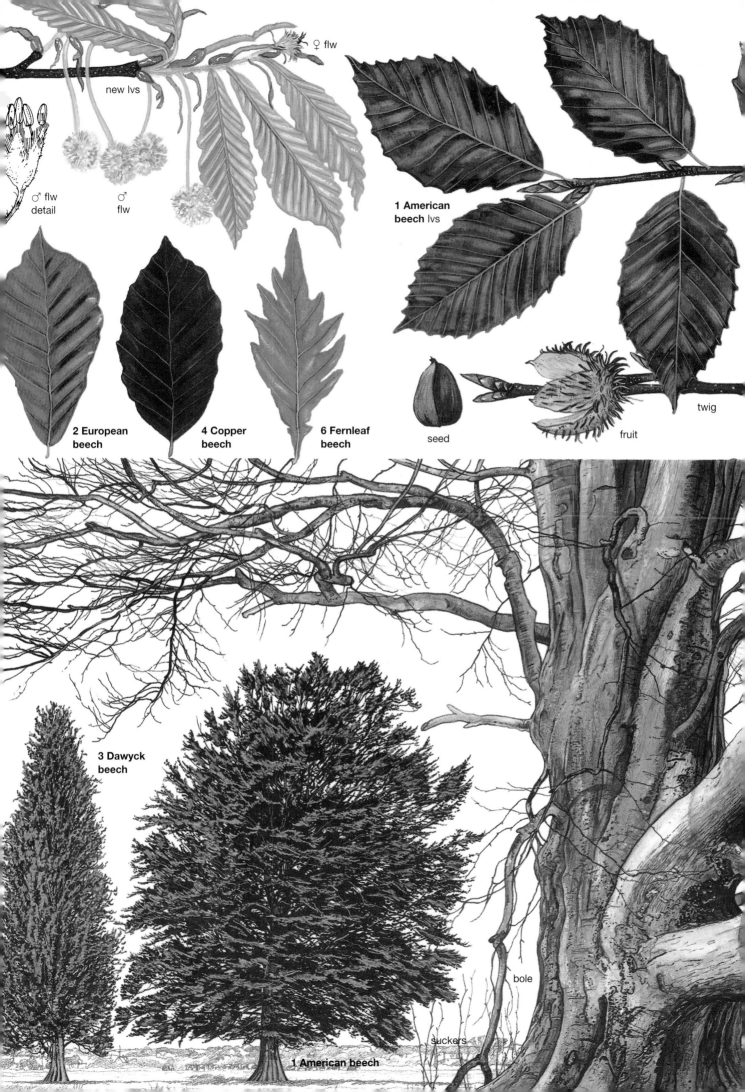

new lvs

♀ flw

♂ flw detail

♂ flw

1 American beech lvs

2 European beech

4 Copper beech

6 Fernleaf beech

seed

fruit

twig

3 Dawyck beech

1 American beech

bole

suckers

Chestnuts, Chinkapins and Tanoak

AMERICAN CHESTNUT (1), *Castanea dentata* has fallen on hard times. Until about 1930 it was the one American species of the four natives to grow into a shapely and big tree, to 100ft tall. Since then, however, it has been devastated by attacks of Chestnut blight, *Endothia parasitica*, and has joined the other three as no more than a shrub and so could be called, as those shrubby ones are, a chinkapin. (The true Chinkapins differ from the chestnut in having woolly shoots and leaves, and only a single nut in each spiny case.) A tiny number of real trees has been found in an occasional remote valley in the Alleghenies, surviving, at least for a time, because of their isolation. Elsewhere throughout its range, from ME, southern ON and eastern IN to northern GA it is seen as sprouts from old stumps and although these grow vigorously to about 40ft they then succumb before bearing seed. Logs of the old trees often still lie beneath the sprouting stumps. Trees planted in the western states may well escape the disease. One by the Cathedral in Victoria BC seemed healthy in 1976 as did a small tree in Revelstoke, BC and one 30ft x 3ft in the University of Washington Arboretum in Seattle. The shoot is slender, shining pale yellow-green ripening to olive-brown then red-brown, finely hairy. The bark is smooth and dark gray until fissured into long, flat, dark gray-brown ridges flaking at the edges. The leaf is 6–7in long.

ALLEGHENY CHINKAPIN (2), *Castanea pumila*, grows from NJ to FL, west to eastern TX, OK and KY. The leaves are 3–5in long, unfold red with thick white hairs beneath and turn dull yellow in the fall.

OZARK CHINKAPIN (3), *Castanea ozarkensis* replaces the Allegheny form in the Ozark Hills and into MO and OK, and has bigger leaves, to 9in long with bristle-tips to its teeth.

CHINESE CHESTNUT, *Castanea mollissima* was sent to the Arnold Arboretum, MA in 1903 and is resistant to the Chestnut blight. It has therefore been grown partly for its nuts and to make hybrids with the American chestnut which could also resist the disease, but also as a foliage tree. Its 8in leaves are bright, glossy green with 13–15in curved teeth each side, reddish veins and with gray-white hairs on the underside. It is infrequent in parks and gardens from southern ON to AL and MO. Many are seen in roadside gardens around Williamsburg and Norfolk, and by US 1 in VA but generally it is confined to collections like Mount Auburn Cemetery, Cambridge, MA, the Bailey Arboretum, NY, the Morris Arboretum and Longwood Gardens, PA; Mount Airy and Dawes Arboreta in OH and Oak Park, Montgomery, AL.

EUROPEAN SWEET CHESTNUT (4), *Castanea sativa* is more scarce and has stout, angled red-brown shoots. With age, the fissures on the bark twist into increasingly flat-angled spirals. In Europe, the buckeyes are called 'horse-chestnuts' and the true chestnut is distinguished as the 'Sweet chestnut' in contrast to 'horse' which probably implies 'coarse and inedible'.

GOLDEN CHINKAPIN (5), *Castanopsis chrysophylla*, more usually now *Chrysolepis chrysophylla*, is of botanical interest as a connecting link between chestnuts and oaks and for being, with its dwarfish relative the **Sierra chinkapin**, *C. sempervirens*, the only ones outside southeastern Asia. It is found from southern WA by the coast in one locality and from mid-OR to mid-CA commonly in the Cascades and by the coast, with small patches in the Sierra Nevada. In OR it is a bush of the understorey, as at Koosah Falls, and it is small in Pygmy Forest, Mendocino, CA but between these places, in the Siskiyou Mountains around Gasquet and elsewhere it is a shapely, tall tree, with a pale gray bark, with a few dark, sharp-edged vertical fissures. The evergreen leaves are 3 x 1in and thick and leathery, often with the only visible vein the pale yellow midrib. The flowers do not emerge and open until midsummer when the new leaves are out. Male catkins 1–3in long are in big terminal bunches, pale yellow-green. Some of them bear a few female flowers near the base but mostly the females, with red-purple stigmas, are on their own short catkins behind. The fruit are in tight bunches of about 10, bright green and spiny.

TANOAK (6), *Lithocarpus densiflorus* is, like the chinkapins, the only member of the genus not in southeastern Asia, and is very much a far-western tree in America. It inhabits the Coast Range from the Umpqua Valley in south OR to the Santa Inez Mountains in southern CA and, locally in the Sierra Nevada south to Mariposa. It is bushy around Grants Pass, OR and in Mendocino, CA, but a tall tree around Gasquet, on Bear Ridge, and among the tallest Coast redwood stands between them and again in Big Basin redwood groves well to the south of San Francisco. It has large, 1in, long-ovoid, pale orange to dark brown acorns in shallow, spiny cups. Young trees stand out in the woods with whitish-gray bark. When 50ft tall it has become dark brown and vertically fissured.

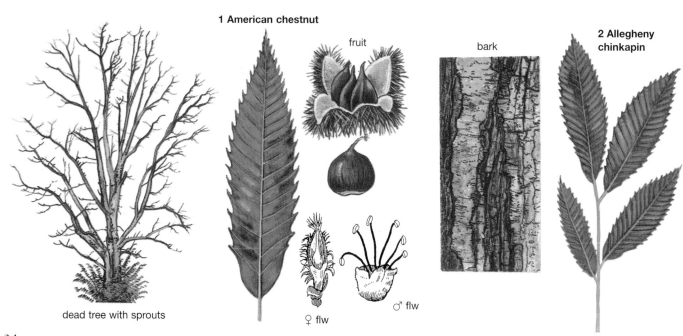

1 American chestnut

fruit

bark

2 Allegheny chinkapin

dead tree with sprouts

♀ flw

♂ flw

bark

3 Ozark chinkapin

5 Golden chinkapin

under

♂ flw

4 European sweet chestnut

fruit

♂ flw

6 Tanoak

seed

bark

fruit

5 Golden chinkapin

6 Tanoak

bole with fire scar

White oaks

The oaks are a huge assemblage of species of the northern hemisphere, extending into the southern only in Colombia, and have been estimated to be 450–500 in number in the genus *Quercus*, omitting the hundred or so *Lithocarpus* species. More than half of these are evergreen trees with two main centres of distribution, China and Mexico, both yet to be fully explored botanically. There are 58 species of full tree form in North America and here they have been particularly liable to hybridise. The crosses resulting can be hard to unravel as to the exact parentage or whether some are in fact hybrid rather than varieties or even true species in their own right. Currently 86 hybrids are recognised and given their formal botanical names and another dozen are probably hybrids. The oaks of North America can usefully be separated as five groups: White, Chestnut, Red, Willow and Live. The Red and Willow oaks are the most given to hybrids, within and between the two groups. Many of the White and Live oaks are very rugged, long-lived trees which reach a great size. Some Red oaks grow much faster when young and make tall trees but not being so long-lived they do not achieve such stout stems. All oaks have acorns for fruit, and every plant that bears acorns is an oak, of one group or another, but leaf shape varies enormously from small, unlobed, untoothed, thin and slender to big, much and deeply lobed with big teeth and, in China, to big hard leaves like rhododendrons.

WHITE OAK (1), *Quercus alba* is typical of the group it heads in having rough, scaly or shaggy bark and in extending its range further north than all but one in the other groups, from PQ and ME to MN and from east TX to the Atlantic coast. It is common almost everywhere from Deering Oak Park, Portland ME to Mankaro, MN to north FL, except near the coast of NC. Tall trees in the open have crowns with a columnar spire of several vertical branches for the top 40–50ft, with few laterals. Old trees can be very broad. A fine example is the famous tree at Wye Mills, MD which has long been an accredited 'champion' and given as 29ft 8in round, but which more fairly measured at 7ft, to avoid huge root-buttresses, is 100ft x 23ft 4in. The leaves emerge stained crimson then turn cream before becoming bright green above, whitish beneath. Before falling they turn bright orange-red, crimson and red-purple. An odd feature is that shade and lower-crown leaves have lobes cut less than halfway to the midrib, and full-light, top leaves are deeply and elegantly cut with curved sinuses nearly to the midrib.

BUR OAK (2), *Quercus macrocarpa* is another White oak, and extends further north and west than any other eastern oak. It is common in woods around Winnipeg and along creeks in SD and just reaches SK and MT. It ranges to the coast in TX but except for tiny patches in LA and AL it is absent in the southeast from MS to north VA. It is the dominant oak west of Madison, WI where it stands out with its dark crown, almost black branches and dark gray bole with bark deeply ridged and sometimes shaggy. Emerging foliage is a distinctive yellow. It is occasionally planted in the west, as in Boulder and Denver, CO and in Vancouver, BC. The acorn is the biggest in American oaks, to 2 x 1½in on a tree in Tulsa, OK at the Art Gallery. The leaf can be 12 x 6in and varies much in the depth of lobing.

OVERCUP OAK (3), *Quercus lyrata* is a somewhat southern White oak growing from the Gulf Coast in TX north to St. Louis, MO and round the south of the Alleghenies to NC and a few outposts in MD and DE. It is the common tall deciduous oak in the Live oak areas as in City Park, New Orleans, LA where there is a fine avenue; from Liberty to Livingston, TX and by US 61 in MS, but there are good trees at its northern limit, in Druid's Hill Park, Baltimore, MD and one 100ft x 14ft in the White House Garden, Washington, DC. It has been little planted beyond range but is in Shenley Park, Pittsburg, PA. The acorn is almost enclosed in the big, globular cup and the leaf can be 9 x 7in.

OREGON WHITE OAK (4), *Quercus garryana* is the only native oak in BC and WA and extends along the Coast Range to the Bay Area, CA with two areas in the Sierra Nevada. It is common from Victoria to Nanaimo on Vancouver Island, around Tacoma, WA, each side of the Willamette Valley and along the Rogue and Umpqua Rivers, OR. It stands out in farmland fields, broad, dark in bark and nearly black in leaf, often encumbered by mistletoe.

POST OAK (5), *Quercus stellata*, stands out wherever it is seen by the way that it hangs its seemingly cross-shaped leaves. It ranges from the coast of MA and Long Island to MO and mid-TX east to the Atlantic Coast, and is a common woodland, roadside tree over most of this range and in old city parks but not in central squares. There are trees of 100ft x 12ft in Memphis Botanic Garden, TN and one in Athens, GA is 100ft x 14ft. The bark is gray-brown, finely fissured into vertical plates, flaking or stripping and sometimes shaggy. The stem is usually straight, bearing rather few lower branches which are twisted. The leaves are 4–8in long and variable in lobing but always broadly a right-angled cross.

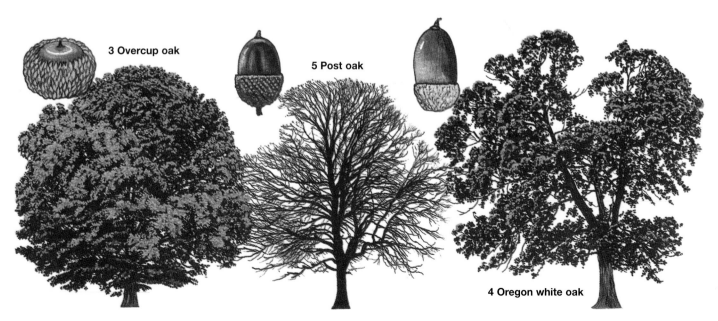

3 Overcup oak

5 Post oak

4 Oregon white oak

4 Oregon white oak

2 Bur oak

1 White oak

leaf variations

acorn

twig

5 Post oak

3 Overcup oak

acorn

2 Bur oak

1 White oak

bole

White oaks

VALLEY OAK or **CALIFORNIAN WHITE OAK (1)**, *Quercus lobata* is confined to that State from Trinity River to near Los Angeles. It is abundant on the dry sandy hills around Paso Robles, where one in the park square is 80ft x 13ft, by Rt 128 along the Navarro River to Albion Bridge, carrying some mistletoe; by Rt 198, Lemmon Cove and 41 to Yosemite in the Sierra Nevada. It has a short, stout trunk with dark gray bark closely cracked into smooth, square plates, and big, curving branches, the upper ones twisting to an often misshapen top and the lower arching down, both with rather pendulous outer shoots. There are fine soft hairs on the upper side of the leaf and a thicker covering beneath, which side is gray-green and much paler than the dark gray-green, subglossy upper side which has dark veins. The leaf is 1–3in long, and the shoot is pale green-brown and very finely hairy.

GAMBEL OAK (2), *Quercus gambelii* takes its name from its discoverer, William Gambel who surveyed the natural history of the southern Rocky Mountains in 1844. It is also known as the Utah white oak. Its northernmost stand is in UT, and there it fails by only 30 miles to reach ID and give that state even one native oak. It ranges south from UT and the adjacent corner of WY through CO, south NV and AZ to NM and western TX. It is common on dry hillsides through much of this area as a small, sinuous tree or a shrub, prominent in the fall as its foliage turns through yellow to orange and rich red-brown and sometimes a good red. It can be seen beside Rt 163 from Monument Valley through Blanding to Monticello, UT; by Rt 64 to Grand Canyon, AZ where it is of good tree-size; above Jerome, US 89Alt. and for long stretches of Rt 104 west of Tucumcari, NM. Gambel oak has a dark gray bark and a slightly ridged, gray-brown shoot reddish on top. The leaf is 2½ x 2in and has dense, short white hairs on its underside and stalk.

CHAPMAN OAK (3), *Quercus chapmanii*, named from the Florida botanist who first distinguished it, is a White oak abundant only in western FL from Tampa to St. Andrews Bays and scarce on sandy barrens north just into SC and west into AL. Its young shoots are covered in dense, bright yellow hairs and shed them to become dark red-brown. Its leaves are thick and hard, 2–3in long and semi-evergreen. The ½in acorns are pubescent on the half which protrudes from the deep cup. It is often a very low shrub but can be a round-topped 50ft.

ENGLISH OAK (4), *Quercus robur* grows right across Europe to the Caucasus Mountains and in North Africa. In America, only in RI and MA, notably around Newport and Manchester NH, Marblehead and Salem MA in the east and Vancouver, Victoria, Sidney and to the border in BC and nearby WA is it variably common in parks, gardens and towns. It is uncommon in parks in ON and south to Washington, DC, in OH and PA, inland in BC and there is one near the Capitol in Denver, CO. A fine tree is near the Capitol in Olympia, WA, 100ft x 12ft. It differs from all American oaks and nearly all others too, in the base of the leaf not tapering to the stalk but curving out from it in an 'ear' each side. The leafstalk is less than ⅛in long, but the acorn, paired or single, is on a stalk 2–3m long. In this White oak, the terminal winter bud on the leading shoot either aborts or is subordinate to one of the laterals beside it, which puts out a strong shoot, ascending at an angle to the axis. Except in woods, long straight stems are thus very unusual.

The Cypress oak (5), 'Fastigiata', is a densely columnar form with bigger, longer leaves. A tree found in Germany was first grafted in 1783. Seedlings raised from its acorns vary from erect like the parent to broad or globular and wineglass shaped and in PA, NJ and around, a form is grown with strong upswept, incurved lower branches. It is on Riverside Drive and in the botanic garden in Ottawa; the Allen Botanic Garden, Toronto; in St. Catherine's and similar parks and towns in ON; in Brunswick, ME; Newbury Street, Boston and other parks in MA, NY, MI, PA (fine trees in Duke Street, Lancaster), in OH (fine trees in Columbus), DC and MD. Further south it is scarce but seen in Memphis Botanic Garden, TN. There is a splendid avenue at the Mormon Temple, Salt Lake City, UT and trees in Wenatchee, WA and around Vancouver, BC and in Eugene, OR.

SESSILE OAK (6), *Quercus petraea* from Europe and a superior tree in Britain to the English oak, has more solid, firm leaves tapering to a 1in yellow stalk and acorns without stalks. It is seldom seen in America. There is a young one in the George Landis Arboretum, Esperance, NY. The erect form, **'Columna' (7)** is more slender than the Cypress oak. This is planted along Sprague Avenue in Spokane, WA and in the Royal Botanic Garden, Hamilton, ON.

HUNGARIAN OAK (8), *Quercus frainetto* grows very fast into a majestic dome of straight branches with pale gray, finely plated bark. It is deplorably little known in America but there is a tree at the School of Horticulture, Niagara Falls, ON and several about 60ft tall at the University of Washington Arboretum, Seattle.

2 Gambel oak

7 'Columna'

4 English oak

5 Cypress oak

8 Hungarian oak

1 California white oak

2 Gambel oak

6 Sessile oak

3 Chapman oak

4 English oak

1 California white oak

1 California white oak autumn

bark

Emory and Chestnut oaks

EMORY OAK (1), *Quercus emoryi* is the common hillside and canyon oak across southern AZ and NM into western TX. It is in the tall mixed woods beside the road through Oak Creek Canyon, among Arizona pine and Arizona smooth cypress, and in the open high above Jerome by US 89Alt to the west. It is evergreen, although it is another White oak, and shrubby, not often over 30ft tall. The bark is black with gray scaly ridges, the shoot stout, pink-brown densely hairy, fading from the red in which it emerged. The leaf is stiff and hard, bright gray-green beneath, 2 x 1in. The paired acorns nearly 1in long are smooth, bright green in summer and ripen to rich purple-brown.

CHESTNUT OAK (2), *Quercus prinus* is one of a small group found nowhere outside eastern North America. They are characterised by large, long leaves with many shallow, usually rounded lobes or teeth and taper usually to slender stalks. Its leaves less closely resemble those of the American chestnut than, for example, does the closely related Chinkapin oak, but they are in the same mould and serve to give this group its name. Several of the leaves of this group are more like the European sweet chestnut and this may have been in the minds of those who named the group. Some works have taken the name *'prinus'*, which was given by Linnaeus in 1753 and included the Swamp chestnut oak, to apply properly only to the latter and so require a name for the more northerly Chestnut oak. The first published name to distinguish this was given by Carl Willdenow in 1805 and he called it *'Quercus montana'* so this name is often used. It occurs from southeast ME and the Hudson Valley just into ON to MI and via eastern OH and southern IL to mid-AL. On the eastern side it does what so many other trees do; it occurs along the coast through Long Island and DE then, from around the Chesapeake Bay, it takes to the hills and continues to GA and AL but not on the Coastal Plain. It is the commonest of the many oaks in much of the Alleghenies and Great Smoky Mountains, along the Skyline and Blue Ridge Drives and to over 4600ft in TN. It has been planted on the Coastal Plain, for example in Savannah and the Callaway Gardens, Lone Pine, GA, but very little elsewhere and none was found in the west. The leaf is to 9in long, gray-white beneath and on a stout 1in, often reddish, stalk. The acorns are shining rich red-brown and begin to germinate very soon after they fall, the sprouting radicle pushing out as they lie carpeting the ground. A tree at Hyde Park, NY, Vanderbilt Mansion is 95ft x 14ft and one in the Tyler Arboretum, Lima, PA is 105ft x 11ft.

SWAMP CHESTNUT OAK (3), *Quercus michauxii* very nearly takes over where the Chestnut oak leaves off, to the south. They overlap in NJ and DE and then where the Chestnut oak keeps to the hills, the Swamp chestnut ranges around the Coastal Plain, through north FL and the Delta, LA into east TX and up the Mississippi Valley to south IN and IL, overlapping again only in the hills of GA and AL. It is common particularly along US 51 and 61, in MI and TN and to Cairo, IL and around Indianapolis, IN where there are good trees in Broad Ripple Park and one at a nearby house is 70ft x 13ft. It differs from the Chestnut oak in having a very pale, silvery or creamy gray bark fissured into small strips and flakes and generally rather larger leaves, darker above and more silvery beneath and more marked lobing and two more pairs of veins, to 16 on large leaves. It grows rapidly.

CHINKAPIN OAK (4), *Quercus muehlenbergii* is a more elegant version of the above two oaks, with its more slender leaves glossy bright yellow-green, slightly curved teeth, edged finely pale yellow, somewhat bluish white beneath and slender yellow stalk. It has about 12 pairs of veins. The bark is dull gray fissured into narrow ridges which flake to leave paler or pink patches. Like the Chestnut oak, this keeps to the hills after leaving the coast in MD but it strikes to the Gulf Coast near Tallahassee, FL and extends to central TX, OK and IA. One at the Philbrook Art Center, Tulsa, OK is 80ft x 10ft. A good specimen is in the Capitol Park, Raleigh, NC out of range, while others in Broad Ripple and Marriott Parks, Indianapolis, IN are within range and could be wild trees.

SWAMP WHITE OAK (5), *Quercus bicolor* is, despite the name, a Chestnut oak, not a White but its leaf is much more like some members of that group and much less like a chestnut leaf than the others in its group. However, that is chance, because the name probably derives from the underside of the leaf. When this first unfolds it is blue-green above and silvery white with hairs beneath. In some trees the silvery underside remains when the hairs have been shed but in others the color is more green than white. The bark is pale gray with a coarse network of thick blackish-gray ridges. The leaf is usually 6 x 3in but may be 10 x 6in. This tree has a rather fragmented range from the junction of PQ and ON, the coast of ME and the Hudson Valley east to OH and then solid to WI and north MO and round to OH, MD, Long Island and MA. One in Highland Park, Rochester, NY is 90ft x 12ft.

5 Swamp white oak

bark

1 Emory oak

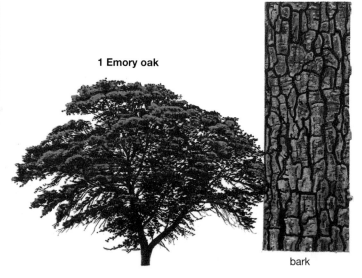

bark

3 Swamp chestnut oak

4 Chinkapin oak

1 Emory oak

5 Swamp white oak

2 Chestnut oak

bark

3 Swamp chestnut oak

2 Chestnut oak bole

Red oaks

The Red or Black oaks are another group found only in North America but this time in both the east and the west. They are more distinct than the other groups, although sharing the features to a small extent with the Willow oaks, their nearest relatives. These features are few large teeth on the leaves all drawn out at the tip to a whisker, and small acorns taking two years to ripen.

NORTHERN RED OAK (1), *Quercus rubra* grows further north in the extreme east than any other oak, in NS and PQ but not as far in the central states as the Bur oak. It extends south to OK and AL and to the east coast from NC northwards but not on the plains of GA and SC. It is very common throughout the Allegheny Mountains and reaches 5500ft at Wesner Bald, and through OH and New England but shows up less in the south where there are so many other oaks. It is widely planted in the west, in Vancouver, Victoria, BC, in Spokane and Seattle and Tacoma, WA, on the campus at Eugene, OR. Exceptional trees are: Marquand Park, Princeton, NJ, 132ft x 12ft and 125ft x 15ft 6in; Longwood Gardens, PA, 130ft x 13ft; Holden Arboretum, Mentor, OH, 90ft x 19ft and Smith College Campus, Northampton, MA, 90ft x 14ft. The bark of very wide, flat ridges and wide fissures is typical of old trees. Young ones, and particularly those in the west, in hot areas, or street tubs, are bright silvery gray and smooth.

BLACK OAK (2), *Quercus velutina* derives its botanical name, 'velutina', from the velvet-like covering of very fine hairs on the shoot, leaf and leafstalk. That on the shoot, stalk and underside of leaf lasts more or less until leaf fall but that on the upper side of the leaf is soon shed and the top becomes shiny. The leaf is hard and tough like parchment and there is a curious tendency for the midrib to fork and give the leaf two outer ends. The range is from ME to GA in the east and from TX to WI in the west. Beyond that it is planted in Denver CO (18th and Stout Streets) and Seattle, WA (4th St.). A fine tree, 135ft x 17ft, is beside Washington St., Princeton, NJ and at Dumbarton Oaks, DC, one is 75ft x 18ft while one at Winterthur, DE is 140ft tall.

SCARLET OAK (3), *Quercus coccinea* ranges from ME to AL and MO away from the coast south of VA, to over 5000ft in the Great Smoky Mountains, TN. It is planted in some collections in WA and at Eugene, OR. A hollow trunk in Highland Park, Rochester, NY is over 18ft round; a tall tree in the Barnes Arboretum, PA is 130ft tall. It is common by much of US 50 from St. Louis, MO to Annapolis, MD and DE and by the Palisades Parkway, NJ.

PIN OAK (4), *Quercus palustris* is wild from RI and VT to KS, OK and TN but is grown widely as a city street tree far beyond that as well as within it. It is much the commonest tree in many city parks like Central Park, New York and Prospect Park, Brooklyn, NY and is in streets from Toronto, ON to Tulsa, OK; in Denver, CO and again commonly in Vancouver and Victoria, BC. Fine trees line Nassau Street, Princeton, NJ. One in Edgewater Park, Cleveland, OH is 100ft x 15 ft. The habit of young trees suits them well to street planting, with their straight clean stem and high skirt of fine shoots below a slender spire.

NORTHERN PIN OAK (5), *Quercus ellipsoidalis* occurs from northern IN to mid-MN and MO and replaces the Bur oak as dominant tree in parts of south MN and into WI. It is also local in MI and is planted in Denver, CO. The leaves unfold pale crimson and turn whitish-green then shiny dark green. One at the University of Wisconsin Arboretum is 80ft x 15ft.

SOUTHERN RED OAK (6), *Quercus falcata*, is very distinct with its dark leaves cut into longer, slender, curved lobes and is common over most of its range from NJ to north FL, west to TX and MO. It is often a tall, elegant tree, and is 100ft x 14ft in McPherson Square, Washington DC; 115ft x 14ft at Middleton Place, SC and 135ft x 12ft in the L.H. Cohn Arboretum, Baton Rouge, LA. The **Cherrybark oak**, var. *pagodifolia* is an interesting form found over much the same range. Its lower crown bears leaves very like the Black oak and the upper bears those of the type, Southern Red oak. It can be recognised by the dark gray to black bark in square plates.

TURKEY OAK (7), *Quercus laevis* has even more deeply cut and curved-back lobes on glossy bright green leaves 6in long. It dominates low sandy hills as a large shrub from SC and LA, inland in GA to Swainshoro and abundant by US 80 to Savannah; by Rt 87 from Brewton, south AL; 399 Santa Rosa Island FL and Pensacola.

SHUMARD OAK (8), *Quercus shumardii* has a larger, less deeply lobed leaf than the pin oak, more like the Northern red oak but with tufts in the vein-angles beneath, like the pin oak, but smaller. The leaf is also like that of the Pin oak in being shiny beneath. This tree occurs from NC round the plains to OH and west to mid-TX, in the variety *texana*, the Texas oak, and an outlier in VA/MD. A tree by the Capitol in Atlanta, GA is 80ft x 15ft. Planted in Highland Park, Rochester, NY it has grown in 60 years to 85ft x 6ft.

1 Northern red oak

2 Black oak

8 Shumard oak

forest tree

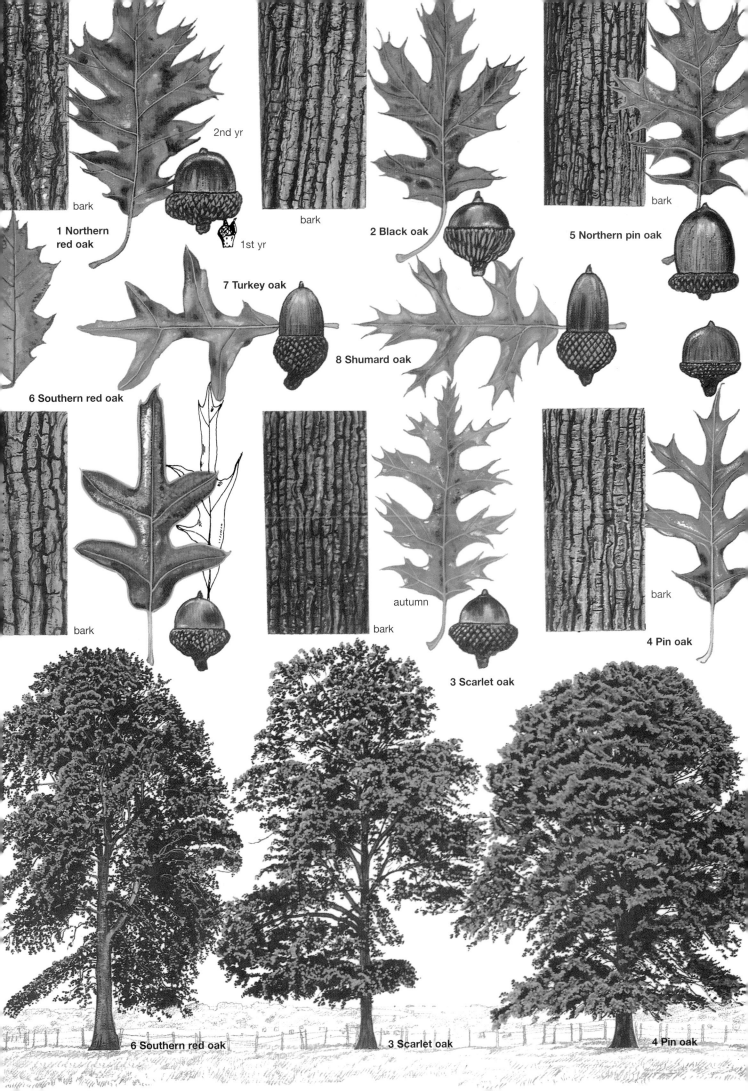

bark

1 Northern red oak

2nd yr

1st yr

7 Turkey oak

2 Black oak

bark

5 Northern pin oak

8 Shumard oak

6 Southern red oak

bark

autumn

bark

3 Scarlet oak

4 Pin oak

6 Southern red oak

3 Scarlet oak

4 Pin oak

Blackjack and Willow oaks

CALIFORNIA BLACK OAK (1), *Quercus kelloggii* is the sole representative of Red oaks in the west. It is common in most of the foothills and valleys in the mountains from southwestern OR each side of the Central Valley, CA to the Mexican border. Although the 1972 Champion was over 120ft x 28ft in the Siskiyou Mountains, OR, it is a tree of very moderate size around Grant's Pass, OR and in Yosemite National Park, CA while in King's Canyon it is bushy, spreading and twisting. These bushes are worked over in October by Steller's jays taking the long-ovoid, chestnut-brown acorns, striped pale brown. The bark is dull gray broken by dark, narrow fissures into pale gray ridges. A tree in Capitol Park, Sacramento CA is 90ft x 9ft. The leaf can be 9 x 6in and the pale green, usually softly hairy underside has a white midrib.

BLACKJACK OAK (2), *Quercus marilandica* is an eccentric among the Red oaks where deeply cut, rather thin leaves are the accepted norm, since it has the broadest, most shallowly cut leaves of any oak, and they are thick and hard. They are 6 x 6in and often curl to show the underside which is pale orange with dense hairs in most of the range but bright yellow in the southeast. The broad midrib divides into three at its halfway point. The tree is rugged and broad with level branching, and a spreading tall shrub in the dry hills in TX and AR. It ranges from mid TX to south IA and east to Long Island, NY skirting south OH and WV. It is often a thicket under Loblolly pine in SC and GA. Planted in Highland Park, NY and in the Coker Arboretum, NC it is 60ft tall and one in Texarkana, TX by a crossroads as US 67 leaves town northeastwards is a fine tree of about 50ft, but anything above 40ft is unusual.

ARKANSAS OAK (3), *Quercus arkansana* is a small-leafed Blackjack oak, discovered in south AR but with its main range through LA and on the Coastal Plain to GA. The leaf is 4 x 4in and dull yellow beneath.

TURKEY OAK (4), *Quercus cerris* belongs to a group not found in the New World and grows across southern Europe. Useful features in identification are the prominent whiskers around not only the terminal buds but the laterals as well; dense hairs on the shoot and a finer covering on both sides of the leaf, and the branches swelling out to join the trunk. It is a good grower in city parks in England and a very vigorous tree in the warmer parts. In North America it is also a city park tree but only in NY where there is a long avenue across Central Park towards the Reservoir and many trees elsewhere, in the New York Botanic Garden and in Prospect Park, Brooklyn. Otherwise, it is seen as a town and garden street only in RI from Middletown to Newport, and as single large trees in the Morris Arboretum and Woodlands Cemetery, Philadelphia, PA. It sows itself in Central Park and the trees there show wide variation in the depth and regularity of the lobing.

WATER OAK (5), *Quercus nigra* is a Red oak with a great tendency to hybridise not only with others in that group but with Willow oaks as well. It also has leaves of variable shape on the same tree, from round-ended spoons to some like small Blackjack oak leaves and others more deeply lobed. There are tufts in the vein-angles beneath. The bark is finely fissured vertically, pale or dark gray in broad, roughened plates. It is native DE to mid-FL and TX, north to AR, TN and the plains of NC. It is common around Dismal Swamp, VA and all along the Coastal Plain and up the Mississippi Valley to Dyersburg, TN. One in Audubon Park, New Orleans was 100ft x 16ft in 1981 but going thin. In Athens, GA, there are fine trees. One on Lumpkin Street is 80ft x 14ft and in Columbus, AR one is 100ft x 13ft. Very few are planted in the west.

LAUREL OAK (6), *Quercus laurifolia* has the same natural range as the Water oak but is much less seen although quite common on the coast of VA and in western LA into TX. This oak is nearly evergreen with very dark red-brown to black slender shoots and spur-shoots at right-angles to the main shoot. It has long, level branches and carries much dead twiggery in its crown.

WILLOW OAK (7), *Quercus phellos* also ranges, broadly, from DE to eastern TX but misses almost all GA, and the mountains of NC. It is much planted in the streets of New York, Philadelphia, PA, Washington, DC and Atlanta, GA and generally in OH. There are also trees in arboreta in Vancouver, BC and Seattle, WA. A big tree by the Capitol in Washington, DC is 110ft x 18ft. Young trees have very smooth, gray bark. New leaves unfold late, yellow with red tinted centres.

SHINGLE OAK (8), *Quercus imbricaria* is like Willow oak but with leaves half as long again and on a stalk three times as long, and like a Laurel oak but again with a ⅛in leafstalk and softly hairy beneath instead of the shiny smooth underside. It is found almost exactly northwards from where the Willow and Laurel oaks fade out from AR to NJ as far as south IA, MI and the whole of PA. It is common along US 50 from IL east; around Baltimore, MD and, planted, in city parks in NY. In the New York Botanic Garden it is 115ft x 9ft.

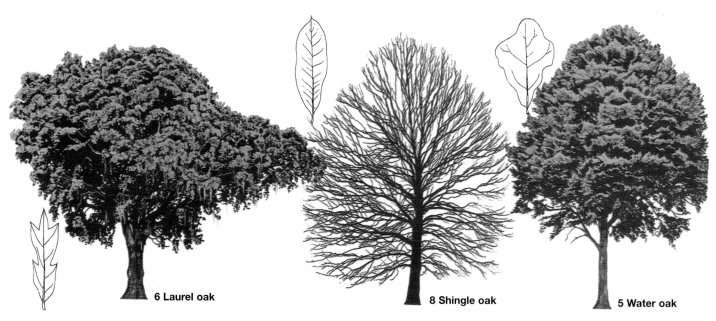

6 Laurel oak

8 Shingle oak

5 Water oak

44

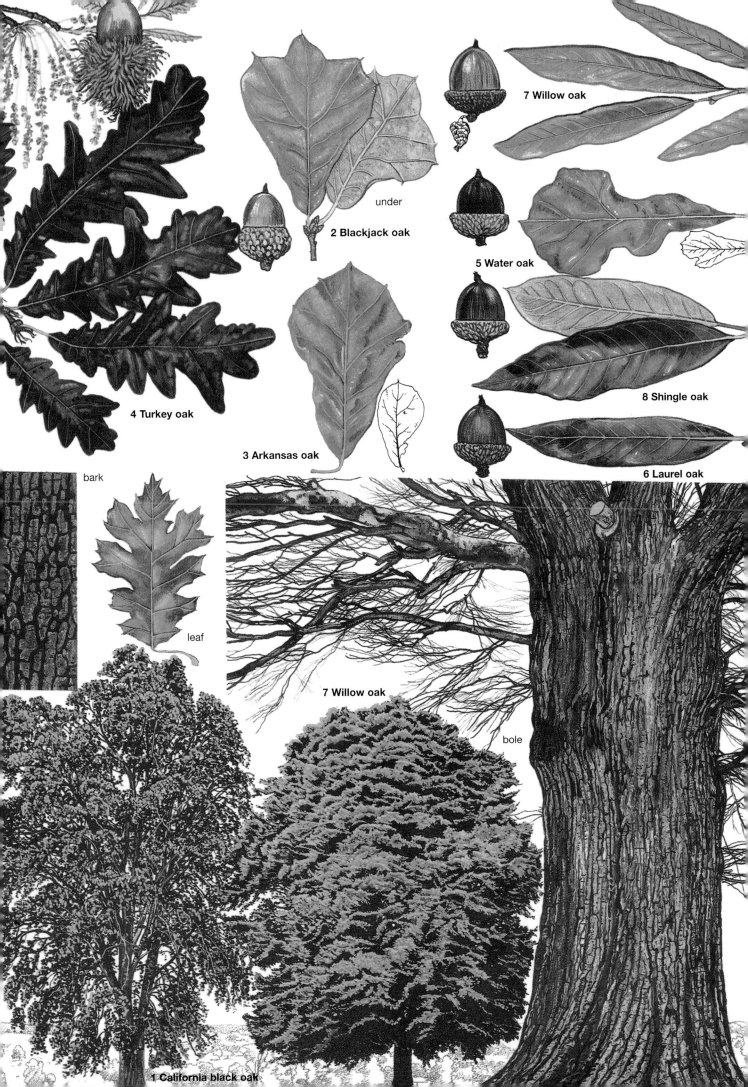

7 Willow oak

2 Blackjack oak

under

5 Water oak

3 Arkansas oak

8 Shingle oak

4 Turkey oak

6 Laurel oak

bark

leaf

7 Willow oak

bole

1 California black oak

Live and Silverleaf oaks

The Live oaks are a small group confined to North America, with many species in the southwest and two in the southeast. They are evergreen, and in America the term is used for any evergreen oak including the European Holm oak which belongs to another group altogether. It does resemble the Live oak of the southeast, and may be planted there, Holm and Live being used seemingly indiscriminately. This suggests, however, not so much the presence of the European tree as of carelessness or ignorance in the writers. The Live oaks were not distinguished as a group by Sargent in his 1905 *Manual of the Trees of North America*, not in its revisions to date. They were partly placed as an evergreen section of the Willow oaks and partly as evergreen sections of White oaks. The division was between those in which the acorn is two years maturing, taken as Willow oaks, and those with a one-year acorn. Live oaks are, in general, long-lived, slow-growing trees with small, thick and hard leaves, entire or spine-toothed and rarely with noticeable lobing. The western species inhabit hot sandy hillsides and dry rocky canyons, while the two eastern trees are on the Coastal Plain with high summer rainfall on sandy, quickly draining soils.

LIVE OAK (1), *Quercus virginiana* has a natural range in a belt close to the coast from VA to south TX, spreading farther inland only across peninsular FL and in central TX. It is common around Williamsburg and Norfolk, VA but begins to dominate as a big countryside tree only towards Charleston, SC south and westward across the Delta and in Big Thicket, TX, to Jacksonville, Athens and Dallas in that state. It is shrubby along the coast around Pensacola, FL but tall trees line the coast road, US 90 towards Biloxi and Gulfport. It extends up the Mississippi Valley only to near Natchez, MS, ending on US 61 near Lorman, a little to the northeast. It is the big tree of the city parks along the Gulf Coast, particularly in New Orleans, LA. Here, in Audubon Park are trees 60ft x 24ft, and in City Park, 75ft x 25ft and 65ft x 23ft. At Bellingrath Gardens outside Mobile it is the vital tree for shelter from the sea winds. This is the tree that gives much of the character to the Plantation mansions and gardens in SC where the approach is usually by a long avenue of Live oaks. Their broad crowns of flatly arching branches and evergreen leaves give shade right across the broadest, and liberally infested with the long gray tassels of Spanish moss (really a plant in the Pineapple Family, a bromeliad, *Tillandsia usneoides*) they give a unique aspect to the place. At Boone Plantation, the avenue dates from 1743 and the best tree in it is 80ft x 18ft 4in (1981). At Middleton House near Charleston, a magnificent tree by the river was 85ft x 29ft 10in in 1975 and another was 55ft x 25ft 9in. The first was reputed to be a marker on an old Indian trail, but some doubt on the trees' antiquity is thrown by the growth of a dated tree in Lafayette, LA. At 541 on East Main Street by the sidewalk, this was planted in 1831 and in 1977 it was 60ft x 19ft 6in. Planting has extended the range of Live oak to Little Rock, AR and to the border of OK and it is in tubs in Tulsa streets. In the east it has been planted inland in AL to Auburn and Tuskegee; in NC to the Capitol at Raleigh and in some gardens in PA. In the west, there is a small tree in the University of Washington Arboretum, Seattle, WA. The leaf shape of Live oak is very variable in the presence of lobes and teeth, and the size from 2 to 5in long. The shoot is covered in dense gray wool.

COAST LIVE OAK (2), *Quercus agrifolia* seems to have been the victim of an error in its botanical name. 'Agrifolia' means 'field-leafed' where 'aquifolia', holly-leafed, must have been intended. It is native to near the coast in Mendocino County, CA south to the border and is much seen from the Bay Area south. Planted in the Los Angeles State and County Arboretum, Arcadia, it is 60ft x 11ft and there is one in the Charles English Gardens, Seattle over 3ft round. The young bark is very smooth and black. The underside of the leaf has tufts of hairs in the vein-angles.

CANYON LIVE OAK (3), *Quercus chrysolepis* grows from the Siskiyou Mountains, OR southward along the Coast Range and Sierra Nevada on the mountains to the Mexican border and east in AZ. The acorn is up to 2in long, chestnut-brown in a flat 2in cup. It is a spreading tree or shrub with both entire and spiny toothed leaves.

INTERIOR LIVE OAK (4), *Quercus wislizenii* has a similar range from northern CA, with smaller, more pointed acorns set deeply in the cup. Unlike the acorn of the Coast live oak and the Live oak, these acorns take two years to mature, as in the Canyon live oak.

ARIZONA WHITE OAK (5), *Quercus arizonica*, is a Live oak of the mountains from the western end of TX through south NM and AZ. It is a small tree with large, twisted branches and its leaves last only the one full year, densely hairy beneath. The bark is pale gray with scaly ridges.

SILVERLEAF OAK (6), *Quercus hypoleucoides* is from the same areas but is less common there. The bark is nearly black and the upper side of the leaf a yellower green. The acorn takes two years to mature, unlike that of the Arizona white oak.

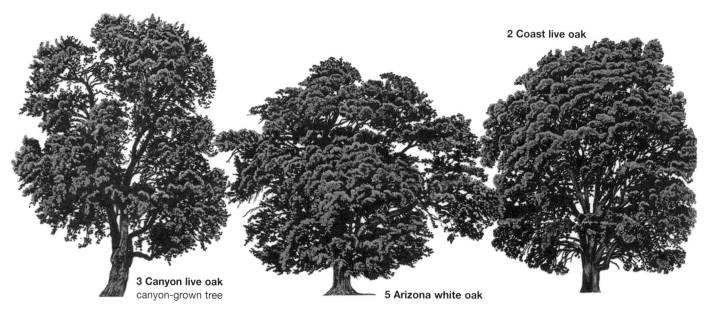

2 Coast live oak

3 Canyon live oak
canyon-grown tree

5 Arizona white oak

4 Interior live oak

2 Coast live oak

3 Canyon live oak

1 Live oak

under

5 Arizona white oak

6 Silverleaf oak   under

Spanish moss

1 Live oak bole

American and Wych elms

The elms are about 45 species found across northern and central Eurasia and in eastern North America, south to Panama. Like the Lindens, they are absent from the Rocky Mountains and the west coast. A few in America and Europe are big trees, important for their timber, but the majority are of medium to medium-small size. The timber is remarkably durable when constantly wet. Logs hollowed out in Roman times and used as water-pipes have been unearthed in good order. Large sizes have been used in lock-gate construction and a traditional use is for coffin-boards. The finely waved grain in a cross-section, hard wearing quality and taking a good polish give it a more useful role indoors for panelling, stair-treads and chair seats. Elms are the first trees in this book not to have their flowers in catkins of separate sexes. Although wind-pollinated like most of the catkin trees, elm flowers are perfect, that is each flower is both male and female, and they are in bunches or on long slender stalks in racemes. They are all dark red, and in all except three species, two American and one Chinese (grown in America), they open well before the leaves come out in spring. The other three open theirs in the fall. Some elms in America and more in Europe are being killed in great numbers, but a visitor sees fine elms in every town and little sign of disease. The cause is a fungus spread by a bark-beetle which breeds in the dead trees that its activities make available to it. With three such differing organisms as a tree, a beetle and a fungus, the effects on the disease of weather and climate are complex and control is difficult. Attacking the beetle by insecticide sprays and the fungus by injections in the tree have been difficult to do well and in large outbreaks have been of short-term effect. The felling of all trees showing signs of disease is a drastic remedy but has been successful where carried out early and persistently. The fungus spread from Central Asia, so the trees from there have some inherent resistance to it, and are planted in America and Europe, where the native elms have not acquired resistance.

AMERICAN ELM (1), *Ulmus americana* ranges from NS and south PQ to SK and the edges of MT and WY to central TX and central FL. Although a woodland tree in many parts, and most noticeably in the north, as around Toronto in ON, Milwaukee to Black River Falls, WI and from Mankato, MN to Des Moines, IA, where there are fewer other trees to hide them than in the south, this elm is most seen in Main Street Eastern America, in small and medium sized towns. Also in city parks, squares and streets, very much the same from Montreal, PQ to New Orleans, LA and Fort Worth, TX to Winnipeg, MB. It is common in shelter-belts from OK to MN and ND. Some fine specimens are: one outside the main gate at the Ottawa Botanic Garden, ON, 80ft x 15ft; one in Queen Victoria Park, Niagara Falls, ON, 100ft x 12ft. In Monument Park, Washington, DC, 90ft x 17ft and one at George Reed House, Newcastle, DE, 100ft x 13ft. This elm is planted fairly widely in the west, in BC in Grand Forks, Victoria and Parksville; in WA at Ferndale. In CO at Denver and Boulder; in WY at Cheyenne; in MT in Missoula. In Salt LakeCity, UT, one in 500 St. is 90ft x 12ft. At the Cathedral in Santa Fe, NM one is 85ft x 16ft at 3ft. In northern woodlands, the tree grows a sinuous, short trunk bearing many sprouts and two or three big, spreading branches. The leaves on sprouts and on some parts of normal lower foliage, here and elsewhere are often 6in long or more and twice as big as those in the upper crown.

WYCH ELM (2), *Ulmus glabra* from Europe, is named 'glabra', smooth, because the branches and trunks keep the smooth, silvery bark long past the size at which in other elms they are broken into ridges and fissures. It has however, a leaf more harsh than the American elm with a much shorter and densely haired stalk. It is rather scarce, in parks in ON and New England, notably in Boston, MA but more seen in BC, from Penticton and Vernon to Sidney. There are two big trees in a square in Olympia, WA, both about 120ft x 14ft and a bigger one in the Capitol Park, Sacramento, CA, 120ft x 16ft. The **Camperdown elm (3)** was found as a seedling in Scotland spreading twisted branches low over the ground. Grafted at 6–10ft on a stem of Wych elm the contorted branching forms a mushroom from the edge of which long-pendulous shoots hang to the ground bearing very harsh 8in leaves. This is quite common in ON, New England, NY, PA and OH and again in BC and near the coast of WA. The **Golden wych elm (4)**, **'Lutescens'** is a very rare broad, vigorous tree seen in the gardens of the School of Horticulture, Niagara Falls, ON and more in the botanic gardens and parks in Vancouver BC.

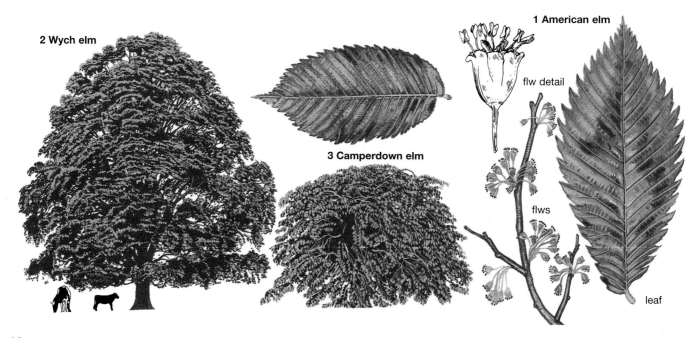

2 Wych elm

3 Camperdown elm

1 American elm

flw detail

flws

leaf

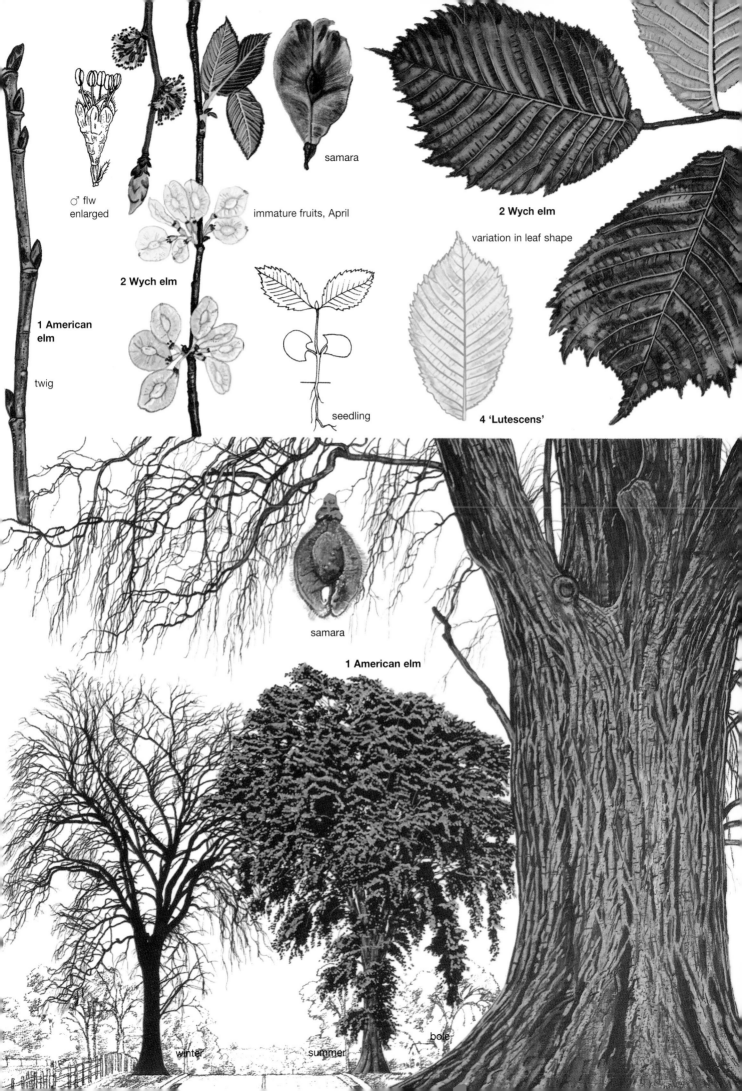

♂ flw
enlarged

2 Wych elm

1 American elm

twig

samara

immature fruits, April

seedling

2 Wych elm

variation in leaf shape

4 'Lutescens'

samara

1 American elm

winter

summer

bole

Rock, Slippery and European elms

SLIPPERY ELM (1), *Ulmus rubra* is very widespread in the east, native from around Montreal, PQ to south MN, mid-NE and KS to east TX via north LA to the coast in SC. It is less seen in woods than as planted trees in parks and squares as in Central Park and Washington Square, New York; the Commonwealth in Boston, MA and the Ellipse, Washington, DC. It is planted in squares a little beyond its range, as at the Capitol in Bismarck, ND and in the Esplanade and Gardens District, New Orleans, LA and far to the west as in Revelstoke, BC and Wenatchee, WA where one is 100ft x 11ft. The bark is brown and sooty gray in coarse ridges and the rounded crown, upright in young trees, is densely hung with big leaves looking very dark from a distance. The leaves are rough above and softly hairy beneath, up to 8in long and with 15–20 pairs of veins. The flowers are crowded in short-stemmed bunches, and the fruit are big, nearly 1in, and smooth.

ROCK ELM (2), *Ulmus thomasii* differs from the Slippery elm in having its few flowers in a loose, open 1–2in long flower-head, and the thicker shoots and small branches growing warts then ridges and finally corky wings. The leaf is smaller, to 5in, but has more veins, to 22 pairs, and is bright pale green above and hairy only on the veins beneath. It is less wide ranging than the Slippery elm although reaching Montreal, round the south of Lake Huron into south MN and MO and to the northern parts only of IL, IN and OH with big outliers in TN. It tends to have an upright crown with a good trunk, shaggily ridged with gray-brown bark. The fruit are nearly round, finely hairy all over with a fringe round the edge. The timber is of particular value in the construction of small ships, and the logs of Rock elm can be distinguished from others readily only by their bark, so to reassure boat-builders importing it, the bark was left on. This sent over the bark-beetles carrying Dutch elm disease which had reached America in about 1930. It had come from Europe, so this would have been no disaster except that it had, in America, produced a strain of greatly enhanced virulence in which the fungus invaded wood of earlier years and spread down the stem and into the roots. It was not only fatal, but it could run through populations of English elm which had spread from suckers. The centres of infection could be traced back to the ports where small ships were made, starting in about 1967. The name 'Dutch' elm disease is unfortunate and unfair. It arose from the pioneer work in control and breeding resistance into elms done in Holland. Some good trees of promise produced there failed in the face of the new strain of disease after 1970.

ENGLISH ELM (3), *Ulmus procera* is rather an enigma. It was, until the disease struck, the dominant hedgerow and landscape tree over most tracts of farmland in England. But it rarely, if ever, sets viable seed, and always spreads by root-suckers, is rarely in any woodland, and cannot be found anywhere else in Europe, from whence all the trees native to England spread after the Ice Ages. It is quite unlike the Field elms of Europe in its multi-domed crown, few huge limbs and harsh upper surface of the nearly round leaf. It will have derived from one or very few trees, thought to have been brought from southern France in the Iron Age. It is infrequent in parks, squares and streets from the Commonwealth in Boston, MA to the parking lot at the Missouri Botanic Gardens, St. Louis, particularly in PA with fine trees in Lancaster, Duke and Orange Streets; Carlisle, and River Drive, Harrisburg and in OH in Clearwater Park, Cleveland and from Canton to Wooster. In MD it is along W. Lombard and Greene Streets, Baltimore. There are trees in Lake Shore Drive, Chicago, IL and by the Capitol at Madison, WI. Until it caught the disease in 1981, a tree near the Capitol in Washington, DC was 120ft x 20ft. The slender crowned, cutleaf form **'Viminalis' (4)** and the golden leafed **'Louis Van Houtte' (5)** are rare forms.

WHEATLEY ELM (6), *Ulmus carpinifolia* 'Sarniensis' is the form of Smoothleaf elm growing in the Channel Islands and is also known as the Jersey or Guernsey elm. It resembles the English elm in its dark rounded leaf and dark brown bark cracked into small squares, but it differs much in its shape. The neat, narrowly conic crown, tapering to an acute spire, recommends it for the planting of formal avenues and in streets. The lack of heavy branches makes it safer in these places than the English elm which may drop big branches without warning. The Wheatley elm can be seen along the Potomac Drive and in McPherson Square, Washington, DC, each side of the western approach to Longwood, PA and by the Park Offices in Rockefeller Park, Cleveland, OH, while a very big one, 100ft x 12ft is at Smith College, Northampton MA.

CORNISH ELM, *Ulmus angustifolia* 'Cornubiensis' is the form of Field elm found in Cornwall, England and Normandy, France. It differs from the Wheatley elm in its branches arching out with foliage held close to them; in bright green, slender leaves and in dark gray bark in long ridges. It can be seen in Mount Airy Arboretum, Cincinnati, OH; in the Capitol Park, Washington, DC and in the west on Richelieu and 99th Street, Vancouver, BC.

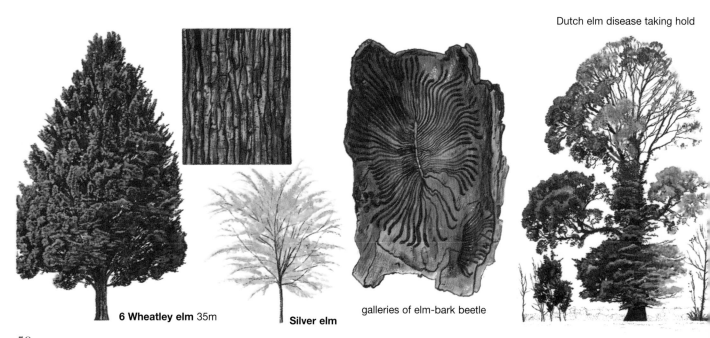

Dutch elm disease taking hold

6 Wheatley elm 35m   **Silver elm**

galleries of elm-bark beetle

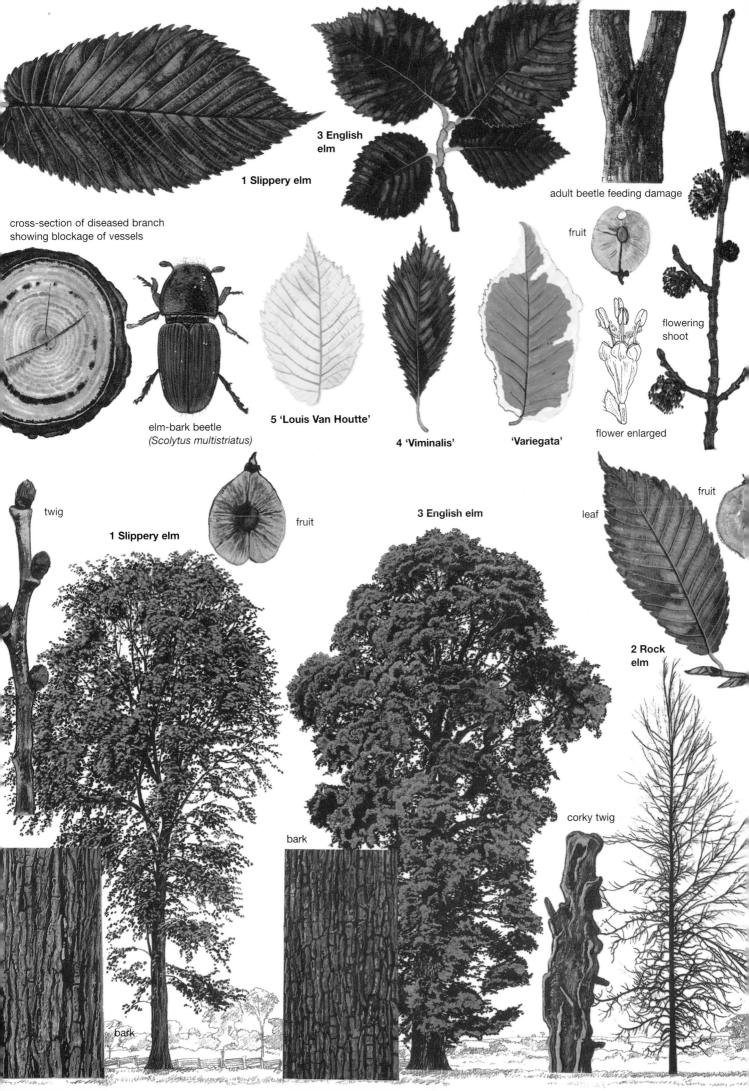

3 English elm

1 Slippery elm

adult beetle feeding damage

cross-section of diseased branch
showing blockage of vessels

fruit

flowering
shoot

elm-bark beetle
(*Scolytus multistriatus*)

5 'Louis Van Houtte'

4 'Viminalis'

'Variegata'

flower enlarged

twig

fruit

1 Slippery elm

3 English elm

leaf

fruit

**2 Rock
elm**

bark

corky twig

bark

bark

Cedar, Winged and Asiatic elms

CEDAR ELM (1), *Ulmus crassifolia* is a strange tree; its leaves are so hard and rigidly stalked that in a wind they remain quite unflexed and the shoot bends with the leaves as one piece. In late summer, before the yellow fall colors show, the dark green leaf assumes a mildewy gray on its hard, whiplike shoots which are thickened after the first year by two opposing dark red-brown corky flanges. The underside of the leaf is covered in hoary white thick hairs and has 7–9 very prominent pairs of veins. Bark is dull pink-gray becoming dark gray deeply fissured. It is a small tree with a short bole, a dome of arching branches and rather pendulous outer shoots. It is very common in TX and AR particularly on low hills in the Ozark Mountains and into OK to Muldrow and much less so to MS and LA. This, like the **September elm**, *Ulmus serotina* of the same area but not in TX, flowers in the fall, beginning in August, the flowers on slender, hairy stalks in heads of 3–5 and by October the fruit, barely ½in long, hang in masses, oblong-elliptic and deeply notched, covered in soft, white hairs.

WINGED ELM (2), *Ulmus alata*, also happily known as the Wahoo, with a town named from it in NE, grows from TX to central FL and south VA. It is a common roadside tree in Cedar elm country in TX, notably from Liberty and Daingerfield to Texarkana and in AR in the Ouachita and Ozark National Forests. It is like the Cedar elm but has a larger, softer leaf, turning yellow earlier in the fall and its thick, blackish shoots with corky wings are not always numerous among the slender smooth ones. The pale gray-brown bark is prominent and less ridged. The winged elm extends in bottomlands to Kansas City then south around the Coastal Plain. Here, it is easily confused with the Siberian elm which is widely planted, and has no winged shoots at all. It is frequent in gardens around Baton Rouge and New Orleans, LA and in the country particularly towards Atlanta, GA and into NC. It also ranges up the Mississippi bottomlands through Dyersburg, TN, Clinton KY and Salem, IL.

SMOOTHLEAF ELM (3), *Ulmus carpinifolia* has an elliptic leaf, smooth leathery bright green above with white tufts beneath in the vein-angles. It has a broadly domed crown with branches of all sizes and slender, often hanging outer shoots. The bark is pale gray distinctively marked by long vertical dark ridges well into the crown. It is a scarce tree, noted in the Allen Botanic Garden, Toronto, ON; in Buffalo, NY, at the John Hopkin University, Baltimore, MD and Franklyn Park, Columbus, OH.

'SAPPORO AUTUMN GOLD' (4) elm was bred in WI for resistance to Dutch elm disease by crossing two resistant Asiatic elms, the Japanese elm and the Siberian elm. So far it has been healthy and vigorous making an upright tree with large, dark green leaves.

SIBERIAN ELM (5), *Ulmus pumila* has long been one of the most widely planted and useful trees in North America. It is often, in the semi-deserts of NM and AZ, the only tree seen for scores of miles, planted for shade at every rest-station. It is similarly planted throughout the Prairie States to SK and as a common shelterbelt, farm and roadside tree, particularly in IA, NE and MN and south through OK, AR and in TX. It is a common street tree as far north as Winnipeg, MB where it is the median tree in the main street, Portage, and eastward through ON to Montreal, PQ. One in the Ottawa Botanic Garden is 100ft x 9ft. It is nearly as common in OH, PA, where in the Morris Arboretum near Philadelphia one is 70ft x 19ft at 1ft, and in NY and MI but is noticed less in these states with so many more trees. It does become scarce south of Washington DC, and one 85ft x 10ft by the Capitol at Richmond, VA is the farthest southeastern tree noted. In the west, it is common through CO to WY and UT. In BC it is an inland town tree, at Grand Forks, Greenwood, Vernon and at Revelstoke where it is cut annually and grows long arching shoots sparsely strung with small leaves. Likewise in WA from Spokane to Chewela. In NV it is common in Reno, Carson City and Las Vegas and in CA by I 8 into the Los Angeles area.

CHINESE ELM (6), *Ulmus parvifolia* is much planted in streets and precincts in Las Vegas, San Bernardino and south CA north to Sacramento. But, oddly, its distribution in the east is very different as it is seen here and there in towns from New Orleans, LA to Montreal, PQ. In the dry heat of southern CA the bark sheds orange-brown scales to leave a smooth, blue-white stem but in the east it is gray-brown fissured into squares. Its prettily leafed, almost evergreen domed crown of stiffly hanging shoots is seen in Poudras Street and the Gentilly Woods area in New Orleans, in Manteo, NC, in Rockefeller and Edgewater Parks, Cleveland, OH; Headhouse Marker, the Penn Center and Main Line District in Philadelphia, PA and in botanic gardens in NY, and a tree from the original Chinese seed in Central Park was 60ft x 12ft in 1981. It is most like the Siberian elm but it flowers in the fall, has smaller, darker leaves and the bark is not ridged.

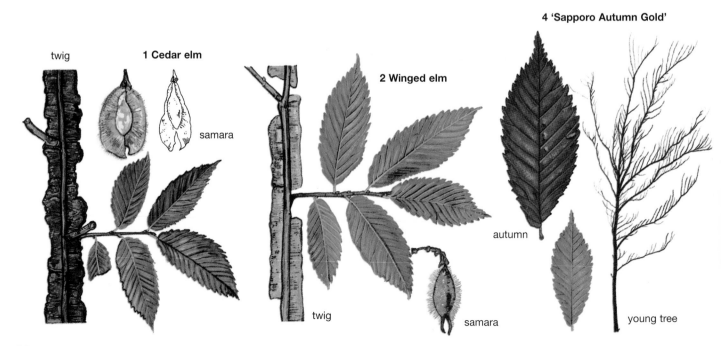

4 'Sapporo Autumn Gold'

twig

1 Cedar elm

samara

2 Winged elm

twig

autumn

samara

young tree

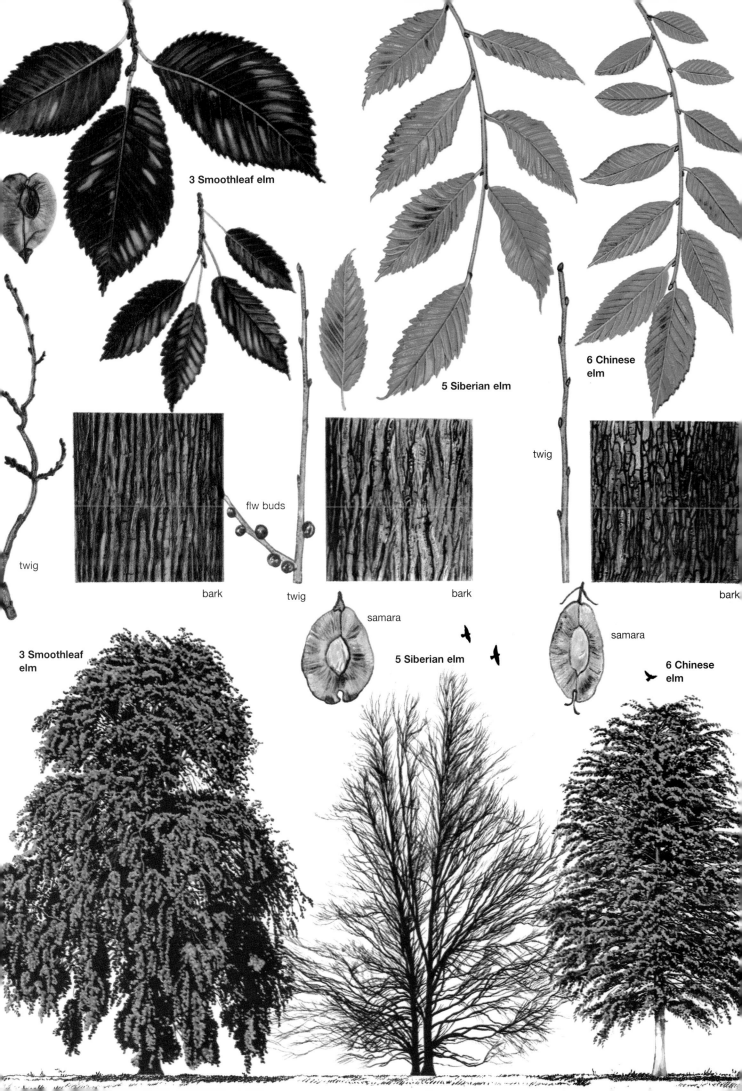

3 Smoothleaf elm

5 Siberian elm

6 Chinese elm

twig

flw buds

bark

twig

bark

twig

bark

samara

samara

3 Smoothleaf elm

5 Siberian elm

6 Chinese elm

Hackberries, Sugarberry and Keaki

The Hackberries or Nettle-trees are placed in the Elm Family but differ from the true elms in having male and female flowers on separate flowerheads on the same tree; in the fruit being a berry-like drupe, and in the bark being generally smooth although in some species this is much knobbed and flanged. There are over 50 species spread across Eurasia and North America, from China to southern Europe and east and western America to Central America. Of the seven in North America, two are shrubs and two are little more, and of very restricted occurrence. Some of the hackberries take a very casual attitude to toothing on the leaf, not bothering with any on one side maybe, yet with the other toothed almost to the base, and, on the same tree, some toothed only towards the tip on one or on both sides. All the leaves are asymmetric at the base, and in nearly all species three main veins diverge from near to the stalk.

HACKBERRY (1), *Celtis occidentalis* is the common *Celtis* species of the northeast, replaced in the southeast by the Sugarberry. There are small populations in the extreme south of PQ and ON and again in NC, GA and AL but the main range is from RI and the Hudson Valley, NY to VA and west, avoiding most of PA and WV to MN and OK. It is a common city park tree in OH and notably in Chicago, IL, Milwaukee, WI and through MN to Des Moines, IA and in eastern NE with big trees beside US 275 west from Omaha. The trees in Cheyenne, WY, although planted, are just within the extreme of the natural range, while those around Denver and Loveland, CO are beyond it. So is a fine tree, loaded with fruit, by Portage Avenue a few miles west of Winnipeg City, MB. In some areas, for example, around Indianapolis, IN, most of the trees are heavily galled and nowhere is this more evident than in Central Park, New York, where every specimen is bedecked with great numbers of 'witches' brooms', clusters of slender shoots which abort at the tips but leaf out every year. Those in Lafayette Square, Washington, DC, are nearly as bad. In Central Park the trees have smooth gray bark but it is normally well covered in dark abrupt, broken ridges 1in thick.

SUGARBERRY (2), *Celtis laevigata* replaces the Hackberry from south MD and VA round the Coastal Plain and up the Mississippi Valley to central IL and southern IN and thus the two overlap a little in VA but widely over northern AR and much of MO, KY, IL and IN. Very generally, sugarberry has a pale ashen or pink-gray bark, smoother among the short abrupt ridges which project to 2in, smaller leaves, often only 2in long, and usually quite entire. But many trees where the species overlap are far from distinct and then, as at the Capitol, Little Rock, AR, there are two trees of the same size and appearance and one is labelled

Sugarberry and the other Hackberry, it must be the color of the fruit which decides. It ripens orange-red on the sugarberry and dark purple on the Hackberry. A huge tree, 80ft x 14ft x 10ft (two stems) at the Robert Carter House, Williamsburg, VA is equally ambiguous. The many good trees along roads from Charleston, SC to Baton Rouge, LA and Memphis, TN are plainly typical Sugarberry. One in a street near the Capitol in Montgomery, AL is 85ft x 13ft. It is a common hedge tree in TX, AR and OK. In the south in small yards in cities it is often cut back and grows annual wands, fanning out and arching with leaves depressed each side, yellowish green.

NETLEAF HACKBERRY (3), *Celtis reticulata* is more or less the western hackberry, growing from ID, WA and OR to KS, CO and TX to CA, on dry hill and canyon sides. There is one in Ottawa Botanic Garden, ON. It is named from the conspicuous network of veins on the underside of the leaf, and is usually shrubby, rarely even 30ft high.

GEORGIA HACKBERRY (4), *Celtis tenuifolia* is more than a shrub only in a few of the southern fringes of its extensive range from ON to FL and TX. Its shoots are slender, dark red-brown and finely hairy.

LINDHEIMER HACKBERRY (5), *Celtis lindheimeri* is confined to one county in TX, Bexar County. It is like the Netleaf except for the pale underside to its leaf and the dark red-brown fruit.

NETTLE TREE (6), *Celtis australis* is from southern Europe. It is easily distinguished from the American hackberries by the long tapering slender tip to the leaf and the soft hairs on both sides of it. It is included here on the strength of three big trees in Sacramento, CA, and there may well be more. There are two in Sutter Park, the larger 75ft x 8ft 2in in 1982, and one in the Capitol Park, 80ft x 8ft 6in.

KEAKI (7), *Zelkova serrata*, an elm relative from Japan, was sent to America in 1860 and has been much planted in parking lots and precincts from ME to DC, including the Pentagon, and there are big trees in Washington, DC. One by 6th and G Streets is 65ft x 14ft and one by the lake near the Capitol is 65ft x 12ft. It is in most of the parks in OH and along the streets of Akron. In the west there is one 70ft x 9ft near the Capitol in Salt Lake City, UT and smaller trees in the botanic gardens around Vancouver, BC. There are few in the southeast, but some in the Callaway Gardens, GA. It is an exceptionally attractive shade tree and the elegant leaves turn yellow, orange and bronzy red in the fall.

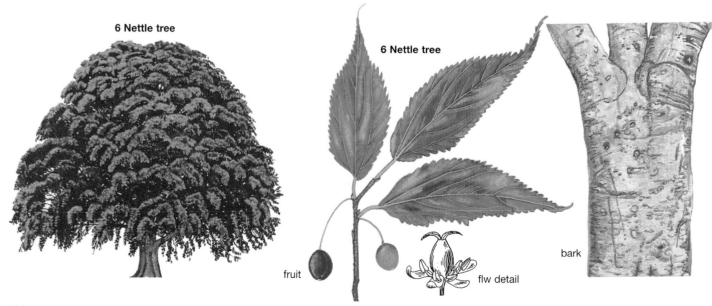

6 Nettle tree

6 Nettle tree

fruit

flw detail

bark

bark

nut

bark

fruit
fruit
3 Netleaf hackberry

flws

1 Hackberry

fruit

2 Sugarberry

fruit
fruit

new lvs

fruit
fruit

♀ flw

♂ flw

4 Georgia hackberry

5 Lindheimer hackberry

twig

7 Keaki

1 Hackberry

7 Keaki

1 Hackberry bole

Mulberries and Osage orange

The Mulberries are about 10 species from Mongolia, China and Japan and two in North America. The White and Black mulberries have been cultivated for so long, for silkworm raising and fruit, that their natural ranges cannot now be defined and the Black may have extended into Asia Minor or even into Europe. Mulberries are deciduous trees of moderate to small size with flowers of one sex only on each spike but the male and female spikes usually on the same tree even if tending to be on different branches. The fruit are peculiar in that each apparent fruit is a cluster of fruits, and the fleshy juicy part is the swollen calyx.

RED MULBERRY (1), *Morus rubra* is found in MA and the Hudson Valley, NY then almost everywhere south of PA and WI to mid TX and is quite common in gardens and woods over most of this region, including the valleys high in the Allegheny Mountains. It is most noticeable in the south in AL and around New Orleans, LA and in the north around Indianapolis, IN, while in MN, IA and east NE it is frequent as a roadside hedge. Trees cut back can throw out shoots 4ft long. The leaves are late unfolding and in MN are still not expanded by mid-May. They can be 10 x 10in and the stalk, usually 3in long, can be over 6in. The biggest leaves tend to be those cut into deep lobes.

TEXAS MULBERRY (2), *Morus microphylla* is a little shrubby plant rarely 20ft tall, found in TX and adjacent parts of OK and NM into AZ. Its leaf is less than 2in long, on a slender, hairy stalk. The trees are usually of one sex only. The shoots are slender and pale orange-red.

WHITE MULBERRY (3), *Morus alba* is a Chinese tree which has been widely planted from north NY, but not New England, to NC and across to TX, CO and UT, NM and AZ to CA. It is less seen in OR and WA but more frequent in southern BC. It is seen in Toronto, ON while in NY it is in Buffalo, in Lyndhurst Garden, Tarrytown to 75ft x 7ft; in Central Park, New York; Prospect Park, Brooklyn and in the streets of Oyster Bay, Long Island. It is common in roadside gardens in OH and PA where one at Longwood is 60ft x 16ft 7in at 1ft. There are big trees in Williamsburg, VA along the streets of the historic area, to 11ft round, but in poor shape (though better than the Paper mulberries with them). The smooth, glossy upper side of the leaf distinguishes this from other mulberries. **Teas' weeping mulberry (4)** extends the range in the north, being seen in the main street, Sherbrooke, in downtown Montreal, PQ, and in New England as well as over the rest of the range, and is more conspicuous. It does not seem, however, to be planted south of Washington, DC in the east. It is found through TX to CA but from Albuquerque, NM through AZ and CA north to Merced and in Reno and Las Vegas, NV it is mostly in the form 'Acerifolia', a non-flowering tree with big, glossy deep green leaves 10 x 8in. Some of these are ovate and some have 3 lobes, the central one long-elliptic tapered to a fine point. It is a prominent tree in gardens around Santa Fe, NM, Phoenix, AZ and particularly, San Diego, La Jolla, and around Los Angeles to San Bernardino, CA. The bark is pale leaden gray with fine dark streaks.

BLACK MULBERRY (5), *Morus nigra* is not often seen but is apparently naturalised from FL to TX and the 1971 champion, an amazing 67 ft x 18ft 7in, was in Westminster, MD. This tree has a reputation in England, where it has been grown since before 1600, of great age and very slow growth. Since the latter is quite untrue and it grows fairly fast, yet none is even 11ft round, it is evidently quite short-lived and the reputed ages are spurious. None of the 'historic' trees has a bole; all are either sprawling or have been mounded up to the spring of branches. The explanation seems to be that mulberries were propagated by 'truncheons', that is big branches sawn into lengths of 5ft and half buried. They sprout well, but the new branches spring from round the sawcut, which decays in 30 years and they need supporting. Very soon the tree looks as if Milton had sat under it. A new truncheon can be made every 100 years or so and passed off as the old tree.

OSAGE ORANGE (6), *Maclura pomifera* is native only to TX and adjacent parts of AR and OK, but that is more than usually irrelevant today when the hedgerows common in OK are equally common in PA, IN and DE and it is a frequent park, garden and square tree from Lake Shore Drive, Toronto and Niagara Falls, ON locally to VA and DE. There are trees in Central Park, New York, and in NM in Tucumcari and Los Arbores Avenue, Albuquerque, but there are few, if any further west. The bark is orange-brown with interwoven ridges which in old trees are pink-gray and stringy. The leaves vary in size greatly on the same shoot, from 2in long on short spurs to 5 x 3in on new growth and 7 x 6in on sprouts. The timber was used by Indians for bows and was found to be superior even to the European yew so was used in sporting bows until largely replaced by laminated wood. The vital features are not only strength and elasticity, but, as in the yew, a marked and visible change from the dark heartwood to the pale sapwood, making easy the cutting of lengths with hard, elastic outsides and compressible inside halves. The big, hard 5in fruit, inconvenient when they litter sidewalks and squares, are inedible tough stringy tissue with milky white juice, and are, as in the related mulberry, really compound groups of small fruit.

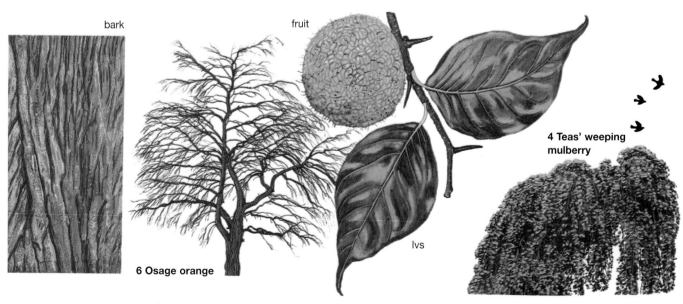

bark

fruit

lvs

4 Teas' weeping mulberry

6 Osage orange

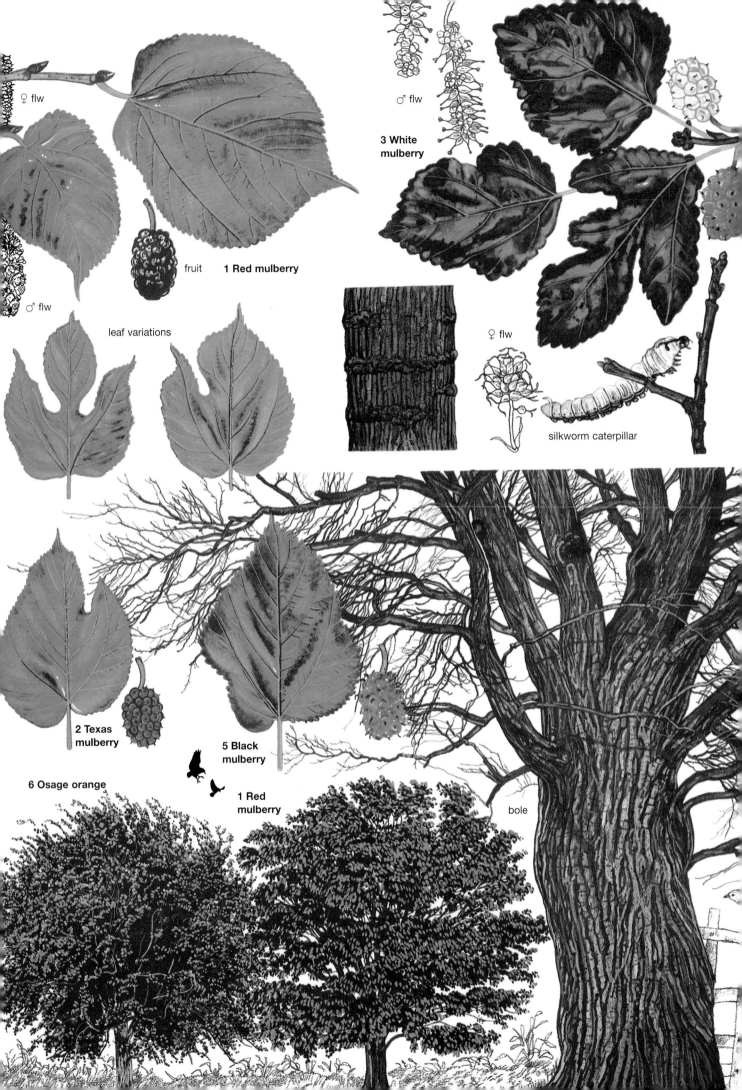

♀ flw

1 Red mulberry

fruit

♂ flw

leaf variations

3 White mulberry

♂ flw

♀ flw

silkworm caterpillar

2 Texas mulberry

5 Black mulberry

6 Osage orange

1 Red mulberry

bole

Fig, Paper mulberry and Katsura

FIG (1), *Ficus carica* has given its name to a genus of some 800 members of the Mulberry family, all evergreen and mostly tropical. It includes some plants of strange habits like the strangler-figs and the Banyan as well as vines like the little *Ficus pumila* grown on conservatory walls. They all have peculiar flowers which are almost entirely enclosed in a cup. Insects are lured into it through a small hole and collect a dusting pollen before they can escape to take it to another flowerhead to fertilize the female flowers within. Then the whole head becomes a succulent fruit with the stamens inside. Certain species of wasp have specialised in visiting fig flowers and are confined to the areas where the figs are native. The Common fig comes from southwestern Asia but the form grown is an ancient selection, a female which is fertile without the need of an insect. It is grown from Washington DC in small numbers south on the Coastal Plain becoming common towards New Orleans and the Delta, LA and in MS to Natchez. In the Central Valley, CA, around Merced, it is grown in orchards for its fruit and is pruned down hard each year.

PAPER MULBERRY (2), *Broussonetia papyrifera* from Japan and China has been widely cultivated there for the paper made from its bark and for high quality linen from its fibers. The leaf can be 8in each way and variably cut into deep, often irregular lobes. It has soft gray hairs all over making a fringe round the margins. Male trees bear bright yellow catkins 3in long and curled somewhat while females bear ½in brown globular flowers. The bark is brown or grayish-purple, broadly ridged and pitted with lenticels, particularly on the young trees in which it is green-gray, striped pink. The wood is brittle and old trees lose most of their branches and become short, craggy hulks. This is very noticeable in Colonial Williamsburg, VA where several streets are lined with them. The tree is planted from NY, where there are trees at Mohonk Mountain and Highland Park, Rochester, one there being 50ft x 6ft, and uncommonly southwards to MD. From there on it is more common southwards, notably on the Delta and around New Orleans, LA and in the Mississippi Valley in AR, OK and IL and in east TX and a few in west OH.

KATSURA TREE (3), *Cercidiphyllum japonicum* is the biggest broadleaf tree in Asia, where it grows in Japan and, discovered only in 1910, in China. The trees in cultivation are probably all from Japan, certainly all the older ones, being sent first in 1865. Botanically, this tree is of great interest, being the only survivor of a group of families of ancient origin related to the magnolias but now quite isolated and hard to place among its possible nearest relatives. In some features it is far more primitive than the magnolias with their bowl-shaped, beetle-attracting, perfect flowers. It has flowers of separate sexes on separate trees, pollinated by the wind, opposite leaves and branching and 'softwood' timber like a conifer. In this wood there are no specialised fiber-cells for strength and rigidity and vessels for carrying sap as in the normal 'hardwood' of broadleaf trees. In the more primitive softwood these two functions have to be combined and the sap is conducted through thick-walled cells, tracheids, joining at long-tapered overlapping ends to allow the sap to cross as freely as possible through a number of holes while maintaining strong unions.

The Katsura tree leafs out bright red, fading to shrimp pink, and at this stage it is liable to damage by late frost, but will leaf out again being fairly hardy. It needs a good summer rainfall or a damp soil and will then grow very rapidly. In America, it makes the best growth from MA to PA and MI but succeeds well enough far to the north and south of these states. It is found in parks and large gardens sparingly from Montreal, PQ to GA, TN and IL with a good tree in the Queen Victoria Park, Niagara Falls, ON, and in smaller gardens also in MA, NH and NY and notably in Newport, RI. One at Smith College, Northampton, MA is over 90ft tall and one in a Manchester, NH, roadside front yard is 70ft x 6ft. There are big trees on Long Island, NY with one at the Bailey Arboretum over 80ft x 9ft, also in MI with one in the Beal Garfield Gardens, East Lansing, 65ft x 9ft. The biggest plant is one dating from 1898 in the Morris Arboretum, PA which is about 80ft x 18ft, measured at 1ft. A good tree grows at Biltmore House, NC and another in the Memorial Garden in Athens, GA but there are few further south. It is planted along Lake Drive, Milwaukee, WI and at the Lincoln Memorial. In the west there are fewer. It is in the botanic garden at Denver, CO but otherwise it is confined to BC and WA, being quite frequent around Vancouver and Victoria and more so in and around Seattle, WA where Sandpoint Way and other streets are planted with it. There is a tree over 50ft x 6ft in Point Defiance Park, Tacoma, WA. Fall color is variably spectacular and may be lacking if drought causes early leaf-fall. Young trees mostly turn scarlet and deep red while older trees vary unpredictably. Some turn brilliant gold and little more while others go on to be pink, red and crimson, or have a mottled look from some leaves remaining green and some turning lilac. Some behave differently from year to year but they are always highly attractive. Seedlings grow rapidly into very shapely transplants and should be put out when young.

2 Paper mulberry

3 Katsura tree

♀ flws

ripe fruit

1 Fig

♂ flws

leaf variant

unripe
fruit

ripe fruit

cross-section
of fruit

3 Katsura tree

3 Katsura tree

1 Fig

Yellow poplar, Sassafras and others

YELLOW POPLAR (1), *Liriodendron tulipifera* was thought to be the only one of its kind in the world until 1875 when the very similar Chinese species was discovered. Yellow poplars or Tulip trees are plainly, from the curious structure of the flower, a sort of magnolia but they differ sufficiently in their buds, shape of leaf and in their fruit to be placed in a genus of their own. The Yellow poplar is native to nearly everywhere from MA to IN and close to the river down the Mississippi Valley to just short of the Delta and to central FL. It is common throughout this region and usually the tallest tree in the locality as it is in the whole region. It has been planted a little in eastern TX but widely and commonly in AR, OK and even more in southern BC, in WA and southern CA, particularly in the streets of Claremont, Arcadia and other parts of Los Angeles. Among the taller ones, a tree at Winterthur Gardens, DE, in Chandler's Wood was 160ft x 16ft 4in in 1987 while many in the garden are over 190ft, and at Longwood PA to 155ft mostly clear of branches for over 60ft. Roadside woods around the PA/DE border are commonly nearly as good. The **Fastigiate yellow poplar (2)**, 'Fastigiatum' was planted first in 1888 in the Arnold Arboretum, MA. The University of Wisconsin Arboretum at Madison, WI has one, but few are seen. The yellow **Golden variegated poplar, 'Aureomarginatum'** is scarce and is in Beacon Hill Park, Victoria, BC and in Point Defiance Park, Tacoma, WA.

CHINESE TULIP TREE, *Liriodendron chinense* has more deeply lobed leaves, more silvered beneath and is growing at the Van Dusen Botanic Garden, Vancouver, BC.

SASSAFRAS (3), *Sassafras albidum* is a tree in the Laurel Family, a group specialising in aromatic foliage, and is one of only three species of Sassafras in the world, the other two being in China and Taiwan. It ranges from ME to mid-MI, south IL and to east TX and central FL. It often spreads by suckers from the roots and runs along the edges of roads and fields making long hedges with trees at varying distances holding up umbrella crowns on twisting branches. This is most seen in parts of PA and in AR. The hedgerow sprouts are prominently pale orange in the bark, while old trees have pale orange or red-brown ridges broken into big blocks by ashen-gray fissures. In SC and GA sassafras forms an undergrowth in the woods and is a good tree only in towns and gardens. The fall colors are spectacular as the leaves turn through yellow and orange to scarlet and crimson. The sexes are usually on different trees and the fruits are 3–4 on an erect, red stalk ripening into clear red berries.

The variation of leaf-shape from unlobed through asymmetrically two-lobed like a mitten to quite deeply 3-lobed occurs on the same tree, the older and less vigorous trees and shoots bear unlobed leaves. This is seldom a tall tree and two of 85ft by the Graduate Faculty at Princeton, NJ and one of 90ft in Highland Park, Rochester, NY are exceptional. So are the boles of two beside US 20 in Madison, OH which in 1975 were 70ft x 16ft 1in and x 14ft 4in. There are almost none planted in the west.

SWEETGUM (4), *Liquidambar styraciflua* is also one of only three of its genus, the others growing in Asia Minor and China and Taiwan. It is in the Witch-hazel Family and shares the family feature of brilliant fall coloring. It has flowers of only one sex, the males in 3in terminal spikes and the females in solitary ½in globular clusters on a 2in stalk from an axil. They are on the same tree although some trees have few females and others are crowded with them. The fruit are hard and woody and hang dark brown on the tree through the winter. A leaf crushed or torn emits a strong sweet aromatic scent. The bark is soon dull gray-brown and deeply ridged, but in streets in the Pacific West it is smooth, silvery gray. Young branches often grow corky flanges for some years. The tree ranges from Long Island, NY to east TX and mid-FL and is common almost throughout, but particularly dominant in east TX and in AR. It is planted in MA and ME and rarely in MI and ON but commonly in Victoria and around Vancouver, BC, in Seattle and coastal WA, less in OR and commonly again around Los Angeles, where it is a boulevard tree in Claremont. The color display in the fall is prolonged and various. In TX and AR this is the mainstay of fall colors and before turning scarlet and deep red, many trees are mottled orange and scarlet.

CHINESE SWEETGUM (5), *Liquidambar formosana* has hard, saw-edged very dark leaves with 3 broad triangular lobes. They turn rich orange and purple late in the fall, or tend to be evergreen. It was introduced in 1907 and a splendid specimen is at the Savannah Plant Introduction Station, GA, 85ft x 8ft.

PERSIAN IRONWOOD (6), *Parrotia persica* is another in the Witch-hazel Family. It flowers in January and is a tall, spreading shrub or small tree, 52ft tall in the Arnold Arboretum, MA, smaller in Willowwood, NJ; the White House Garden, Washington, DC; at Mill Creek Center, Youngstown, PA; at Michigan State University and in the two botanic gardens in Vancouver, and the Butchart Garden, Sidney, BC.

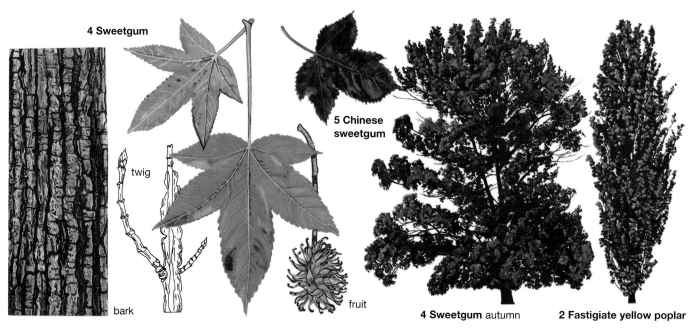

4 Sweetgum

twig

bark

5 Chinese sweetgum

fruit

4 Sweetgum autumn

2 Fastigiate yellow poplar

bark

fruit

3 Sassafras

bark

flws

6 Persian ironwood

fruit

twig

lvs

flw

1 Yellow poplar

fruit

seedling

1 Yellow poplar

3 Sassafras

1 Yellow poplar
bole

1 Yellow poplar

Cucumber tree and other Magnolias

The Magnolia Family is divided strictly between America and Eastern Asia, with 10 of its 80 species in America and the rest in China and Japan with a few along the eastern Himalaya. In America one grows in northern South America, one in Mexico and 8 in the USA, one extending just into Canada. The family has some very primitive features. Although the flowers are sufficiently advanced to comprise both sexes in the one flower, they are curiously constructed and the conic centre of carpels may be a direct development from the coniferous cone which it slightly resembles. There is no true distinction between the sepals and the petals and the bowl shape of the open flower was evolved to make landing easier for beetles, which are not precision flyers, before there were any bees and flies to carry pollen. All American magnolias flower when in full leaf while most from China open theirs well before there are any leaves to hide them, and they are large pink and white flowers, so it is these trees which are planted for early spring color.

CUCUMBER TREE (1), *Magnolia acuminata* is the one that ranges into Canada, just into ON and keeps largely to the hills from there to GA and in MO and AR with small areas on the plains in AL, MI and LA. It is at 5020ft altitude by Rt 19 in NC and is common from OH and PA southwards in the mountains. It has been planted quite widely in New England and north to Montreal, PQ; in IA and in the west it is grown in the Charles English Garden, Seattle, WA and the Los Angeles State and Country Arboretum, CA. The leaf is sometimes 1ft long and is variably silvered beneath. The seeds, typically of magnolias, protrude on white stalks from the bright pink-purple fruit and being scarlet they make a colorful clash. **Yellow cucumber tree (2)**, var. *cordata* is wild only in GA where it is said to be a small bush.

ASHE MAGNOLIA (3), *Magnolia ashei* is confined as a native to the northwestern corner of FL but as an outstanding tree for handsome foliage it is planted in a few gardens like Biltmore, NC and north to the Ford Foundation at Gladwyne, PA. The silver undersides of the leaves, which are 16 x 4–8in, are well shown and rather spectacular. The shoot is pale green bloomed gray-blue.

BIGLEAF MAGNOLIA (4), *Magnolia macrophylla* has a leaf with 'ears' at the base and silvery beneath like the Ashe magnolia but it is about 3ft long. The flower has nearly 500 stamens where the Ashe has fewer than 200. It is rare and local from the VA/NC border and south OH to AR, LA and GA.

FRASER MAGNOLIA (5), *Magnolia fraseri* has leaves like the two above, but smooth, not hairy beneath and less than half the size, to 17in long. It is confined to the mountain valleys from VA southwards.

UMBRELLA MAGNOLIA (6), *Magnolia tripetala* has a big leaf, to 20in long, tapering to the stalk and prominently veined. The flower is white, 6in long. Native to the mountain valleys from PA and OH to GA and to the coast in VA and NC and the hills of AR and OK, it is planted in gardens in ON; at Mohonk Mountain; Highland Park, Rochester; the New York Botanic Garden and at Planting Fields in NY. It is common in roadside woods in AR around Royal on US 270.

SWEETBAY (7), *Magnolia virginiana* is deciduous in the north of its range, in MA, on Long Island, NY and along the Coastal Plain, and evergreen in the south, by the Gulf Coast to south FL and east TX. It is highly attractive in the fall where miles of the slender shrubby trees line the roadside, as around Dismal Swamp, VA, with shiny green and bright blue-white foliage surrounding the 2in scarlet fruit. It is much planted in OH and MI. Although usually 30ft or less, there are trees over 60ft in GA and LA and over 50ft near the Capitol in Olympia, WA.

SOUTHERN MAGNOLIA (8), *Magnolia grandiflora* has the biggest flower of any native tree, up to 10in across, and with a strong, sweet, fruity fragrance. Although native only to the southern ends of the states from NC to TX, on the plains, it is planted extensively northwards to DE and PA, OH and IL and particularly in town main streets in AR and in OK. It is also very common in southern CA around Los Angeles, in Tustin, Arcadia, Claremont and Pasadena and in the streets of Oceanside.

SAUCER MAGNOLIA (9), *Magnolia × soulangeana* is a hybrid between two Chinese species raised near Paris, France and first flowered in 1826. It is the common, bushy magnolia in small gardens, flowering early on bare shoots and very freely even when young. **'Lennei' (10)** is of unknown Italian origin, a form with larger, darker leaves and superior flowers. When the petals droop they show the very white inside surface.

CAMPBELL MAGNOLIA (11), *Magnolia campbellii* from Nepal and Assam is the biggest of all magnolias. It rapidly grows a stout short trunk with elephant-gray nearly smooth bark. In Strybing Arboretum, Golden Gate Park, CA a form selected for flowers avoiding early frosts, **'Late Pink'**, is 62ft x 6ft.

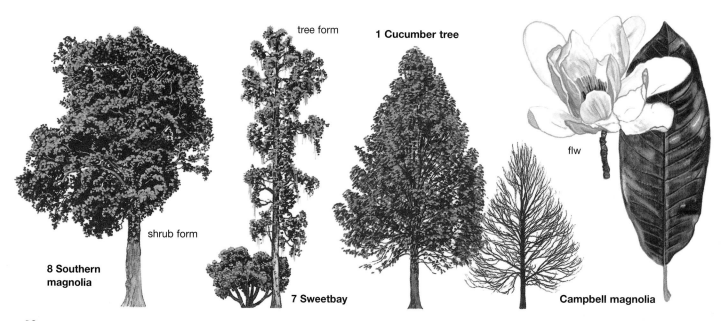

tree form

1 Cucumber tree

flw

shrub form

8 Southern magnolia

7 Sweetbay

Campbell magnolia

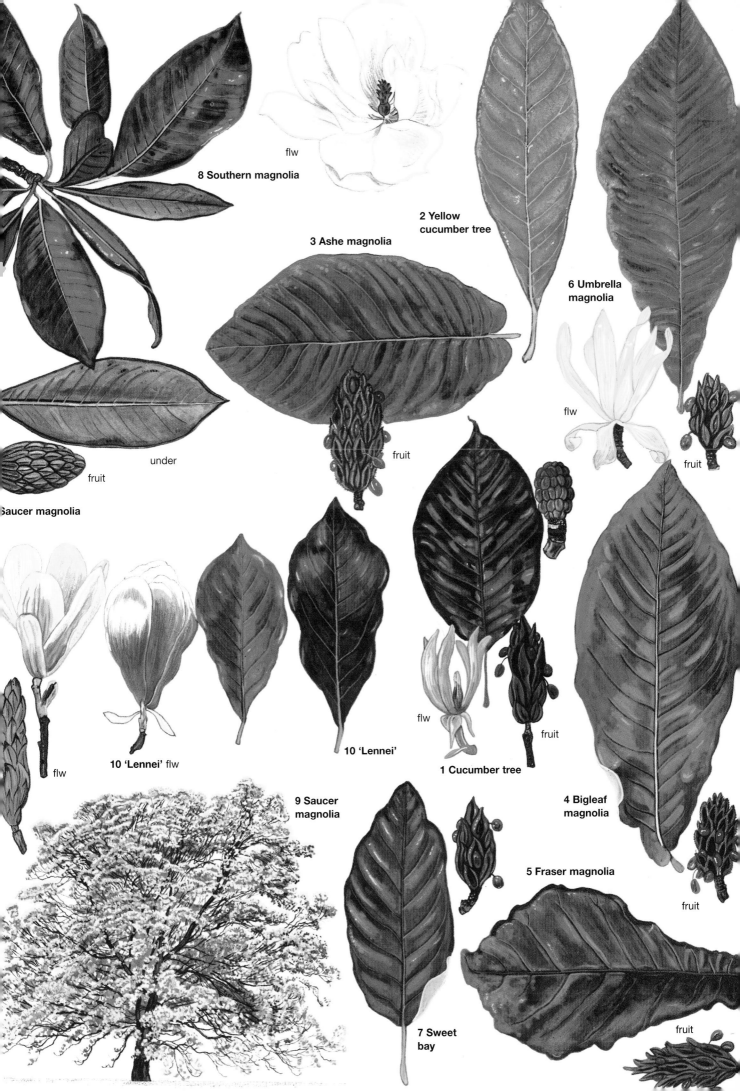

8 Southern magnolia

flw

2 Yellow
cucumber tree

3 Ashe magnolia

6 Umbrella
magnolia

flw

fruit

fruit

under

fruit

Saucer magnolia

10 'Lennei' flw

10 'Lennei'

flw

fruit

1 Cucumber tree

flw

9 Saucer
magnolia

4 Bigleaf
magnolia

5 Fraser magnolia

fruit

7 Sweet
bay

fruit

Hawthorns

The Thorns or Hawthorns, *Crataegus* are in the great Rose Family, *Rosaceae* and in a group of tree genera related closely enough to hybridise with or be used as understock in grafting. Serviceberries, Medlar, Mountain ash and Pears. By 1899 only 17 American species had been recognised. By 1910 there were 1100. Charles Sprague Sargent, founder of the Arnold Arboretum, had soon described 700. William Ashe of NC described 170 more. The Department of Agriculture, Forest Service Checklist of 1979 reduces these to 35 with 46 hybrids. In this the Cockspur thorn includes 25 former 'species'. After a few years of moderately rapid growth, thorns grow slowly and make dense, hard wood with a high fuel value. Many are easily raised from cuttings, and being strong and usually well-spined they are used for stockproof hedging. They are long-lived and decorative in flower and fruit, making good park and garden trees.

COCKSPUR HAWTHORN (1), *Crataegus crus-galli* has close rows of curved, 2–5in pale brown spines. It occurs at wood-edges or in open, low woods from southern PQ, ON and WI to MA, northern FL and GA to TX. It is seen planted in parks and gardens but less frequently than its hybrids and other less ferociously armed species. It is nonetheless planted beyond its range in parks in Chicago, IL, Milwaukee, WI and Norfolk, NE and is in Denver Botanic Garden, CO. The bark is brown or pale gray in thin plates, crumbling to orange. The flower and fruit-heads are without hairs, unlike those of its hybrids with which it is often confused, particularly the Plumleaf thorn.

SCARLET HAWTHORN (2), *Crataegus coccinea* is a fine sturdy tree with handsome big leaves, flowers and fruit, popular in northern parks and fairly readily recognised, but by no means a simple species botanically. The original basis for the name 'coccinea' by the Swedish botanist, Linnaeus, in 1753, is thought by many botanists to apply to what were later named *C. pedicellata* and the Biltmore hawthorn, *C. intricata* and has also been used to cover *C. ellwangeriana*, *C. holmesiana*, *C. chrysocarpa* and the Downy hawthorn. *Coccinea* can be used as a name which includes the large-leafed trees with big fruit and thorns 1in long in which the shoot, underside of leaf and the leafstalk are smooth, without hairs soon after emerging.

DOWNY HAWTHORN (3), *Crataegus mollis* then includes 11 more one-time species in which the underside of the leaf is downy or its veins are, the shoot and the fruit usually also. In one form, the Arnold hawthorn

from MA and CT, the spines are 3in long and the shoot becomes bright orange-brown and this form is often planted. The Downy hawthorn is wild from NS and PQ to AL and TX west to ND. It is common in city parks in New York, Chicago and most eastern cities.

FROSTED HAWTHORN (4), *Crataegus pruinosa* grows from VT to DE and IL as a small, usually shrubby plant distinct in its leaves unfolding reddish and maturing blue-green above and pale beneath and its fruit being 5-angled and apple-green with a plum bloom, ripening very shiny dark red, heavily speckled. It has hairless foliage and flowerstalks.

BLACK HAWTHORN (5), *Crataegus douglasii* is a largely western species with a range from AK to north CA and a broad arm across to WI and MI and another in the Interior Rockies to NM. Spines are often absent and when present only 1in long. The fruit are ⅜in long and black.

PLUMLEAF HAWTHORN (6), *Crataegus × prunifolia* is a hybrid between the Cockspur hawthorn and an unknown species and may have arisen in the wild. It differs from it very markedly, having few thorns and these dark, shining purple like the shoot, and a glossy dark green, broad leaf. It is infrequent in city parks and in botanic gardens from ON to WI. Its fall colors take it from yellow and orange to dark red through the color of burnished copper.

WASHINGTON HAWTHORN (7), *Crataegus phaenopyrum* is an attractive little tree unusual in the wild from VA to FL and AR to IL but escaped from cultivation from OH to MA and planted frequently in cities. It is in most cities in PA and OH, IN and IL as well as KS and WA.

ONE-SEED HAWTHORN (8), *Crataegus monogyna* has long been introduced and is so easily raised, useful as a stockproof hedge and hardy that it has been spread and then seeded itself across wide areas from PQ to NC, OK and NE and in OR and BC. It is planted in many city parks. One by the river in Santa Fe, NM is 20ft x 2ft 2in. The erect form, 'Fastigiata' is grown in the Royal Botanic Garden, Hamilton, ON; at the Greensburg Garden Center, Mill Creek Park, Youngstown and in Carlisle, PA.

PAUL'S SCARLET HAWTHORN (9), *Crataegus oxyacantha* 'Paul's Scarlet' arose as a branch sport in England in 1858. It is widely planted in ON and New England and in the west in MT, ID, WA and BC.

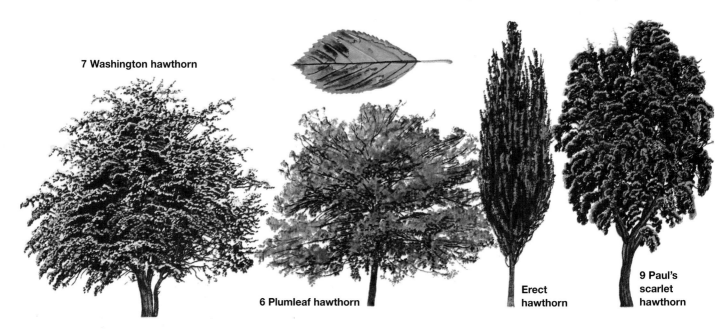

7 Washington hawthorn

6 Plumleaf hawthorn

Erect hawthorn

9 Paul's scarlet hawthorn

8 One-seed hawthorn

flws

9 Paul's scarlet hawthorn

flws

fruits

5 Black hawthorn

flws

flw detail

Broadleaf cockspur hawthorn

1 Cockspur hawthorn

2 Scarlet hawthorn

fruits

fruits

twig

fruits

3 Downy hawthorn

fruits

fruits

7 Washington hawthorn

fruits

5 Black hawthorn summer

winter

5 Black hawthorn bole

Sycamores

The Sycamores, the sole members of the Family *Platanaceae*, are also called Planetrees and Buttonwoods. In England they are 'planes' and the Sycamore is *Acer pseudoplatanus*, which translates as 'the false-plane maple'. In Scotland, however, this maple is called 'the plane', completing the circle. In all three countries, the maple named botanically *Acer platanoides*, that is 'the plane-like maple', is called the Norway maple. This mix-up between planes and maples, trees not related to each other at all, is only part of the muddle, for 'sycamore' is derived from *'Ficus'*, the fig, and *'Morus'*, the mulberry, and is also the English name for the oriental tree with edible fruit known also as the Fig mulberry, *Ficus sycamorus*. The word 'plane' is derived from the Greek word for 'broad', referring to the leaf. There are three species in North America, one in southern Europe and Asia Minor and about four in Mexico and Central America, but one hybrid between the Sycamore of Eastern North America and the Eurasian tree is the most widely planted in northern parts of Europe and is common in North America. The sycamores are large trees and long-lived, with male and female flowers in separate heads on the same branches. The timber is hard and dense, with beautiful dark freckles in a cream to pink background, known as 'lacewood'.

SYCAMORE (1), *Platanus occidentalis* grows wild by streams and in damp soils on the plains and in the mountains from ME through southern ON, MI and WI to IA and eastern TX. It is planted in city streets in all parts of this range and a little beyond, west to Boulder and Denver, CO, in Wenatchee, WA and in Reno, NV. In the north there are small trees in the botanic gardens at Montreal, PQ, and Ottawa, ON. A fine tree at the Brandywine battlefield in PA was 108ft x 22ft 1in in 1981. A very tall one 138ft x 14ft grows at nearby Hagley Mill. A tree with a very fine bole, 115ft x 15ft is in a garden in Colonial Williamsburg, VA. There is a tendency to call most of the sycamores in streets 'London plane' even where they are, plainly to a Londoner, American sycamores, and one at Smith College Campus, MA by the lake, 115ft x 13ft, is labelled 'London plane' but is a sycamore, distinguished by the larger longer-stalked, single fruit-ball, the shallowly lobed leaf and the straight branches with white patches of bark.

The sycamore in general has a very open crown of few straight branches at a low, rising angle and upper branches nearly vertical to a spire top. In the wild particularly, the bark is blue-white on the branches and scaly orange-brown on the bole. A notable feature in summer is the clusters of new leaves emerging white among the dark green foliage. Fully open large leaves are 10 x 12in. In WA, trees cut back annually to the bole grow shoots over 10ft long. In the fall the foliage turns from bright orange to orange-brown.

CALIFORNIA SYCAMORE (2), *Platanus racemosa* grows from the Upper Sacramento River along the lower Sierra Nevada and in the Coast Range from Monterey to Mexico. It is common in towns from San Bernardino, Victorville and Riverside through Encinitas and El Cajon to Alpine. It differs from the Sycamore in having about 5 small fruit strung down the stalk and a leaf with 3 deeply cut main lobes, either entire at the margin or with small, peg-like teeth.

ARIZONA SYCAMORE (3), *Platanus wrightii* grows by streams in the mountains of southern AZ and NM. It is prominent in Oak Creek Canyon in AZ and planted in Tucson, because its foliage is a deep glossy green and hangs, showing the very long 3 main lobes. The fruit-balls are 3–4 on a stalk.

LONDON PLANE (4), *Platanus × acerifolia* is a hybrid between the Sycamore and the Oriental plane, *Platanus orientalis*. It seems to have arisen in Spain or France in about 1650 and has been grown in England since 1680. It possesses hybrid vigor, adding to the exceedingly robust constitution inherited from both parents, a remarkable tolerance to polluted air and bad rooting conditions, and a very long life. It often becomes too big for its position and its roots may lift sidewalks. The City of Philadelphia claims to be responsible for half a million London planes and they are the cause of most of the claims for damages due to trees, and the City wants fewer of them. It is a very fertile hybrid and seedlings spring up in London window-boxes.

It seems likely that seedlings raised in America will often have the Sycamore as the father species and so be back-crosses more like the Sycamore. This could explain in part the occurrence of plantings regarded as London plane yet really, in effect, Sycamore. True London plane is common in cities in the northern USA, in New England, NY, OH, PA and MI. A line in Central Park, New York runs from 72nd 80th Street on the west side. Three in Woodlands Cemetery, Philadelphia are about 110ft x 14ft, and one in Bartram Park a few miles to the south is 128ft x 13ft 6in (1987). It is in Swift Current, SK and common in Victoria and Vancouver, BC. One in Penticton is 75ft x 8ft. It is in the Parkade in Spokane; in Wenatchee, Seattle, Tacoma and Bellingham, WA. This tree differs from the Sycamore in the variably deeply 5-lobed leaves, brown and yellow bark and 4–6 fruit on a stalk.

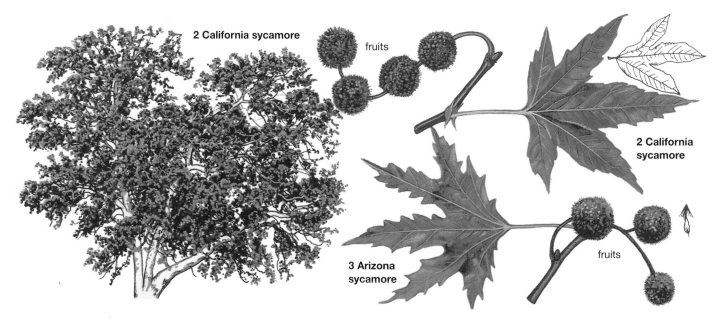

2 California sycamore

fruits

2 California sycamore

3 Arizona sycamore

fruits

♂ flws

new lvs

♀ flws

4 London plane

fruit

seed

leaf variations

1 Sycamore

seed

fruit

1 Sycamore

twig

bole

1 Sycamore

Mountain ash

The genus *Sorbus* is divided into two remarkably differently foliaged groups, and one of hybrids between them, variously intermediate. The Mountain ash group has large compound leaves with a dozen or more leaflets, the Whitebeam group has simple rather rounded leaves, so do the Hybrid service trees. The genus is in the Rose Family and has the usual five-parted calyx and five petals, and is sufficiently close to the pears to have made a hybrid when the European whitebeam crossed with a Common pear in Alsace, France, before 1650, producing the Bollwyller pear. Although so peculiarly diverse in foliage, *Sorbus* is maintained as a single genus because of similarities in the floral parts and fruit. The wood is generally quite hard, close-grained and white but since none of the species reaches timber sizes, it is used only in turnery and marquetry. The flowers are white except in the Asiatic Kashmir rowan in which they are pale pink, and they are fragrant, pleasantly sweet to most people although some find a noseful from near the massed flowers in a head of the mountain ash kinds borders on the offensive. The majority of the 100-plus species are mountain ashes in Eastern Asia. There are seven native to North America, four of them shrubby. The Whitebeams are confined to the Old World and so, therefore, are the hybrids.

AMERICAN MOUNTAIN ASH (1), *Sorbus americana* is scarcely more than a shrub and the European species is preferred for planting in parks and gardens. The American one is also known as Roundwood and grows into a round-topped, spreading low tree seldom 30ft tall, with pale gray, scaly bark. It has resinous winter buds, dark red above and greenish beneath, glossy with a few long, silky gray hairs, on stout red-brown, hairy shoots. The leaf is up to 8in long with usually 13–15 leaflets but sometimes as few as seven, entire for most of the basal half and sharply toothed beyond. In the fall the leaflets turn orange and the central stalk is bright red. It is found from NF to Chesapeake along the coast, along the Allegheny mountains just into GA, through MI and WI to southeastern MB. It grows on the top of Sharp Mountain, VA, at 5000ft at Buck Springs Gap Overlook and at 6000ft at the summit of the Blue Ridge Drive in NC.

EUROPEAN MOUNTAIN ASH (2), *Sorbus aucuparia* is wide ranging over the cooler parts of Europe and Asia so it is very hardy. It grows rapidly in youth into a quite upright tree sometimes over 60ft tall but is not long-lived and is rarely 8ft round the trunk. The bark can be silvery gray but in the north it is often coppery brown and, in either case, smooth until net-worked by a pattern of scaly ridges. The winter bud is dark purple densely set with long, gray, appressed hairs on a dull purplish gray shoot. The leaf usually has 15 leaflets, with a range of 9–19, and they are entire only for ½in of rounded base. This tree is common in parks and gardens from Montreal, PQ to Winnipeg, MB, and BC and south to OR, CO, OH and PA. The **Upright mountain ash (3)**, **'Fastigiata'** was raised in Ireland before 1840 and is sometimes seen.

SHOWY MOUNTAIN ASH (4), *Sorbus decora* is so named because of its splendid heads 6in across of large, ½in berries. It is in effect a northern and high altitude form of the American mountain ash, occurring over much the same range but not extending south beyond MA, NY and northeast IA while occurring further north in NF, Labrador, PQ and ON and even, in possibly a distinguishable variety, in southern Greenland. Where the two species overlap, the Showy mountain ash is higher on the hills, and there are probable intermediate forms. It has relatively broader, more round-ripped or abruptly tapered ends to fewer leaflets, up to 13. It is equally often shrubby but as a tree is no smaller than the American mountain ash.

SCARLET MOUNTAIN ASH (5), *Sorbus commixta* 'Embley' has had a rough passage before arriving at this name. It seems that in about 1890 some seed was sent to Britain by the Arnold Arboretum as *Sorbus discolor*, a Chinese species with white fruit. The trees grew to flowering size and bore large orange-red fruit. Meanwhile, another batch of seed from Japan received as *Sorbus matsumurana* yielded very similar trees and these were later found to be *Sorbus commixta* from Japan, Korea and Sakhalin. Both origins were grown and marketed under the early, erroneous names for many years, and often still are. One particularly good tree of 'discolor' grew at Embley Park, Hampshire, England and this was renamed *Sorbus* 'Embley'. It is at first an upright tree, then the branches arch out holding the very distinctive slender leaflets on an open crown in fern-like sprays. In mid-fall each leaflet has a broad margin of dark purple before turning bright scarlet all over, then deep red. In view of the source there should be some planting in MA and New England.

KOREAN MOUNTAIN ASH (6), *Sorbus alnifolia* grows also in Japan and China and is occasionally planted in North America. It has smooth, pale gray bark like a beech and dense heads 3in across of flowers which last for two weeks in late spring. As well as attractive foliage, in a dense crown of slender shoots, it has a time when its fruits are an unusual pink-orange as they ripen slowly to scarlet.

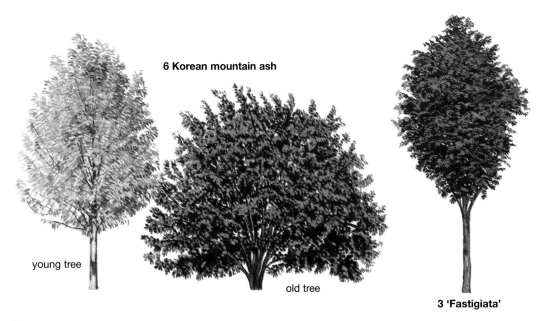

6 Korean mountain ash

young tree

old tree

3 'Fastigiata'

Mountain ash bark

6 Korean mountain ash

fruits

flw detail

twig

2 European mountain ash

fruits

'fructu-luteo'

1 American mountain ash

5 Scarlet mountain ash

fruits

autumn

2 European mountain ash

1 American mountain ash

Finnish service tree

bole

Whitebeams

The other part of the genus *Sorbus* is very different from the Mountain ash group in general appearance. Instead of compound leaves with many slender leaflets, its foliage is of simple leaves, rounded and broad, silvery beneath with a close mat of hairs. They also have fewer flowers in a cluster and fewer but larger berries. The name 'whitebeam' from the Anglo-Saxon, 'white wood', is equally apt if taken to be 'white tree', for when the leaves emerge they show at first the silvery undersides, then the upper sides as they bend over are also silvery from long hairs, which are soon shed. For the rest of the season in leaf, the underside shows when the foliage is disturbed by the wind. The whitebeams are only Old World trees, native right across the northern parts of the Eurasian landmass from the British Isles to Japan. They are little grown in North America but as hardy, attractive trees some of those given here should be found in parks and small gardens in the cooler parts, from PQ and New England to BC and WA.

COMMON WHITEBEAM (1), *Sorbus aria* is native to southern England on chalk soils and to Central Europe. It is a tree of moderate size, to 60ft, but of robust constitution, withstanding the hard conditions of town streets well, and is common in city suburbs in Europe. For these positions, the form **'Lutescens' (2)** is well suited by its neatly egg-shaped crown. The name, literally 'growing gold', refers to a yellow tinge in the silver as the leaves open, but against the dark purple shoots they appear as white as in the type. The large-leaf form **'Majestica' (3)** arose in France and grows strongly into a very handsome tree with leaves 6in long. This tree is similar to the hybrid **'Wilfrid Fox (4)'**, which is the Common whitebeam crossed with the Himalayan, but this is fairly strictly upright as a young tree and its fruit do not ripen red, as in 'Majestica' but pale orange to brown.

HIMALAYAN WHITEBEAM (5), *Sorbus cuspidata* is a vigorous, tall-growing tree with foliage similar to the last two but distinguished by thicker and longer leaves, to 9in, with only about 10 pairs of veins instead of 15, shallower toothing and slight lobing. It has large flowers for a whitebeam and they have a strong scent of hawthorn. The large fruit ripen pale brown.

TIBETAN WHITEBEAM (6), *Sorbus thibetica* 'John Mitchell' was long thought to be a form of, or hybrid from, the Himalayan whitebeam raised by John Mitchell at Westonbirt Arboretum, England. Trees originating from Westonbirt are called 'John Mitchell' to distinguish them from those raised from seed from the wild. It has even larger, thicker leaves than the Himalayan, many of them almost circular, to 8in across, and grows very fast.

CHINESE WHITEBEAM (7), *Sorbus folgneri* has, in the best form, almost metallic silvering under the leaf. The foliage turns scarlet and deep red late in the fall.

SERVICE TREE OF FONTAINEBLEAU (8), *Sorbus × latifolia* is a hybrid of the Common whitebeam and the Wild service tree, first known and described from a small population confined to the Forest of Fontainebleau near Paris, France. It has handsome glossy foliage.

SWEDISH WHITEBEAM (9), *Sorbus intermedia* breeds true and has been spread by birds beyond man-made plantings. It is a sturdy tree excellent in towns and is most likely to be seen in urban streets and parks. It bears more flowers than other whitebeams, the bunches, 5in across, being densely set along the shoots, giving the tree in flower the aspect of a hawthorn. The trunk is straight, usually clear for 6ft or more, and has dull purplish-gray bark, smooth between shallow, scaly fissures. The foliage rarely shows much color in the fall but some leaves turn yellow.

FINNISH WHITEBEAM or **BASTARD SERVICE TREE (10)**, *Sorbus × thuringiaca* is of unknown origin, apparently a selection from the hybrids that arise between the European mountain ash or rowan and the Whitebeam in Europe, in which the whitebeam was a long-leafed form. These hybrids do not breed true and the Finnish whitebeam is propagated by grafting on to rowan rootstock. It is a very sturdy, upright tree with substantial leaves up to 6in long, rather hanging, in dense masses concealing the interior crown. Leaves on strong shoots have 1–2 pairs of free leaflets at the base. This tree is useful for moving at a good size into a car-lot and the even more strictly erect form, **'Fastigiata'**, is favoured for such places.

MEDLAR (11), *Mespilus germanica* from Europe and Asia Minor has 1in thorns and is closely related to the thorns, hybridises with them and is often grafted on to one. It differs in having large solitary flowers and fruit. It was once grown in orchards as the fruit, kept until almost rotting, were regarded as edible. The leaves are to 5in long, downy both sides but more beneath, and turn an attractive pale yellow for a good while in the fall. The tree is usually broader than it is tall and grows slowly.

flw

11 Medlar

5 Himalayan whitebeam

bark

fruit

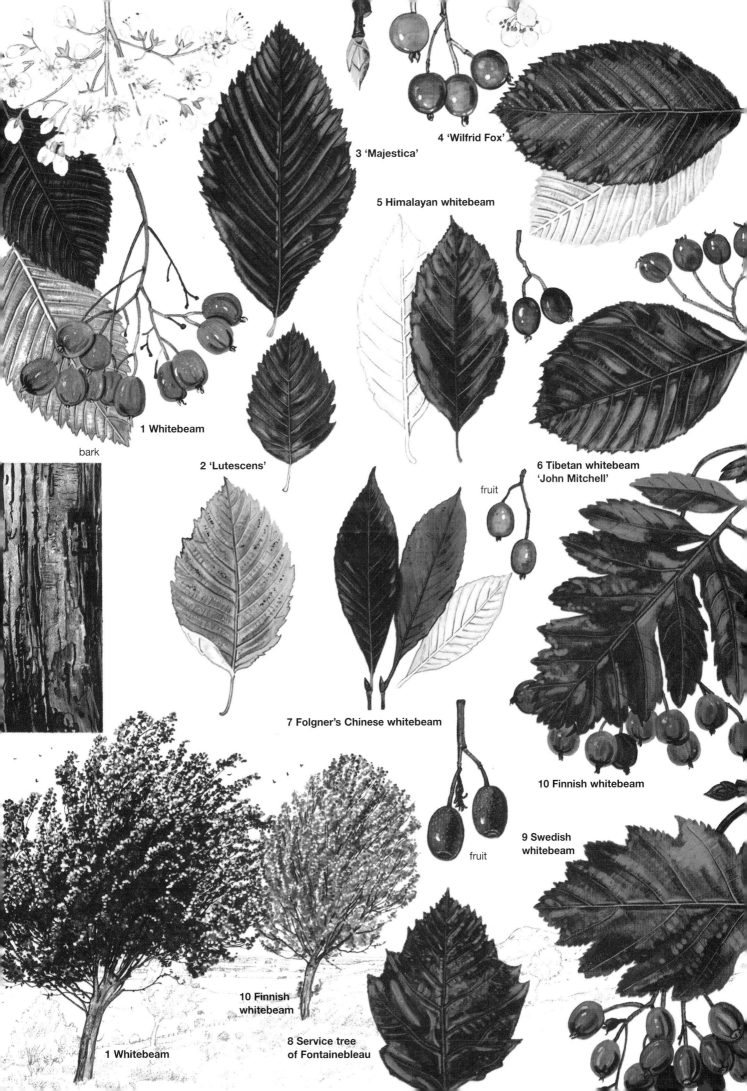

3 'Majestica'

4 'Wilfrid Fox'

5 Himalayan whitebeam

1 Whitebeam

bark

2 'Lutescens'

6 Tibetan whitebeam
'John Mitchell'

fruit

7 Folgner's Chinese whitebeam

10 Finnish whitebeam

fruit

9 Swedish
whitebeam

10 Finnish
whitebeam

1 Whitebeam

8 Service tree
of Fontainebleau

Crab apples

The Apples are medium–small trees of the cooler parts of the northern hemisphere. They are typical of the tree-members of the Rose Family in having numerous intergrading variants and hybrids between the species and causing botanists much work and controversy. But unlike most of the others, the genus *Malus* has not been found crossing with any other genus, nor will it graft readily on to any of them. The wood is hard and dense and has a sweet fragrance when burning. The trees are mostly very hardy and able to grow in difficult soils.

SWEET CRAB APPLE (1), *Malus coronaria* includes about five forms which have been classed at times as separate species. It is wild from NY and IL to AR and GA along streams and woodland edges. It has red-brown bark shallowly fissured into broad, scaly ridges. The flowers are rose-scented more strongly in the form **'Charlottae' (2)** found by de Wolf in Waukegan, IL in 1902. This has flowers in bunches of six, double, with 16 petals, and in full flower looks more like a Japanese cherry than an apple. It is widely planted in parks and gardens.

PRAIRIE CRAB APPLE (3), *Malus ioensis* is the mid-western Sweet crab from IN and WI to OK and AR. It is a low, bushy tree with level branches that have leaden gray bark while that on the trunk is in narrow, brown strips. The shoots are dark red with a gray bloom and the leaves are softly hairy white beneath or yellowish green. This tree is planted in gardens in WI, MN and south to CO. A far better garden tree, however, is the form **Bechtel's crab apple (4)**, **'Plena'**, which bears abundant flowers so double that they have over 30 petals and looks remarkably attractive with the pink droplet-shaped flowers among the leaves.

OREGON CRAB APPLE (5), *Malus fusca* ranges from the Kenai Peninsula, AK along the coast to northern CA. It is the only American apple to show bright fall colors and the thickets in WA and CA shine out in mid-October orange and scarlet.

PURPLE CRAB APPLE (6), *Malus × purpurea* is a hybrid raised in Orleans, France before 1900, involving the purple Siberian *Malus pumila* 'Niedwetskyana' which has dark red pigment in all its parts and is extremely hardy. The Purple crab is too, and being very floriferous it is valued for amenity in cold northern areas and also as a pollinator in orchards. It has been selected and crossed with other species in Europe, Canada and in the Prairie States so a great array of floriferous red to purple forms is now widely planted.

JAPANESE CRAB APPLE (7), *Malus floribunda* was brought from Japan in 1862 and is a common tree in town gardens from ON to DE in the east and in CA. It comes into full leaf very early, bright green but in May the red buds foam out and the pink and white flowers smother the crown, followed in some years by masses of tiny yellow fruit. **Hall's crab apple (8)** was brought from Japan in 1863 by Dr. G. R. Hall in the single or semi-double form and in the more double form 'Parkmanii'. It is like the Japanese Crab apple but its rich pink flowers are less abundant.

RED SIBERIAN CRAB APPLE (9), *Malus × robusta* is one of several similar hybrids of the wild Siberian crab, *Malus baccata* and is grown for its persistent, large fruit and for its sturdy vigor in cold areas. The Yellow Siberian crab differs only in the color of the fruit.

'GOLDEN HORNET' CRAB APPLE (10) holds the calyx on its fruit, on a protruded tip which is wrinkled, distinguishing it from other yellow-fruited crabs. It also weeps more strongly and the weight of the fruit, in bunches of 6, bears the arched branches down to vertical. It was raised in a nursery in Surrey, England, in about 1940 from a selection of a cultivar of the Japanese *Malus zumi* and is grown in many northern parks and gardens. Its long-pendulous shoots are wreathed in white flowers.

PILLAR CRAB APPLE (11), *Malus tschonoskii* was brought from Japan in 1892 to the Arnold Arboretum. It is one of the very few tree species fastigiate in the wild populations. Unselected seedlings grow into variously upright trees from columnar to broadly avoid with spreading lower branches. Ed Scanlon of Cleveland, OH recognised this tree as a useful one for planting in streets because it is neat with brilliant fall colors, exceedingly tough and resistant to compacted and dry soils; and it bears few and small fruit, which is a good point in a tree for precincts and streets. The scarlet leaf-buds open with foliage silvered by fine hairs.

HUPEH CRAB APPLE (12), *Malus hupehensis*, sent from west China in 1900, is a triploid and hence has great vigor and comes true from seed, as it will not cross with any other species. Seedlings grow 3–4ft in each of the early years and it makes a tree to 60ft x 8ft. A few flowers are borne in the 4th year from seed, a few hundred in the 5th and a thousand or more in the 6th. After that the tree is a cloud of big gold-bossed flowers spraying out in elegant bunches every May, and densely set with little glossy dark red fruit in September. A pink-flowered form is equally common in the wild and is frequent in parks and gardens.

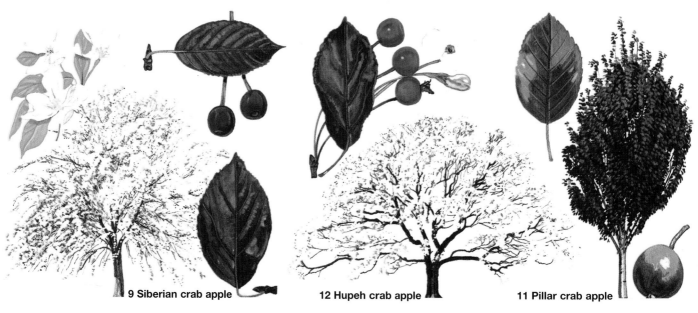

9 Siberian crab apple   12 Hupeh crab apple   11 Pillar crab apple

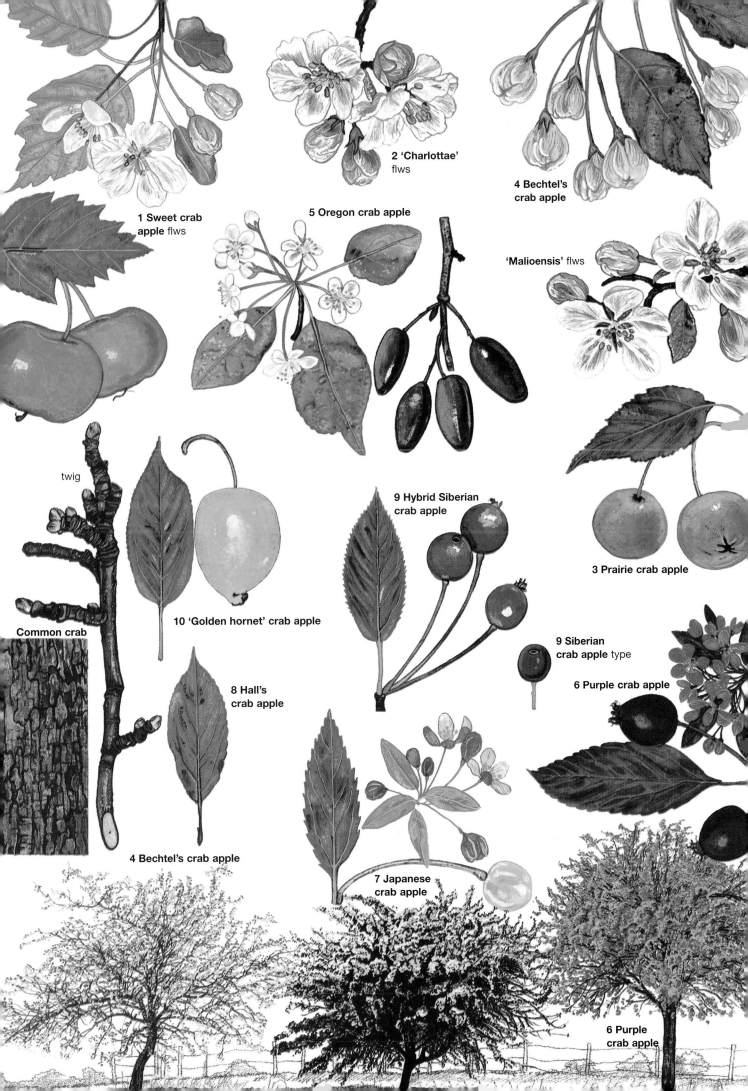

2 'Charlottae' flws

4 Bechtel's crab apple

1 Sweet crab apple flws

5 Oregon crab apple

'Malioensis' flws

twig

9 Hybrid Siberian crab apple

3 Prairie crab apple

10 'Golden hornet' crab apple

Common crab

9 Siberian crab apple type

6 Purple crab apple

8 Hall's crab apple

4 Bechtel's crab apple

7 Japanese crab apple

6 Purple crab apple

Serviceberries, Loquat and Pears

The Pears, *Pyrus* are an Old World group widely grown for their large fruit with a peculiar texture deriving from grit-cells. The Serviceberries are small trees and shrubs in the Rose Family closely related to the hawthorns, on which they can be grafted, and the Mountain ash group with which they make a hybrid. This is a bush found growing wild in many parts of the Rocky Mountains. Although only a very small group, the Serviceberries, with between two and 16 species worldwide in Eurasia and North America, have sown great confusion among botanists and it is those in North America which are the source of the trouble. They show many variations and hybrids in the wild and in cultivation.

DOWNY SERVICEBERRY, *Amelanchier arborea* can be taken to include the **Allegheny serviceberry (1)**, *Amelanchier laevis* a form with hairless leaves and flowerheads. It may also be seen labelled *A. × grandiflora* which is considering it to be a hybrid between the Thicket serviceberry, *A. canadensis* and the Allegheny form. The bark is light brown or gray-brown and very smooth and the buds slender and sharp. The flowers are profuse unless the tree is shaded, and all open within a few days. The bloomed dark purple-red berries are soon eaten by birds and the seeds, after this brief stay in the hot, acid stomach, are prevented from germinating at once when voided by a need to be frozen first. Although usually shrubby, the Downy serviceberry is 65ft tall in Mount Cuba garden, PA. It grows from southern NF to MN south to LA and FL.

WESTERN SERVICEBERRY, *Amelanchier alnifolia* grows from AK and Mackenzie to north CA with a band across NE and MN to ON and PQ. It differs in its much more coarsely toothed and round-tipped leaf and ovoid bud. It is now usually made to include the **Pacific serviceberry (2)**, *Amelanchier florida* which is probably restricted to the Rocky Mountains, east only to ID, and has slightly larger flowers to 1¼in across. Neither is much more than a shrubby thicket.

LOQUAT (3), *Eriobotrya japonica* from China and Japan is also in the Rose family, an evergreen too tender to be grown outside the warmest, most frost-free regions. It makes a broad-topped low tree to 30ft with spreading, upcurved branches and few, stout shoots, handsome with big dark, crinkled but shiny leaves to 1ft long. The flower head is 6 x 8in covered in dense brown hairs and the fruit is edible, ripening in the spring after the late summer flowering, where it is grown for the fruit in Mediterranean countries. The underside of the leaf is softly hairy with a prominent yellow mid-rib and veins. It is frequent in small gardens, courtyards and on walls from Charleston, SC near the coast to the Delta and Baton Rouge, LA and TX, north through Dallas and less frequent to Little Rock, AR. In the west it is in Columbus Avenue, San Francisco, CA and the Bay Area generally, in small town-gardens; in Arcadia and around Los Angeles to San Diego, also in Phoenix, AZ and Las Vegas, NV.

COMMON PEAR (4), *Pyrus communis* is an upright tree with a long, straight trunk and dark brown bark broken into small squares. It can be over 60ft tall and is long-lived, with very strong, durable and finely grained timber which turns well and makes excellent fuel. In city parks its small, globular fruit ripening dark green remain unmolested by the public. Like all pears, its flowers open as the leaves are only beginning to unfold. In this one the leaves are then pale yellowish brown partly hidden by the large flowerheads fairly early in spring.

USSURI PEAR (5), *Pyrus ussuriensis* has leaves at first covered in dense, silvery white hairs adding to the white of the flowers. This tree from Korea and Mongolia is very hardy. A few of its slender, very hard shoots end in spines. As a shapely 45ft tree in Willowwood Arboretum NJ shows, it is an attractive tree with pleasant late fall colors. The American collector Frank Meyer sent the **Callery pear**, *Pyrus calleryana* from China in 1918. It is a sturdy tree of robust constitution and good foliage coloring well in the fall but of rather shrubby habit. Ernest Wilson had sent it in 1908, but it had then attracted little interest. Meyer's seed, however, was given to the Glenn Dale Plant Introduction Station in MD and here they raised and selected the exceedingly attractive and shapely **Bradford pear (6)**. This has become one of the most useful trees in city plantings, in precincts and streets from ON to GA. The neat, dense, upright, ovoid crown is held on a trunk with pale gray smooth bark darkening with age and becoming lightly fissured and scaled. The shoot is brown with a bluish bloom. The flowers are white with broad, rounded petals in a large head opening among silver-haired unfolding leaves which in the fall turn a fine mixture of yellow, orange and red. The tree is prominent in many cities in ON, NY, NJ, NH and PA through OH, WI, GA, LA and OK. So far it has not been planted much in the west beyond Denver, CO.

Some 30 years ago, Ed Scanlon in Cleveland, OH raised and distributed the slender, more upright form, **'Chanticleer' (7)**. This is even brighter in the fall when it turns from gold to scarlet and crimson with a few leaves usually green until the end of the year and sometimes opens some flowers at the height of the coloring.

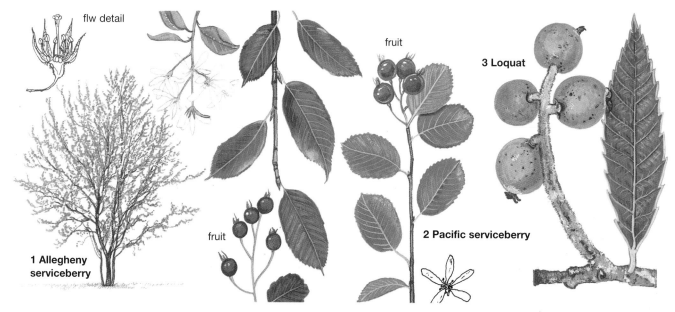

flw detail

fruit

1 Allegheny serviceberry

fruit

2 Pacific serviceberry

3 Loquat

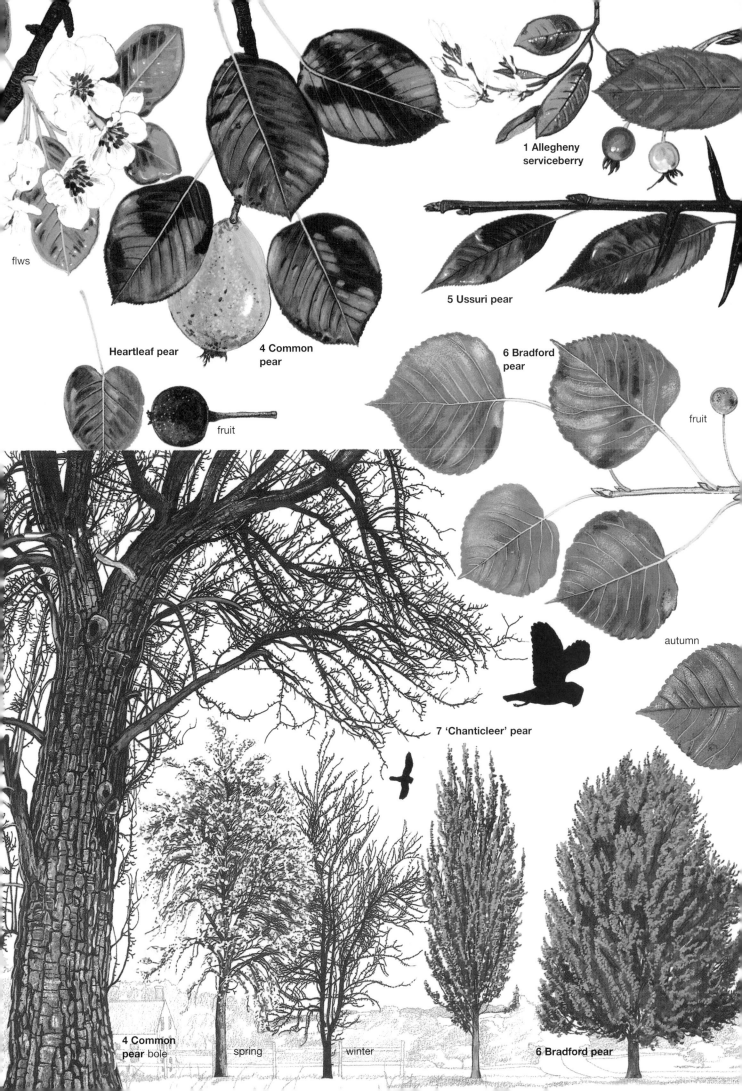

flws

Heartleaf pear

fruit

4 Common pear

1 Allegheny serviceberry

5 Ussuri pear

6 Bradford pear

fruit

autumn

7 'Chanticleer' pear

4 Common pear bole

spring

winter

6 Bradford pear

Cherries and allied fruits

The genus *Prunus* includes cherries, plums, almonds, apricots, peaches and cherry laurels as well as bullace, sloe and damson. They all have the basic Rose Family flower of five sepals and five petals like the apples, hawthorns, serviceberries and other rosaceous trees, but differ from them in having a fruit with a single seed, the hard, central 'stone'. This is surrounded by thick, fleshy more or less edible tissues in all except the almonds, in which it is dry and stringy. The genus contains some low shrubs like the Blackthorn and the Russian almond, but is largely of medium–small trees, rarely long-lived since they are susceptible to silverleaf fungus and other diseases despite the defence, very unusual in broadleaf trees, of exudation of gum.

BLACK CHERRY (1), *Prunus serotina* is in the bird cherry group with the flowers in spike-like racemes at the ends of leafy shoots. 'Serotina' means 'late' and refers mainly to the ripening of the fruit in comparison with other cherries. The foliage has little groups of orange or white hairs on the midrib beneath, straight and perpendicular to it. The bark is dark purplish gray peeling in curved strips and ageing to brownish-pink, broadly fissured. The leaf is 5in long and has a thickened, waved margin. The glands at the base, found in most of the cherries, are enlarged into several wings or lobes, green at first, then dark red. In the fall most of the leaves turn clear, bright yellow, a few are red and some remain green until very late. This tree is native to the region south of a line from NS to MN and east around Houston, TX, but is scarce from SC to AL where the **Alabama black cherry**, var. *alabamensis* is in a few hills, and the **Southwestern black cherry**, var. *rufula* is the form in the mountains of western TX and in AZ. Over the main range, the Black cherry is common in woodlands and is frequently planted.

PIN CHERRY (2), *Prunus pensylvanica* flowers from early May to late June depending on latitude and altitude and ripens fruit in July and August. Its shining bright red shoots bear in their second year, short, thick spur-shoots. The bark of old trees is broken into dark red-brown, papery, horizontal plates. This tree, usually low or shrubby, is found almost all across Canada and southwards in mountains to GA and CO.

CHOKE CHERRY (3), *Prunus virginiana* is another bird cherry like the Black cherry and almost a shrubby version of it. The underside of the leaf has tufts of white hairs in the vein-angles. The tree has a remarkable range, all across Canada from Labrador to BC and across the USA south to Chesapeake, TN, MO and NM to CA. It is common by roadsides.

BITTER CHERRY (4), *Prunus emarginata* is very like the Pin cherry with broader, more round-tipped leaves with one to four large dark glands at the base. It forms dense thickets at high altitudes and is found from BC to ID and south in the hills to CA, AZ and NM.

CATALINA CHERRY (5), *Prunus lyonii* is confined in the wild to the islands off the coast of South CA where it grows on the four biggest and on Anacapa, but it has been planted widely on the mainland of CA. Its evergreen, hard, leathery leaves are usually abruptly narrowed to a short point and it makes a low, bushy tree but with a stout trunk.

ALMOND (6), *Prunus dulcis* when grown in orchards for fruit is often a white-flowered form. The nuts contain poisonous prussic acid but are innocuous unless a large sackful is eaten at a sitting. For decorative planting in more northerly gardens, the larger, rosy-pink-flowered forms are grown as well as **Pollard's almond**, *Prunus × amygdalo-persica*.

PEACH (7), *Prunus persica* in orchards in Central Valley, CA has escaped along roadside hedges. In gardens the cultivar **'Klara Mayer' (8)** is grown for its superior flowers.

APRICOT (9), *Prunus armeniaca* is widely planted for its fruit. The broad, rounded leaves are distinctive.

MAHALEB CHERRY or **ST. LUCIE CHERRY (10)**, *Prunus mahaleb* opens its small flowers late in attractive sprays along the shoot. They are strongly and sweetly scented. It has escaped from cultivation and become naturalised from ON to DE, IN and KS and from ID to CA.

MANCHURIAN CHERRY (11), *Prunus maackii* is a bird cherry grown for its bark which in young trees is shining honey-gold becoming with age dark orange. It grows rather too fast to give the best results, since in 40 years it can be 8ft round and by then the shining orange areas are being squeezed between big, broadening, rough gray fissures. There are trees in the Arnold Arboretum, MA and in the University of Minnesota Landscape Arboretum at Chaska, MN.

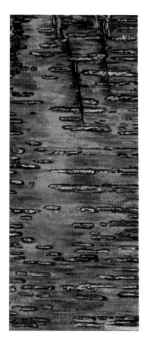

11 Manchurian cherry

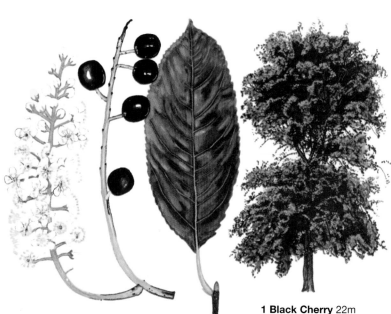

1 Black Cherry 22m

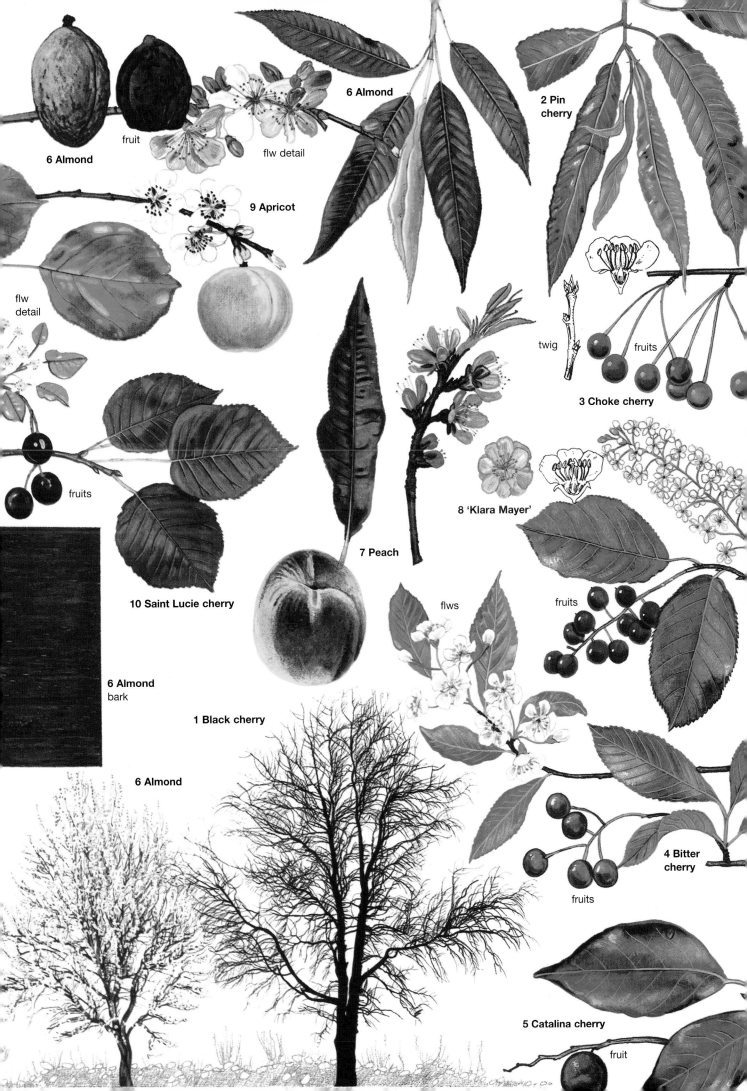

6 Almond

fruit

flw detail

6 Almond

6 Almond

9 Apricot

2 Pin cherry

flw detail

twig

fruits

3 Choke cherry

8 'Klara Mayer'

fruits

10 Saint Lucie cherry

7 Peach

flws

fruits

6 Almond
bark

1 Black cherry

6 Almond

4 Bitter cherry

fruits

5 Catalina cherry

fruit

Plums and Cherries

MAZZARD (1), *Prunus avium* is the Gean or Wild white cherry of Europe. It is one of the several species from which eating cherries derive but its unimproved fruit are small, and are eaten by birds before ripening fully. Hence the Latin *'avium'* and the value of the tree in planting for wildlife. It is also a tree of great amenity value, for its clouds of white flowers in late spring and its yellow, orange and crimson leaves in late fall. This species is used as understock for the grafts of all the Japanese 'Sato' cherries and other forms needing to be grafted. The growth pattern of the tree is highly unusual in broadleaf trees, with the branches confined to whorls at the ends of each year's growth, until it becomes broadly domed with age and the outer shoots hang. This tree has escaped from cultivation and become naturalised in many regions as well as being planted in parks and gardens. It is particularly common around Vancouver and Victoria, BC and Seattle, WA. **Double-flowered mazzard (2)**, 'Plena' has dense rows of flowers opening two weeks later than the single-flowered, and lasting a week or two longer. It can be over 80ft tall, unlike the slightly more opulently flowered similar double white Japanese cherries which flatten out at 25ft.

MYROBALAN PLUM (3), *Prunus cerasifera* is the first spring-flowering tree in bloom, starring in January or February, with its green leaves opening at the same time. The little plums are edible. This is rarely planted but can arise where it has been used as understock for a variety and has grown away. The common variety is **Pissard's purple plum (4)**, 'Pissardii' found in Iran in 1880. Its fuzzy crown is a shapeless mass of twigs and its foliage, a brownish-red or muddy purple, casts gloom over huge areas of suburbs from south ON to IL and NY. It is pleasantly scarce southwards, in the Mississippi Valley and the midwest but there are bad infestations in Houston and Amarillo, TX, in Tulsa, OK, Wichita, KS and Ames, IA also near Omaha, NE. In the west it is common to abundant in BC and WA. OR is largely free of it but it starts again in southern CA. The much improved form 'Nigra' arose in North America and is mixed with the other form everywhere. It has flowers opening three weeks later and lasting longer as well as leaves of shiny, dark red.

DOUBLE APRICOT-PLUM, *Prunus × blireana*, a hybrid between Pissard's plum and a double form of Japanese apricot, is a shrub or small tree of great beauty when in flower. A superb little bush was in full flower in late May at over 5000ft in a garden in Rawlins, WY but nearer sea level it may flower in February.

SARGENT'S CHERRY (5), *Prunus sargentii* from northern Japan and Sakhalin was sent to the Arnold Arboretum in 1890. As a seedling it may spread into a broad bush but it is usually grafted on to mazzard to make a tall tree. It provides a great display of massed rather small flowers in middle-early spring and another of scarlet foliage very early in the fall. It is grown from ME to DE and, less frequently, in parks in Vancouver, BC and Seattle, WA, but mostly in New England. At Smith College, Northampton, MA it is over 50ft x 8ft and it is a street tree in Amherst. It is grown in 38th Street and the Penn Center in Philadelphia and near Harrisburg, PA. Seed of Sargent cherry sent abroad from the trees at the Arnold show that it crosses readily with other cherries nearby. **'Accolade' (6)** is one such, a cross with the Rosebud cherry from seed raised in England, a singularly beautiful bright soft pink in flower, opening well before Sargent cherry and rather sparse leaves turning orange and dark red. Another is **'Spire' (7)** from seed sent to Hampshire, England, perhaps a cross with the Yoshino cherry.

YOSHINO CHERRY (8), *Prunus × yedoensis* from Japan has not been found wild and is probably a hybrid of relatively recent origin. It is early into flower and long shoots are wreathed in the dense masses of fragrant flowers which open from pink buds. In warm weather, as in San Francisco, they tend to remain pink but in cooler places they are soon pure white. It is a tree of poor shape and the foliage is dull and coarse. The most famous planting is that at the Tidal Basin, extending to Haynes Point, Washington DC, made with plants sent from Japan in 1912. Equally frequent in the north and almost replacing this tree southwards to GA is the low hummock of the **Weeping Yoshino, 'Perpendens'**.

HIGAN or **ROSEBUD CHERRY**, *Prunus subhirtella* is common only as the **Weeping rosebud cherry (9)**, 'Pendula' sent from Japan to the Arnold Arboretum in 1862. It is common in MA, CT, NY and PA, OH and DC and is often 60ft tall, a fountain of delicate pink in March. It is in the large gardens and parks in BC and frequent in WA.

REDBARK or **TIBETAN CHERRY (10)**, *Prunus serrula* from China and Tibet was first sent in 1908 to the Arnold Arboretum. It is scarce but one is in the University of MI Botanic Garden at East Lansing and others in the Van Dusen garden, BC and the University of Washington Arboretum. Unless planted by a path where it can be seen and stroked, it is liable to lose the glossy bark under dark scales.

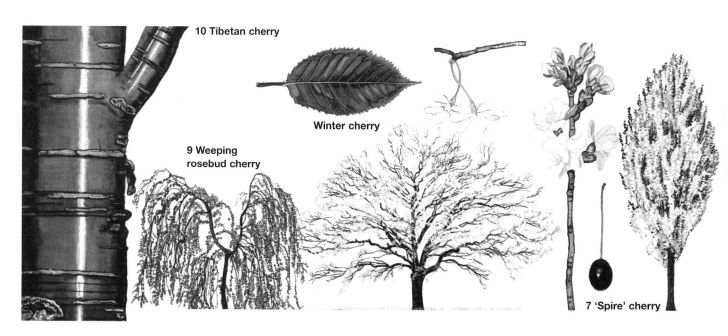

10 Tibetan cherry

Winter cherry

9 Weeping rosebud cherry

7 'Spire' cherry

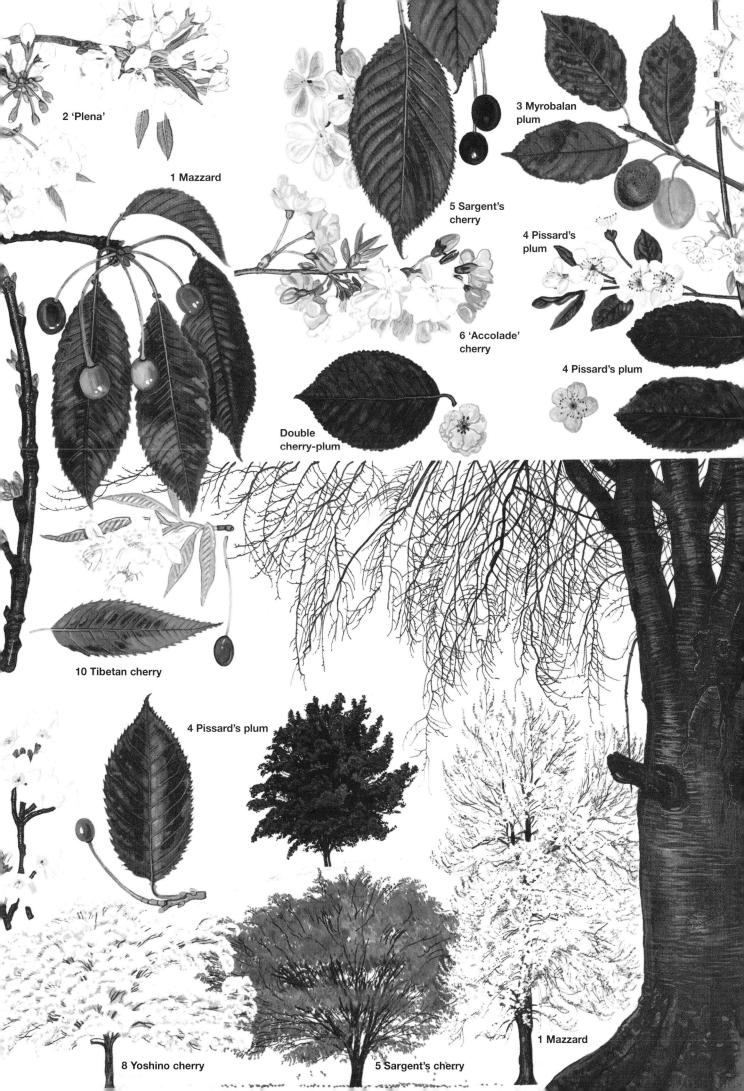

2 'Plena'

1 Mazzard

3 Myrobalan plum

5 Sargent's cherry

4 Pissard's plum

6 'Accolade' cherry

4 Pissard's plum

Double cherry-plum

10 Tibetan cherry

4 Pissard's plum

8 Yoshino cherry

5 Sargent's cherry

1 Mazzard

Japanese 'Sato' cherries

The 'Japanese' cherries were produced over a long period some 300 years ago in an old tradition of crossing and selecting among decorative plants in Japan with some also from China. There are no records of the parentages of these trees but the bristle-tipped teeth on their large, long-pointed leaves derive from the Oshima cherry, *Prunus speciosa* and the copper red-brown young leaves of many of them are from the Hill cherry, *Prunus serrulata* var. *spontanea*. Until recently these flowering cherries, usefully gathered under the Japanese term 'Sato' cherries, meaning 'domestic' or garden cherries, were named as varieties of *P. serrulata* but modern practice is to use a cultivar name, the old Japanese one where it is known, without any attribution to a species. This removes the problem of their unknown precise origins. A study at the Arnold Arboretum changed some of the names in 1985 but the previously accepted names are used here. All are grafts, usually low down and grow heavy spreading branches. In this book some known plantings will be given as examples rather than as definitive attempts at a full cover of the ranges. They are relatively scarce in North America but may be found in parks and gardens from PQ to MD in the east, especially in ON and New England, OH and PA to MI and WI and in BC, WA, ID and MT in the west with a few in OR and CA.

'KANZAN' (1) is probably the commonest cherry in North America. The strong, rising branches drooping with years of being bowed down by the weight of the superabundant flowers, and the pale, whitish green underside of the leaf identify it in summer. Fall color is amber, pink and some red. It is planted in ON, NY, CT, RI, OH, BC and WA.

'HOKUSAI' (2) opens its similar bunches of flushed pink flowers several weeks before 'Kanzan' and turns red and crimson in the fall.

'TAIHAKU' (3) has an extraordinary history. In 1923 a woman took the flowers from a dying tree she had bought in a job-lot from Japan in 1900 to a show where Collingwood Ingram was a judge, in Sussex, England. He took what shoots he could to make grafts and four years later was shown a silk embroidery in Japan dating from about 1750. The embroidery showed the 'Great White cherry' lost 200 years ago. He said he had one in his garden in Kent and then sent some buds by air to be matched with the embroidery picture. Every 'Taihaku' in the world derives from that dying tree. The flowers can be 3in across and the hard, dark leaf 8in long. Growth is very strong with stout branches rising at a flatter angle than in 'Kanzan'. Flowers open early for a Sato cherry.

'SHIROTAE' (4) is the first Sato in flower with its large single and semi-double flowers among bright green leaves which identify the tree in summer together with its flat crown.

'UKON' (5) is also early into flower and like a smaller-flowered 'Taihaku' when the yellow fades and the red eye shows, but it is semi-double and the leaf is very oblong. A tree is in the Brooklyn Botanic Garden, NY.

'CHEAL'S WEEPING' (6) has over 50 petals, more double than any other cherry, and opens its flowers early.

'SHIMIDZU' (7) is among the last to open its frilled, very white flowers from long sprays of pink buds hazed in lilac hairs below leaves of yellowish-lilac, soon green, and is very spectacular but a poor grower.

'ICHIYO' (8) is a very strong grower with big rising branches spreading widely. Late in the season the wide open, green-eyed soft pink flowers open beneath green leaves 6in long and well spaced.

'SHIROFUGEN' (9) is another among the last to open its flowers and makes very strong growth, soon level then drooping at the branch-ends. The pink buds among dark red leaves open pink then turn white, striking beneath the large leaves, then as these turn green the flowers go pink again and last a long time.

'AMANOGAWA' (10) is a Lombardy poplar cherry late into flower with apple-blossom-like flowers sweetly scented.

'PANDORA' (11) is a cross between the Yoshino and Higan cherries and very vigorous. It is a vast improvement on Pissard's plum which it resembles in its early masses of small pink-budded white flowers but it has green slender leaves turning orange in the fall.

'OKAME' (12) opens clusters of narrow-petalled flowers on bunches of shoots from branches and trunk, very early. It is a hybrid raised by Collingwood Ingram in Kent, England from the Himalayan Bell-flowered cherry, *Prunus campanulata*.

'KURSAR' (13) from the same source is a hybrid from the Japanese Alpine cherry, *Prunus nipponica* opening a week or two later its much richer pink, broad-petalled cup-shaped flowers.

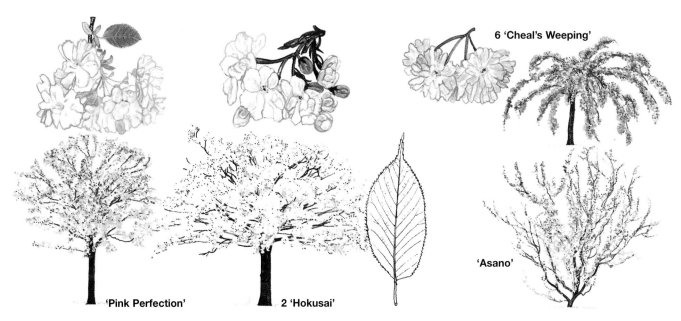

6 'Cheal's Weeping'

'Asano'

'Pink Perfection'

2 'Hokusai'

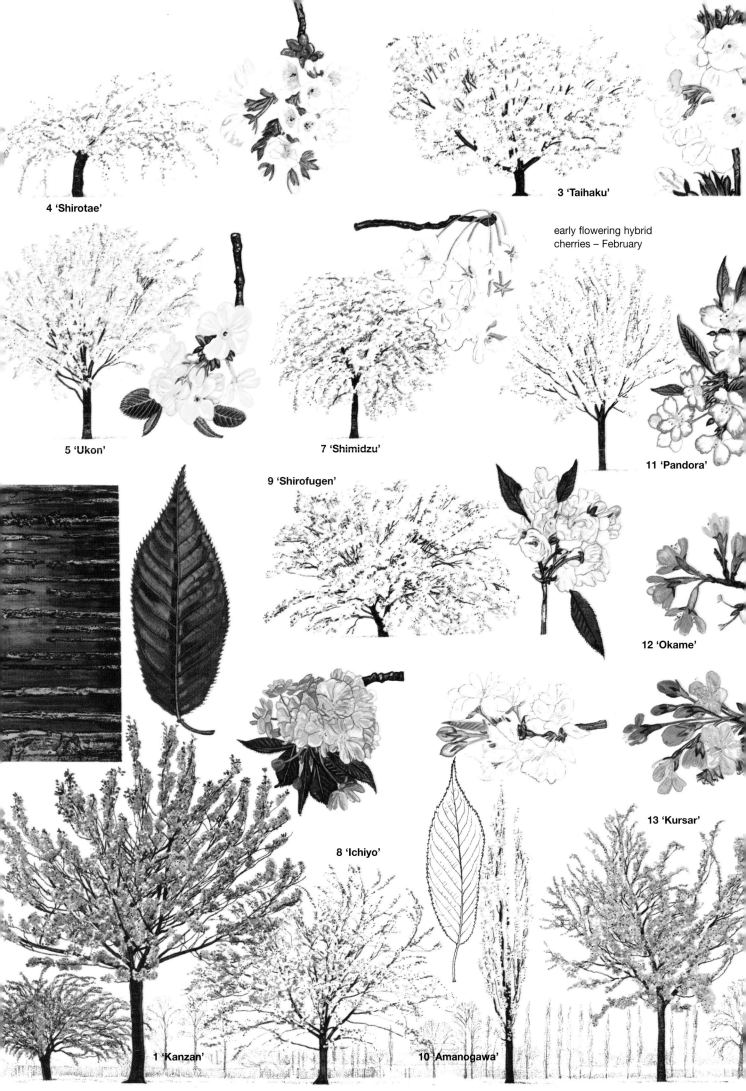

4 'Shirotae'

3 'Taihaku'

early flowering hybrid cherries – February

5 'Ukon'

7 'Shimidzu'

11 'Pandora'

9 'Shirofugen'

12 'Okame'

13 'Kursar'

8 'Ichiyo'

1 'Kanzan'

10 'Amanogawa'

Redbuds, Silk trees and others

The Pea Family, *Leguminosae*, is a huge one uniting all the plants in which the fruit takes the form of a legume, a pod with the seeds arising along one margin, and splitting open along both when dry. It includes all peas and beans, lupins and locusts, wistaria and redbuds, many edible fruit and seeds and some highly poisonous. Stature varies from tiny herbs through bushes like Gorse and Broom to very large trees. Features other than the legume fruit are variable to a high degree for even the pea-flower structure, with five petals, one 'Standard', two 'wings' and two forming the 'keel', uniform across a great diversity of plant forms in the family, is replaced by normal radial flowers in Honey locusts, Jerusalem thorn and Kentucky coffee trees and the pinnate or trifoliate leaves of the great majority are not invariable.

EASTERN REDBUD (1), *Cercis canadensis* is an upright, bushy-crowned, flat-topped small tree on a short, slender trunk, seldom much more than 30ft tall. The bark is gray, sometimes red-brown and darkens with age becoming scaly. The tree ranges from south NY, south MI and IA to TX and everywhere to the east except FL, and is a fairly common woodland tree over most of that area. It is also common in gardens notably in OK, AR and along the Gulf Coast. It is planted north of its range in large gardens in ON and MA and as a street tree in NY and CO. From PA to NC, increasingly from north to south, it is attacked by a canker and many branches hold dead, brown leaves in summer.

CALIFORNIA REDBUD (2), *Cercis occidentalis* is only a shrub, rarely 20ft tall, with deep red-purple shoots and a smaller leaf often notched at the tip. It grows from south UT and NV through CA to AZ and is common by streamsides from Merced to El Portal, CA.

SCOTCH GOLDEN CHAIN TREE (3), *Laburnum alpinum*, is native to SE Europe. It has 15in, sparsely flowered racemes opening late, and large, 5in leaflets shiny and smooth. **Voss's golden chain tree (4)**, *Laburnum × watereri* 'Vossii', a hybrid between the Scotch and Common golden chain trees, has an abundance of long, dense chains of flowers and good foliage. It is commonest in ID, WA and BC.

SILK TREE (5), *Albizia julibrissin* or mimosa, is a southern Asiatic, spreading, low tree popular in small roadside gardens where the winters are not too severe. This is from Long Island, NY, where it is common but at, or a little beyond the limit for good growth, the Coastal Plain, TX and north into MO and IL in the east, and north to Seattle in the west, but seldom in OR. The form 'Rosea' is the usual one but a hardier, unnamed origin from Korea and very similar, is grown at the Arnold Arboretum, MA. Roadside garden trees are about 25ft, very flat-topped with big branches springing at about 1ft on the trunk. They are also often pruned back hard to stumped main branches or to the trunk annually. The bark is dark, greenish gray, striped vertically with prominent brown speckles. The leaf is 12–18in long and turns dark gray-green in late summer then yellow and sometimes orange. The flowers have the scent of sweet hay and open throughout the summer. There are trees in Phoenix, AZ, Los Arbres Avenue, Albuquerque, NM and Las Vegas, NV.

FLAMBOYANT TREE (6), *Delonix regia* from Madagascar is the most spectacular tree of the Pea Family when in flower. It makes a broad umbrella of twisting branches bearing doubly compound leaves 2ft long, each with some 1200 leaflets. It may flower twice a year and ripens pods 20in long ribbed by about 40 seeds. It is grown in south FL, commonly in Miami, more sparingly to Orlando.

CHINABERRY (7), *Melia azedarach*, from India and China, makes a low, rounded crown densely set with 2ft dark green leaves. A few are as far north as Odessa, MD and Washington, DC and by the coast of VA but it becomes common, one each side of the door in small gardens, from GA to TX and AR, north to Covington, TN but not into OK. It has run wild in GA and LA. It is common in AZ and in south CA. The bark is dark purple-gray with fine, pale brown fissures. The single bony seed in each fruit has been used for beads.

TEXAN UMBRELLA TREE (8), 'Umbraculiformis' is a lower-domed, more dense plant with a more spreading crown which is said to have arisen on the battlefield of San Jacinto, TX. It replaces the Chinaberry to some extent in AZ and southern CA to Riverside, Barstow and Alpine, and there are few in Las Vegas, NV.

TALLOW TREE (9), *Sapium sebiferum* is in the Euphorbia Family and was sent from China in 1850. It is common in streets and parks along the Gulf Coast from AL to TX, running wild around Kenner, New Orleans and west LA as hedges. One in Barrack Street is 56ft x 8ft. It extends upstream to Natchez, MS and Little Rock, AR and east through GA and the coast of SC to south NC. It is in the streets of Saratoga, CA. The leaves with their slender driptip unfold yellow. The flowers open in May and June.

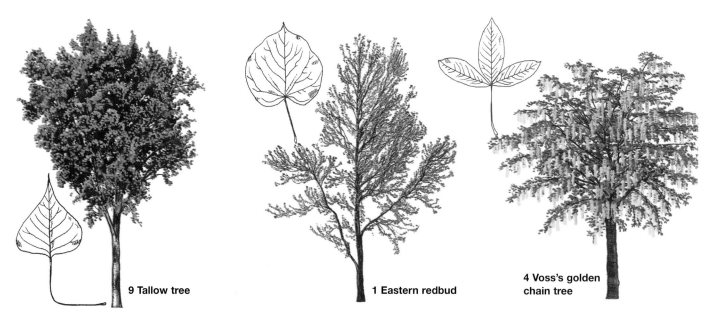

9 Tallow tree

1 Eastern redbud

4 Voss's golden chain tree

flws

fruit

1 Eastern redbud

Camphor tree

fruit

flws

4 Voss's golden chain tree

♂ flw

fruit

9 Tallow tree

3 Scotch golden chain tree

flw

2 California redbud

flws

5 Silk tree

7 Chinaberry

flws

fruit

8 Texas umbrella tree

6 Flamboyant tree

5 Silk tree

6 Flamboyant tree

Locusts and Pagoda trees

The Locusts, *Robinia*, are a few suckering trees and shrubs native only to the USA and Mexico. The hybrids believed to have arisen in the wild bring the total to 14 but excluding those and the low shrubs, four tree-species are accepted for the USA. They form no terminal buds and the axillary buds are naked, three to four together under a membrane beneath the base of the leafstalk. There is a pair of short spines where each leaf arises, derived from stipules, and some species have soft, clammy spines in great numbers on the new shoot.

BLACK LOCUST (1), *Robinia pseudoacacia* is the biggest species and has become by far the most widespread. The bark of young trees and of vigorous suckers is smooth, bright brown which soon becomes fissured and matures to dark dull brown or pale gray, networked by deep, broad ridges. The leaves unfold yellow and towards the end of summer are dull, gray-green, often scorched by early frosts in the north, to dark gray before being shed. The timber is exceedingly strong, durable in the soil and hence valued for fenceposts. It was once sought for ships' masts, and a form, var. *rectissima*, Shipmast locust, cultivated for this purpose because it has a good, straight, long trunk, is still seen from NJ to New England. The natural range of Black locust is now even less meaningful than that of most trees in North America, as it is far more common almost everywhere else. It was in the Appalachian Mountains from mid-PA to GA and AL and in the Ozark and Ouachita Mountains of AR into MO. Most of this has been cut over and the trees are grown-on suckers, several from a stump, or are bushy at high altitude, as at Wesner Bald, NC/TN at 5600ft. A few unlogged valleys in the Great Smoky Mountains, TN, have single-boled trees of no great size. It is common from PQ everywhere to the south except along the Gulf Coast but common again in TX and north to NE where it is a farmland hedge tree. Further west, it is running wild in the lower Fraser River Valley, BC, and abundant in the Okanagan Valley and around Vancouver and Victoria. It is frequent in WA, ID and MT and common in north west NV in Austin and Carson City, in south UT and west CO. It is frequent in Santa Fe and Albuquerque, NM and Phoenix, AZ but scarce in CA where there are some in Boonville, Felton and Saratoga. In NY, the trees are notably slender-crowned with narrow flat tops at around 100ft. These may be Shipmast locust.

The **Golden locust (2)**, **'Frisia'** arose in Holland in 1935. In cool summers it maintains the bright yellow in which the leaves open until they turn orange in October but in hot, dry seasons they become nearly green and do little in the fall. It is frequent only in BC. The **Umbrella locust (3)**, **'Umbraculifera'** is thornless and a grafted mophead, occasional in TX, OK, BC and WA. The **Single-leaf locust (4)**, **'Unifoliola'** arose in France before 1855 and is a curiosity which grows to the same size as the normal tree. The **Upright locust (5)**, **'Fastigiata'** is too strictly fastigiate to be attractive and is not long-lived. The **Decaisne locust (6)**, once thought to be a selection from Black locust, is now regarded as a hybrid between that and the Clammy locust, *R. viscosa* and has the name, *R. × ambigua* 'Decaisneana'. It grows to the same size as the Black locust.

IDAHO LOCUST (7), *Robinia* 'Idaho' is a hybrid between the Black locust and, probably, the Downy locust. Neither is native to anywhere near Idaho but the tree is planted as an ornamental from ID to NM.

ROSE ACACIA (8), *Robinia hispida* is a suckering shrub which has rarely been known to set seed. Grafted on to a leg of Black locust it forms a bushy-topped plant with the biggest and best flowers of any locust.

PAGODA TREE (9), *Sophora japonica* comes from China and Korea but was described first, in 1750, from plants seen cultivated in Japan. In China it is one among the hierarchy of trees allotted to planting by the graves of citizens and rulers of various ranks. This one was for the schoolmaster's grave and hence is known also as the Scholar's tree. Somewhat like Black locust at first glance, the Pagoda tree has a more open, spreading crown and less deeply ridged bark, but it differs more in several details. The buds are similarly hidden in the leafstalk base, but the shoots are without spines and are blue-green. More noticeably, the leaflets taper to a point, and the big, open, flowerheads stand at the shoot-tips in September. The leaves also emerge white. This tree is much planted in squares, parks and streets from south ON to VA and west through MI and OH to MO and in BC and WA. There was a vogue for planting it in Washington DC some 40-50 years ago. Some big trees are in: Public Gardens, Boston, MA, 70ft x 13ft; Fairmount Park, Philadelphia, PA, 65ft x 11ft; Capitol Park, Washington, DC, 95ft x 13ft and a broken tree 17ft 3in round in 1981; The Ellipse, 95ft x 14ft. There are trees in the streets of Wichita, KS. One in the Capitol Park, Salt Lake City, UT and one in the Capitol Park, Sacramento, CA is 82ft x 7ft 4in. It is grown in Denver, CO in the botanic garden, and in Albuquerque, NM in Los Arbores Avenue. The **Weeping pagoda tree (10)**, **'Pendula'** makes a mound, sometimes 40ft tall, of contorted branches from which the outer shoots hang. It seldom flowers.

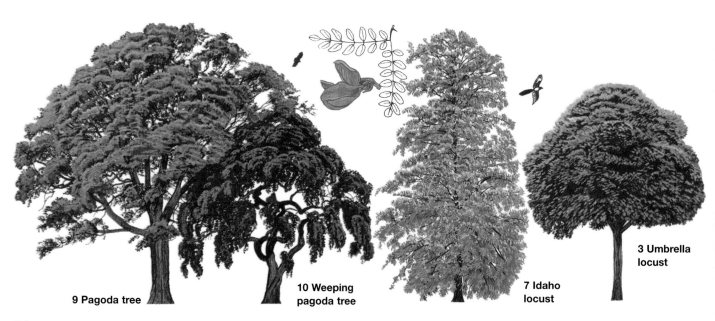

9 Pagoda tree

10 Weeping pagoda tree

7 Idaho locust

3 Umbrella locust

8 Rose acacia

4 Single-leaf locust

6 Decaisne locust

9 Pagoda tree

2 'Frisia' golden locust

5 Upright locust

1 Black locust 30m

Honey locusts, Coffee tree and others

The honey locusts are some of the few members of the huge Pea Family which have ordinary shaped flowers with 3–5 oval petals, not the peaflower with standard, wings and keel. They are remarkable for the branched thorns growing from the trunk increasing annually. Two of the world's 14 species are native to the USA.

HONEY LOCUST (1), *Gleditsia triacanthos* usually has bunches of ferocious thorns fairly thickly spread on its trunk, but a thornless variant, **'Inermis'**, occurs also in the wild. This is exceptionally fortunate, for the honey locust is invaluable in tolerating the heat, dust and drought of downtown city streets, and it is planted among skyscrapers from Montreal, PQ and Toronto, ON in every city to Atlanta, GA and Seattle, WA. Its native range is only from PA along the western flanks of the Alleghenies to AL and TX and north to IA and NE, but it has spread from cultivation east and north to New England. It has been planted commonly in BC and from Spokane, WA in cities east and south through WY, UT and CO; in Las Vegas, NV; Santa Fe and Albuquerque, NM; Flagstaff, Sedona and Mesa, AZ and in Bishop, CA. The fruit, 12–15in long, can be a nuisance where, as in Central Park, New York by the Zoo, they fall in quantity on the paths. So non-fruiting forms have been bred, of which **'Moraine' (2)** raised in 1949 is the most frequent. Before 1954 the splendid gold-leafed form **'Sunburst' (3)** was raised in the Middle West. Arising from 'Inermis' it too can be planted in streets without impaling passers-by and it is now more common than the greenleaf form on the Coastal Plain.

WATER LOCUST (4), *Gleditsia aquatica* grows in swampy bottomlands from SC to TX and up the Mississippi Valley to IL and IN. It has a broad, flat-topped crown from a short trunk but the main distinction is the obliquely ovoid 2in fruit.

TEXAS HONEY LOCUST (5), *Gleditsia × texana* is a hybrid between the Water locust and Honey locust with fruit intermediate, flattened, 5in long. It grows in a few places where the parent species overlap from the Brazos River, TX to LA and IN.

KENTUCKY COFFEE TREE (6), *Gymnocladus dioicus* also has nearly regular flowers but with the sexes on separate trees. Males, on 4in spikes, are white and green striped in bud, opening to 5-petalled starry white with orange anthers. Females, about 50 on bright green racemes 10-15in long, open greenish-white and cup-shaped in a ribbed, dark red calyx.

The leaf can be 45in long and 25in across, and unfolds late and pink, turning white then green, then yellow and orange before being shed, the main stalk persisting many days longer. Native from west NY and PA to TN and east OK, NE and SD, it is seen more in parks and gardens beyond its natural range than in woods. It is in Ottawa, Toronto, ON, and NY gardens, to the Capitol at Raleigh NC and in Oak Park, Montgomery, AL. At Charlottesville, VA on the campus in Pavilion III it is 102ft x 9ft 3in. In Winterthur DE March Bank it is 135ft tall.

JERUSALEM THORN (7), *Parkinsonia aculeata* is also a regular-flowered member of the Pea Family, a spreading, open, bright green shrubby plant. The young leaf 12in long has tiny leaflets which are soon shed leaving the evergreen stalk. Native to near the Mexican border in TX and AZ, it is widely planted from Charleston, SC by the coast through Savannah, GA and New Orleans, LA usually by buildings but west of that, often as a hedge, and through AZ to CA where it is in the median of 115 for miles around Baker.

YELLOWWOOD (8), *Cladrastis kentukea* (*C. lutea*) has the standard pea flowers, white, fragrant and on an open panicle 10–15in long. It has very smooth dull gray bark with rings of folds around branch-scars and is a fragile tree, for even in deep valley bottoms few achieve much age or size before the main stem is broken. The widely spaced leaflets are mainly alternate, not opposite. The side-buds are hidden in the base of the leaf-stalk and there are no terminal buds. It is native to one area around KY, TN and another around the borders of MO, AR and OK but is widely planted in small numbers from Montreal, PQ to DC, most commonly in Manchester, NH and in MA. Winterthur Garden, DE has one 65ft x 12ft 9in at 3ft and it is in most big gardens in PA, OH and MI.

TREE OF HEAVEN (9), *Ailanthus altissima* from north China has been planted in almost every city in North America from Montreal, PQ to Victoria, BC and Charleston SC to Los Angeles, CA. Only parts of OR, north CA, and south FL seem to be relatively free of it. In many cities like Washington, DC and Memphis, TN it ramps around inner suburbs, seeding and suckering and erupting in sidewalks, medians and yards and it runs wild in the Allegheny Mountains to 2,500ft. Male trees have large greenish panicles of flowers, red in bud opening after midsummer to cream, unpleasantly scented 5-petalled flowers. Female trees have 12 x 12in panicles soon becoming big bunches of scarlet fruit with 1–5 wings, turning brown and hanging late, well into winter in the south.

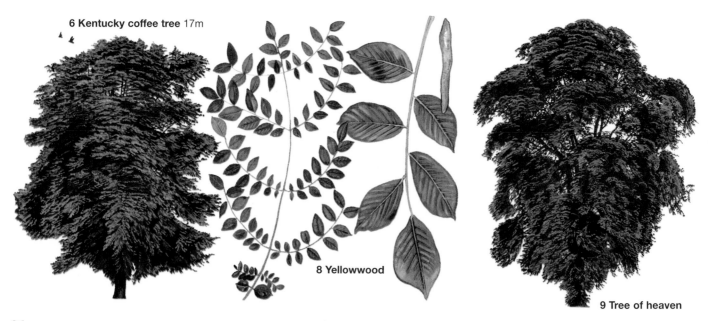

6 Kentucky coffee tree 17m

8 Yellowwood

9 Tree of heaven

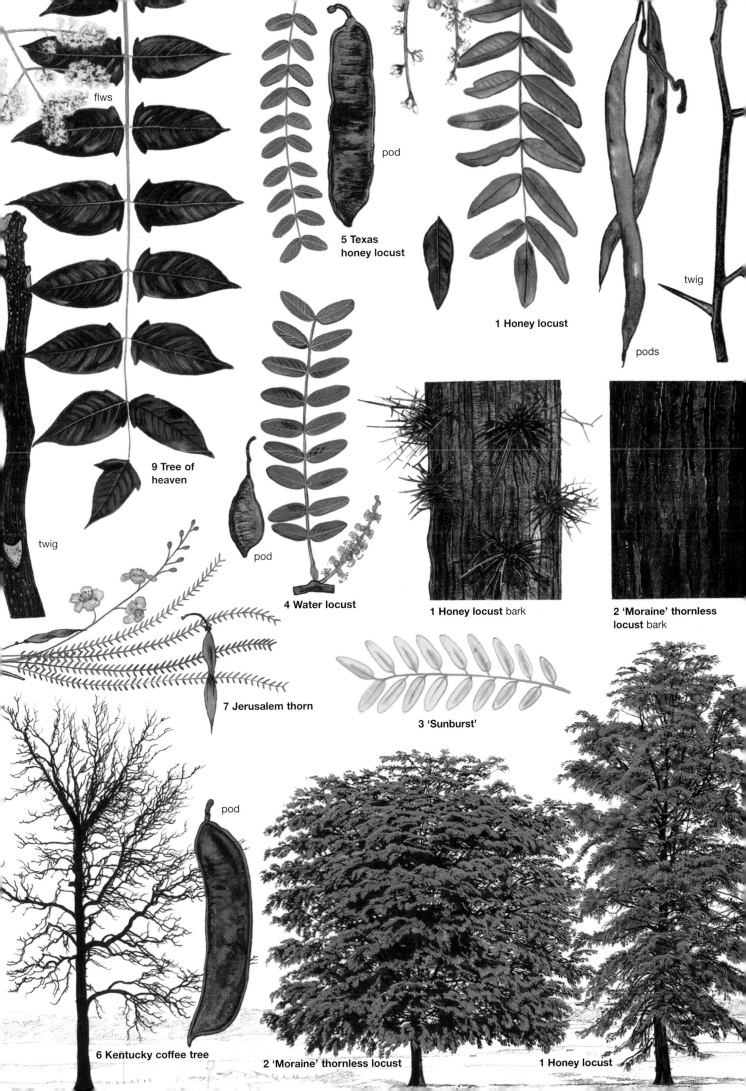

flws

5 Texas
honey locust

pod

1 Honey locust

twig

pods

9 Tree of
heaven

pod

4 Water locust

1 Honey locust bark

2 'Moraine' thornless
locust bark

twig

7 Jerusalem thorn

3 'Sunburst'

pod

6 Kentucky coffee tree

2 'Moraine' thornless locust

1 Honey locust

Hollies and Box

The hollies comprise several hundreds of species from both hemispheres, in the tropics and in temperate regions, in which they range across the world, except western North America. There are 13 species in eastern North America, mostly very small trees. Hollies are mostly evergreen with hard, firm leaves, but a few are deciduous, two of them in North America. Unlike most plants, in which annual leaf-shedding is a defence against severe winters and therefore the evergreen species are those in the warmer regions, the deciduous hollies tend to be of southern distribution and the most northerly are evergreen. The European one, quite commonly grown in North America, is the most northerly ranging broadleaf evergreen of all in Europe. The leaf has a thick cuticle covered in wax which protects the interior tissues and gives the surface in several species and forms a high polish.

AMERICAN HOLLY (1), *Ilex opaca* grows wild in scattered patches by the coast from MA to Long Island, NY and inland in southeast PA and more commonly and widely spread from NJ to mid-FL and east TX north through AR and TN to WV. It is planted in OH, in Central Park, New York and in the Hudson Valley, NY but is only a small tree in those parts, and also in the Morton Arboretum, IL and in collections in Vancouver, BC and in Seattle, WA. It is a common, quite large roadside tree, to 50ft in western LA and through eastern TX into AR and in many places from VA to GA. It is a shapely conic tree 50ft tall in many places but in the wild many trees have 2–3 stems. The bark is smooth dark gray finely striated dark yellow-green.

TAWNYBERRY HOLLY (2), *Ilex krugiana* is restricted to Dade County, south FL, with nearly all white bark until it darkens in old age.

DAHOON (3), *Ilex cassine* spreads on the Coastal Plain from NC to LA mostly on swampy land. The shoots are covered in dense silky hairs for a few years then mature dark brown. It is a low, shrubby tree with a roughened, dark gray bark. It is planted in medians in Little Rock, AR. **Foster's holly** is a hybrid between the American holly and the Dahoon. A low, rounded shrub, it has broad shining dark leaves and is frequent in the southeastern states. It is in the median of some main roads around Oakridge, TN.

YAUPON (4), *Ilex vomitoria* ranges on the Coastal Plain from VA to TX and north into AR and OK. The leaves persist for two years on pale gray shoots arising from stout, level branches. This is a small, branchy tree.

POSSUMHAW (5), *Ilex decidua* sheds its leaves in the fall except for a few on strong young shoots. It is usually a tall, straggling shrub with spreading branches and silvery gray bark. It is wild from MD to central TX and north to KS, IL and IN in lowland and foothill bottomlands.

EUROPEAN HOLLY (6), *Ilex aquifolium* grows as far north as Norway and to 1800 ft in Scotland. It is hardier than all but one American species and is planted each side of the US–Canadian border but cannot survive the winters of PA, DE or NJ and is common only in the west, around Vancouver, and by the coast of WA, OR and CA. Having been cultivated for hundreds of years, this holly has given innumerable variant seedlings and these are more frequent in many gardens than the type tree. The **Yellow-berried holly (7)**, **'Bacciflava'** is a highly attractive form when in fruit. The **Hedgehog holly (8)**, **'Ferox'** with rows of spines on the upper surface of the leaf can be 30ft tall and has a form with white margins. These are male forms so they bear no berries. The **Pyramidal holly, 'Pyramidalis'** is very female, a shapely conic tree with smooth, pale green leaves. **'Madame Briot' (9)** is female with purple shoots. The **Weeping holly (10)**, **'Pendula'** is female too and was found in Derby, England in about 1830. **Perry's weeping holly (11)** is female and so is **'Handsworth New Silver' (12)** which has purple shoots. **'Golden Milkmaid' (13)** is one of many similar forms with spiny, pale yellow blotched leaves. **Madeira holly** was grown in the conservatories of Victorian mansions for its winter berries. In the summer the tubs were moved out onto the terrace so when berries were sown from these plants, many had been pollinated by bees from flowers of the common holly and a series of hybrids arose. They were named as a group after Highclere, the home of the Earls of Caernarvon near Reading, *Ilex × altaclerensis*, and many are robust trees, smoke- and salt-resistant and reaching 60ft. The **Camellia-leaf holly, 'Cameliifolia'** is one, a tall, conic, leafy tree.

BOX (14), *Buxus semperivirens* from southern Europe and southern England is a member of a genus not native in North America. It is found around public buildings, with a large planting below the Capitol at Washington, DC, and in large gardens, often trimmed or shaped and some may be found labelled 'American box, *Buxus americana*'. These are usually a form with long, narrow leaves, probably **'Longifolia'**. The wood is the only temperate wood which is more dense than water, and so a block of it will sink. It is very hard and suited well to precision instruments and, carved on the endgrain, blocks for woodcuts. Trees in Odessa, DE and in Bartram Park, Philadelphia are 25ft tall.

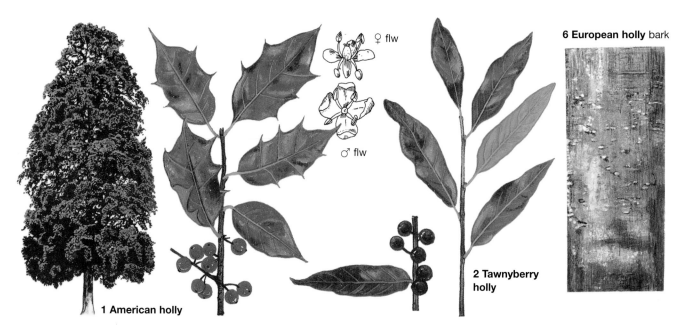

♀ flw

♂ flw

6 European holly bark

2 Tawnyberry holly

1 American holly

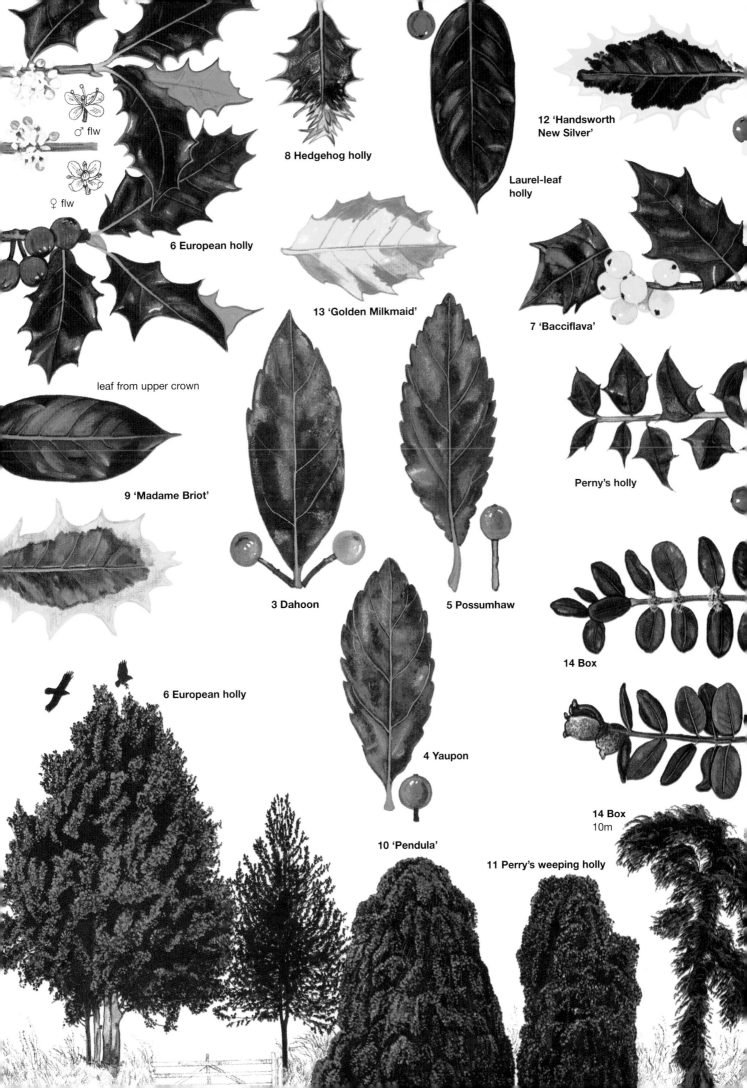

8 Hedgehog holly

6 European holly

12 'Handsworth New Silver'

Laurel-leaf holly

13 'Golden Milkmaid'

7 'Bacciflava'

♂ flw

♀ flw

leaf from upper crown

9 'Madame Briot'

Perny's holly

3 Dahoon

5 Possumhaw

14 Box

6 European holly

4 Yaupon

14 Box
10m

10 'Pendula'

11 Perry's weeping holly

Sugar and allied Maples

The maples are the equal of the oaks in their ubiquity in North America, their value as timber, ornament and amenity, and the diversity of their foliage and bark. They are, however, fewer in number, with 13 species native to North America and about 150 worldwide. They have opposite leaves and fruit while the flowers are either in catkin-like racemes or in umbels. The sexes can be arranged in every possible combination and a few have entirely male or female trees.

SUGAR MAPLE (1), *Acer saccharum* has the most vibrant orange-scarlet fall color of any maple and is very common as a woodland and town tree over its range from south PQ, NS to MN and IA south to MO and in the mountains to TN and NC where it can be seen at 4300ft. A tree by Black Locust Trail in the Great Smoky Mountains, TN is 130ft x 10ft. At Vanderbilt Mansion, NY, one is 100ft x 14ft. Many Main Street trees are nearly as big and it is planted, often mixed, intentionally perhaps, with the similar Norway maple, a little beyond its assumed natural range, from a small tree in Winnipeg, MB to a large one in Tulsa, OK. It is rare in the west, although planted in Beacon Hill Park, Victoria and in Revelstoke, BC; in Wenatchee, WA and by the Capitol in Helena and in Missoula, MT. The pencil-slim **'Newton Sentry' (2)** arose in 1871 and is in parks from ON and MA rarely to MN and IL and most often in NY. One in Brooklyn Botanic Garden is a branchless, feathered pole over 50ft tall which grew only one side-shoot and that was removed. **'Temple's Upright' (3)** has many vertical stems and is less scarce in MA, NY and PA. One in the old Ellwanger and Barry Nurseries where it arose, now Rochester University House, planted in 1909, is 85ft x 8ft.

BLACK MAPLE (4), *Acer nigrum* is very closely related to the Sugar maple, with larger, darker leaves more thinly spread over a more open crown, turning rich yellow in the fall. They can be 6 x 9in on a 6in stalk, and have soft hairs on their underside. It has a similar range to the Sugar maple but is less common and extends not so far north. At the School of Horticulture, Niagara Falls, ON, it is 75ft x 8ft and in MI it is known to 116ft x 16ft. It is planted in the Ottawa Botanic Garden, ON; Lincoln Park, Chicago, IL; Waterworks Park, Des Moines, IA; in Lake Shore Park, Ashtabula and the Secrest Arboretum, OH.

CANYON MAPLE, *Acer grandidentatum* is also closely related to the Sugar maple but always a smaller tree. It has dark brown, scaly bark and bright red smooth winter-buds. The flowers are like the Sugar maple but with a more prominent yellow calyx. It is a tree of damp canyons in the southern parts of the eastern crests of the rocky Mountains from the ID/WY border south through east UT and CO to NM, AZ and into Mexico, with eastern outliers in the Wichita Hills, OK and the Edwards Plateau, TX. It is planted in Beacon Hill Park, Victoria, BC and in Highland Park, Rochester, NY.

CAPPADOCIAN MAPLE (5), *Acer cappadocicum* is remarkable for its range from the Caucasus Mountains through the Hindu Kush and along the Himalaya to China and Japan. It also is the champion for growing suckers, trees being surrounded by thickets of them and sometimes outgrown by their reaching 85ft. The entire margins to the lobes are distinctive and butter-yellow color in the fall is reliable. This tree is reasonably frequent only around Vancouver and Victoria, BC where it lines a few streets. One in Point Defiance Park, Tacoma, WA is 60ft x 10ft. In the east it is rare but it has grown very rapidly in Highland Park, NY where one planted in 1902 was 62ft x 11ft 5in at 1ft in 73 years and in Queen Victoria Park, Niagara Falls, ON it is 56ft x 10ft at 2ft. The form **'Aureum' (6)** is more scarce and is seen at Langley and the Van Dusen Botanic Garden, BC. Its new leaves are a bright, fresh gold fading slowly to light green. Since young trees add new leaves throughout the summer, their exterior crown is always gold.

NORWAY MAPLE (7), *Acer platanoides* ranges through northern and central Europe to the Caucasus Mountains. It is quite like the Sugar maple and is so often planted mixed with it in streets that the suspicion arises that the species have been mixed in nurseries. The fine avenue of Sugar maple leading to the Gateway Arch in St. Louis, MO ends, possibly by design, in a pair of Norway maples. The Norway has a smooth, very finely fissured bark becoming shallowly networked by ridges, where the Sugar maple has a coarsely scaling bark becoming platey and shaggy. The sap of Norway maple is milky, not clear; the flowers have prominent yellow petals, are in umbels, out before the leaves. The Norway maple is a common street and square tree from PQ to WI south to MD and frequent from there to GA and AL with fewer in OK, AR and IA. In the west it is scarce in BC and frequent in WA notably in Wenatchee and Grand Coulee, and in ID and MT with a few in UT, WY and CO. At Swarthmore College, PA it is 95ft x 11ft. **'Crimson King' (8)** is usually really the duller, more offensively miscolored **'Goldsworth Purple'** arising in England in 1936. It is common in PA, OH, IN and IL but ranges into PQ, ON, ME south to GA and west to SD, MT and UT and is common in BC and coastal WA.

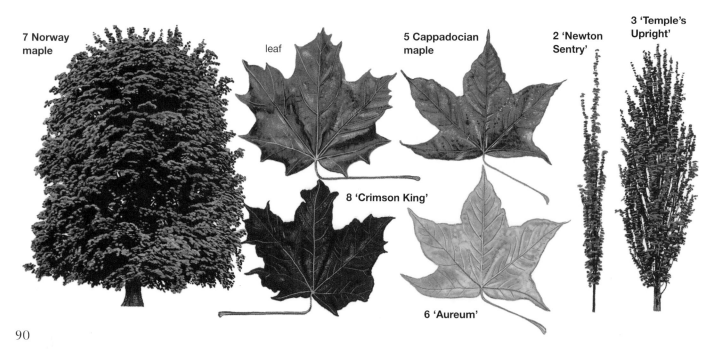

7 Norway maple

leaf

5 Cappadocian maple

2 'Newton Sentry'

3 'Temple's Upright'

8 'Crimson King'

6 'Aureum'

flw detail

flws

twig

Bigtooth maple

4 Black maple

leaf variant

7 Norway maple

5 Cappadocian maple

1 Sugar maple

fruits

bark

4 Black maple

autumn

1 Sugar maple

bole

Planetree and other Maples

PLANETREE MAPLE (1), *Acer pseudoplatanus* is the Sycamore of England and the 'plane' of Scotland. It is not native to either country but to a swathe of countries from the Caspian Sea to France. Taken to North America long ago, it is, like some other European trees which are reputed to be common in the northeastern USA, really common only in Newport and Middleton, RI. Elsewhere it is no more than locally frequent in NY, PA and DC in the east. In the west, it lines streets in Missoula, MT and Tacoma, WA. Although it is a rather coarse European tree with negligible fall colors and there are many superior native species, it is imperturbably robust in the face of smoky air, sea winds and poor soils, and grows very fast in youth. Planetree maple timber is white, bone-hard and strong. It neither stains nor takes up taint from food. The long flower-racemes have male flowers on the outer half which is soon shed and the females nearer the base remain to ripen into fruit.

Leopold's maple (2), 'Leopoldii' from Belgium, a rather blotchy tree rarely effective, is 45ft x 5ft at the garden of the School of Horticulture, Niagara Falls, ON and 40ft x 6ft at the old Ellwanger and Barry nursery, now Rochester University, NY. The **Variegated planetree maple (3)**, 'Variegatum' is an old cultivar or group of similar forms with examples in Washington Park, Albany, NY; Fairmount Park, Philadelphia, PA and is quite common around Vancouver, BC. The **Purple planetree maple (4)**, 'Purpureum' is inexcusably dreary, but is frequent in BC and WA. The leaf underside has a gray cast like an attack of mildew. The **Erect planetree maple (5)** is a coarse and dull imitation of the 'Temple's Upright' Sugar maple and is rare. The **Golden planetree maple (6)**, 'Worleii' is rather splendid, but is also rare. In the east, one is in Highland Park, Rochester, NY. In the west, there is one at Penticton, BC.

MOUNTAIN MAPLE, *Acer spicatum* is a shrub or little tree in the shade of woods from south Labrador, NF and central PQ to SK, IL and in the mountains to GA. It can be seen by the roadside on Rt 2, MA from Greenfield to North Adams and at 5900ft in NC by Bear Trail Ridge. It is planted in Revelstoke BC, and the University of Washington Arboretum. Its little pale, yellow-green flowers are on an erect, spike-like raceme 2in long.

CHALK MAPLE (7), *Acer leucoderme* is an elegant small tree, closely related to the Sugar maple, from NC to AR and OK. It is rare and local. There is one in the University Arboretum in Seattle, WA. The pale gray bark becomes chalky with age and the leaves are whitish beneath.

CRETAN MAPLE (8), *Acer sempervirens* is an evergreen maple from the Eastern Mediterranean with leaves entire or variously 3-lobed and should be in a few gardens.

MONTPELIER MAPLE (9), *Acer monspessulanum* from southern Europe looks evergreen but is not, although the leaves stay on late and dark green. New leaves are bright fresh green, followed by bright yellow-green flowers on short drooping racemes. One in Point Defiance Park, Tacoma WA, is 40ft x 6ft.

TARTAR MAPLE (10), *Acer tataricum* from around Asia Minor is a bushy little tree, pretty when its abundant bunches of fruit are scarlet during the summer. It is grown in collections like those at the School of Horticulture, Niagara Falls, ON; Mount Airy Arboretum in OH; the Morton Arboretum IL and that of the University of Minnesota at Chaska, MN.

AMUR MAPLE (11), *Acer ginnala* is a near relative of the Tartar maple from China and Japan, and is much hardier. It is a common tall bush with wand-like rising and arching stems, in Winnipeg, strung with little bunches of brown fruit after leaf-fall. It is in tubs in Montreal, PQ, in Bishop Street and is grown in Ottawa in Wellington Street and the Botanic Garden; in Portland, ME in the big gardens in New England and the Hudson Valley, NY, the Calloway Gardens, GA and in Wichita, KS. In the west, a widely forked low tree is prominent on a street corner in Revelstoke, BC and young plants thrive in Genoa, NV.

TRIDENT MAPLE (12), *Acer buergerianum* is a leafy attractive little tree from China and Japan. In the fall, good trees turn orange and coccineal crimson. In spring, the little bunches of yellow flowers are numerous. It is in Brooklyn Botanic Garden NY, and the Bailey Arboretum, Long Island. In the Morris Arboretum, PA it is 60ft. There is one 20ft tall in the Strybing Arboretum, San Francisco, CA.

HORNBEAM MAPLE (13), *Acer carpinifolium* has a surprising leaf for a maple. It is unlobed, lanceolate, 8in long with 20 or more pairs of parallel veins. The green flowers are strung down a 5-in stalk and the sexes are on separate trees. The leaves turn a good gold in the fall. It is a small, bushy tree from Japan and is very rare in America. There is a good one in the Brooklyn Botanic Garden, NY.

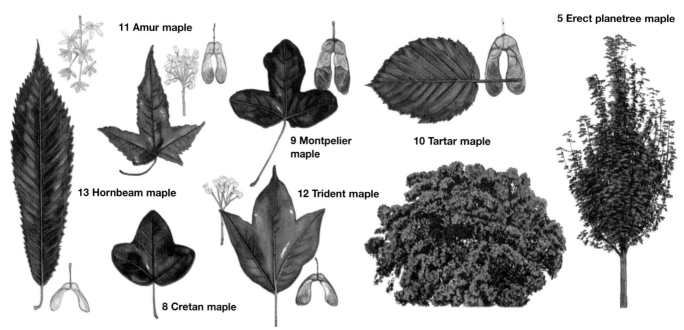

11 Amur maple

5 Erect planetree maple

9 Montpelier maple

10 Tartar maple

13 Hornbeam maple

12 Trident maple

8 Cretan maple

flw

2 Leopold's maple

1 Planetree maple

fruit

twig

7 Chalk maple

'Brilliantissimum'

6 Golden planetree 'Worleii'

1 Planetree maple 35m

4 Purple planetree maple

bole

3 Variegated planetree maple 24m

'Brilliantissimum'

Box elder, Vine and other Maples

BOX ELDER (1), *Acer negundo* is better called the Ashleaf maple since it has no similarities to either a box tree or an elderberry. It often shows some indecision as to the number of leaflets that it will have, the terminal one being lobed in various depths, some almost to the base, often on one side only. Across the extraordinary native range there is a great variation with the region, in size, color and hairiness of leaf and shoot. The range is, broadly, from NY south of the Great Lakes, sweeping north to central MB, SK and AB then southeast to TX with large areas in the eastern and central Rocky Mountains from MT to NM and AZ and outliers in CA, Mexico and Guatemala. In general, the foliage declines in size and fades from rich glossy green to yellowish and acquires soft hairs from northeast to southwest. The var. *violaceum* with blue-bloomed smooth shoots and 5–7 leaflets occurs at random amongst the populations from MA through OH to MN. The **Arizona** form, var. *arizonicum*, has blue-bloomed shoots and only 3 small leaflets, which turn yellow and orange in the fall. This is well seen around Flagstaff, in Oak Creek Canyon and in NM.

    Californian box elder, var. *californicum* has a brown or gray shoot covered in soft hairs like the underside of the 3 leaflets and grows in small numbers scattered around the Central Valley and in the San Bernardino Mountains, most numerous around the Bay Area and the Santa Ynez Valley. The type Box elder has leaves to 8 x 6in, rich glossy green on pale green, smooth shoots. It grows very fast in youth, becomes sprouty and dies young. This form, which is common in Winnipeg, in the cottonlands of SD and in the Mississippi Valley in AR, KY and TN, has been planted in Montreal, PQ and in the only large region that is beyond its native range, the Pacific Northwest. It is common in BC and northern WA. This maple has the sexes on separate trees and the flowers opening before the leaves. The male trees have dense bunches of slender threads, each one tipped by a tiny flower of a few yellow stamens. The threads turn from white to pale brown and look like beards. Female trees have only 6–10 in a bunch also 5in long. The fruit hang brown after the leaves have fallen. **'Variegatum' (2)** arose in 1845 in Toulouse, France and is the most extravagantly white variegated of any tree and even the fruit (for it is female) is largely white. Like the fine golden **'Auratum' (3)** from Germany, it is little planted in North America.

FLORIDA MAPLE (4), *Acer barbatum* is the form of Sugar maple growing in damp woods from the coast of VA along the Coastal Plain to TX and north to AR and OK. It is uncommon but can be seen wild in the Callaway Gardens, GA and from Tuskegee to Montgomery, AL. It has a whitish, smooth bark with pale gray horizontal bands, and the 4 x 5in leaf with 3 main lobes is blue-white beneath.

ROCKY MOUNTAIN MAPLE (5), *Acer glabrum* is a low bushy tree of the understorey in western woods which occasionally has 3 leaflets but normally a leaf divided into 3 lobes of varying depth. They are deeper in the typical form which grows from MT and the Black Hills of SD to the Mexican border in NM and AZ and in the Sierra Nevada, CA, and shallower but more coarsely toothed in var. *douglasii*. This is the northwestern form, from south AK to WA, OR and north MT, called the **Douglas maple**, and has its fruit wings more parallel. In the fall, the leaves turn orange. The flowers are about 6 on an drooping raceme.

VINE MAPLE (6), *Acer circinatum* has an orbicular leaf with 7–9 triangular lobes turning bright yellow, orange and scarlet in the fall. It is scarcely a tree, rather a big shrub with long slender branches which lean on other, bigger trees, as is well seen in Stanley Park, Vancouver, BC. It grows from mid-BC to Mendocino County, CA.

EUROPEAN FIELD MAPLE (7), *Acer campestre* is an uncommon tree in city squares and parks from ON to MI and IL south to GA and in Wichita, KS, and in BC and WA, where it lines a street in Seattle. The leaves unfold pink in spring and red in second growth, then in the fall they are gold, turning orange. The fruit, 2–3in across the widely spread wings, are stained crimson during the summer.

VINELEAF MAPLE (8), *Acer cissifolium* is a 3-leaflet tree from Japan, not to be confused with the Vine maple. Its bark is pale gray, and its leaves are on wire-thin smooth, red stalks. It makes a broad, flat-topped crown, flowers copiously and colors pale orange in the fall. It is very rare but one planted in 1907 in Highland Park, NY was 35ft x 7ft when 68 years old and there is one in the Bailey Arboretum, NY, 35ft tall.

ROUGHBARK MAPLE (9), *Acer triflorum* is another Asiatic 3-leaflet tree, this time from Korea. Apart from the bark and smaller leaf, it is very like the Nikko maple and colors even brighter red in the fall.

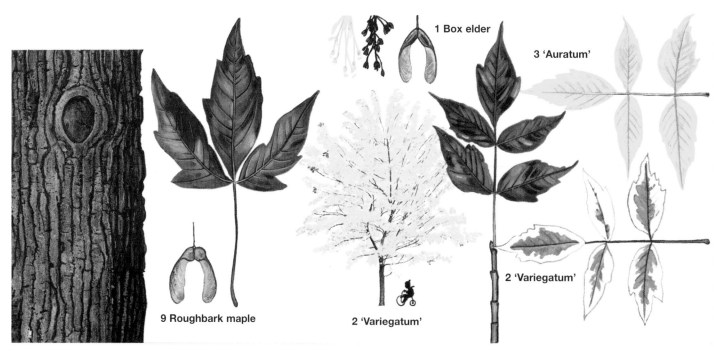

9 Roughbark maple

2 'Variegatum'

1 Box elder

3 'Auratum'

2 'Variegatum'

♀ flw

♂ flw

flws

4 Florida maple

flws

Oregon maple

8 Vineleaf maple

7 European field maple

1 Box elder

bole

5 Rocky mountain maple

6 Vine maple

Silver, Japanese and other Maples

SILVER MAPLE (1), *Acer saccharinum* has leaves with silver undersides. The same silver flashes out when the upper side of the leaf is the pale yellows, biscuit and some red of fall colors. The flowers open about two months before the leaves and the fruit are shed in early summer. New leaves unfolding in summer are white or yellow and by then the older leaves in hot, dry places are becoming bright yellow. Planted in streets where summers are hot, the bark is smooth and silvery gray. On old trees it is dark, flaking and shaggy and trunks bear numerous sprouts. The native range is from NB and south PQ to NY then in the hills to MS, west to AR and ND, but it is a common street and park tree beyond this to east TX, CO, NM, UT, NV, ID, MT and particularly in WA and BC. It is scarce in OR and in CA. The biggest trees are in parks within the natural range as in the Allen Botanic Garden, Toronto, ON, 92ft x 11ft; Arnold Arboretum, MA, planted 1881, 105ft x 14ft 8in (1975); Highland Park, Rochester, 98ft x 14ft 8in; and Lakeshore Park, Ashtabula, OH, 102ft x 13ft. At the extremes of planting, there is one in Winnipeg, MB and trees in Flagstaff, AZ. In the wild populations, there is an occasional tree with much more deeply lobed leaves. Some have been propagated as **Cutleaf silver maple (2)**, **'Laciniatum'** and a form with very deep, slender lobes and long-pendulous shining pink-brown shoots, found by D. B. Wier in 1873, was grown in the Ellwanger and Barry Nursery in Rochester, NY and sent out as 'Wieri'. Others of this form are at Mohonk Mountain, 82ft x 8ft and at Vanderbilt Mansion, both in NY, 98ft x 9ft.

SMOOTH JAPANESE MAPLE (3), *Acer palmatum* was brought out of Japan in 1820 when the country was still closed, by Phillip von Siebold who had privileges in return for his skill as an eye-surgeon. This maple had been bred and selected for an extraordinary diversity of forms for hundreds of years but von Siebold's introduction was probably as near to the wild form as any in cultivation and the first distinct cultivars began to arrive in the west in 1861. Relatively few were known here until the 1970s when J. D. Vertrees of Oregon imported some hundreds. At present, however, it is the trees near the type and the older forms which are seen, and predictably, most often those with dreary so-called purple foliage all summer. These slow-growing trees are popular for planting in even the smallest yards, and are common from south ON and New England to OH and more sparingly, south to GA and from Vancouver, where they are notably abundant and depressingly often dull muddy purple, in decreasing numbers southwards. The best form is **'Osakazuki' (4)** with large green leaves above scarlet fruit in the summer and blazing scarlet foliage in late fall, even in shade. The **Coralbark maple (5)**, **'Singo-kaku'** or **'Sen-kaki'** is striking in the winter and has elegantly cut small leaves turning orange and amber. The **Korean maple (6)**, var. *coreanum* has extra good and reliable fall color and **'Atropurpureum' (7)** has attractive deep purple leaves.

FULL-MOON MAPLE, *Acer japonicum* is a bigger tree with smooth gray bark and a form **'Vitifolium' (8)** with big leaves turning gold, scarlet, crimson and purple. The **Golden full-moon maple (9)**, **'Aureum'** was taken as a form of *Acer japonicum* until 1984 when Brian Mulligan of Seattle suspected otherwise and Tom Delendick of Brooklyn Botanic Gardens determined it as a golden-leafed *Acer shirasawanum*. It is a bright, neat, low and very slow plant often grown in rock-gardens.

ZOESCHEN MAPLE (10), *Acer × zoeschenense* is named from the German nursery in which it arose before 1870 as a hybrid between the Hedge or Field maple and the Cappadocian maple. Like the latter it grows a thicket of suckers around its trunk and grows fast. In leaf, the dark ruby-red stalk to the blackish leaf identifies it.

NIKKO MAPLE (11), *Acer nikoense*, later found to grow also in China, was sent from Japan to the Arnold Arboretum in 1890. There is one there dating from 1892 planting, 42ft tall. This maple has thin, smooth, hard-looking dark gray bark and comes into leaf late and yellowish as the flower-buds hang in threes. It is late with its crimson fall color too and valued as it will grow and color in a chalky soil.

PAPERBARK MAPLE (12), *Acer griseum* was sent from Central China in 1901 and except for the remarkable bark is very like the Nikko maple. It is slower growing and more inclined to grow several trunks or some strong vertical branches. These should be removed as soon as they show and a single bole, clean of branches for 6ft, will show the bark best. This tree is grown in collections and large gardens from south ON to VA and MO. At the Arnold Arboretum, MA, planted in 1907 it was 50ft x 4ft and 36ft x 5ft when 68 years old, and there are trees at Smith College, Northampton and Mount Auburn Cemetery. In NY at Highland Park, trees date from 1914. Others are in the Beal Garfield Garden, East Lansing, MI; the Secrest and Dawes Arboreta in OH; in Winterthur Garden, DE; the Morton Arboretum, IL, the Missouri Botanic Garden, St. Louis and on the campus at Charlottesville, VA.

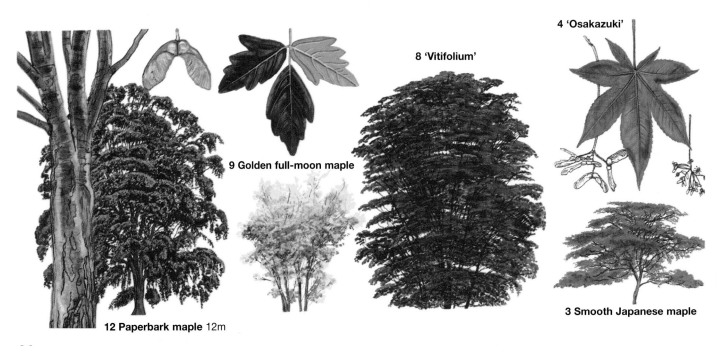

4 'Osakazuki'

8 'Vitifolium'

9 Golden full-moon maple

12 Paperbark maple 12m

3 Smooth Japanese maple

3 Smooth Japanese maple

leaf variant

7 'Atropurpureum'

6 Korean maple

5 Coralbark maple

4 'Osakazuki'

1 Silver maple

8 'Vitifolium'

10 Zoeschen maple

2 Cutleaf silver maple

1 Silver maple 30m

11 Nikko maple

7 'Atropurpureum'

Red and Snakebark maples

RED MAPLE (1), *Acer rubrum* is named for its early spring show of bright red flowers on bare shoots. When the flowers begin to open they are in short-stemmed clusters and they stay open for weeks, joined by others in the cluster, until they are all on slender 2in stalks. Their sexual arrangements are complex. It had been accepted that each cluster was of either male or female flowers and that the two were mixed on most branches but there may be some wholly male or female branches and even entire trees. Recent studies show that more often a cluster which opens as male will be female a week or so later and perhaps male again later still, partly from new flowers opening but also from the delayed development of the alternative sex organs in the same flowers. The fruit mature rapidly and are shed before midsummer. Fall color can vary even among adjacent trees in a small wood where a bright gold tree may be between one of rich deep purple and another scarlet, but the hillsides often appear scarlet for miles. The bark of young trees in streets in hot cities, as in some other maples, is very silvery gray. The Red maple has a greater north–south range than any other North American tree, from the eastern end of NF to very near the southern tip of FL. Westward it crosses south PQ and mid-ON to WI and southward it curves to exclude MO and IL and swings back to east TX. It grows at over 5000ft on rocky ridges of the Allegheny Mountains but is most abundant in wet lowland areas and is a feature of the swampy woods each side of valley and Coastal Plain roads from Quebec to FL and TX. It is commonly planted in cities and towns throughout the range and to a smaller extent in BC and WA, with very few in OR and the Prairie Stares.

The **Fastigiate red maple (2)**, **'Columnare'** was found in Flushing, NY, when 80ft tall before 1894 and grafts from it are grown in a few collections. In the Arnold Arboretum, MA one planted in 1910 was 72ft x 4ft 6in when 65 years old but another planted in 1921 was 75ft x 6ft 6in when only 54 years old. There is a specimen in the University of Washington Arboretum, Seattle.

STRIPED MAPLE or **MOOSEWOOD (3)**, *Acer pensylvanicum* is the only species of Snakebark maple outside China and Japan. The Snakebark maples comprise about 20 rather small trees distinguished from other maples less by their red shoots thickly striped white and maturing into green, or gray bark patterned with chalky white stripes, than by their stalked buds and long racemes of flowers usually of one sex. They mostly have broad leaves with only three lobes but several grow some leaves quite unlobed. The Striped maple has the biggest leaves of any, to 9 x 8in. Its natural range extends from NS and PQ along the coast to VA, along the mountains to GA and west to MN but it is rarely seen west of the Alleghenies. It is a common understorey in the woods of New England and NY, rarely as big as those in the Bailey Arboretum, NY. The flower and fruit racemes arch out in pairs from every joint in the shoots and the leaves turn pale bright yellow early and briefly.

GRAY-BUDDED SNAKEBARK MAPLE (4), *Acer rufinerve* from Japan is the Asiatic snakebark most like the Striped maple. It has smaller leaves with fine red-brown hairs along the veins on the underleaf, persisting only in the main angles at the base. The fall colors are scarlet and crimson late in the season. It may be found in some collections in the northeast.

RED SNAKEBARK MAPLE (5), *Acer capillipes* from Japan was brought first to the Arnold Arboretum, MA by Professor Sargent in 1892. It has a dominant, long central lobe to its shiny leaf, with distinctive parallel veins, and is prolific in flower. The underside vein-angles have tiny red pegs and the leaves turn orange and crimson in the fall.

HERS'S MAPLE (6), *Acer grosseri* var. *hersii* has vein-angles with dark purple spots and the bark, young shoot, leaf, bud and flower are olive-green. The wings of the fruit are distinctively broad. This is grown in the Morton Arboretum, IL, in the Burchart Garden, BC, in the University of Washington Arboretum and in tubs in the streets of Seattle, WA.

PÈRE DAVID'S MAPLE (7), *Acer davidii* has been sent from China in at least five forms since 1879, with leaves varying from 2in to 6in long, slender and unlobed, to one named **'George Forrest' (8)** with dark leaves 6 x 4in with or without small lateral lobes. The vein-angles beneath have small red pegs.

FORREST MAPLE (9), *Acer forrestii* has deeply lobed and toothed leaves with pale veining and scarlet stalks and is very rare.

HAWTHORN MAPLE (10), *Acer crataegifolium* from Japan makes a slender-stemmed little tree with a thin crown showing much red in the leaf and young fruit as well as on the shoots.

BIRCHLEAF MAPLE (11), *Acer tetramerum* is not a true Snakebark although similar. It grows numerous slender stems like suckers. They start away very rapidly but decline before they are of any size.

LIMELEAF MAPLE (12), *Acer distylum* from Japan has thick dark leaves and is notable for its erect racemes of yellow flowers followed by pink and brown fruit. Again, this is not a true Snakebark and it is very rare.

7 Père David's maple

5 Red snakebark maple

3 Moosewood

6 Hers's maple

4 Gray-budded snakebark maple

'Ernest Wilson'

8 'George Forrest'

small leaf form

7 Père David's maple

11 Birchleaf maple

3 Moosewood

5 Red snakebark maple

4 Gray-budded snakebark maple

12 Limeleaf maple

1 Red maple

9 Forrest maple

10 Hawthorn maple

6 Hers's maple

1 Red maple 23m

7 Père David's maple 15m

1 Red maple

2 Fastigiate red maple

Horse chestnuts

The buckeyes are about 15 species of botanically very distinct plants of the northern hemisphere spanning the range from a suckering shrub 10ft tall to tall and massive trees. They have rather restricted ranges in the mountains of Japan, China, India and southern Europe but a few in North America are more widely spread, with six species and 11 natural hybrids in the east and one species in the west. The chief botanical distinctions of buckeyes are oppositely placed leaves and buds; compound leaves of five to seven leaflets which radiate from the tip of a stout stalk, making a palmate or digitate leaf; flowers in terminal panicles and fruit a single seed or two large, smooth seeds in a leathery husk. The seeds germinate keeping the cotyledons below ground and send up a shoot tipped by a pair of adult leaves. In Europe these trees are known as 'horse chestnuts' in place of the prettily descriptive American term, 'buckeye', which refers to the shiny brown seed with a whitish circular patch. 'Horse chestnut' is probably a dismissive term for the seeds, implying coarse, inferior and inedible as opposed to the true chestnut, or Sweet chestnut, *Castanea*. The leaf-scar is the shape of a horseshoe complete with nail-holes, and it may be legendary that the seeds were used in and around Greece, where the native woods are, as a cure for coughing in horses.

HORSE CHESTNUT (1), *Aesculus hippocastanum* is confined as a wild tree to a few mountains between Greece and Albania and was unknown to botany until 1596. It was rapidly spread by planting almost all over Europe and was an early colonist in North America. It differs from all the American buckeyes in its shiny orange-brown glutinous terminal buds, bigger leaves with completely stalkless leaflets, 1ft tall heads of predominantly pure white flowers and very prickly husks around the glossy, grained mahogany seed. Each flower opens with a broad splash of yellow near the base of each petal and once the flower has been pollinated by a bee, this turns rapidly orange and then crimson. Although this is a fine tree spectacular in flower, it is rather a coarse one, dull in summer and unreliable in its gold or red fall colors, so it is astonishing that in the land of such superb trees as the Yellow buckeye,

its hybrids and others, the Horse chestnut should be planted anywhere except in a few parks. But it is almost the only species planted at all in streets and in some entire regions. It is a common street tree from ON and VA to IA and WI and from MT and ID to BC. It is abundant in Newport, RI, and very common in MA where one in Salem is 14ft round the trunk. At the University House, Rochester, NY one is 75ft x 12ft and it is common in Central Park, New York, throughout OH and in Baltimore, MD. In the west, it spreads down the coast from BC and WA to Adria, Raymond and Long Beach but there are few in OR. It is in Salt Lake City, UT, Santa Fe, NM and Boulder, CO.

The wood of this species is soft and weak but straight grained, and fairly light, turning well and nearly white. These features suit it well to use in toys and artificial limbs, particularly because its fracture lacks the hard, often sharp spines of many woods, which could be dangerous in these uses. The weakness is, however, a liability in that a tree in full leaf may, during a sudden summer rainstorm, drop a large branch.

RED HORSE CHESTNUT (2), *Aesculus × carnea* is a hybrid of the Horse chestnut crossed with the Red buckeye. The tree has coarse, dark foliage and dull flowers. It develops big cankers on its twisting branches and, after all too long, falls to pieces. No organism can be found in the cankers. The tree breeds true, unlike normal hybrids in which the offspring range from nearly one parent to the other, because of spontaneous doubling of the chromosomes in one branch, probably in the original tree. So most of the trees are seedlings. Where a tree is an evident graft it is usually of the superior form, **'Briotii' (3)**, which has shiny-leaves and flowers of a good bright red. Both forms are common from ON and NY to MN, in southern BC and northern WA. The fruit husk is nearly smooth, thin, and contains dull, dark little seeds, often three. In a nursery in France, a seed raised from a Horse chestnut had been pollinated by a Red horse chestnut, so giving a backcross hybrid, **'Plantierensis' (4)**. It is a superb tree with large heads of pink flowers and no fruit.

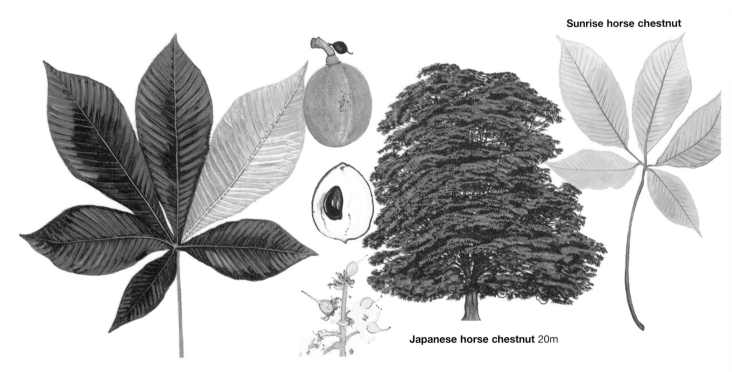

Sunrise horse chestnut

Japanese horse chestnut 20m

2 Red horse chestnut

1 Horse chestnut

3 'Briotii'

4 'Plantierensis'

2 Red horse chestnut 22m

1 Horse chestnut 35m

Buckeyes

The Buckeyes or American horse chestnuts consist of one quite distinct one that keeps itself to itself out in the far west and the others in the east which can be sorted into 5 species, one variety and ten hybrids or about a dozen species, according to taste.

CALIFORNIA BUCKEYE (1), *Aesculus californica* is the western species and grows in low, dry foothills from Shasta to the Coast Ranges south to San Luis Obispo and the length of the western slopes of the Sierra Nevada. It has low branches spreading from 1–3ft up the trunk with scaly, thick, pale pink-gray bark and very resinous red-brown buds. The 5 well-stalked leaflets turn yellowish in summer and black in early fall. The 5–10in flower panicle opens the top few flowers so much ahead of the others that often when the lower flowers open, it is crowned by a few smooth, pear-shaped projecting fruit. When the black leaves have fallen, the fruit remain prominent and pink-brown for weeks. Very attractive in full flower, it is surprisingly not seen planted anywhere.

YELLOW BUCKEYE (2), *Aesculus octandra* is the finest of the group. It does not achieve quite the massive stem or broad crown sometimes seen in the European horse-chestnut, but it can be taller, with a superior stem and foliage of an elegance and brightness unknown in that tree, as well as brilliant fall colors. It is remarkable and deplorable that the Yellow buckeye is so rarely planted in parks, even within its range, while the European horse-chestnut replaces it entirely as a street tree. The shoot is a shining gray-buff with a few small pale lenticels and the leaflets have stalks from 1–2in long and are finely toothed and 4–8in long. A variant with red flowers occurs at White Sulphur Springs, WV and is grown at Mount Vernon, VA where it is 70ft x 7ft as var. *virginica*. The species ranges from southwest PA and south IL in valleys and on hills in the Alleghenies just into GA. A fine long-boled specimen at Newfound Gap, TN is 100ft x 11ft and an even finer one on the Black Locust Trail is 140ft x 10ft. One at Rochester University House, NY is 75ft x 9ft 6in. The tree is also in Queen Victoria Park, Niagara Falls, ON; in the Ellipse and the White House Garden, DC; in Planting Fields, NY and there is one 10ft in girth in Me Kwa Mooks Park, Seattle, WA.

HYBRID BUCKEYE (3), *Aesculus × hybrida* may sometimes be seen in a garden as a grafted tree probably labelled '*Aesculus × discolor*' or as a variant of Yellow buckeye. It has some Red buckeye in its parentage and its flowers may be red or pink. The foliage is coarser than Yellow buckeye, the leaflets being broader with short, stout stalks.

RED BUCKEYE (4), *Aesculus pavia* is only a small tree, often little more than a shrub with a slender crown of rising branches and, in the open, pendulous outer shoots, but in flower it puts the Red horse-chestnut to shame. The slender panicle, 5–8in long, holds flowers which are a good bright dark red without the muddy tone of those of the ordinary Red horse-chestnut, and the leaflets are shining dark green. It is native to the Coastal Plain from south NC to mid-FL and TX, inland in AL and up the Mississippi Valley to OK, MO and IL, but is not much seen and is seldom planted.

OHIO BUCKEYE (5), *Aesculus glabra* has much the most extensive range of the buckeyes and has two other features not found in the other native species. Its leaflets have scarcely any stalk, and its fruit husk has short spines. In both these aspects the tree approaches the European horse-chestnut. The bark is dark gray, shallowly and coarsely fissured into big, square, scaly plates, but in MO and AR the bark of old trees is white and roughly scaling. By late summer the yellow-green leaflets with yellow midrib turn shining gray and by the fall they are yellow. The flower panicle is 5in long and hairy, densely set with flowers in bunches of 5. The range extends from west PA to TN in the Allegheny valley bottoms and from IL and IA to west AR and, as **Texan buckeye**, var. *arguta*, through mid-TX. It is locally frequent, planted in city parks and squares within the range or near it, as in Chicago, IL, Madison WI and at the Capitol in Des Moines, IA and in Omaha, NE. It is occasionally planted in the west, as in Grand Forks and Vernon, BC and at the Capitol, Helena, MT. The Texan form differs mainly in having 7 more coarsely serrated leaflets.

PAINTED BUCKEYE (6), *Aesculus sylvatica* is native to the Coastal Plain from VA to central GA, northeast AL and east TN. It is planted in Ottawa Botanic Garden, ON and in Fort Collins, CO. The bark of young trees is pale gray-pink, roughened and knobbly, and of older trees, dull gray to brown with lifting scales. The leaflets have very short, stout stalks, softly hairy at first, and the central eye has small, purple dots.

BOTTLEBRUSH BUCKEYE (7), *Aesculus parviflora* is a suckering shrub making thickets of vertical stems about 12–15ft tall, very rarely a small tree on a single stem. It is the last buckeye to flower, doing so at a useful time, in late summer, and abundantly. The leaflets, 3–9in long, turn orange and dark red in the fall. It is local in AL and southwest GA but is fairly widely planted.

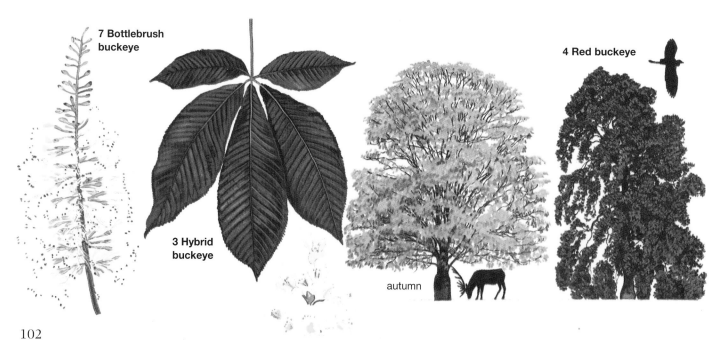

7 Bottlebrush buckeye

3 Hybrid buckeye

4 Red buckeye

autumn

6 Painted buckeye

5 Ohio buckeye

2 Yellow buckeye

twig

4 Red buckeye

1 California buckeye

fruit

seed

flws

5 Ohio buckeye

2 Yellow buckeye

bole

Basswoods and Lindens

The Lindens, basswoods or limes are some 30 species around the northern temperate region with the exception of western North America. The species native to eastern North America are now generally taken to be 3 but have at various times been split into 18. They are all deciduous, alternate-leafed medium to large trees requiring damp, quite rich soil. The flowers are perfect and in little bunches spreading from about half way along a stalk that is protruded from half way along a leafy bract.

AMERICAN BASSWOOD (1), *Tilia americana* is distinguished by its apple-green buds and shoots and the prominent series of parallel pale veins on a glossy leaf which is almost the same color above and beneath and has hairs beneath confined to tiny tufts in the vein-axils. It is a very shapely conical young tree, handsome in leaf. The leaf is normally some 8 x 7in but on sprouts and some young trees it may be 15 x 12in. The bract with the flowers is 4 x 1in and has a pink midrib. The native range of this tree is extensive, from NB north of Lake Huron to southeast MB and east SD in the north and from east KS and north AR, TN and the highest ranges in NC in the south. In the east it reaches the coast from MB and NJ then keeps to the hills to NC, overlapping with the White basswood from NC to PA. It is at 4300ft by US 19 in NC and is rare, both as native and as planted trees on the Coastal Plain. Within the main range and to some extent beyond it to the west and north, it is a universal town and city tree. It is common in Winnipeg, MB and in Montreal, PQ. One in the main street of Granville, OH is 85ft x 10ft. One in the Hoyt-Scott Arboretum, Swarthmore College, PA, planted in 1887 was 108ft x 7ft 4in in 1976. In the west it is in Boulder, CO; Salt Lake City, UT; in Cheyenne, WY and Helena and Missoula, MT. In WA it is in Seattle, Everett and Wenatchee but it is fairly frequent only in BC.

EUROPEAN LINDEN (2), *Tilia × europaea* is a hybrid between the Broadleaf and the Small-leaf lindens and has a strong tendency to large bunches of sprouts around the base and on burls on the trunk. The untidy growth distinguishes the tree in winter from the American basswood. It is said to be common in North America but this must be from a failure to separate it from the Small-leaf linden, which is seen at times labelled 'European linden'. It is in fact, common, like several other European trees, only in Newport, RI. There are a few in the Public Gardens, Boston, MA; in Toronto, ON; one 92ft x 10ft at Lyndhurst Garden, NY; in Washington Square, Philadelphia, PA; one 102ft x 12ft at St. John's Annapolis, MD and in some collections in OH, with even fewer in the west. Outside Vancouver by Rt 99, there is a large planting and some are in Stanley Park. It is a very rare tree.

CRIMEAN LINDEN (3), *Tilia euchlora* with its lime-green shoots, glossy leaf with big buff tufts in vein-axils beneath and late flowers on pale yellow bracts, has been planted at times in streets. It is usually free from the swarms of aphids which make the other European lindens messy in streets. The crown is domed with branches curving down making a mushroom shape. There are trees in the Genesee Valley, Rochester, NY and at Richmond, VA.

MONGOLIAN LINDEN (4), *Tilia mongolica* is related to the Small-leaf linden and holds its flowers in the same way, spreading or erect, not hanging. Its distinctively sharply lobed little leaves are dark and hard and it is a tough tree only now becoming appreciated for planting in cold places. It is still very rare and apart from a tree in the Arnold Arboretum, MA the main public plantings are by Lake Washington Boulevard, Seattle, WA and a tree by the Capitol at Helena, MT.

SILVER LINDEN (5), *Tilia tomentosa* comes from the southeastern parts of Europe, the Caucasus Mountains and Asia Minor. It is a very sturdy, fast-growing tree rapidly building a stout trunk and a remarkably regular hemispheric, domed crown. The shoot is covered in dense white down until the summer when it wears off. The very oblique leaf is 5 x 4in, crinkled and thick, densely covered beneath in gray-white hairs. The margin is often curled up. The flowers are late and highly fragrant. It is an infrequent tree in city parks from ON and PA to OH with a few in NC, IA, MO and IL. There are several trees in Prospect Park Brooklyn and in Central Park, NY. In the west it is scarce from BC to CA with trees in Beacon Hill Park, Victoria, BC, in Seattle streets and Point Defiance Park, Tacoma, WA, in Eugene, OR, the Strybing Arboretum, San Francisco, CA and in Salt Lake City, UT.

SILVER PENDENT LINDEN (6), *Tilia petiolaris* is of unknown origin, propagated only by grafting on to European or Broadleaf lindens, usually at 6ft. From this height, it grows 2–3 slightly sinuous vertical stems. The leaf differs from that of the Silver linden in its slender stalk as long as the blade and in being thin and flat. It is occasional from ON and MA to PA, OH, DE and MD. At Swarthmore College, PA two are 120ft x 14ft 2in and 110ft x 17ft 5in (1987).

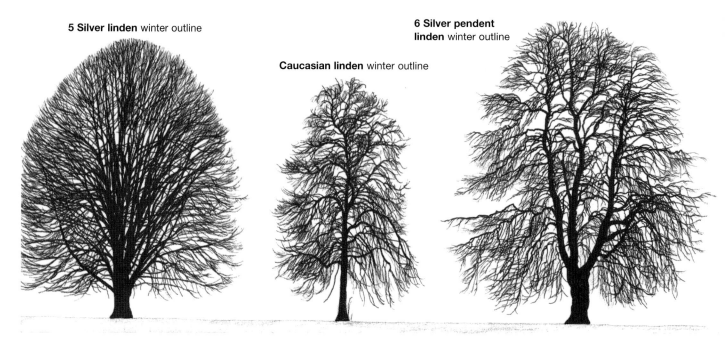

5 Silver linden winter outline

Caucasian linden winter outline

6 Silver pendent linden winter outline

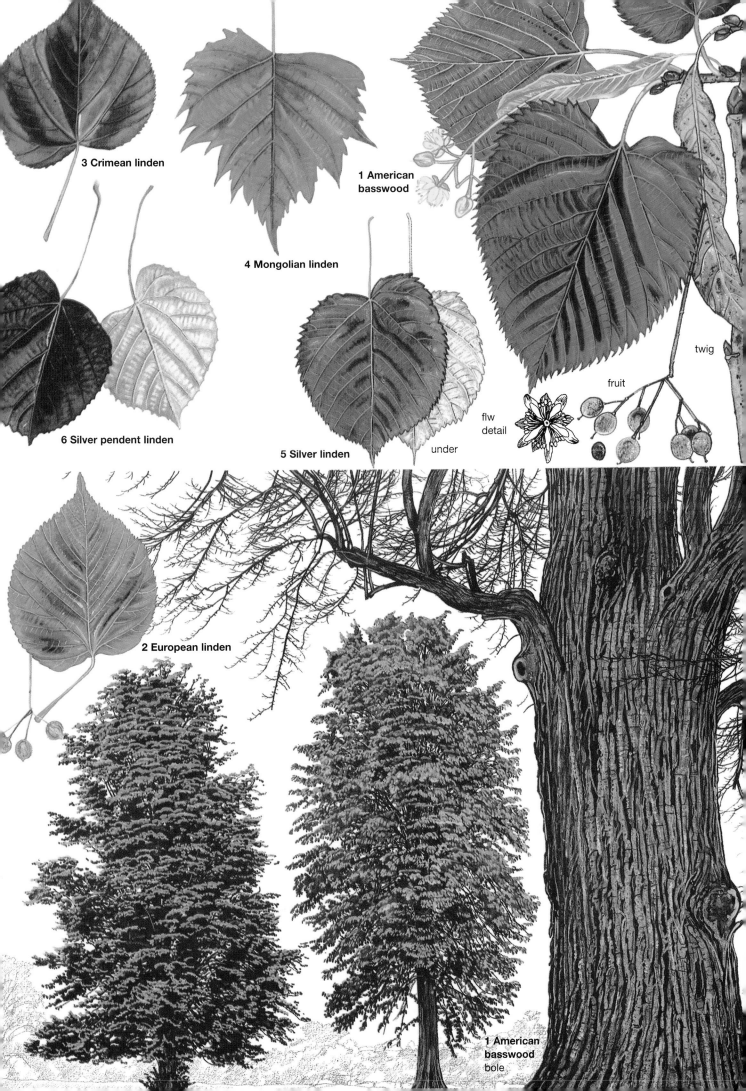

3 Crimean linden

1 American basswood

4 Mongolian linden

6 Silver pendent linden

5 Silver linden

under

flw detail

fruit

twig

2 European linden

1 American basswood bole

Basswoods and Lindens

WHITE BASSWOOD (1), *Tilia heterophylla* is closely related to, and overlaps range in parts, with the American basswood but is, from a distance, rather more like the Silver linden because of the white underside of the leaf. It also has many more flowers in each bunch than the American basswood, up to 25, and lacks the gloss and rich green of the upper side of the leaf. In the hills of WV, and noticeably from US 50 from Bond's Creek to Gormania on the PA border, the silver flashes on the windblown leaves in the roadside woods. The range extends south to AL and has outliers in MO. It is planted in the streets of Trenton, IL and in other cities in the region but is not a commonly seen tree further south. Beyond range it is in residential areas of Memphis, TN; Rochester, NY; Wye Mills, MD; and Newcastle Green, DE. Further afield it is in Waterworks Park, Des Moines, IA and in Helena, MT.

CAROLINA BASSWOOD (2), *Tilia caroliniana* is a variable species widespread across the south and includes six other species which were accepted by Sargent. The **Florida basswood (3)** is, rather oddly, the name by which the more northerly populations were known and is distinguishable by the leaves losing the white hairs on the underside during the summer. As a group these small basswoods extend from NC coast and foothills to TX, OK and AR. The shore of Colonel's Island, near the mouths of the North Newport and Medway rivers in GA, is a good place for them. They all have rusty brown hairs beneath the leaves.

VON MOLTKE'S BASSWOOD (4), *Tilia* 'Moltkei' is a hybrid between the American basswood and the Silver pendent linden, arising in Berlin, Germany and marketed in 1883. It has the hairless shoot and bud and the size of leaf of the American basswood and the whitish underside of leaf with hairs of the Silver pendent, but less white and more sparse hairs. It has also some hybrid vigor in most places and can make annual shoots 6ft long and a tree of over 80ft.

OLIVER'S BASSWOOD (5), *Tilia oliveri* was sent from Hupeh Province to England in 1900 by Ernest Wilson. It can be a difficult tree to establish but where it grows well it is exceedingly handsome. It holds its large, 6in leaves out level and very flat from down-curved 3in slender stalks on drooping shoots, and when it is 60ft or more tall, the upper leaves can be 8 x 7in. It has a smooth bark, soft gray, finely streaked brown with dark Chinaman moustaches over the branch-scars. There are 2–4 fruit on a 2in stalk from a 4in bract, bright green above and whitish beneath. The fruit are large, ½in, globular, gray-green with short, dense hairs.

SMALL-LEAF LINDEN (6), *Tilia cordata* is native to Europe and the Caucasus Mountains. Its attractive features are the pretty foliage of small, nearly round leaves and the abundant bright yellow starry little flowers which spray out at various rising angles. It has been widely adopted as a street tree in American cities. However, it tends to be overlooked, as exotic trees are little known by the public, and where trees are labelled it is all too likely to be 'European linden', the coarse hybrid which is in fact not much planted. The Small-leaf linden is one of the most numerous city street trees from PQ to WI south to NE and VA, and slightly less so in BC and WA. It lines streets in East Lansing and Detroit, MI; Columbus, Cleveland and Cincinnati, OH: Indianapolis, IN; Bloomington, IL; Madison and Milwaukee, WI; Ames and Des Moines, IA; Omaha, NE; Independence Avenue, Washington, DC; Odessa Main Street, DE; and Washington Square and 6th Street, New York, NY. There are trees in Salt Lake City, UT and in Denver, CO. A recent selection in America is **'Greenspire' (7)** with an extra neat, conic crown and orange shoots. This is much planted now, particularly in ON, OH and IA and by the Legislative building in Winnipeg, MB, which shows that it is very hardy.

BROADLEAF LINDEN (8), *Tilia platyphyllos* from Europe and Asia Minor, has a leaf no larger or broader than that of the Common European linden, and in one form it is considerably smaller. It is distinct, however, in being softly hairy all over, and with harder, larger hairs on the veins beneath, and at least until late summer, the leafstalk and shoot are variably densely hairy. This is a cleaner tree than the Small-leaf and the Common European, and rarely has any sprouts around the base or on the trunk, making a fine domed crown, often hemispherical. It flowers before any other basswood, with large, pale flowers, three to five hanging from a prominent large and pale bract. It is locally frequent from ON to mid-VA and OH, and uncommon west to St. Louis, MO. It is most frequent and large in the streets and parks of Baltimore, MD. In Ottawa Botanic Garden it is 75ft x 6ft and one in Highland Park, Rochester, NY, planted in 1915 was 66ft x 7ft when 61 years old. In the west, it is frequent in BC, seen in Revelstoke, Vernon, Osyoos and near the Cathedral in Victoria, and from the border to Tacoma in WA.

The **Cutleaf linden (9), 'Laciniata'** bears so many flowers that the big bracts with them overwhelm the flimsy foliage and the tree looks pale yellow all over. It attracts bees by the thousand. Older trees are liable to throw branches of foliage reverted to the type but a big one in Lyndhurst Garden, NY 56ft x 5ft, is in good order.

5 Oliver's linden

under

bark

summer

4 Von Moltke's linden

winter

under

1 White basswood

fruit

8 Broadleaf linden

under

bark

2 Carolina basswood

fruit

9 'Laciniata'

under

3 Florida basswood

fruit

6 Small-leaf linden

7 'Greenspire'

1 White basswood

bole

Tupelos, Rain trees and others

The Tupelos are a small group related most closely to the dogwoods and conform with the pattern of so many genera in which there are species native to eastern North America and Mexico and in eastern Asia but none at all anywhere between them. Of the 10 species five are trees and three of these are American. The ranges of the three vary from extensive through fairly restricted to the highly restricted.

BLACK TUPELO or **BLACKGUM (1)**, *Nyssa sylvatica* is the wide-ranging one, native in woods from ME and on the ON shore of Lake Erie to TX and mid-FL, and common in the hills over much of this range. It is scattered in small numbers, as understorey in taller woods of mixed hardwoods, and occurs at 4–5000ft along the Blue Ridge Drive in VA and NC. Even when in a fair degree of shade it achieves its scarlet fall color, after being mottled by a mixture of yellow, orange and red leaves. Its craggy bark and elliptic leaves are shared by the Sourwood which grows to a similar size in the same woods from PA southwards, but that has finely toothed leaves while those of the tupelo are entire, and smooth and glossy. They are 2–5in long generally but very mixed in size and some of 7in may be found with them but more often on the frequent sucker-shoots on the trunk or around its base. The male and female flowers are on separate heads but the same tree, the females two to four together. The Black tupelo is often planted in parks from NY to TN.

WATER TUPELO (2), *Nyssa aquatica* differs from the Black in its longer leaf, more tapered to the tip and often with a few blunt teeth, and in its single female flower. It often grows among Bald cypress in the same range from Richmond, VA to Houston, TX and up the Mississippi to Cairo, IL. It is in the woods at Middleton Place, SC, beside US 61 in bayous and bottoms in MS and TN.

OGEECHEE TUPELO (3), *Nyssa ogeche* is a small tree or shrub with dark brown, plated bark and large, 7in leaves, thick, and on a stout, grooved 2in red stalk. The fruit are red ovoids nearly 2in long. It is confined to a few swamps near the coast from Savannah, GA to the Apalachicola River, FL.

GOLDEN RAIN TREE (4), *Koelreuteria paniculata* from eastern Asia is unusual in holding its 12–16in long widely branching panicles clear of the top of the crown, and in the flowers maturing into bright pink or red 2in bladders. Each contains three black seeds. This tree is widely planted in parks and squares from Newport, RI and MA to SC, TN and AR, most commonly south from PA on the Coastal Plain and in OH, less frequently from ON to IN. It is a street tree in Arkansas City, AR and occasional in OK and IA. It is frequent in Vancouver, BC, Seattle and Tacoma, WA and in CA it is common in Central Valley towns and San Diego. It is grown in Carson City, NV and Tucumcari, NM.

FORMOSAN GOLDEN RAIN TREE (5), *Koelreuteria formosana* largely replaces the Golden rain tree to the south of Charleston, SC and along the gulf Coast into TX north to Lufkin. It is a more opulent species with more doubly compound leaves 20–30in long and flowerheads bearing dull purple-red fruit while others still bear flowers. The foliage of a tree without flowers resembles a luxuriant Chinaberry. It is grown in a few places in southern CA but is common and prominent in New Orleans, LA, on the Delta and in Baton Rouge.

IDESIA (6), *Idesia polycarpa* from Japan and China, looks like a Catalpa in leaf but the bark is smooth, the leaves have hooked teeth and scarlet stalks and the fruit and flowers are quite different. Male and female are on separate trees, small, yellow and fragrant on terminal panicles spreading or drooping 4–10in long. The leaf is 8 x 8in on a 5–12in stalk and is pale, whitish green beneath with tufts of white hairs in the axils of the veins. This tree is seen in some collections in the northeast, as in Brooklyn Botanic Garden and the Bailey Arboretum, NY and the National Arboretum, Washington, DC, and in southern CA.

DOVE TREE (7), *Davidia involucrata* can, perhaps be called the Ghost tree but the deplorable common name of Handkerchief tree should be forgotten. It is related to ivies, dogwoods and tupelos but is now accorded a family of its own. It was discovered by the Abbé David Armand in 1869 in west China and it was largely in order to bring back seed of this tree that Ernest Wilson was trained for collecting in China in 1899 and duly sent some in 1903. This first described form has soft white hairs densely set on the leaf underside and a 6–8in stalk to the fruit. To Wilson's later chagrin, Père Farges had already sent seed to Paris in 1897, one of which germinated and flowered in 1905 and this was grafted and distributed. It differs in having a shiny, smooth green underside to the leaf, a fruit-stalk only half as long and more purple bark. It is this form, also sent later by Wilson, **Vilmorin's dove tree (8)**, that is seen in collections in MA, NY and PA and in parks and gardens in BC and WA.

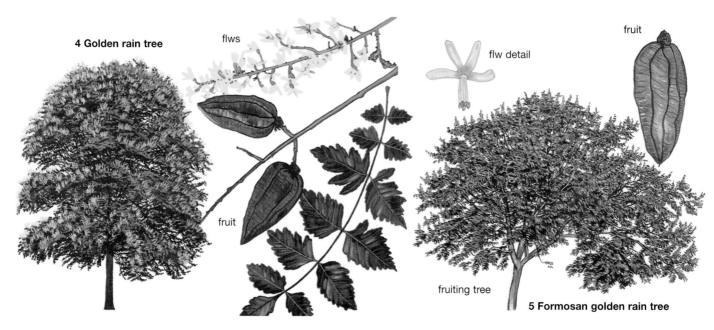

4 Golden rain tree

flws

fruit

fruit

flw detail

fruit

fruiting tree

5 Formosan golden rain tree

♂ flws detail

♀ flws detail

♀ flws

fruit

seed

1 Black tupelo

fruit

2 Water tupelo

bark

3 Ogeechee tupelo

fruits

seed

6 Idesia

7 Dove tree

flw

bract

8 Vilmorin's dove tree

fruit

fruit

seedling

7 Dove tree

bark

bark

1 Black tupelo winter

1 Black tupelo autumn

Eucalyptus and California laurel

The Gumtrees or Eucalypts are a remarkable group of trees in many ways. This single genus, in the Myrtle Family, provides the dominant trees across the entire continental mass of Australia but is absent from New Zealand. Although confined as a native to Australasia, it now provides the tallest trees and the fastest growing, in almost every warm country throughout the world, and, in native woods in Tasmania, the tallest broadleaf tree known, 338ft tall. The ranges of many gums are slender ribbons of riverside woods, which leads to splitting into several species since exchange of pollen is limited over a distance. So there are about 600 species and many are very similar. These aromatic, evergreen trees set no winter bud and grow continuously in climates with no cold period. They have juvenile foliage of broad, opposite leaves, often clasping the stem, but nearly all soon grow adult leaves alternate and slender. The flowers are enclosed in hard capsules with lids that open to allow bunches of stamens to protrude.

BLUEGUM EUCALYPTUS (1), *Eucalyptus globulus* from Tasmania was introduced by a San Franciso nurseryman in about 1875. Flowering and seeding throughout the year and with seedlings growing 6–8ft a year, this very aggressive species escaped into the hills to the south and has taken over extensive areas to 2000ft. Its northward spread is stopped only by hard frosts and extends some 80 miles into OR near the coast. Near Fort Bragg, CA, the banks above the Noyo River are silver-blue with rampant seedlings and it is a common tree through Big Lagoon and Crescent City to Port Orford, OR. In Central Valley it is common north to Fresno and Merced. Huge trees line US 1 in Guadalupe and it is common in medians and windbreaks south to San Diego and east to Alpine, CA but not beyond. It spreads inland up to just south of Cajon Summit and there are trees in Las Vegas, NV.

LONGBEAK or **REDGUM EUCALYPTUS (2)**, *Eucalyptus camaldulensis* is unique in its natural range, from coast to coast across northern Australia. It is less hardy than the Blue gum and likes hotter summers so it ranges less northwards in CA, only to the Bay Area, but further east, into AZ where it is common around cities from the border through Mesa, Phoenix and Tucson to Superior. In CA it is common from Yuma to San Diego and around Los Angeles as shelterbelt and shade tree, and occasionally north in the Central Valley to Wasco. It is also, unlike the Blue gum, seen in the southern half of Peninsular FL, up to Lakeland, Orlando and Disney World, although it is far from common there. It is a tree of much less dark and heavy aspect than the Bluegum, its adult leaves being 5–6 x 1in, pale green with a white midrib, against 8–10 x 3in and dark blue-green in Bluegum. It is not unlike a willow, and old trees have pendulous outer shoots. The flowers are in bunches of 5–6, globular in bud with a stout beak and ripe fruit open out to brown 5-pointed stars. In Bluegum, the solitary flowers ripen to big, top-shaped capsules bloomed blue-white and falling to carpet the ground beneath.

SILVER DOLLAR TREE (3), *Eucalyptus polyanthemos* from New South Wales and Victoria, Australia, is the only gum seen in the eastern states outside southern FL. It is uncommon from Atlanta, GA to west of New Orleans, LA and from near Yuma to the Bay Area and Central Valley to Three Rivers and Wasco, CA. In inland GA and AL it is often cut to the ground by frost and re-grows as a many-stemmed bush, bright blue-white with opposite orbicular leaves. Adult foliage is similar, with alternate leaves and the biggest trees are nearly as blue. It is most frequent along the coast from Pensacola, FL through Foley and Fairhope.

RED FLOWERING GUM (4), *Eucalyptus ficifolia* from Western Australia is spectacular but small and mopheaded with hard, thick foliage. It can be grown only in the most favoured areas. A line stands in Montgomery Street, San Francisco and some streets in Berkeley are planted with it. There are trees in Monterey and Santa Barbara, CA.

LEMON GUM (5), *Eucalyptus citriodora* from Queensland, Australia is rather like the longbeak eucalyptus in its fine, slender foliage but has a more open crown, without hanging outer shoots and shows the bark, coffee-brown in young trees, shedding long strips of brown, gray and purple in old trees. It is grown only in southern CA, from Santa Barbara and Ventura around Los Angeles to San Diego. It is a common shade and shelterbelt tree in the southern part. It is 120ft in the Los Angeles State and County Arboretum.

CALIFORNIA LAUREL (6), *Umbellularia californica* is here placed among other evergreen trees with highly aromatic foliage but belongs botanically with the Sassafras. It is native to the Coast Ranges from OR all through CA and on the western flanks of the Sierra Nevada, and in the southern cross-ranges. It tends to grow with many stems from near the base, at least in cut-over woods, but is known to 150ft x 34ft and in Tallest Tree Redwood Grove a fine tree is 120ft x 17ft 6in. The aroma from crushed leaves is spicy and pleasant but over indulgence is paid for by a sharp headache. Nonetheless, the leaf can be used to flavour stews.

6 California laurel bark

lvs

1 Bluegum eucalyptus bark

fruit

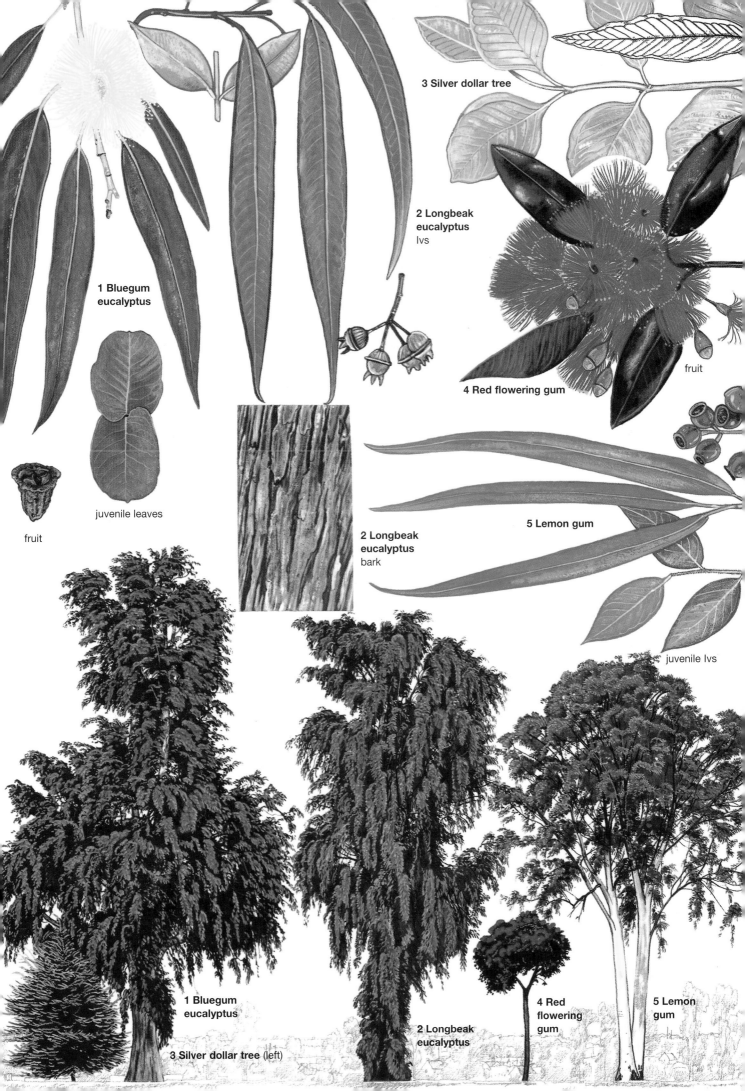

3 Silver dollar tree

1 Bluegum eucalyptus

2 Longbeak eucalyptus lvs

juvenile leaves

fruit

2 Longbeak eucalyptus bark

4 Red flowering gum

fruit

5 Lemon gum

juvenile lvs

1 Bluegum eucalyptus

2 Longbeak eucalyptus

3 Silver dollar tree (left)

4 Red flowering gum

5 Lemon gum

Silverbell, Snowbells and Dogwoods

MOUNTAIN SILVERBELL or **SNOWDROP TREE (1)**, *Halesia monticola* generally has 6 x 3in leaves but some are 10 x 4in. They are thin with the veins deeply impressed and softly hairy beneath. The variety *vestita* is sometimes distinguished, growing in the hills of AR and OK, separated from the main Allegheny population, with soft hairs all over the underside and stalk and sometimes with pink flowers. The finest trees are in the valleys among the Great Smoky Mountains in TN.

JAPANESE SNOWBELL (2), *Styrax japonica* makes a small, rounded tree with level lower branches bearing in June masses of small white flowers which soon mature into little smooth green acorn-like fruit in a starry calyx. It is scarce but should be in some northern gardens.

FRAGRANT SNOWBELL (3), *Styrax obassia* is related to the shrubby **Big-leaf snowbell (4)** which ranges from FL to TX. The Fragrant snowbell, from Japan, Korea and northern China has better claim to the name 'big-leaf' as its nearly circular leaf is usually 6–8in across and often 10in long. On young plants they have two or three large triangular teeth near the tip and may be cut across like the leaves of Yellow poplar. This makes a sturdy, broad tree, seeding itself freely in nearby flowerbeds in the Bailey Arboretum, NY where it is 42ft and 40ft tall. It is grown also in the Brooklyn Botanic Garden; Fairmount Park, Philadelphia, PA; Winterthur Garden, DE; Stanley Park, Vancouver, BC, and the Charles English Garden, Seattle, WA. **Hemsley's snowbell (5)** is the equivalent tree in South China, and grows taller with narrower leaves and, when the winter buds are revealed from within the swollen base of the leafstalk, a feature of *Styrax*, they are orange.

FLOWERING DOGWOOD (6), *Cornus florida* is by far the commonest of the Dogwoods, which comprise about 40 mostly temperate area trees ranging across North America, Europe and Asia (14 trees and shrubs are American). Its wide natural range, from Portland, ME south of IL to east TX, is extended by planting, including south BC and north WA, and within its range it is a common woodland tree and a very common town and garden tree. The streets of Philadelphia, PA; Tulsa, OK; many towns in the Ozark region of AR and in LA and Pensacola, FL, are notably planted with it. It makes a bushy, open, upswept low crown and grows slowly to no great age so it achieves no great size. The square-blocked red-brown bark is highly distinctive and a useful feature in separating this and the otherwise similar Kousa dogwood, especially in winter. In these dogwoods the large 'flowers' are in fact a central bass of minute true, four-petalled flowers surrounded by showy 2in bracts usually four in number. They are usually white, but the form *rubra*, **Pink flowering dogwood (7)**, has soft pink bracts and is more common in the west. The glossy, bright red berries are at their best when the leaves are turning through white and pale pink to become curled and rich dark red.

PACIFIC DOGWOOD (8), *Cornus nuttallii* has the splendid habit of opening a second crop of flowers when it is in full fall color, the 4–6 unnotched white bracts prominent among the scarlet and deep red leaves. It has dark purple-brown, smooth bark, shedding fine scales. The flowers are prominent greenish-white in bud at the shoot-tips all winter. This grows, often under Douglas fir, from Vancouver Island and the parallel coast of BC, along the Coast Range to south CA and on the western flanks of the Cascade-Sierra Nevada to the San Gabriel Mountains but is little seen in CA and is common only in BC.

TABLE DOGWOOD (9), *Cornus controversa* from the Himalaya, China and Japan holds its branches out level with 4in wide bunches of white flowers standing in dense lines erect above drooping leaves, which are alternately held, unlike the opposite leaves of the foregoing trees. It is grown in a few collections, as in Highland Park, NY and the University of Wisconsin Arboretum. The smaller and much prized variegated form, **'Variegata'**, is even more scarce and is grown in Victoria, BC.

KOUSA DOGWOOD (10), *Cornus kousa* from Japan is an exceedingly floriferous bushy tree somewhat similar to the Flowering dogwood but growing taller with a more open crown, smooth gray bark and crinkled margins on the leaf. The form *chinensis* has even more crowded flowers, lasting long as they turn pink. There are Kousa dogwoods in the Bailey Arboretum and Planting Fields, Long Island, NY, and many in PA/DE.

CASTOR ARALIA (11), *Kalopanax pictus* is a strange, gaunt, stoutly branched tree with short but sharp spines on the trunk and many more, soft-tipped and bright blue-green on the new shoots. Its terminal flowerheads, 1ft across, have some 50 white radiating spokes each tipped by a cluster of 25 small white flowers in August and by small black berries until after leaf-fall. The usual form, from China, Korea and Japan has a leaf 5 x 8in on a slender 5in stalk, and the **'Maximowiczii' (12)** variety from Japan has 8 x 8in leaves on stout, rough, hairy red-brown stalks, but there are many trees intermediate. This tree is grown in large gardens and parks from MA to OH and in the Strybing Arboretum, CA.

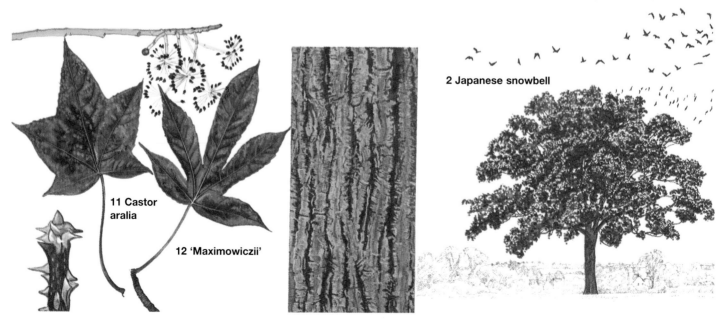

11 Castor aralia

12 'Maximowiczii'

2 Japanese snowbell

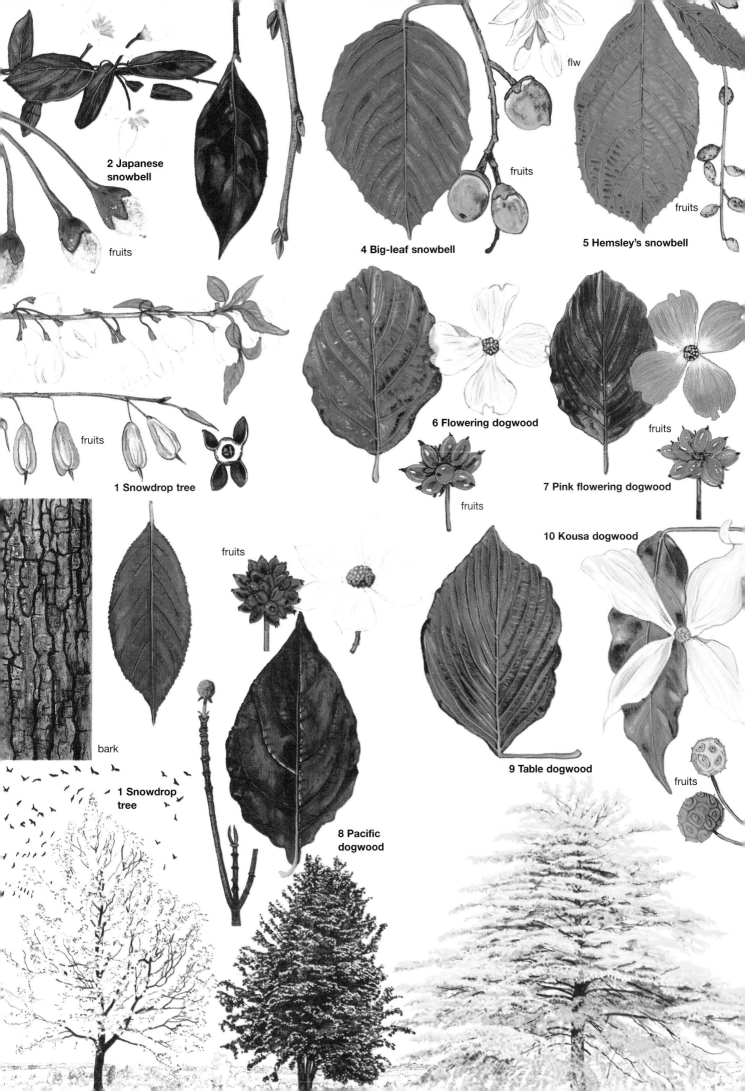

2 Japanese snowbell

fruits

4 Big-leaf snowbell

fruits

flw

5 Hemsley's snowbell

fruits

fruits

1 Snowdrop tree

6 Flowering dogwood

fruits

7 Pink flowering dogwood

fruits

10 Kousa dogwood

fruits

bark

1 Snowdrop tree

9 Table dogwood

fruits

8 Pacific dogwood

Madrones, Sourwood and others

The Heath Family includes such diverse plants as heathers, rhododendrons and azaleas, the Sourwood, Farkleberry, manzanitas and the Madrones, all with a very similar structure of the flower. The Madrones are the biggest in stature.

PACIFIC MADRONE (1), *Arbutus menziesii*, which occasionally exceeds 100ft, is the biggest of the Madrones. The shoot is stout, yellow-green for the first season then bright orange and, as the bark thickens, deep red. The evergreen leaf is 2–6in long and blue-white beneath. Seedlings have finely toothed leaves. The flowers open in March in CA and in May in BC on erect, conic panicles 8in long. The ⅓in fruit are green until most of them turn through orange to scarlet by October. This tree is native from the southern half of Vancouver Island and the corresponding coast of BC along the coast and hills to south of Los Angeles, CA. It is very common in the woods from Alberni to Victoria, BC, around Ashland, OR, Grant's Pass, the Rogue River valley and south of San Francisco, CA.

ARIZONA MADRONE (2), *Arbutus arizonica* is a smaller tree, to 50ft, with thinner, slender leaves, found at 6–8000ft in south AZ and southwest NM.

STRAWBERRY TREE (3), *Arbutus unedo* differs from the Pacific madrone in the smaller, finely toothed leaves, 2–4in long and pale green beneath, and in the October flowering in drooping sprays. It is occasional in western gardens in WA, TX and CA. There is a pink-flowered form, **'Rubra' (4)**.

SOURWOOD or **SORREL TREE (5)**, *Oxydendrum arboreum*, the only species in its genus, has gray bark with thick, interwoven ridges and a high-domed, flat crown on sinuous branches. The underside of the finely toothed leaf is smooth gray-green with only the white midrib showing. The fruit are ivory colored like the flowers and make it hard to see if it is late flowers or fruit with the scarlet fall color. It is native from south PA, MD and DE to near New Orleans, LA but not by the coast. It is planted northwards in OH, NY, MA and WA.

COMMON PERSIMMON (6), *Diospyros virginiana* is native over a wide area of the east, from NJ to the tip of FL and from the southern parts of PA to TX and the Gulf Coast. It is most common, forming miles of hedges of small trees in AR and OK and is planted sparsely to the north in ON, MA and NY. The female flowers are on different trees from the male and are solitary but the fruit are so numerous that they appear to hang in bunches, conspicuous and pale orange in late summer as the hanging leaves turn blackish green.

DATE PLUM (7), *Diospyros lotus* is a Chinese persimmon grown in warm parts of the USA. It has a dark gray bark soon deeply cracked into small square blocks and very glossy leaves.

TEXAS PERSIMMON (8), *Diospyros texana* is a small tree with smooth, pale gray bark and 1⅓in glossy, thick leaves with most of its range in Mexico, spreading into south TX.

RUSSIAN OLIVE (9), *Elaeagnus angustifolia* is an Oleaster, not an olive, from western Asia, very resistant to heat, drought and cold, valued for planting in the middle-west and southwestern regions. It is common from Winnipeg, MB, ND and SD, around Chicago, IL and through the prairies to NM and AZ and west in MT, UT and CO and in the dry interiors of BC and WA. It is less planted east and south of Chicago.

CRAPE MYRTLE (10), *Lagerstroemia indica* is in the Loosestrife Family, *Lythraceae*, and comes from China and Korea. It is an upright, bushy little tree on several stems, smoothly ribbed with pretty bark, pink and gray, flecked green and with bald pink areas. The leaves are opposite, alternate or in threes. It has a long season bearing flowers which are as often white, pink or scarlet in selected forms grown more in the far south, as the normal purplish red. It is common round the Coastal Plain from PA and DE to TX and north in the Mississippi Valley to Cairo, IL and particularly varied and good in the streets of Natchez, MS and the towns of AR and OK. It is occasional in CA in the east, in Bishop and Mariposa and more common around Los Angeles.

CHINESE PARASOL TREE (11), *Firmiana simplex* comes from Taiwan, south China and the Ryuku Islands and makes a curious tree. The smooth dark green trunk holds aloft a single mophead of huge leaves to 22 x 16in on stout stalks 1–2ft long and has no branch or other foliage until it matures with a few short, level branches making a broad, flat top, or, as often happens in GA especially, it is broken and becomes misshapen. A flowerhead at the top, 2 x 1ft with four to six main branches, bears white flowers, chrome yellow anthers and a red eye. The seeds are held on the margins of leafy carpels opening out from a bladder. It is common from SC to LA north to Natchez, MS and in AR.

10 Crape myrtle

flws

flws

9 Russian olive

11 Chinese parasol tree

3 Strawberry tree

flws

4 'Rubra'

5 Sorrel tree

6 Common persimmon

1 Pacific madrone

fruit

flws

fruit

7 Date plum

fruits

flws

2 Arizona madrone

flws

8 Texas persimmon

fruit

1 Pacific madrone

bark

bark

6 Common persimmon

European and Asiatic ash trees

The Ash trees have no botanical relationship with the Mountain ashes, whose popular name merely reflects a broadly similar leaf and ignores the completely different growth, bark, flowering and fruit. The Mountain ash is in the Rose Family whereas the true ashes are in the Olive Family, *Oleaceae*. This is unexpected for two reasons. First, the greater part of that Family is, like the Olive itself, of a southerly distribution, evergreen and tender, unable to grow where winters are severe. Yet ash trees are all deciduous and two in North America range north in MB and SK where few broadleaf trees are hardy. Second, the Olive Family is well represented in northern gardens by shrubs and these are nearly all grown for their showy and often sweetly scented flowers: the lilacs and privets for example, yet the common species of ash have all dispensed with petals and scent, relying on wind pollination, and only a few remain which need to attract insects.

About 70 species spread across the Northern Hemisphere with one as far south as Java and one in Guatemala. Most of them are trees of medium size or fairly small, but several are very large trees. North America has 16 native species, 10 of them confined to the southwestern USA. The ash trees, in conformity with the entire Olive Family, have their buds and hence their leaves and branches in opposing pairs, excepting only a few strong shoots in a few species, in which the leaves are in whorls of three. In the large-growing common species the pattern of rigidly opposite branching is simplified to avoid congestion as the crown ages, by the abortion of the bud or the death and shedding of the shoot on one side. The 'flowering ashes' have perfect flowers, but in the wind-pollinated majority, where the flowers open well before the leaves and are without petals, the sexual side is more complex and varied. Some, like the White ash, have male and female flowers on separate trees and others, like the European ash, have perfect, male and female flowers in various combinations. The wood of ashes is very strong, elastic and shock-resistant and is now used mainly in the making of sports goods. For these uses, the wood must be grown as fast and as evenly as possible, any marked slowing down with age having a deleterious effect on the elasticity. In general ashes grow fast in youth and need full light to mature properly, and they have extensive and greedy root-systems.

EUROPEAN ASH (1), *Fraxinus excelsior* extends to the Caucasus Mountains and Asia Minor in the east and to the far north of Scotland and west of Ireland in the British Isles. It differs from all the other species in its coal-black buds, and from American species in its large leaf, to 14in long with more leaflets, 9–13. It has flowers in chaotic sexual arrangement, some perfect, some male or female, mixed in the flowerheads or separated, with some branches of a single sex so that some branches are loaded with fruit and others without any, and occasional entire trees are of one sex, but the sex of a branch or tree may change from year to year. It has little fall coloring, a fleeting bright gold at times but often the leaves all fall while green, when they are much appreciated by sheep. They are pale green beneath, less white than in the White ash and have short, dense, white hairs each side of the midrib. The terminal buds on young trees and on suckers and sprouts which are frequent on or closely around old trees, open late in the season, uncurling like bracken-fronds, and often tinged purple or brown. This ash has not been much planted in North America and is seen only in some large parks from ON and MD to WI in the east, in Tabernacle Square, Salt Lake City, UT, near the Cathedral in Victoria, BC and in the University of Washington Arboretum and in Madrona Park, Seattle, WA in the west. Two trees in Queen Victoria Park, Niagara Falls, ON are 80ft x 8ft. There are trees in the Public Gardens, Boston, MA and at Vanderbilt Mansion, NY one is 90ft x 10ft. There are several quite big trees in Druid's Hill Park, Baltimore, MD, in Mitchell Park, Milwaukee, WI and one in the Morton Arboretum, IL was 50ft x 6ft when 50 years old.

Golden ash (2), **'Jaspidea'** is a full-sized tree, unlike the little golden-leafed 'Aurea', and grows as fast as the type. Its leaves open gold and are a good gold in the fall but are nearly green in the summer and it is the shoots which give it the name, shining out gold in the winter and spring. It is in most of the collections in ON, NY and OH. **Single-leaf ash (3)**, **'Diversifolia'** grows even more vigorously than the type, with smoother silvery bark on the branches and a more open crown. **Weeping ash (4)**, **'Pendula'** needs to be grafted high on a stem to be graceful. As sometimes seen grafted at about 6ft its shoots reach the ground in about three years and have nowhere to go.

MANNA ASH (5), *Fraxinus ornus* from Asia Minor is one of the 'flowering ashes' with slender petals and sweetly scented flowers at midsummer. It is scarce, but a very large one, 9ft 6in round the trunk, is in Mount Pleasant Cemetery, Seattle, WA and smaller ones are in most of the parks there and in Victoria, BC it lines Quadra and Douglas Streets. There are trees in Point Defiance Park, Tacoma, WA. In the east there are fewer. Fairmount Park, Philadelphia; Prospect Park, Brooklyn and Queen Victoria Park, Niagara Falls, ON, for example.

5 Manna ash

1 European ash

4 'Pendula'

flws

5 Manna ash

3 Single-leaf ash

two forms of leaf

1 European ash

2 'Jaspidea'

American ash trees

Of about 70 species of ash in the world, 16 are native to North America, three of which extend over huge areas east to west and two of them cover also very wide north–south spans.

WHITE ASH or **AMERICAN ASH (1)**, *Fraxinus americana* is one of these last, growing from Cape Breton Island and NS broadly to WI and mid-TX, and is a common woodland, park and city tree over most of that area. It has also been planted well beyond this range in small numbers. White ash has male and female flowers on separate trees; towards the end of summer the leaves turn pale yellow, then orange before becoming bronzy purple all over.

BLACK ASH (2), *Fraxinus nigra* is a largely northern tree growing from NF to Winnipeg MB, and south to IA, WV and NJ, not a large tree nor prominent but planted in streets in Winnipeg and other northern cities. The terminal leaflet often extends very narrowly down its stalk. Leaflet undersides are variably pale but greener than in the White ash, and fall color is pale yellow.

GREEN ASH (3), *Fraxinus pennsylvanica* now includes the **Red ash (4)**, var. *anceolata* with hairy shoots and leaves, and together they have a huge range, from NS to around Lake Winnipeg into AB and south to the Gulf Coast in East TX missing only Peninsula FL and some inland parts from PA to ME. It is much planted in streets west of this, in MT, ID, WY, CO, UT, NM, AZ and WA. The shoot is stout and shining green in the Green ash form grading to more slender and covered in dense gray hairs in the Red ash form. The leaves always differ from the White ash in the leaflets being almost stalkless, more tapered, slender and green beneath.

BLUE ASH (5), *Fraxinus quadrangulata*, so-named from its four-angled young shoots growing four gray wings before shedding them in their fifth year, and the common name from a blue dye made from the inner bark, has a relatively small range. It occupies a rough arc from east TN round through west OH and mid-IL to MO. It is recognisable in these areas in woods by its relatively small, bright green foliage. It is planted on a small scale north and east to MA, NY, PA and DC. This tree has perfect flowers and the foliage turns pale yellow in the fall.

CAROLINA ASH (6), *Fraxinus caroliniana* grows from VA to TX and AR. It is a small tree with male and female flowers on separate trees, pale gray, scaly bark and chestnut-brown winter buds.

TEXAS ASH (7), *Fraxinus texensis*, also confusingly called 'Mountain ash', is found only in TX and south OK. It has firm, thick leaves and stout, twisting branches. The winter buds are orange and the sexes are on separate trees.

VELVET ASH (8), *Fraxinus velutina* is a small, slender tree with small, 6in leaves and velvety soft hairs on the shoot, leafstalk and leaf. It is highly variable and has three extreme forms: **Smooth ash**, var. *glabra* with no hairs at all; **Leatherleaf ash**, var. *coriacea* with dark, thick leaves almost without hairs; and **Toumey Ash**, var. *toumeyi* with slender, longer-stalked, gray-green leaflets with a fine velvety upper surface. Since all intergrades among these are now known and there seems to be no geographical zoning noted, these forms are no longer botanically distinguished. The Velvet ash extends from Mexico into west TX across much of NM and AZ with a loop round through south UT and south NV into the Providence Mountains area of CA. It is planted in streets in these states.

OREGON ASH (9), *Fraxinus latifolia* is native to bottom lands from the border north of Seattle, WA down the Coast Range to the Bay Area and along the western flanks of the Sierra Nevada, with a patch in the San Bernardino Mountains. Its stout bright green shoot is covered densely in pale brown hairs, like the buds. The almost or quite stalkless, broad leaflets are unusual in American ashes, as is the leaf, being often over 1ft long. This tree is common only in the lowland woods of WA and OR and has been planted in Victoria and Vancouver, BC. The male and female flowers are on separate trees.

SINGLE-LEAF ASH (10), *Fraxinus anomala* is a shrub with twisting branches rarely aspiring to be a tree. It grows in the hills of north AZ and adjacent parts of CA, NV, UT, CO and NM. Its leaf is normally a simple one 2in long but there are frequent compound leaves of three or even five leaflets, which are then only about 1in long. The flowers are perfect and female mixed in each head, and the shoot is slightly winged and four-angled. The bark is scaly ridges, dark brown tinged red.

MORAINE ASH (11) is a selection raised in 1958 from the Balkan ash, *Fraxinus holotricha* and used in street planting because of its rapid growth and shapely ovoid crown, mainly in OH and states in that region. It has chocolate-colored buds and gray shoots and makes an attractive tree with elegant 8in white-stalked shiny leaves and gray bark.

9 Oregon ash

bark

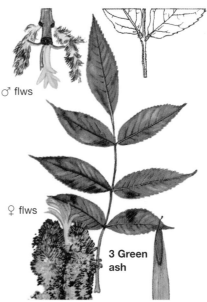

♂ flws

♀ flws

3 Green ash

4 Red ash

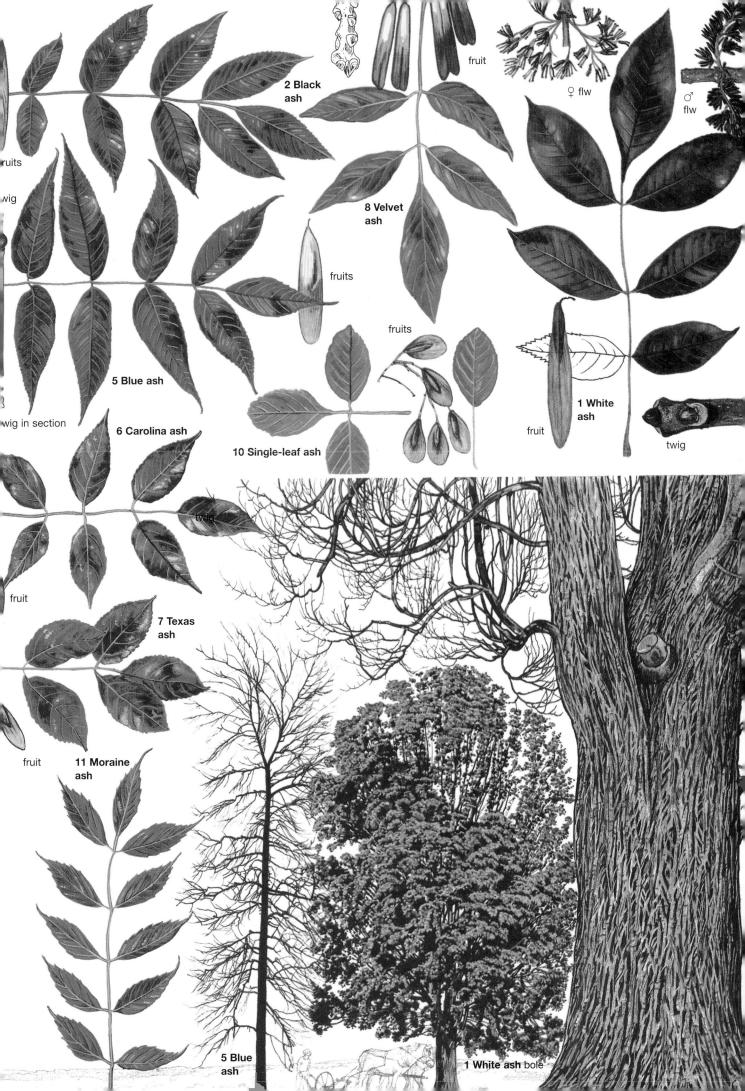

2 Black ash

fruit

♀ flw

♂ flw

ruits

wig

8 Velvet ash

fruits

5 Blue ash

fruits

fruits

1 White ash

wig in section

6 Carolina ash

10 Single-leaf ash

fruit

twig

twig

fruit

7 Texas ash

fruit

11 Moraine ash

5 Blue ash

1 White ash bole

Catalpa, Paulownia and Pepper tree

SOUTHERN CATALPA (1), *Catalpa bignonioides* is in the Bignonia Family with the Trumpet vine and is one of 11 species of Catalpa divided among North America, the West Indies and China. With its close relative the Northern catalpa it is a prime example of how grossly misleading the use of 'natural range' maps can be in North America, for both are found now apparently wild in many parts and with the Southern as common within the range of the Northern as that tree itself. Its original natural range was mainly in the southern parts of MS and AL near the coast and probably into Gulf Coast GA and FL. It is common in hedges today also westward in LA and TX. It is common in parks in Chicago, IL and at Martinsville, IL it is planted alternately with the Northern within whose range this is. It is common from PA and OH to KS, OK and AR; occasional in BC and more frequent in WA, CO, NM and east CA. The bark is not ridged but scales and crumbles in patches, orange-brown or dull pink-brown. A densely mop-headed form, **'Nana'**, is the common form in AZ and is seen occasionally north through UT and WA to one in Oliver, BC. The **Golden catalpa, 'Aurea'** is slower, more tender, susceptible to sunscorch and rare.

NORTHERN CATALPA (2), *Catalpa speciosa* makes a much taller, tougher tree than the Southern, distinguished as much by the stature and dark gray coarsely ridged bark as by the long-tapered drip-tip leaf which is not always very marked. It is in flower three to four weeks before Southern catalpa in the same place, around midsummer, and from about then its leaves take on a marked yellow-green and pale yellow, most evident west of OH and TN in the drier, hotter areas. The native area is a small one around the Ohio and Missisippi rivers in IL, IN, MO, AR and KY where it is very common in hedges, parks and gardens. It is seldom in the east south of DC and MD. It is common in BC and WA, along the coast of OR and is in Carson City, NV. One by the Capitol in Sacramento, CA is 77ft x 12ft and by the County Courthouse in Salt Lake City, UT it is 80ft x 12ft.

FARGES' CATALPA (3), *Catalpa fargesii* from China has the smallest leaves in the genus, 4in long, and hairy beneath, densely so on the stalk and shoot, and masses of small flowers, 10–15 on a 6in panicle. It is rare, in some collections.

YELLOW CATALPA (4), *Catalpa ovata* from China has pale, dull yellow little flowers and hard, dark foliage with red leafstalks, the leaves with well-marked side-lobes. Grown at Bayville, IN in the nursery of J.C. Teas'

this crossed in 1874 with the Southern catalpa to give **Teas' hybrid catalpa (5)**, *Catalpa × erubescens* with tall stature and willow-like fibrous, ridged dark gray bark like the Northern catalpa. The leaves have lobes and are very large, to 15 x 12in. The flowers are smaller and later, widely set on much bigger, more open, panicles 13 x 8in. The fruit are 16in long, ripening dull brown but contain no seed and the tree must be grafted. The new leaves unfold purple. This is a rare tree and can be seen at Queen Victoria Park, Niagara Falls, ON; in Granville, OH and Williamsburg, VA.

ROYAL PAULOWNIA (6), *Paulownia tomentosa* is a Chinese tree usually assigned to the Foxglove Family, *Scrophulariaceae*, but sometimes put in *Bignoniaceae* with the Catalpas. It differs from them in its smooth gray bark, later dark gray and shallowly ridged, and in its flower buds forming in summer, small, and orange-haired, passing the winter at the branchtips to open before the leaves in May. The leaves are opposite as in Catalpa but never also in threes as those are on strong shoots. The fruit are ovoid, shiny and very sticky and persist in large brown bunches through winter. This tree grows very fast, making in its second or third year from seed a thick shoot to 8ft long with 18in stalks bearing leaves 18in long with a few triangular teeth. It soon becomes fragile and liable to lose big branches. From ON to New England and NY this is found only in parks but from there south it is common and often seeding itself. It does this abundantly on roadsides along the Skyline and Blue Ridge Drives in VA and NC and at the higher altitudes it is cut to the ground annually by frost. Tree No. 72 in Central Park NY was 50ft x 10ft 8in in 1975. One in Marquand Park, Princeton, NJ was 50ft x 13ft in 1981, the same size as one in Fairmount Park, Philadelphia, PA where one on Society Hill was 60ft x 12ft. There is a fine avenue in Longwood Gardens. It is common in KY, AR and OH but much less so in the west where it is in the large parks and gardens only, in BC, WA and a few in CA.

PEPPER TREE (7), *Schinus molle* from Brazil and Peru has taken over much of south Mexico and may do the same in the hot, dry south of CA where it is a common roadside tree west of Los Angeles from Tomonga and Moor Park, where one is 70ft x 14ft in Main Street, to Hollister, Salinas, Carmel and Monterey. It is also grown in TX. The hanging, pale, alternate 8in leaves with 15–20 leaflets, on hanging shoots to 30ft long, and hanging slender 1ft bunches of dark pink to dark red fruit like currants are very distinctive.

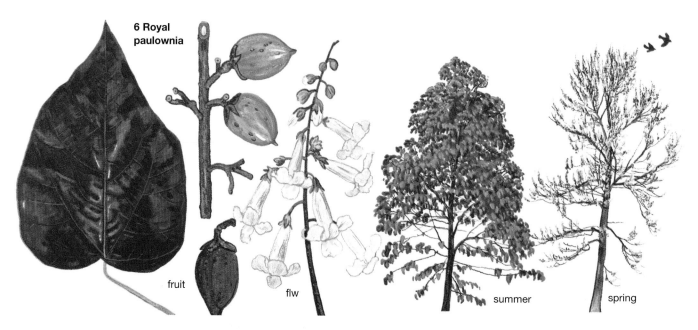

6 Royal paulownia

fruit

flw

summer

spring

1 Southern catalpa

2 Northern catalpa

5 Teas' hybrid catalpa

3 Farges' catalpa

4 Yellow catalpa

twig

fruit

flws

7 Pepper tree

2 Northern catalpa

bole

CONIFERS

Podocarps and Gingko

The Yellowwoods or, better, Podocarps (to avoid confusion with the Yellowwood, *Cladrastis*) are a large and widespread Family of primitive conifers, highly unusual in ranging from the southern hemisphere in Chile to the northern in Mexico and in the eastern hemisphere from New Zealand to Japan. Large numbers are tropical trees in Africa. In some of them the fruit-stalk swells and becomes fleshy and purple or bright blue-white.

BIG-LEAF PODOCARP, *Podocarpus macrophyllus* from Japan is commonly grown against buildings from Sacramento southwards to CA and is also the common podocarp from Charleston, SC to Baton Rouge and beyond in LA and is grown in Phoenix, AZ and in Southern CA, to Mariposa. It is often clipped as a hedge.

PODOCARPUS NAGI (1) from Japan has broader leaves than the Bigleaf and grows in the streets of the Bay Area and San Diego.

KUSAMAKI var. *maki* is a form from China with slender leaves and upright growth often trained against a wall in towns from Charleston along the Gulf Coast and north to Little Rock, AR.

WILLOW PODOCARP (2), *Podocarpus salignus* from Chile has glossy dark green leaves to 6in long and is less frequent. There are trees at Sebring and in Disney World, FL; in Bellingrath Gardens, AL 50ft tall, and in the Strybing Arboretum, CA.

GINKGO or **MAIDENHAIR TREE (3)**, *Ginkgo biloba* is the odd tree out in this book, as it is in any book of plants, as it is neither a broadleafed, 'flowering' tree nor a conifer. It is a Ginkgo and the only one left of a whole Order of plants which were the dominant tree-form worldwide 150 million years ago. Unrelated to any living plant, it shares a few features with only the Cycads, the dwarfish, hard-leafed palm-like plants seen in town plantings along the Gulf Coast, bearing big central cone-like structures. The Ginkgo is by far the most primitive landplant and evolved before a branching, network system of veins became available, so a broad leaf had to be made from a close fan of radiating veins. Like the most primitive conifers, it has the sexes on separate trees, but it has one slightly advanced feature – it sheds its leaves in winter. In the early or middle fall they turn bright pale yellow, then rich gold and some may be pale orange before falling. In PA, it is claimed that female trees (as in the Morris Arboretum near Philadelphia) bear long, low, sinuous branches and the males are slender and tall. Since the tree lines streets in large numbers, the planting of females would block the traffic. Yet elsewhere males and females stand side by side the same shape.

Crown shape is widely various regardless of sex or location, although in hot, dry areas trees tend to be slender, with few branches, and in cool, wetter areas many have dense hemispheric crowns of long, rising branches. The fruit is abundant on female treews in most areas and this does make their use in streets undesirable, for the fruit not only tread into a messy pulp but rot with a singularly foul smell. It is paradoxical that the most primitive plant on earth should be the one most adapted to growing in the most extreme modern environment. From Montreal to New Orleans the Ginkgo is a downtown tree and the taller and closer the skyscrapers the more it dominates. In Manhattan there are places where only the Ginkgo and the Honeylocust seem able to survive. Older and bigger trees are in big gardens from MA to AR and MO and WI with few in the Prairie States and Rocky Mountains and rather few in CA and OR but more again in WA. Among the oldest and finest are one planted in 1817 at Longwood Gardens, PA, 128ft x 13ft 10in in 1987, and one dating from 1830 at Vanderbilt Mansion, Hudson Valley, NY, 92ft x 14ft in 1976.

The 'Sentry' ginkgo (4) is much more restricted in distribution and outside NY and PA it is quite scarce. It is a male form selected for its neat, narrow crown and can be raised from cuttings but is probably usually a graft on an ordinary seedling Ginkgo. In Philadelphia it is common, for example along the Roosevelt Boulevard and in Fairmount Park, while a line at the airport stands in gaps in the entrance canopy. There is a fine group in Pitt Park, Pittsburg. In NY there is an avenue in Brooklyn Botanic Garden and many trees in Central Park. There are a few around DC and in Williamsburg, VA. To the west, there are several in Garfield Park, Chicago, IL, two in the Boerner Botanic Garden, WI and a big one in Forest Park, St. Louis, MO.

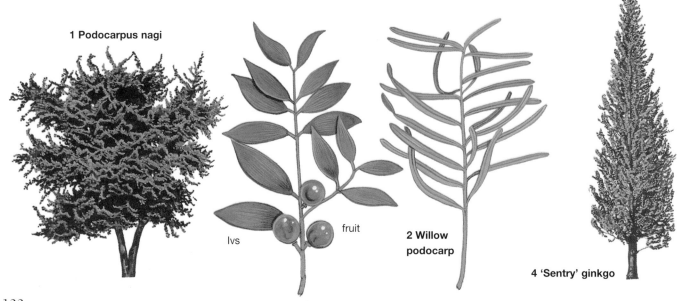

1 Podocarpus nagi

lvs

fruit

2 Willow podocarp

4 'Sentry' ginkgo

♂ catkins emerging

3 Maidenhair tree

♀ flws

leaf from old, weak shoot

3 Maidenhair tree

4 'Sentry' ginkgo

tree in autumn

Yews

The Yews are the only widespread trees in a very primitive Order of conifers separated from the others, together with the Torreyas and Plum-yews or Cowtail pines. There are ten yews across the northern temperate regions from Japan to Honduras all rather similar and only two, the European and the Japanese, exceed 60ft in their home range while several are low shrubs. They tolerate heavier shading than almost any other tree and the most scanty soil among rocks, but must be in a moist place. The timber is extraordinarily hard, strong and durable, although, being that of a conifer, it is classed technically as a 'softwood'. Growth is soon slow, then very slow until almost imperceptible, so very old trees are of no great size and the strength of the timber holds the tree together long after the trunk is very hollow, so it is a very long-lived tree. All parts of the tree except the sweet red flesh of the 'berry' contain a powerful poisonous alkaloid, taxine, including the large seed, which must therefore be ejected by anyone enjoying the pleasantly edible fruit.

PACIFIC YEW (1), *Taxus brevifolia* grows in the shade in damp woods from around Prince Rupert, BC and AK in a broad belt along the Pacific Slopes to mid-CA in the Sierra Nevada and in another from interior south BC to MT and ID. Its leaves are about ½in long. In the interior areas it is only shrubby but in coastal BC, WA and OR it can exceed 50ft.

ENGLISH YEW (2), *Taxus baccata* grows from southern Scandinavia to North Africa and the Caspian Sea and is the biggest of the yews. In England some are 90ft tall and many in old churchyards are 30ft and more round. These big ones far pre-date the Norman churches and the Saxon ones that these often replaced, and Christianity. The churches were to take advantage of the shelter of the tree which had been the meeting place on holy ground a thousand years before. The biggest are nearly all hollow; a few have seedling trees growing up within. This yew is planted in towns and gardens and often clipped into a hedge from Montreal, PQ through New England, NY and PA to DC and west through OH and IL to WI and, more rarely south to TN where it is common in the residential districts of Memphis. It is very common and quite tall in Salem, MA, particularly. It is the shrub along the median in Rock Creek Parkway, Washington, DC and seems to be in every town in OH. In the west there are plants in Salt Lake City, UT and in Victoria, BC but it is scarce. One in Forest Park, Everett, WA is 5ft 3m round and it is seen in Tillamook, OR and Sacramento, CA. From long cultivation in Europe, many forms have arisen many of which are in collections specialising in them, in ON, NY, PA and OH particularly, and a few are shown here.

The **Irish yew (3)**, **'Fastigiata'** was found in Northern Ireland by 1770 and is a female form with the leaves in whorls around the vertical shoots. Curiously, it is very scarce in the east and common in the west. There are trees in the Tyler Arboretum, Lima and in Mill Creek Center, Youngstown, PA; at Planting Fields, NY and in Newcastle, DE. But it is a common town and garden plant on Vancouver Island, around Vancouver City, through Seattle, WA and the coast through OR and CA, infrequent in the south but with an avenue in Sacramento and trees in Monterey, Union Square, San Francisco and Paso Robles, and also in UT in Salt Lake City. The **Golden Irish yew (4)**, **'Fastigiata Aurea'** is seen in Honeyman and South Bend, OR. In 1777 a yew was bought at the door by a John Dovaston to plant by his house in **West Felton (5)**, England where it now is 12ft 3in round. Its peculiarity was to grow long, level branches from which the shoots hung in lines. It can be a male like the original, or a female from one branchsport, and make a handsome spreading tree. It is in the New York Botanic Garden, and some other collections. The **Yellow-berried yew (6)**, **'Fructu-luteo'** arose in Ireland before 1800 and might be found in any collection of yews.

CHINESE YEW (7), *Taxus sumatrana* is found across Eastern Asia from Assam, India and China to Indonesia and Taiwan. If the populations are taken to be a single species, as they are by John Silba, taxonomist of New York, that is the correct botanical name where previously this has been taken to be separable as *Taxus chinensis* or one with *Taxus celebica*. A broad bushy tree with an open crown and sparse foliage, this may also be in a few collections.

JAPANESE YEW (8), *Taxus cuspidata* is hardier than the English yew and so is planted more, it is said, than that species in the cold regions. In fact it is little seen, unlike the English yew, north of NY or west of Chicago, where the dwarf form, **'Nana'**, is clipped into a hedge. A broad, 26ft tree is by the office in the Bayard Cutting Arboretum on Long Island, NY. There is one in the George Landis Arboretum at Esperance, NY and one in the Lyndale Park near Minneapolis, MN, and many in NJ and PA. The bark is dark purple-brown and the fruit are more numerous, bunched and slightly larger than in the English yew. It makes a broad, low tree and has golden-tawny color on the underside of the more raised, stiffer abruptly short-spined leaves. This species has yielded several variant forms, mostly in the USA. **'Adpressa' (9)** arose in a nursery in Chester, England in 1838 and makes an attractively foliaged tree spreading widely from a central stem. The golden form **'Aurea' (10)** is more bushy and is one of the best conifers for winter color.

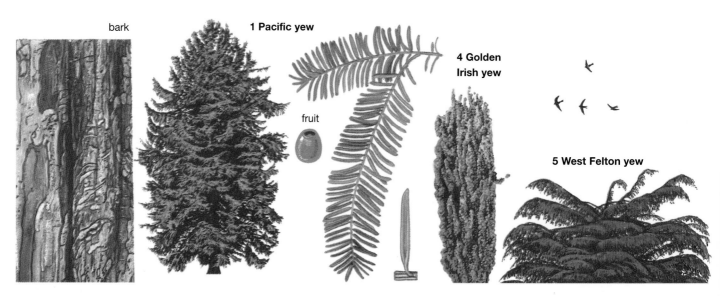

bark

1 Pacific yew

fruit

4 Golden Irish yew

5 West Felton yew

♀ flws

10 'Aurea'

♂ flws

6 Yellow-berried yew

7 Chinese yew

9 'Adpressa Variegata'

♂ flws

8 Japanese yew

9 'Adpressa'

2 English yew

2 English yew

3 Irish yew

♂ flws

Torreyas and Monkey puzzles

The Torreyas or Nutmeg trees are in the Yew Family and Order, and are a typical element of the old Tertiary Age flora once worldwide and now surviving only in North America and Eastern Asia. There are 5 species, one in California, one only just hanging on by one river in FL and GA, two in China and one in Japan. In Torreyas, the fleshy aril growing up around the seed, which in Yews is thick, scarlet and forms a deep cup, is thin, encloses the seed completely and ripens dark purple. The trees are aromatic with an oily, sage-like scent. The Araucarias, Monkey puzzles or Chile pines are a southern hemisphere primitive group now found in South America, Australasia, and Oceania. They have whorled branches on stout, nearly cylindric bales, and leaves hard, often spine-tipped and large and leathery, or small and scale-like. The cones are large, globular and spiny and normally on separate trees from the thick, drooping male catkins. Of the 19 species, 14 are found only on the Island of New Caledonia in Oceania.

CALIFORNIA TORREYA (1), *Torreya californica* is found in two separated areas, one near the coast from Mendocino to the Santa Cruz Mountains, in little canyons running down to the sea, as near Parlins Fork, and the other along the lower foothills of the Sierra Nevada from Eldorado to Tulare Counties and seen by US 49 around Mariposa and Rt 140 to El Portal. It is rarely planted, but there is one 55ft tall in Beacon Hill Park, Victoria, BC and south of the range, in Sorter Park, Sacramento, 40ft tall and one in Paso Robles, CA. In the east it is very rare indeed, with one in Fairmount Park, Philadelphia, PA.

FLORIDA TORREYA, *Torreya taxifolia* has narrower leaves, richer green and lacking the pale margins and has its own Torreya State Park at Rock Bluff by the Apalachicola River in FL and a few trees grow from there upstream into GA but it is plagued by disease. It is planted in Tallahassee and there are trees in the Henry Foundation garden at Gladwyne, PA and the National Arboretum in Washington, DC.

JAPANESE TORREYA (2), *Torreya nucifera* has smaller foliage and is seen in the Bailey Arboretum, Locust Valley, NY, 50ft x 6ft at Swarthmore College, PA and other arboreta.

MONKEY PUZZLE (3), *Araucaria araucana* from the Andes on the border between Chile and Argentina was brought to Kew, England in 1795 by Archibald Menzies who took five nuts from the dessert at a banquet in Valparaiso, Chile, and raised them in pots on the way home. It is the hardiest of the family but in North America it is barely hardy in the northeast, where the only trees are a small planting said to survive on Long Island, NY. Further south the summers are too hot, but it is well suited to the west coast where it is common in BC, the Olympic Peninsula and coastal WA becoming less frequent through OR to mid-CA. There is a fine male tree in Nanaimo on Vancouver Island and trees in all the big parks and gardens from Sidney to Victoria and around Vancouver. There are many around Seattle and Tacoma and one in Olympia is 60ft x 6ft. It is seen along the coast at Raymond and Long Beach, WA and at Reedsport and Florence, OR into CA at Orick, Philo and Yachata and in the Golden Gate Park, San Francisco. This is one of the few conifers to grow sprouts from the roots, near the base of the trunk, which in old trees resembles an elephant's foot.

BUNYA-BUNYA PINE (4), *Araucaria bidwillii*, from Queensland, Australia, is a monkey puzzle with a more open, broader crown from which grayer shoots are nearly pendulous. There are some in FL from Lakeland southwards but it looks much more happy in southern and mid-CA. One in the Capitol Park, Sacramento is 135ft x 10ft 5in. There is a fine tree in the middle of Berkeley and a few in San Francisco and more around Monterey, Los Gatos and Ventura, a good 50ft tree in Paso Robles and some around Los Angeles.

NORFOLK ISLAND PINE (5), *Araucaria heterophylla* is grown in the same areas. It comes only from Norfolk Island, north of New Zealand, and is widely grown in the subtropics. In the city square of Jalapa, Mexico, one is 150ft x 11ft. In FL it is growing in Miami, Sebring and Lakeland but is not very big. Unlike the Bunya-bunya, it is also in LA being frequent in the Gardens District of New Orleans and in Audubon Park. In CA it is frequent from San Diego and La Jolla around Los Angeles with indifferent specimens in Ventura, but better trees northwards in Monterey, Hollister, Santa Cruz and San Francisco.

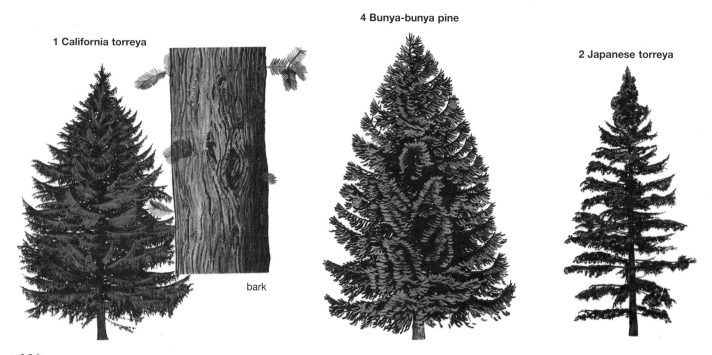

1 California torreya

bark

4 Bunya-bunya pine

2 Japanese torreya

♂ flws

♀ flws

3 Monkey puzzle

seed

cone

2 Japanese torreya

1 California torreya

♂ flws

3 Monkey puzzle

4 Bunya-bunya pine

5 Norfolk Island pine

juvenile foliage

5 Norfolk Island pine

3 Monkey puzzle young

seedling

False cypresses

MONTEREY CYPRESS (1), *Cupressus macrocarpa* grows wild only in two little patches of low cliffs, one each side of Carmel, near Monterey, CA. The southern grove, Point Lobos, is slowly spreading south past the parking-lot as young trees of bizarre shapes with long slender branches at flat angles densely and closely covered in foliage so that each looks like a thick rope. Trees planted south through Big Sur and Lucia hold many such ropes nearly vertical and one a few miles north at Fisherman's Wharf, Monterey is a 40ft spike from a platform of spreading branches. Yet outside this area, the trees planted are of conventional shapes and the more recent plantings near the sea to San Diego are slender, conic trees. There are a few by the coasts of OR and WA and good, tall slender trees by the harbor at Sidney, Vancouver Island, BC. Trees are seen inland as far as Hollister, Los Gatos, Saratoga and Ben Lomond, in the south and Cloverdale and Orick in north CA. The foliage has a sweet lemon-verbena scent when crushed.

ARIZONA CYPRESS (2), *Cupressus arizonica* is a rare and local tree in the Chisos Mountains of west TX, Cook's Peak in NM and nearby mountains in AZ. It seems not to have been planted. The bark is much ridged and fissured, unlike that of the **Arizona smooth cypress (3)**, var. *glabra* in which it is smooth and dark purple at first, then big flakes fall to leave pale yellow and dark red patches. In the wild in Oak Creek Canyon and nearby parts of AZ it is brown, flaking and stripping. Planted in Central Valley, CA, it has numerous, long level lower branches and a slender spire above, but in the eastern states, where it is infrequent but seen in gardens on the Coastal Plain from DC southwards, it forms an upright, neatly ovoid crown. It is planted in Las Vegas, NV and at Bishop, CA but is mainly in shelterbelts in the Central Valley and in gardens through southern CA. The foliage is variable speckled with white resin-spots and gives the scent of grapefruit when crushed. A selection, **'Pyramidalis' (4)**, has more upright shoots and white spots.

GOWEN CYPRESS (5), *Cupressus goveniana* is even more rare and restricted than the Monterey species and is found very near it, in two tiny groves near Carmel, CA. They make spiky trees with a few wandering slender branches. The foliage, in short, rectangular sprays, has a richly aromatic scent. The **Mendocino cypress**, var. *pigmaea* is the form found on the White Plains in the Pygmy Forest. It was named from the little trees common among the dwarfed Shore pine, Coast redwood and Douglas firs in this extremely inhospitable soil.

TECATE CYPRESS (6), *Cupressus guadalupensis* var. *forbesii* is the form of Guadalupe cypress found on a few mountains in Orange and San Diego counties, CA and on Mount Tecate on the Mexican border. Its very rapid healthy growth in cultivation inland encouraged some planting in shelterbelts and gardens in southern CA.

BAKER CYPRESS, *Cupressus bakeri*, Modoc or Siskiyou cypress, is native to southwest OR and north CA. It is planted in roadside gardens south across Mendocino County but a tree as good as any is in NY, perhaps the only one in the eastern states, at the Castle Garden Center, Highland Park, Rochester. The fine shoots are thickly speckled white and when crushed give the scent of sage, or cigars.

MACNAB CYPRESS (7), *Cupressus macnabiana* is the only American true cypress that has a normal sort of range and is not confined to a couple of tiny groves or a few mountainsides. It is found along the Sierra Nevada at around 2500ft, in the Shasta region and on the inner northern Coast Ranges. The foliage gives a scent of camphor mixed with sage, and is more in flattened sprays than in other American true cypresses.

ITALIAN CYPRESS (8), *Cupressus sempervirens* has foliage and cones very like the Monterey cypress but the crown is very different, being slender, columnar with a conic top, darker, with upswept minor shoots which are nearly scentless when crushed. This is a favourite tree for planting one each side of the front door, especially in NC and TN. It is more frequent in New Orleans and west LA into TX as far as Dallas. It is common in Las Vegas, NV and in much of southern CA.

INCENSE CEDAR (9), *Calocedrus decurrens* is related most closely to the Western red cedar and grows the same conic, level-branched shape over much of its range from mid-OR through CA. Planted further north, it has more upright branching and one in Point Defiance Park, Tacoma, WA, 95ft x 13ft, has huge, steeply ascending branches. In the east, where it is planted at Winterthur, DE, Longwood, PA in Princeton, NJ and some gardens in OH, it is narrowly columnar and tightly upright. One exception is a remarkable tree in the Coker Arboretum, NC which is conic with level branches drooping at their tips. In Merced Grove, CA one is 170ft x 16ft 3in and one near the 'General Grant' Giant sequoia, is 150ft x 14ft. On the CA side of Lake Tahoe, trunks of Incense cedar are as rich red as redwoods. There are a few big trees in Reno, NV.

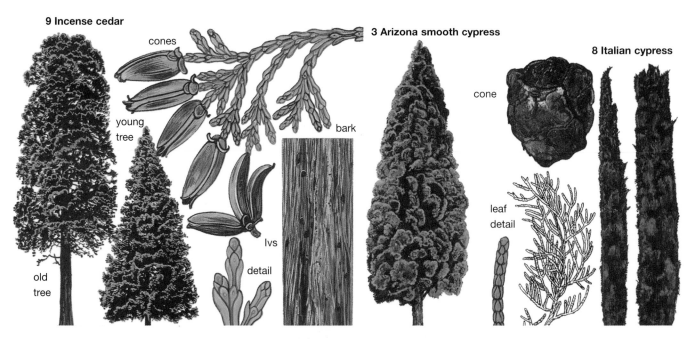

9 Incense cedar — cones — young tree — bark — lvs detail — old tree

3 Arizona smooth cypress — cone

8 Italian cypress — leaf detail

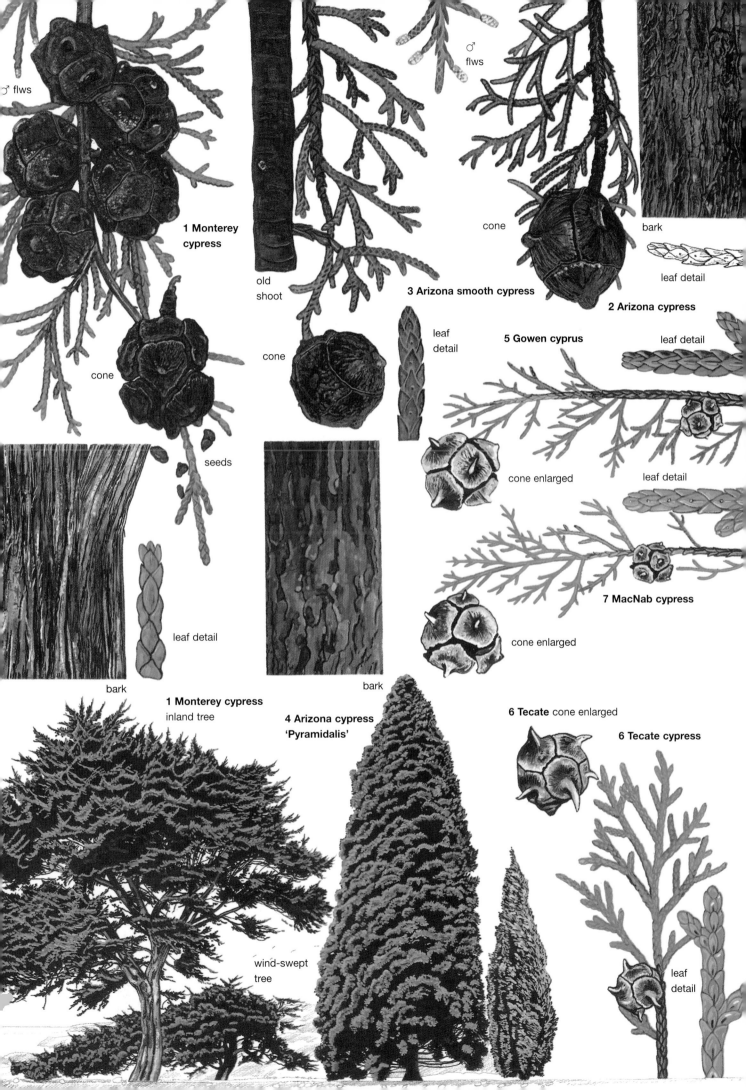

♂ flws

1 Monterey cypress

old shoot

cone

seeds

cone

leaf detail

♂ flws

cone

bark

leaf detail

3 Arizona smooth cypress

2 Arizona cypress

5 Gowen cyprus

leaf detail

leaf detail

cone enlarged

leaf detail

cone enlarged

7 MacNab cypress

bark

bark

1 Monterey cypress
inland tree

**4 Arizona cypress
'Pyramidalis'**

6 Tecate cone enlarged

6 Tecate cypress

leaf detail

wind-swept tree

True cypresses and Incense cedar

The cypresses are of two general kinds, the 'True cypresses' and the 'False cypresses'. The early European botanists knew only the cypresses with big cones and with the small shoots making bunches, so the genus *Cupressus* was founded on those. The cypresses with small cones and foliage in flattened sprays are found only in North America and eastern Asia. When it was decided to put them in a genus of their own, a new name had to be coined; this is *Chamaecyparis*, 'False' or 'Dwarf' cypress.

ATLANTIC WHITE CEDAR (1), *Chamaecyparis thyoides* has the most finely divided foliage of them all, in flattened sprays held in dense, upcurved bunches. When crushed, these have a gingery scent. It is a tree of swampy bottomlands from ME to NC and from northwest FL to southern MS. The bark is dark brown separating into layers of long strips, often in a spiral.

ALASKA CEDAR or **NOOTKA CYPRESS (2)**, *Chamaecyparis nootkatensis* has hard, thick foliage which is hanging and dark, relieved only through the winter and spring by an abundance of pale yellow male flowers. The fine points on the scale leaf tips are stiff and make it difficult to rub the foliage the wrong way. Crushed foliage has an oily, rather unpleasant turpentine scent. A feature of the tree is its unfailingly regular conic crown, in the wild and in cultivation. The crown is open inside with curtains of foliage hanging on the outside, and in thinly foliaged, old or sickly trees it is transparent. In the wild, the tree is more pendulous than it is when grown in other parts, and also broader. The tree is native from the Anchorage area in AK along the coast and islands to the Puget Sound area of BC and then takes to the hills in the Olympic Mountains and Cascades of WA and OR to the Siskiyou Mountains where it is just in CA. It is rarely planted in the west. In the east it is planted in many northern collections in ON, NY and NJ and, although growth is poor, in OH. The **Weeping Alaska cedar (3)**, **'Pendula'** has sharply raised branches from which the foliage hangs in curtains.

HINOKI CYPRESS (4), *Chamaecyparis obtusa* is one of the two Japanese species of false cypress and has foliage bright green above and strongly patterned blue-white beneath. It is common in town gardens only in Newport, RI and in the Main Line area of Philadelphia, PA. In Fairmount Park there, it is 50ft tall; at Planting Fields, NY, it is 60ft and at Winterthur, DE it is 55ft x 5ft. The **Golden hinoki (4), 'Crippsii'** is a squat, conic tree as bright a gold as a tree can be, which arose in 1900 in Kent, England. There is a prominent planting by Rt 9 at Stony Point, NY

and it is frequent in Newport, RI and Washington, DC. It is in big gardens in NY, ON and OH; more rarely and south into NC. In the west it is sometimes seen in WA.

The **Fern cypress (5), 'Filicoides'** hangs long, flat sprays from a gaunt crown in the Bailey Arboretum, NY. The **Club-moss cypress (6), 'Lycopodioides'** has congested, upright tufts showing much blue underside. **'Tetragona Aurea' (7)** from Japan in 1873, grows slowly into a 35ft tall column, green in the interior, bright gold outside. It is in Winterthur Garden, DE; Planting Fields, NY and in a few gardens in WA.

SAWARA CYPRESS (8), *Chamaecyparis pisifera* is the other Japanese species and bears masses of cones like small, crinkled peas, hence 'pisifera', pea-bearing. It is common in DC, in Baltimore, MD and in the Hudson Valley, NY where one at Vanderbilt Mansion is 85ft x 6ft. There are 70ft trees in Marquand Park, Princeton, NJ and one 80ft x 6ft by the Speer Library. **'Filifera'** and **'Filifera Aurea' (9)** are frequent in New England, NY, ON and OH, often broad and bushy but thinly crowned, occasionally tall and slender. **'Plumosa' (10)** and **'Plumosa Aurea'** are frequent town-garden trees from ON to DC and OH and around Vancouver, BC and in WA. The green form is commonly seen around Washington, DC and Philadelphia, PA partially reverted to the flat-foliaged type and partially intermediate. The **Moss cypress (11), 'Squarrosa'** is a juvenile form with bright chestnut-red bark, infrequent in small town gardens from ON to DE and more frequent south in lowland VA and NC. It is common around Vancouver and scarce in OR with one at Glide, and there is one in Scotia, CA. Trees over 70ft tall are in the Cutting Arboretum, NY, 85ft in Winterthur, DE, and one 60ft x 10ft is in Olympia, WA.

LEYLAND CYPRESS (12), × *Cupressocyparis leylandii* is a cross between the Alaska cedar and the Monterey cypress with a total of 12 separable seedlings. One of them has flat, frondlike sprays like Alaska cedar, **'Leighton Green' (13)** from Wales in 1911, picked from a Monterey cypress. Another is **'Haggerston Gray' (14)** from the Nootka cypress, which has branches of gray foliage in several planes. There are Leyland cypresses in the botanic gardens in BC and in CA, where the rare blue-foliaged one **'Naylor's Blue' (15)**, also of 1911 origin, is 50ft in the Strybing and 56ft x 3ft in the Huntington Gardens, CA. Two Northern Irish forms are both golden, **'Castlewellan Gold' (16)**, a primrose yellow-tipped foliage turning orange in winter, and **'Robinson's Gold' (17)**, flat-foliaged brighter yellow.

4 Hinoki cypress

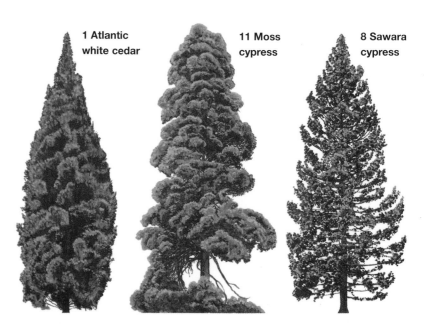

1 Atlantic white cedar

11 Moss cypress

8 Sawara cypress

4 Hinoki cypress

cone enlarged

5 Fern cypress

11 'Squarrosa'

7 'Tetragona Aurea'

6 Club-moss cypress

10 'Plumosa'

9 'Filifera Aurea'

4 Golden hinoki

Formosan cypress

8 Sawara cypress

cones

2 Nootka cypress

cone

2 Alaska cedar bark

2 Alaska cedar

3 Weeping Alaska cedar

16 'Castlewellan Gold'

17 'Robinson's Gold'

1 Atlantic white cedar

14 'Haggerston Gray'

bark

13 'Leighton Green'

15 'Naylor's Blue'

14 'Haggerston Gray'

Port Orford cedar and forms

PORT ORFORD CEDAR or **LAWSON CYPRESS (1)**, *Chamaecyparis lawsoniana* is one of the flat-foliaged, small-coned cypresses in the group often called the 'false cypresses'. The generic name *Chamaecyparis* is derived from the name for a low shrub, the cotton-lavender, which has cypress-like foliage, and *Chamae-* 'dwarf', so the group is also called the 'dwarf cypresses'. No member of it makes this name for the group less appropriate than does the Port Orford cedar. In the early days after its discovery, trees were found 200ft tall. John Jeffrey discovered it in 1851 when he was working for the Oregon Society, founded by Scottish landowners for the purpose of obtaining more seeds of the trees first sent by David Douglas between 1826 and 1833 and to find more.

The Port Orford cedar was first collected in quantity by William Murray in 1854. He sold the seed to the Edinburgh nurseryman Peter Lawson, who sent out the first plants and after whom the tree was named '*lawsoniana*'. Murray found the tree in the inland outlier from its main range, in groves between the Trinity River and the Upper Sacramento River in the Trinity Mountains. The main population was from Coos Bay, OR near the coast to Mad River, CA, near Arcata, and inland in the Klamath and Siskiyou Mountains in OR and CA. Disastrous fires in early days and, in 1936 at Camp Hill, OR together with intensive logging in the limited stands of pure woods reduced its occurrence to scattered old timber and larger areas of second growth. There was a large trade to China and Japan in timber for coffins, and it was the choicest timber for quality yachts, Venetian blind slats, batteries and clothes chests.

Today some big trees remain among other conifers in small areas, like some 140ft tall among Brewer spruce and others on Bear Ridge, CA at 5000ft, above Gasquet, and second growth is common along US 101 in many places from del Norte, CA to near Dune City, 24 miles north of Coos Bay, OR. Between Bandon and Port Orford where the highway has recently been widened, new banks and ditches are covered in seedlings. The range has been extended by planting relatively little southward; a tree here and there, in Sacramento and Berkeley and one at Big Sur, but greatly in the north. It is common in coastal WA and abounds in Vancouver and Victoria, BC, inland at least to Oliver. In the east, a tree in Highland Park, NY, is one of the very few north of DC where there are many in parks and cemeteries and a few in TN and GA but many of these are bushy garden forms. They can all be told from any similarly shaped forms of the two Japanese species by the scent of the crushed foliage. In all Port Orford cedar forms this is, at the first sniff, like parsley, then more resinous. It is extraordinary that this cypress, so uniform in shape and dark yellowish green color in the wild, with only an occasional roadside seedling blue-gray, has rapidly become in cultivation in Europe by far the most variable conifer in the world. One of the seedlings from the first seed arose in 1855 in Surrey, England, as the tightly erect, bright green **'Erecta Viridis' (2)**, now common in Vancouver, BC and through Sedro Wolley, Snohomish, Everett, Seattle, and Tacoma to Raymond and Adria, WA. It grows into a big tree and becomes very untidy as wet snow bends branches out permanently to ruin the shape until they are cut out.

In 1869, Lawson's Nurseries raised **'Intertexta' (3)**, a slender column of hanging, curiously open, sparsely divided, hard, dark foliage. It is slow at first, raised as a cutting, then grows fast to over 80ft, although the one in the Queen Elizabeth Gardens, Vancouver, is young yet. In British and Dutch nurseries a stream of new forms arose, until it seemed that every nursery had its own named form. There are some 230 named, fully distinct forms now and more added every year, dwarf, medium, big, gold, gray, blue, every shade of green, thread-foliaged, tufted, juvenile, erect, pendulous or spreading.

The first good gold was **'Lutea' (4)** from London in 1870. It is slender-conic with pendulous outer shoots and is commonest in Victoria, BC and frequent through Seattle and Tacoma to Raymond, WA. A very different golden form **'Stewartii' (5)** arose in Hampshire, England, a sturdy, conic tree with long, fernlike sprays of golden shoots slightly downwards from each side of the main shoot, and a bright green interior. This is grown at Planting Fields, NY in the east and more commonly in the west, in Osyoos, Penticton, Vancouver and Victoria in BC, and around Seattle in WA.

Around 1880, the erect, gray-blue **'Allumii' (6)** arose in England. It is at Olympia and in gardens between Startup and Sultan in WA; in Revelstoke, BC, and in the east, in the Bailey Arboretum, NY; in Winterthur and at Christiana, DE and in collections in OH. The narrower, brighter blue **'Columnaris' (7)** arose in Holland in 1940 and the big-growing **'Triumph of Boskoop' (8)** from Holland, a broad cone growing faster than the wild type.

'Wisselii' (9) from Holland in 1886, with brilliant masses of crimson male flowers, is in the big gardens in BC and WA. **'Fletcheri' (10)** from Surrey, England in 1911, has fluffy, juvenile foliage and is common by the coast from BC to South Bend, OR. **'Ellwoodii' (11)** from Hampshire is tighter erect, grayer and with larger adult foliage. It is in the University of Wisconsin Arboretum. **'Pottenii' (12)** from Kent, England, is a soft green, flame-shaped tree to 50ft. **'Green spire' (13)** is a much improved **'Erecta Viridis'**. **'Fraseri' (14)** is a grayer, less strictly upright **'Allumii'** from England by 1891. The very finely divided pale green foliage of **'Filifera' (15)** is, like the last two, rarely to be seen in America.

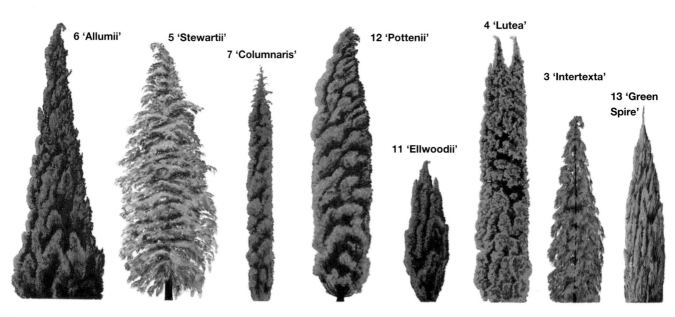

6 'Allumii' 5 'Stewartii' 7 'Columnaris' 12 'Pottenii' 4 'Lutea' 3 'Intertexta' 13 'Green Spire' 11 'Ellwoodii'

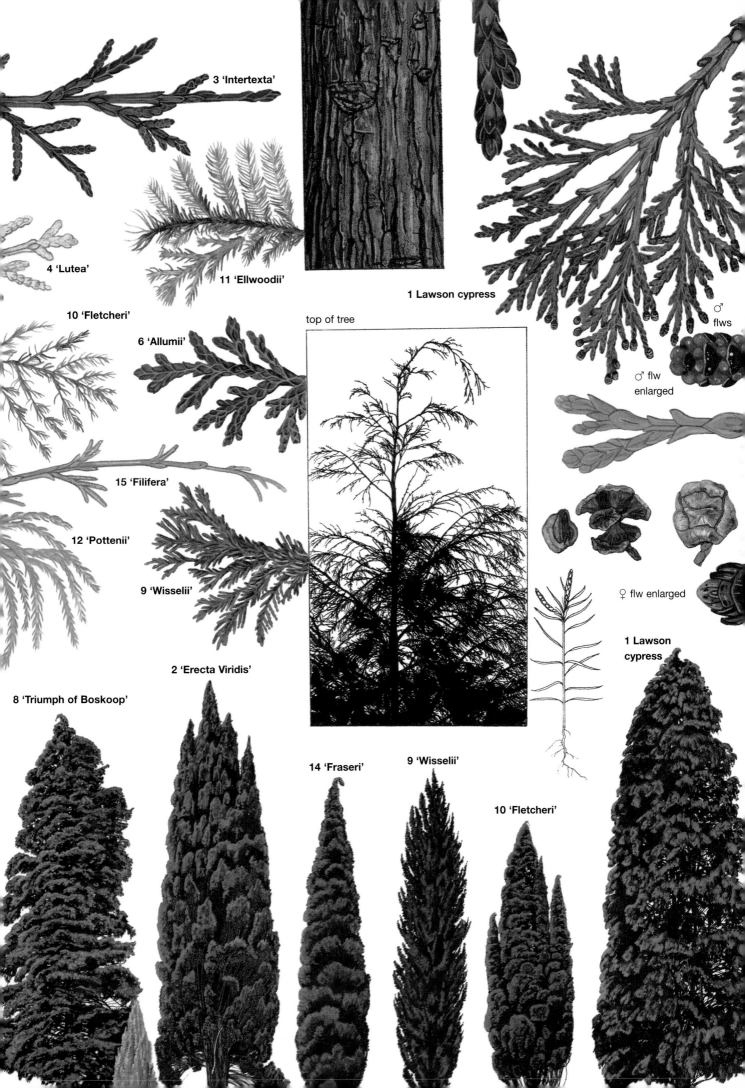

3 'Intertexta'

4 'Lutea'

11 'Ellwoodii'

1 Lawson cypress

♂ flws

♂ flw enlarged

10 'Fletcheri'

6 'Allumii'

top of tree

15 'Filifera'

12 'Pottenii'

♀ flw enlarged

9 'Wisselii'

1 Lawson cypress

2 'Erecta Viridis'

8 'Triumph of Boskoop'

14 'Fraseri'

9 'Wisselii'

10 'Fletcheri'

Junipers

COMMON JUNIPER (1), *Juniperus communis* is the most widespread tree species in the world, and its low scrubby forms range the furthest north. It grows from Alaska, Greenland and Iceland across Europe and Asia to the Bering Sea and south in America to the Olympic Mountains, Sierra Nevada, AZ and NM and in the east to NC. In America it is a low shrub except in a few eastern locations where it can be 15ft tall. The **Irish juniper (2), 'Hibernica'**, is seen in some parks and small town gardens from ON, MA and NY to MD, PA and OH and in the west, on Vancouver Island, BC. The **Swedish juniper (3), 'Suecica'** differs only in the shoot tips curving sharply out.

EASTERN RED CEDAR (4), *Juniperus virginiana* is the common juniper of the eastern half of North America from ME to TX and SD. Older trees are common from MN to SC in pairs by cemetery gates and in front of rural houses, and in shelterbelts in SD and NE. The bark peels in brown strips from the fluted trunk. Spiny little juvenile leaves radiate from the terminal inch of weak shoots of adult scale-foliage and from the base of stronger shoots. Male and female flowers are on separate trees and female trees can be blue-white in summer from the abundance of the bloomed little fruit, which ripen more purple in the one season. There is great variation from dark green to pale blue-green in the foliage, but a distinct form, **'Glauca' (5)** with a narrow, upswept crown of gray-blue and white, mostly adult foliage is in some gardens, notably in MN and NE.

ROCKY MOUNTAIN JUNIPER (6), *Juniperus scopulorum* takes over westward where the Eastern red cedar leaves off, but was separated in 1897 only because the male flower has six stamens instead of 12. This is rarely possible to see but there is a wide gap between the ranges east of the Rocky foothills so location is the key. Further west it is common from AB to WA, WY and CO where it is much planted in towns.

WESTERN JUNIPER (7), *Juniperus occidentalis* is frequent from WA to the southern cross-ranges, CA on dry hillsides usually as a slender, thinly branched tree growing under ponderosa pine. On the granite of the Sierra Nevada, however, some huge, low trees stand out with orange bark on short massive boles, known up to 43ft round and probably 3000 years old. The crushed foliage gives a scent of sage and turpentine.

UTAH JUNIPER (8), *Juniperus osteosperma* is a common desert tree seen for miles as little candelabra-shaped trees, none above 20ft tall from WY and UT through NV to CA and AZ around the Grand Canyon. The bark is gray-brown spiral strips and the foliage is thick and rounded.

ONE-SEED JUNIPER (9), *Juniperus monosperma* is similar to and replaces the Utah juniper in east AZ, NM, CO and west TX. It differs in the fruit retaining its blue bloom where the Utah fruit becomes red-brown, and containing a single large seed. This is used in the Pueblo necklaces sold in Sedona, AZ.

ALLIGATOR JUNIPER (10), *Juniperus deppeana* is easily known by its bright blue-gray foliage and by its bark. It ranges from southwest TX to Guatemala, where the bark is dove-gray.

DROOPING JUNIPER (11), *Juniperus flaccida* is also a mainly Mexican tree, extending into the Chisos Mountains of west TX, at 6–8000ft. Its foliage hangs in long sprays unlike any other American juniper.

MEYER'S BLUE JUNIPER (12), *Juniperus squamata* 'Meyeri' is a Chinese garden selection of a variable juniper, brought to the USA by F.N. Meyer in 1910. It grows fast for a juniper, spreading out long arms in irregular low fans, but begins as a shapely little conic plant. It has pink-brown bark adhering in papery flakes and the interior crown holds much dead, pink-brown leafage. It is most frequent in Victoria, BC in large and small gardens, and from Vancouver through Seattle to Tacoma and Merilo, WA. In the east it is rare except in OH.

CHINESE JUNIPER (13), *Juniperus chinensis* from China and Japan, differs from the Eastern red cedar chiefly in the fruit being twice as big, the juvenile foliage harder, more prickly and largely at the base of the shoot, not at the tip, and the sour scent of crushed foliage, in place of the fresh paint smell of red cedar. The cultivars are found only in the warmest parts of the USA. The one that is most in the public eye is the **Hollywood juniper (13), 'Kaizuka'** or **'Torulosa'** which was sent from Yokohama in 1920. It is seen against the walls of city buildings commonly in the Bay Area, Salinas, Saratoga and south to San Diego, CA and eastward in Las Vegas, NV, Salt Lake City, UT and Florence, AZ. North of the Bay Area it is scarce as far as Coos Bay, OR and Seattle, WA. In the east it is seen from Brewton and Castleberry, AL and from FL and New Orleans, where there are many, and to Tulsa, OK. It is female and often covered with violet bloomed fruit. **Keteleer's Chinese juniper (14)** is a shapely conic form with dense, almost entirely adult, scale foliage, seen in a few collections. At Morton Arboretum IL it is 35ft tall. The **Golden Chinese juniper (15), 'Aurea'** raised in England in 1855 is rare in North America. A male form, its abundant yellow flowers from August to April enhance its color.

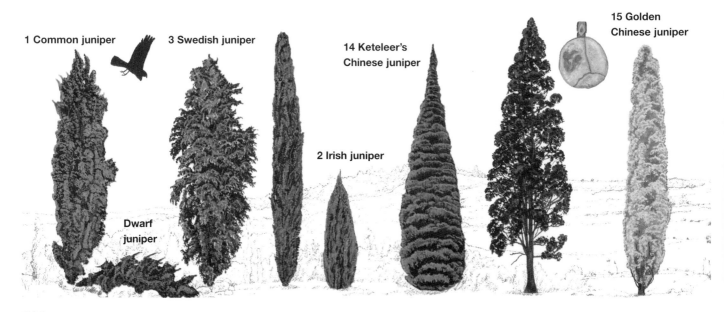

1 Common juniper

3 Swedish juniper

14 Keteleer's Chinese juniper

15 Golden Chinese juniper

2 Irish juniper

Dwarf juniper

Swedish
niper

2 Irish
juniper

13 Chinese
juniper

15 Golden
Chinese
juniper

bark

bark

1 Common juniper

6 Rocky Mountain juniper

7 Western
juniper

12 Meyer's blue juniper

foliage in
3s and 2s

♂ flw

11 Drooping juniper

9 One-seed
juniper

bark

8 Utah
juniper

5 Eastern
red cedar
'Glauca'

10 Alligator juniper

6 Rocky Mountain juniper

7 Western
juniper

4 Eastern
red cedar

13 Hollywood
juniper (right)

10 Alligator
juniper

Western red cedar and Arborvitae

The Thujas or Arborvitae, 'trees of life', have difficulty with their popular names since 'thuja' is not yet in that category. The three commonest in North America, two native and one exotic, are known as White cedar, Red cedar and Arborvitae. None is a true cedar and all are Thujas, members of a small genus divided between North America and Eastern Asia. They are in the Cypress Family and related most closely to the Incense cedar, and similarly resinous and aromatic.

NORTHERN WHITE CEDAR (1), *Thuja occidentalis* received the name 'occidentalis' meaning 'western' in 1753, when it was the only American species known, but it seems odd today, when it is very much the 'eastern' cedar 2000 miles east of the other American species. It is a small and not long-lived tree of swampy ground from the mouth of the St. Lawrence River and Anticosti Island to the shores of James Bay to SK south around Lake Michigan to NY and locally as a smaller tree in the Alleghenies to TN. Its foliage is distinguished by the uniform matt, pale yellow-green underside, the upper side roughened by a raised gland on most of the scale-leaves and a scent, when lightly crushed, of apple. The bark is dull orange-brown, ridged and shredding. The branches leave the stem level or slightly depressed and within a short distance turn sharply upwards.

'Spiralis' (2) is a slender, neat, acute-topped columnar little tree with deep green foliage, bronzing only a little in winter, in short flat sprays arising in spirals around erect shoots. It is said to be of unknown American origin, first described in 1923, but a broken-topped specimen in the Arnold Arboretum, MA, is labelled as dating from 1883.

WESTERN RED CEDAR (3), *Thuja plicata*, 'discovered' by the Malaspina Expedition at Nootka Sound in about 1790, had long been used by the Indians for canoes, houses, utensils and totem-poles. The timber is light, quite strong, but soft and easy to work and with a remarkable resistance to decay in water. Since it splits evenly it is also ideal for shingles, needing no paint, and 80% of shingles used are of this thuja. It grows from Baranoff Island, AK along the coast and western slopes to Mendocino, CA and on the eastern ranges from AB to ID and MT. In the east, it is common in Newport, RI and it is in many large gardens from ON and NY. **Golden-barred thuja (4)**, **'Zebrina'** was raised in England around 1900 and is seen in the west only, commonly in BC and less so in WA, and one each at Orick and Berkeley Campus, CA.

ORIENTAL or **CHINESE ARBORVITAE (5)**, *Thuja orientalis* has its foliage in erect flat sprays and is thus the same color on both sides. It has only the faintest, vague scent when crushed. The cones have a large, hooked beak on about four of the scales and are bloomed blue-white in the summer, and as it cones freely this is often its main feature. It is common each side of the front door on the Coastal Plain from MD to TX and west through NM and AZ to CA and NV. It is scarce north of MD in PA, NY and OH to WI, MT and WA and common in AR, OK, KS and UT. It is also common in cemeteries and small town parks. It was found first in North China before 1750. **'Elegantissima'** (6) bronzes during cold winters and is greenish until the new growth emerges yellow. It is scarce from PA to NC in the east and from BC and MT to CO in the west.

JAPANESE ARBORVITAE (7), *Thuja standishii* has stripping bark with smooth patches of rich dark red, on coarse, lifting plates often in a spiral. Its foliage is hard, rounded in section with new shoots often dusted silver. The underside has narrow gray-white streaks and crushed foliage gives a sweet lemon and eucalyptus scent. This tree is growing in collections from ON to DE and OH. One in the Arnold Arboretum, MA, planted in 1890 was 42ft x 9ft 6in when 86 years old.

KOREAN ARBORVITAE (8), *Thuja koraiensis* is a rare, small, upswept tree with either pale, fresh green or dark blue-gray foliage, brilliantly white beneath and giving, when crushed, a strong scent of rich almond-cake. It is very hardy but slow growing.

HIBA ARBORVITAE (9), *Thujopsis dolabrata* is better known as 'Thujopsis'. This means 'like a thuja' and was coined for the genus of this single species differing in globular cones, instead of the small, flask-shaped leathery ones of Thuja. It also has broad, flat, hard foliage with a pattern of thick white streaks on the underside. The likening of the lateral streaks to the blade of a hatcher, 'dolabra' is the origin of 'dolabrata', which is liable to be erroneously given as 'dolobrata' or 'Weeping'. This small Japanese tree needs cool, moist summers and is nearly confined in America to parks and big gardens in BC and WA, as in Beacon Hill Park, Victoria and Forest Park, Everett, but there is one prominent in Manchester, NH.

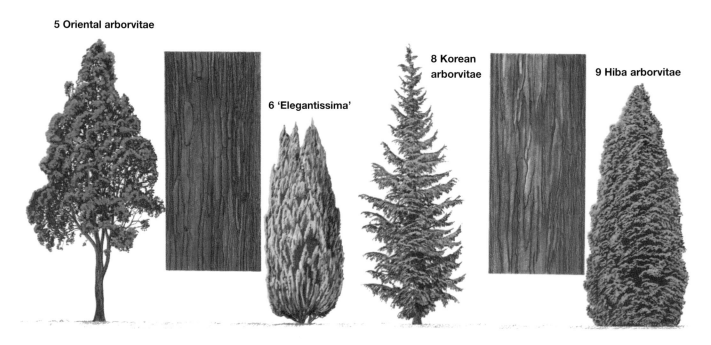

5 Oriental arborvitae

6 'Elegantissima'

8 Korean arborvitae

9 Hiba arborvitae

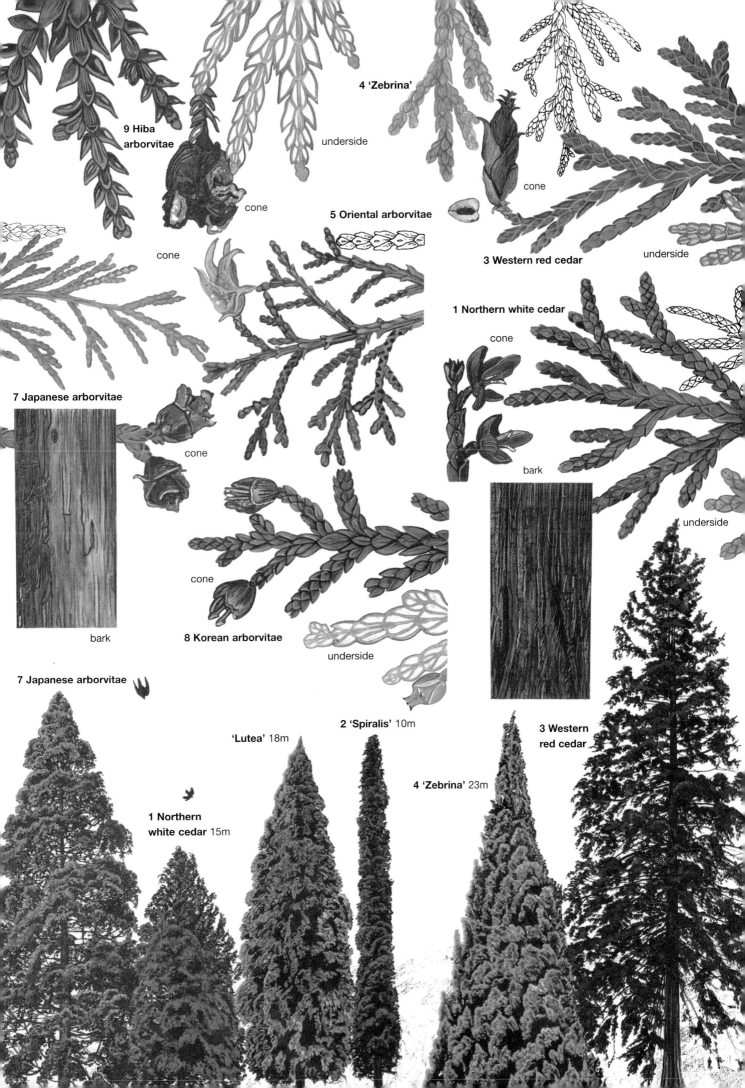

9 Hiba arborvitae

cone

4 'Zebrina'

underside

cone

5 Oriental arborvitae

3 Western red cedar

underside

cone

1 Northern white cedar

cone

7 Japanese arborvitae

cone

bark

cone

8 Korean arborvitae

underside

bark

underside

7 Japanese arborvitae

2 'Spiralis' 10m

'Lutea' 18m

4 'Zebrina' 23m

3 Western red cedar

1 Northern white cedar 15m

Giant Sequoia and Redwood

GIANT SEQUOIA (1), *Sequoiadendron giganteum* is today wild only in the western foothills of the southern half of the Sierra Nevada, CA in 72 groves; many of them having fewer than 20 adult trees, but all now fully protected. In 1852 the most northerly large grove, Calaveras, was discovered by a hunter employed to cater for workers at the goldfields of the 1849 goldrush. The biggest groves are further south, in Sequoia and King's Canyon National Parks. The Giant sequoia is not quite the tallest, biggest in bole nor oldest tree in the world but it is the biggest in volume of timber, with 'General Sherman' **(2)** the champion, and is among the oldest, 'Grizzly Giant' being estimated to be over 3500 years.

It is now known that recurrent fire is necessary for the growth of groves. In these woods, it takes about 25 years of growth of brush and young trees after one fire before there is enough fuel to sustain the next. This is started by lightning and burns briefly, the heat opening the cones, which remain for 30 years with live seed inside. Seedlings grow in the ash-covered, cleared soil with White and Douglas fir which outgrow the Sequoias but the next fire comes while their bark is still thin and resinous so they are mostly killed leaving the already thickly fibrous-barked Sequoias, to grow on. Success in controlling wildfire caused brushwood fuel to increase so that the inevitable eventual fire burned longer and more strongly, causing great damage. Now the Park authorities have instituted a 25-year controlled fire-cycle.

A few of the best specimens, from south to north, measured in 1980–2 are: Sequoia NP, Giant Forest Village, entrance, 'Sentinel', 255ft x 68ft 9in; Round Meadow, 290ft x 75ft 6in 'General Sherman', 290ft x 79ft 10in; Office, 262ft x 59ft; King's Canyon NP, 'General Grant' **(3)**, 255ft x 79ft 10in at 7ft; 'Robert E. Lee', 277ft x 74ft 3in (with burl) 'Oregon Tree', 276ft x 64ft 8in; Yosemite NP., Tuolumne Grove, first tree down loop road, 255ft x 62ft 4in; Merced Grove, log cabin, 282ft x 39ft 5in; below, 260ft x 49ft; Mariposa Grove, (1971) entrance, 240ft x 46ft 3in; 'Grizzly Giant' 205ft x 72ft 4in at 8ft. Outside the natural range the tree is quite common in BC coastal parks and gardens to 120ft x 20ft in Beacon Hill Park, Victoria and through Seattle to Point Defiance Park, Tacoma, WA and sparsely through OR. At Sacramento Capitol, CA one is 125ft x 18ft and there are small trees inland at Exeter, Wasco, Independence and a good row on the southern outskirts of Reno, NV. In the east the only respectable tree is in the Tyler Arboretum, PA, 88ft x 10ft 5in in 1976 and there are bushy ones in the Public Gardens, Boston and the Arnold Arboretum, MA; at the George Landis Arboretum; Brooklyn Botanic Garden and Planting Fields, NY. Better trees are at Prospect House, Princeton, NJ; at Longwood Garden and in Lancaster, PA, Mill Creek Center, Youngstown, OH, and small ones in Washington, DC but few, if any further south.

The **Weeping giant sequoia (4)**, **'Pendulum'** seems to be planted only in the west, in parks and gardens around Victoria and Vancouver, BC and in Point Defiance Park, Tacoma, WA.

COAST REDWOOD (5), *Sequoia sempervirens* is the sea-fog tree of the hills a little back from the coast from a few miles into OR for 550 miles south to beyond Big Sur, CA. In the high rainfall northern parts of this belt, trees over 300ft tall stand in close formation and around Weott there are big woods of trees around 350ft tall and still growing. South of the Bay Area where there is no summer rain, the trees are above 250ft only where the shape of the land holds the sea-fog for the morning as at Big Basin and the Henry Cowell Redwood Park, west of Saratoga. Then the big trees are much further apart. Further south they are confined to sheltered watercourses near the coast as in the Nacimienta Valley and rarely exceed 180ft. The tallest tree in the world is now probably 'Dyerville Giant', 367ft in 1986, since the 'Tallest Tree' by Redwood Creek has died back to 355ft. In Giant Tree Grove, another 'Tallest Tree' was 360ft x 42ft in 1981. Others near Weott are as tall. A far bigger tree is near US 101 a few miles north of Orick in Prairie Creek Grove, which was 315ft x 59ft. By the same road to the south near Benbow a tree by the stores in Richardson Grove is 335ft x 38ft and many beside the 49 miles of Avenue of the Giants are around 310ft x 45ft. One by the track beyond 'Founders' Tree' (345ft x 39ft 2in, 1980) was 360ft x 35ft. In the Henry Cowell Redwoods, 'The Giant' was 270ft x 50ft 6in in 1982 and in the same year in Big Basin, 'Father of the Forest' was 260ft x 53ft and 'Mother of the Forest' was 310ft x 46ft 8in.

This tree is common as a slender, tall tree in gardens around the Los Angeles area, dusty gray-blue in foliage, and occasionally inland in the Central Valley. Northwards it is rare with a small one at Forks, WA. In the east it is very scarce, and one at William and Mary Hall, Williamsburg, VA 95ft tall and a group in Norfolk Botanic Garden, VA are the only large ones. 'Fire trees' are often seen where the trunk was shorn of branches by lightning or fire and has a close cover of green sprouts instead. **'Adpressa' (6)** arose in France around 1865 and makes a slender, sparsely crowned tree with oval leaves bright blue-white.

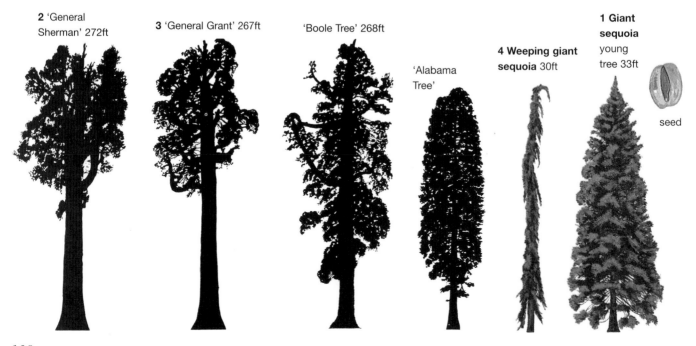

2 'General Sherman' 272ft

3 'General Grant' 267ft

'Boole Tree' 268ft

'Alabama Tree'

4 Weeping giant sequoia 30ft

1 Giant sequoia young tree 33ft

seed

♂ flws

young
cones

underside
of leaves

♂ flws

**1 Giant
sequoia**

mature
cone

mature cone
having shed seed

**5 Coast
redwood**

6 'Adpressa'

seedling

Japanese red cedar and Chinese fir

JAPANESE RED CEDAR (1), *Cryptomeria japonica* is no more a cedar than the many American trees called by that name, but a Redwood most closely related to the Giant sequoia. There is only the one species of Cryptomeria and it occurs also in Yunnan Province in southwest China in a form with more lax, open foliage, var. *sinensis* sometimes called *C. fortunei*. It was this that was brought first to Europe, by Fortune, in 1842 and 1844 but it is the two Japanese forms with the foliage in shorter, more dense bunches which are seen in North America normally, with var. *sinensis* in a few collections like the Bailey Arboretum and New York Botanic Garden, NY.

The Japanese tree is common only in RI at Newport, and in NH at Manchester and along the coast of CT. On low, rocky cliffs here it looks under stress with its foliage yellow. It is frequent in east PA and there are trees in Annapolis, MD, Middletown and Newcastle, DE, as well as in OH on Lake Shore Boulevard, Cleveland; in the Holden Arboretum and Spring Grove Cemetery, Cincinnati. To the south it is very scarce and mainly in botanic gardens in TN and TX, and in Bellingrath Garden, AL. In the west it is also rare, noted in Beacon Hill Park, Victoria, BC; Charles English Garden, Seattle, WA; Sacramento Capitol Park and on the campus at Berkeley, CA. It is a tree that needs cool wet summers for its best growth, and thrives only in some areas of the Pacific Coast. The only big tree of the form **'Lobbii' (2)** is in Point Defiance Park, Tacoma, WA where it was 85ft x 12ft 8in in 1976. This form, with short tufts of foliage and a brush-top, is the common form around Philadelphia, West Chester, Lancaster and Greensburg, PA. In the Tyler Arboretum, Lima, PA it is 60ft x 5ft. It is also grown in west OH, in Baltimore and Wilmington, MD, at Williamsburg, VA and in the Duke Gardens, NC.

'Elegans' (3) is a stabilised juvenile form raised long ago in Japan and brought out in 1861. Bushy as a young plant, it becomes top-heavy as it grows tall and may bend down in a hoop. But this will rarely be seen in America and not for many years as there are very few planted. In the east the Bailey Arboretum, NY, has one and in the west there is one in Victoria, BC. **'Cristata' (4)** is another Japanese oddity, making quite a slender tree to over 50ft and bright green.

CHINESE FIR (5), *Cunninghamia lanceolata* is another Asiatic redwood and shows it in its bark and cones. The male flowers, in big terminal clusters, will on some trees frequently break the rule universal among conifers, that male and female flowers be quite separate, and grow round the base of a female flower. The tree can grow a fine single trunk, but often it is seen as a close group of several stems, probably after frost or grazing damage in its first few years. The crown holds internally a great deal of dead foliage which is rusty brown and contrasts with the bright green of the live, outer foliage. Although tapering to a very sharp point, and hard in texture, the foliage is not really prickly as each leaf is pliant. The cones, though, are spiny, each scale narrowing to a rounded tip with a small, hard, brown spine.

This tree is occasional in NY and NJ. At Longwood Gardens, PA it is 50ft x 7ft. In the Secrest Arboretum, OH it is 35ft x 2ft. But it is from DC southwards that it becomes common, outside almost every town in roadside front gardens all round the Coastal Plain and up the Mississippi Valley to Memphis, TN, Hot Springs and Russellville AR and Lincoln, TX. There seem to be none in New Orleans itself, but some not far west, in Janetville and New Iberia, LA. In the Alleghenies it is in only a few gardens, as at Biltmore, NC. In the west the Van Dusen Botanic Garden, Vancouver, BC has one and some roadside gardens near Olympia and Tacoma, WA grow it. There is one at Glide, OR and in CA it is grown in Arcadia, while the Capitol Park at Sacramento has one 95ft x 7ft. The form **'Glauca'** is even more silvery, dusty blue in hot areas, south of NC, than it is elsewhere. It is occasional among the type trees. At Kenilworth Aquatic Garden, DC it is 45ft tall, and in the Tyler Arboretum, PA, 20ft. Good trees are in Biltmore, in the Cypress Gardens, SC, on Auburn Campus, GA and by US 29 a few miles south.

JAPANESE UMBRELLA PINE (6), *Sciadopitys verticillata* is not a pine of any sort but is another redwood, so remote from any other now living that it is completely unlike any other plant. It has redwood-like cones, although more fragile, but its bark is dark brown, coarsely stripping and becoming gray with age. The bare shoot between whorls has little brown knobs which are the tips of long, tightly appressed scale leaves. The whorls themselves are supported by crowded rings of similar leaftips and contain the 4–5in apparent leaves. Each of these is a pair of leaves fused together, as shown by their being grooved above and beneath, not keeled. This tree is in many gardens in NY, with 50ft trees at the Bayard Cutting Arboretum and the Bailey Arboretum, and in New England it is almost common. It is planted along the main street in Storrington, CT and is in small gardens in Manchester, NH and Newport, RI. It is more a big-garden tree in MA and PA with one tree as far south as Charlottesville, VA. In the west it is scarce, with a fine tree on the Sloane Estate, Nanaimo, and small ones in the Butchart and Van Dusen Botanic Garden, BC. In WA it is in Everett Cemetery, by the road east of Bellingham and in Point Defiance Park, Tacoma.

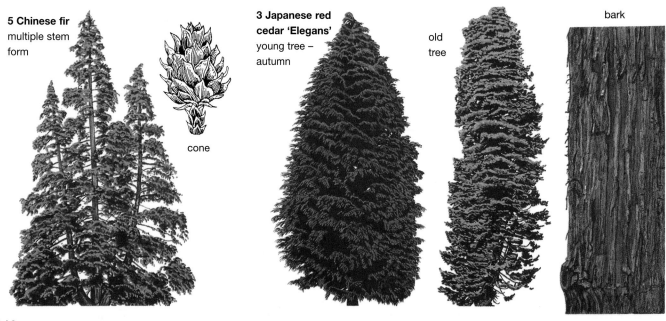

5 Chinese fir
multiple stem form

cone

3 Japanese red cedar 'Elegans'
young tree – autumn

old tree

bark

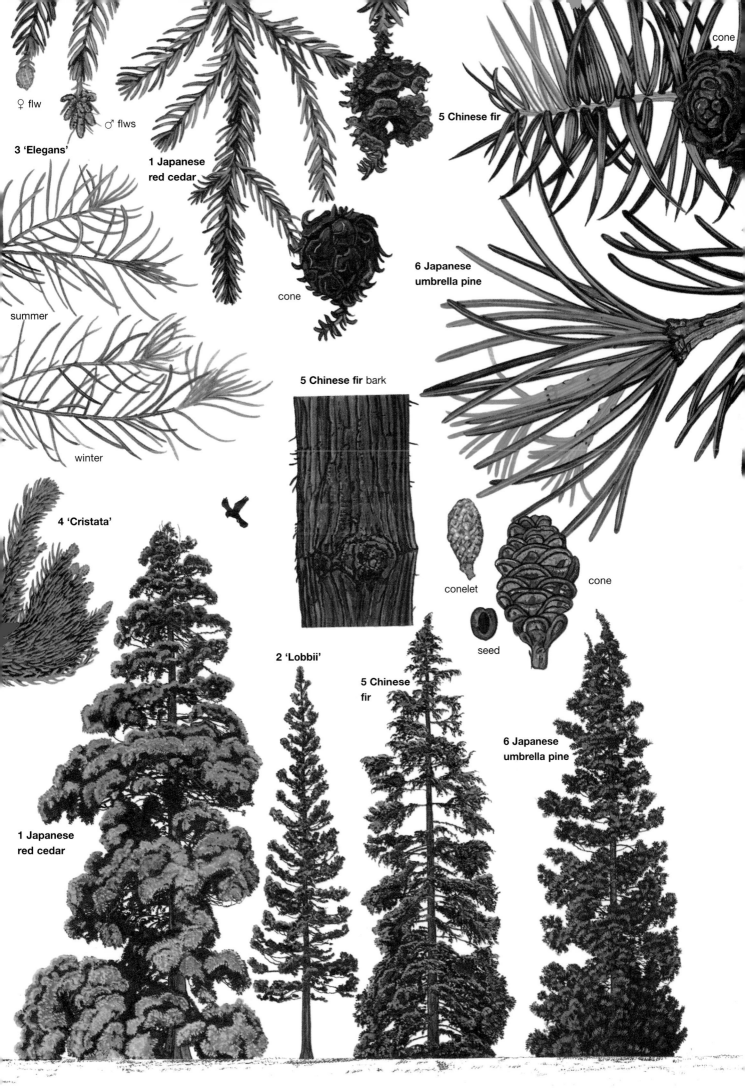

♀ flw

♂ flws

3 'Elegans'

1 Japanese red cedar

5 Chinese fir

cone

6 Japanese umbrella pine

cone

summer

winter

5 Chinese fir bark

4 'Cristata'

2 'Lobbii'

conelet

seed

cone

5 Chinese fir

6 Japanese umbrella pine

1 Japanese red cedar

Bald cypresses and Dawn redwood

A few members of the old Redwood Family evolved the deciduous way of life in which the leaves are thin-skinned and more efficient in the growing season but cannot survive cold winters and are shed in the fall. In the enthusiasm, perhaps, of such a bold move in early conifers, these redwoods shed not just the leaves but also the side-shoots which bear them. Two of these trees are the Bald cypresses in eastern North America and two are in China.

BALD CYPRESS or **SWAMP CYPRESS (1)**, *Taxodium distichum* is confined in the wild to swamps, flooding river-plains and the edges of tidal, brackish lagoons and in these places it grows 'knees' or pneumatophores. These arise from the roots at 20 or more yards from the tree, each a broad little pillar eventually 4–5ft tall, rather like a termite mound, with the typical bark of the tree trunk and with the top a dome rising from a recess inside a thick, rounded rim. It takes some 50 years for a tree to show knees, which contain spongy wood tissues and must help to provide the roots with oxygen. Trees growing in the tidal waters of Chesapeake and similar bays have trunks which flare out towards the base to a diameter disproportionate to the small trees. Male and female flowers are on the same tree but many trees have few flowers of one sex and great numbers of the other. The range is from DE and the Pine Barrens of NJ and Dismal Swamp, VA along the coast and inland along river bottoms, westward of the I95 in NC, SC and GA, to around Orlando, FL. South of this it appears to be replaced by the Pond cypress but it continues along the plains into TX, inland through AR and by the Mississippi in MO and IL and the Ohio in IN. It is widely planted north of its range in parks and big gardens in NY, MA, PA, MI and OH.

Big trees are in Spring Grove Cemetery, Cincinnati, OH, 82ft x 11ft and 115ft x 10ft; in the Ellipse, Washington, DC, 110ft x 11ft; and at Biltmore House, Asheville, NC, 60ft x 6ft. In the Morton Arboretum, IL a tree was 62ft x 7ft 7in when 51 years old. In the far west there is a swamp planted with Bald cypress outside Seattle visible from the I 5; it is grown in the botanic gardens in Vancouver and Seattle. In Point Defiance Park, Tacoma it is 70ft x 7ft but there are very few between this one and those on the campus at Berkeley, CA.

POND CYPRESS (2), var. *nutans* or *Taxodium ascendens* at its most distinct has its new shoots arising vertically and thread-like as the leaves are closely held to them, and in the form **'Nutans' (3)** they arch over from the ends of the branches, but trees intermediate between these and the Bald cypress can easily be found. The Pond cypress is wild from VA to eastern LA and is dominant in the Everglades and south FL generally. It is planted from MA, with trees in the Arnold Arboretum and one at Smith College, Northampton over 50ft x 6ft; and NY, PA to OH where in Franklyn Park, Columbus it was 66ft x 3ft 2in in 1975 and there are plots in the Secrest Arboretum. A fine tree at Biltmore, NC was 77ft x 4ft in 1974. Trees of the 'Nutans' form are at Rochester University, NY; the Tyler Arboretum, Lima, PA; and in the Ellipse, Washington, DC.

MONTEZUMA BALD CYPRESS (4), *Taxodium mucronatum* extends from its Mexican range just into TX. This is the species with the biggest bole in the world, the tree at the Church of Sta. Maria del Tule, near Oaxaca, being 135ft x 117ft 8in. It is evergreen and has slender, pendulous shoots. Trees planted in the Huntington Gardens, Pasadena, CA in 1912 were to 80ft x 12ft 3in in 1977.

DAWN REDWOOD (5), *Metasequoia glyptostroboides* was only a well-known and widespread fossil until details of trees found in 1941 in Hupeh, China, were published in 1945. Seed collected by an expedition from the Arnold Arboretum was sent in January 1948 to all the botanical institutions of the world. Trees from this seed, planted 1949–50, are in big gardens and parks from ON and MA to Houston, TX but not south of mid-GA or along the Gulf Coast or in the Mississippi Valley much south of St. Louis, MO. It seems to grow best on Long Island, NY and in DE and PA, but some tall trees are in southern CA. Growth is so exceptionally rapid that dimensions quoted without their dates are meaningless. The biggest known outside of the native areas in China is in the Bailey Arboretum, Long Island. In 1976 when 26 years planted this was 74ft x 10ft 1in. By 1981 summer it was 85ft x 12ft 10in. The tallest and the first in cultivation to 100ft is one of the two at James Blair Hall, Williamsburg, VA, which was 104ft x 9ft 7in in 1981. Two by Carnegie Lake, Princeton, NJ were 100ft in 1981. One at Willowwood, NJ was 98ft x 11ft 3in in 1987. In the west, the biggest in the University of Washington Arboretum in Seattle was 65ft x 4ft in 1975. In Los Angeles State and County Arboretum one was 88ft x 4ft 4in in 1977. The Dawn redwood differs from the Bald cypress in the leaves and shoots being opposite, the crown more open and the leaves bigger, broader and unfolding some two months earlier.

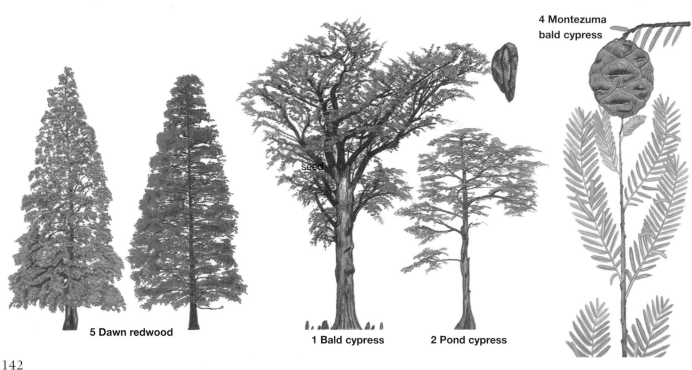

4 Montezuma bald cypress

seed

5 Dawn redwood

1 Bald cypress

2 Pond cypress

cone

♂ catkin

5 Dawn redwood

2 Pond cypress

♀ flw

♂ flw

1 Swamp cypress

cone

3 'Nutans'

1 Swamp cypress

2 Pond cypress

1 Swamp cypress 'knees'

European and N. African silver firs

EUROPEAN SILVER FIR (1), *Abies alba* grows in the Pyrenees Mountains, where some fine stands on the French side are reminiscent of the big woods in WA and OR, through the Alps and south into the Balkan Mountains. It was early into cultivation in England where one is known to have been planted in 1603 and after about 1750 it was widely planted as a forest tree. It is not happy in North America and only a few may be found in collections in NY, MA, PA, OH and DE. The bud is brown and non-resinous and the shoot gray with a little scatter of small dark hairs. Unlike the Caucasian fir, which is very similar, it has the leaves well parted above the shoot and sparsely set. The crown has a tendency to become fan-topped as the main stem fails, or broad with big branches growing out level then turning abruptly vertical. In the Balkan Mountains, this silver fir becomes involved with a group of related species, the relicts of larger populations once widespread around the Mediterranean Sea and now scattered on mountains, and forms some hybrid populations through Greece into Asia Minor.

GRECIAN FIR (2), *Abies cephalonica*, however, is a good separate species in the mountains of southern Greece and a very sturdy, vigorous tree too. It comes into leaf too early to escape frost damage in most years when grown in northerly parts like Britain and probably in some frosty sites in New England although there at about the same latitude as its home in Greece. The leading bud flushes last in all silver firs and the time-lag is enough for the leading shoot to emerge unscathed while the lower sideshoots have their new growth scorched back. For some years this may make the tree narrower in the lower crown than it would otherwise be but vigorous growth of the branches above the frostline soon makes a sturdy tree with strong, raised branches in a broadly conic shape. It is quite rare but is evidently well suited to many places between ON and VA in the east and WA and mid-CA in the west as there are some very big trees but none is very old. A young one is at the School of Horticulture, Niagara Falls, ON, and the state of New York has some big trees. At Lyndhurst, Tarrytown, one was 77ft x 9ft 10in in 1975 and at the Cutting Arboretum on Long Island the biggest of four was 108ft x 12ft 10in in 1981 and another was 95ft x 12ft. At Highland Park, Rochester, growth has been variable, at 70ft x 5ft 3in in 69 years, and 88ft x 7ft 0in in 55 years. There is a tree in Charlottesville, VA, 87ft x 5ft 10in in 1981 and one at Prospect House, Princeton, NJ, 46ft x 4ft. In the Secrest Arboretum, OH it was 75ft x 5ft when 58 years old. There is a tree at the University of Wisconsin Arboretum, Chaska, WI. In the west there is a 50ft tree at Sacramento, CA near the Capitol. The variety **'Apollinis'** grows on Mount Parnassus in Greece and is an even more vigorous tree with hard spined leaves as in the Grecian fir and dark orange-brown shoots but instead of the leaves radiating fairly evenly all round the shoot, they lie mainly along the top with only a few radiating below. There are two in the Bayard Cutting Arboretum, NY, the larger 84ft x 7ft 7in and two much bigger in the west, in Point Defiance Park, Tacoma, WA. These were 85ft x 13ft 6in and 108ft x 13ft 8in in 1976.

SPANISH FIR (3), *Abies pinsapo* is a relict species reduced to six small stands around the town of Rondo in the Sierra Nevada in southern Spain. These woods were in constant danger from fire and from goats until efforts were made to preserve them. The name *'pinsapo'* is an abbreviation of *'Pinus saponis'*, the soap pine, because the inhabitants of those parts beat and crushed branches in water to make a detergent solution. It is also called 'Hedgehog fir' from the spiny leaves closely surrounding the young shoots. On older trees the leaves are blunt and rounded, although still hard if less rigid, and on some shoots those along the centre of the shoot are nearly as broad as they are long. Silver firs in general grow best, fastest and tallest in the cool moist air of northern parts and the Spanish fir does too but it grows better than most in hotter, drier and often lime-soiled areas, although not long-lived and becoming twiggy with much dead wood in the crown when some 80 years old. Trees raised from seed are variably gray-blue to dark green in leaf and the bluest are selected as **'Glauca'**. At the Cutting Arboretum there are two of these, one 46ft x 8ft 9in. Another in Prospect House, Princeton, NJ is 42ft x 3ft 3in. There are trees of nearer the type, greener leafed, at Planting Fields, Long Island, NY 60ft x 5ft 6in and 60ft x 5ft in 1976. In the west there are small trees in the Butchart Garden, Sidney and Beacon Hill Park, Victoria, BC and in the University of Washington Arboretum in Seattle, WA.

ALGERIAN FIR (4), *Abies numidica* grows only on Mount Tabor in the Atlas Mountains and was discovered and brought into cultivation in 1864. Like the Spanish fir, to which it is closely related, the leaves have blue-gray stripes on the upper surface and can be very broad, and densely set. Those along the midline of the shoot can be broader than they are long. The shoot is orange and the bark dull orange-brown cracked into a pattern of regular, round-cornered square plates. It is a sturdy and shapely tree growing fast on the right sites, to 100ft tall and is not fussy about soils. A fine tree at Rochester University House, NY, is probably an early planting in the Ellwanger and Barry nurseries that were there originally and received early seeds from Europe. In 1977 it was 72ft x 7ft 10in. This is a rare tree in America and the only other public trees noted are one in the Bayard Cutting Arboretum, NY, 70ft x 8ft 1in and one in the Strybing Arboretum, San Francisco, CA, 33ft x 5ft in 1982.

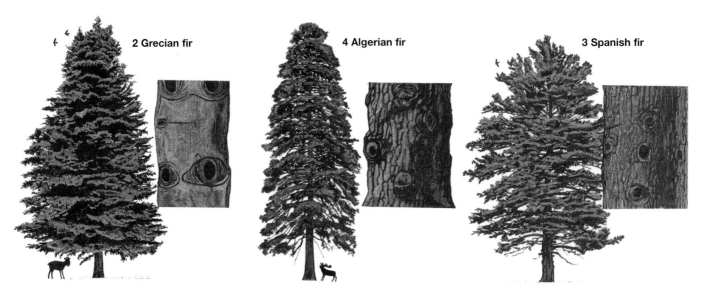

2 Grecian fir 4 Algerian fir 3 Spanish fir

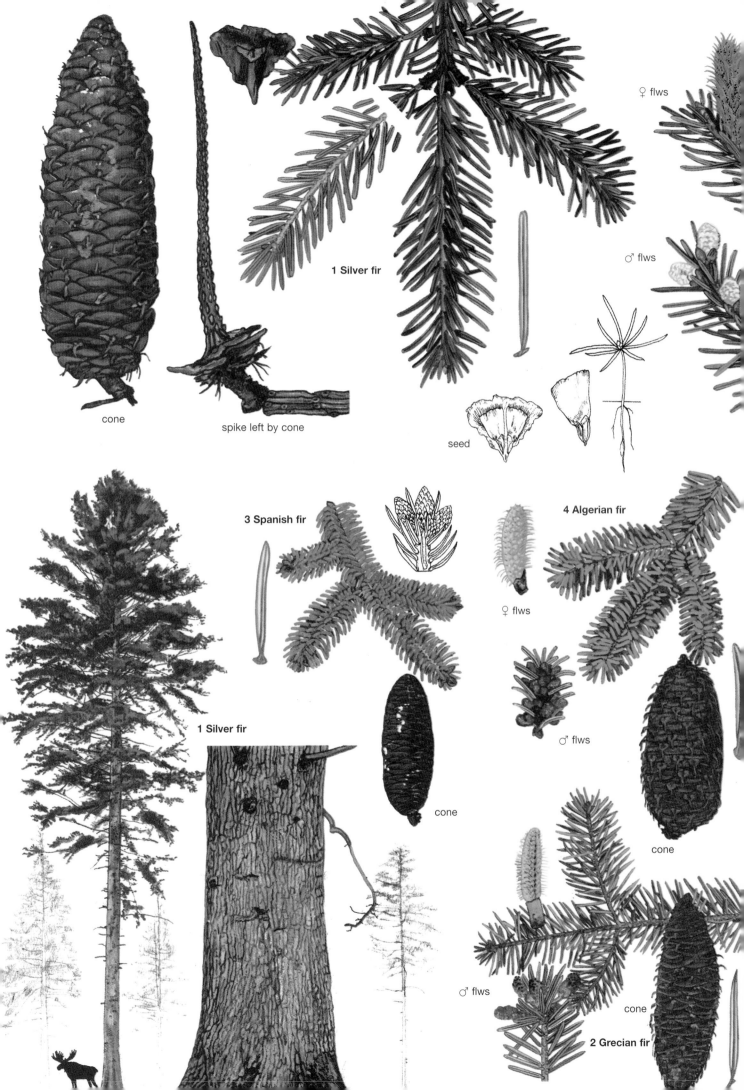

cone

spike left by cone

1 Silver fir

♀ flws

♂ flws

seed

3 Spanish fir

4 Algerian fir

♀ flws

1 Silver fir

♂ flws

cone

cone

♂ flws

cone

2 Grecian fir

Grand, Red and other Silver firs

GRAND FIR (1), *Abies grandis* was the tallest of all silver firs, once exceeding 300ft, although today none is as tall. The foliage when bruised gives a strong scent of oranges. The cones are rarely seen because they grow only on a few of the top branches of trees over a hundred years old, and so are 150–200ft above the ground and disintegrate on the tree. It grows from the north of Vancouver Island and the coast of BC along the coast to mid-CA where the last stand is at Caspar and a few single trees a little to the south by the Albion River. It is in large stands only on the eastern slopes of the Cascade Mountains, and extends eastwards in ID and MT where, by Rt 200 it stops abruptly at Plains. There are big trees in the Siskiyou Mountains. In the Cathedral Grove remnants of the vast superb forests that have been felled on Vancouver Island, trees over 230ft x 14ft remain. One by Cornwall Park, Bellingham, WA is 150ft x 12ft and small young trees are frequent in gardens in BC, WA and ID but it is very little planted outside its range beyond CA.

BRISTLECONE FIR or **SANTA LUCIA FIR (2)**, *Abies bracteata* is an oddity with no close relations in the genus, within which its cones and slender, acute buds are unique. The sharply spined leaves 2in long are distinctive. The tree is wild only in small groups scattered at the heads of narrow canyons in the Santa Lucia Mountains for about 40 miles from near Point Sur, CA. Small specimens are in the Strybing Arboretum, San Francisco and the University of Wisconsin Arboretum, Madison, WI.

CALIFORNIA RED FIR (3), *Abies magnifica* ranges from around Diamond Lake in the Cascade Mountains of mid-OR and the Shasta area and Siskiyou Mountains to the southern parts of the Sierra Nevada, CA. The name 'Red fir' comes from the deep rich red of the bark of the older trees at high elevations, as around Crater Lake, but they are mixed with trees with nearly black bark thickly ridged pale gray as are most of the trees on the CA side of Lake Tahoe and in Yosemite National Park. The tree grows only above 5000ft altitude, mainly between 6000 and 8000ft, and many superb specimens are seen at places popular with tourists. At Glacier Point, Yosemite, below the car-lot one is 165ft x 15ft 6in but far better is a short line by a meadow and pullout five miles down the road where the biggest is 175ft x 20ft. In King's Canyon a prominent tree near Cedar Lodge is 180ft x 15ft 5in and in Sequoia National Park, General Sherman Grove one is 230ft x 16ft 4in. None seems to have succeeded when planted elsewhere. The **Shasta red fir**, var. *shastensis* is identical except for the projecting bracts of the cone.

SUBALPINE FIR (4), *Abies lasiocarpa* comes into view wherever a road in the Rocky Mountains climbs in a pass to 10,000ft. It ranges from Yukon, AB and UT to AZ and is a snow-line tree, at its most slender where the snowfall is heaviest as at Paradise Center on Mount Rainier, WA and on Hurricane Ridge in the Olympic Mountains. A fine tree stands in a street in Revelstoke, BC and one is in a beach-house garden at Long Beach, WA. There are fine stands at the top of the Cameron Pass, CO/WY and in the Tetons National Park around Jenny Lake and almost all the 40 miles into Yellowstone National Park to Old Faithful Inn. It is also well seen beside the Sunday Pass, BC on RT3 and there are small areas in the Wasatch Mountains above Ogden, UT.

Corkbark fir (5), var. *arizonica* which grows from central CO to AZ soon grows wide pink corky fissures in its bark, which becomes thick and yellow-gray. This form is more successful in the east and is grown in the Royal Botanic Garden, Hamilton, ON, in the Dawes Arboretum, OH; at Cornell University and Highland Park, Rochester, NY; at the Arnold Arboretum, MA, the University of Minnesota Landscaping Arboretum, Chaska, MN and at the University of Wisconsin Arboretum, WI.

MANCHURIAN FIR (6), *Abies holophylla* is a handsome, very hardy tree seen in some collections in the east. In the Ottawa Botanic Garden it is 40ft x 4ft and in the Arnold Arboretum, MA it is 30ft x 3ft. There are several in the George Landis Arboretum NY and in OH there are four in the Dawes Arboretum to 55ft x 4ft and some in the Secrest Arboretum.

KOREAN FIR (7), *Abies koreana* as grown from seed from Quelpaert Island flowers and bears rows of cones when it is only 5ft tall, and remains a small tree, but seed from the trees found later, in 1917, on the mainland of Korea grow into good, shapely trees like those at the Arnold Arboretum over 50ft tall. A smaller tree is in the Queen Victoria Park, Niagara Falls, ON. The underside of the leaves is thickly chalky white often obscuring the green midrib.

CILICIAN FIR (8), *Abies cilicica* from Asia Minor and Syria is similar to the Caucasian fir but has nearly black bark ringed by prominent branch-scars. A superb specimen at the Bayard Cutting Arboretum, Long Island was 121ft x 13ft 2in in 1981. Specimens at the George Landis Arboretum, NY and at Smith College, Northampton, MA bore other labels in 1976, and there are more at the Secrest Arboretum, OH, at Longwood Gardens, the Morris Arboretum and at Westtown School, PA.

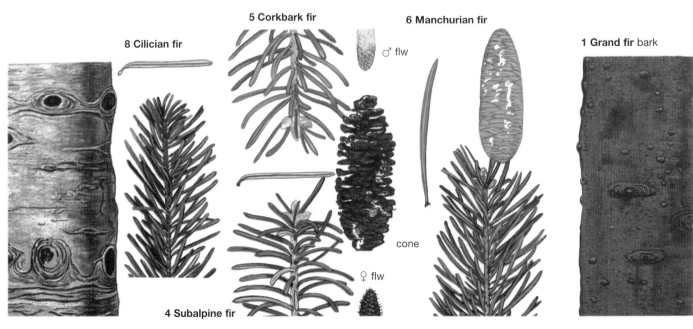

8 Cilician fir

5 Corkbark fir

♂ flw

6 Manchurian fir

1 Grand fir bark

cone

♀ flw

4 Subalpine fir

1 Grand fir

2 Santa Lucia fir

♂ flws

♀ flw

3 California red fir

♀ flw

cone

♀ flws

♂ flws

cone

1 Grand fir 55m

4 Subalpine fir 20m

2 Santa Lucia fir 36m

3 California red fir 37m

7 Korean fir 10m

Balsam, Fraser and allied Silver firs

The Silver firs, *Abies*, are about 40 very resinous, usually tall trees, with regular conic crowns and whorled branches. They grow all round the northern hemisphere from Alaska to Eastern Siberia, south to Mexico, the Mediterranean Sea and south China. They differ from Spruces in their leaves being leathery and rarely spined and in their female flowers and cones standing erect until they disintegrate on the tree. Also the leaves arise from sucker-like bases which go with them when they fall, leaving the shoot smooth. Spruce leaves arise from pegs moulded at their bases into the shoot as ridges, and the falling leaf snaps off leaving the peg behind and the shoots coarsely roughened.

BALSAM FIR (1), *Abies balsamea* is among the most resinous of all the silver firs; large blisters of resin in the bark persist to a greater age and the foliage needs only slight bruising to yield its highly aromatic balsam scent. This tree is the main source of Canada balsam, used for mounting microscopic specimens. It grows from the coast of central Labrador to PA and some of the mountains of VA, across the middle of PQ to SK and northeast AB south to IA, WI and MI. It is very common over huge areas of hillside in the Adirondack Mountains, NY, New England, ON and WI with bushy little trees seeding down banks to the roads and very shapely small trees growing up behind them. There are some plantations, notably in WI and between Ogden and Boone, IA, and a plot in the Secrest Arboretum, OH. There are few specimen trees in parks or squares but there is one in Hyde Park Mansion, NY, one 60ft tall at Smith College, Northampton, MA and one in Spring Grove Cemetery, Cincinnati, OH, 60ft x 5ft. At Big Meadow Center in the Blue Ridge, northern VA, the Balsam fir is var. *phanerolepis*, halfway to, or a hybrid with, the Fraser fir. The bracts protrude a little from the cone and the smooth, cream-brown shoots bear Fraser fir's short leaves with gray stripes.

FRASER FIR (2), *Abies fraseri* grows at the highest points of mountain ridges through NC. At Bear Ridge Trail it is 100ft tall at an altitude of 5870ft. The summit of Clingman's Dome, 6617ft, is covered in it and the ground in many such places is carpeted densely with seedlings. It is seen planted in a few town gardens in the valleys, as at Boone, NC. There and on the hills, young trees are shapely, with slender, open crowns and two-foot leading shoots but they cone early in life and die young.

PACIFIC SILVER FIR (3), *Abies amabilis*, or Beautiful fir, is also a resinous tree with blisters on the bark, but only when young, and the fragrance arising from bruised foliage is a citrous, fruity one like tangerines. The stout shoot has a light covering of fine, brown hairs and the globose buds are purple, soon white with exuded resin. It grows from the extreme south of AK to the Olympic Mountains, WA and inland along the Selkirk and Cascade Mountains to OR with small areas on the Coast Range in OR and the Siskiyou Mountains in CA. It stands out among other tall silver firs for its narrow crown of blackish foliage on short, level branches from a silvery stem.

MARIES'S FIR (4), *Abies mariesii* is remarkably like the Pacific fir. Its shoot has a denser cover of orange-brown short hairs; its leaves are barely half as long and its bark is dull gray, heavily freckled. It is grown in a few collections, as at the George Landis Arboretum, NY and the Secrest Arboretum, OH.

SICHUAN FIR (5), *Abies fargesii* from China is growing in Highlands Park, Rochester, NY and has leathery, glossy leaves on shoots which vary from orange and mahogany brown to purple, and a slender crown.

VEITCH'S SILVER FIR (6), *Abies veitchii* from Japan has foliage similar to the Pacific fir but the leaves are held more forward and do not fan out flat around the shoot-ends. The cones are smaller, more slender and borne more freely especially on young trees. It is always identifiable by the deep flutes, rounded ridges and hollows under the branches on the trunk. In the Bayard Cutting Arboretum, Long Island, NY a forked tree is 52ft x 4ft and another 41ft x 4ft 4in (1981). At Rochester, NY a tree at Highland Park Center is 62ft x 5ft and one in the pinetum is 60ft x 6ft and there is a tree at Cornell University. At the Arnold Arboretum, MA the form var. *olivacea* with green cones is over 3ft round.

CAUCASIAN FIR (7), *Abies nordmanniana* is a rather more luxuriant form of the European silver fir, although not at its best in North America. The bark becomes pale gray and broken into small squarish blocks and the crown usually remains regularly conic to a good height. A bushy little tree in Ottawa Botanic Garden is evidently a little too far north, but at Mohonk Mountain, NY it is 82ft x 6ft while several at the Vanderbilt Mansion, Hyde Park are good trees and one was 93ft x 9ft 7in in 1976. In 1981 one at the Bayard Cutting Arboretum, Long Island was 88ft x 6ft 10in. At Highland Park, Rochester, it had grown to 84ft x 9ft in 74 years. It is in many collections, parks and large gardens in PA and in DC it is at the Tidal Basin. It is in the Secrest Arboretum in OH and in the far west, at Point Defiance Park, Tacoma WA.

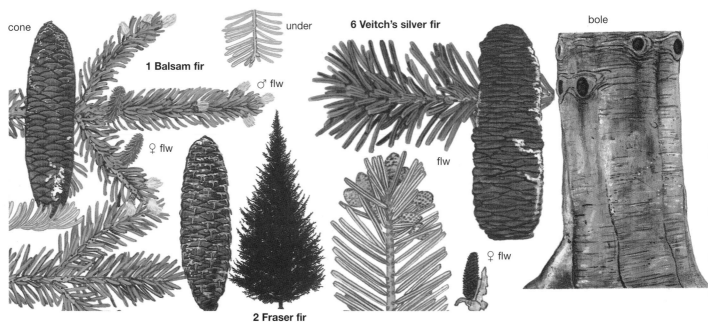

cone   under   **6 Veitch's silver fir**   bole

1 Balsam fir

♂ flw

♀ flw

flw

♀ flw

2 Fraser fir

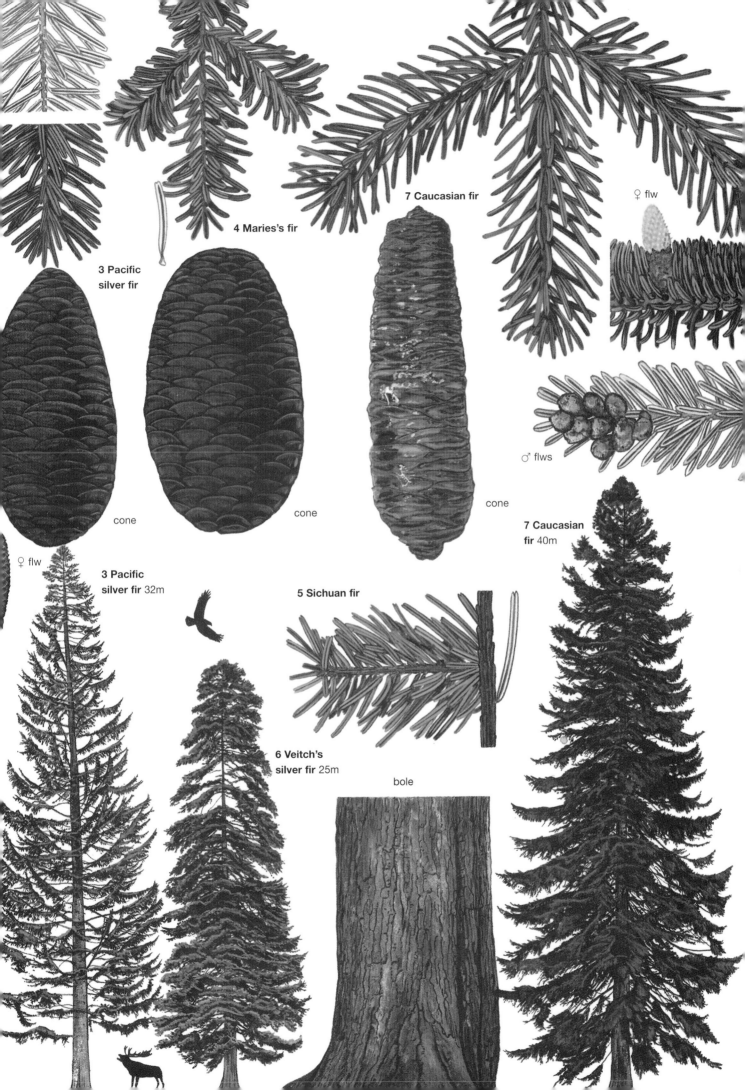

7 Caucasian fir

4 Maries's fir

♀ flw

**3 Pacific
silver fir**

cone

cone

cone

♂ flws

**7 Caucasian
fir** 40m

♀ flw

**3 Pacific
silver fir** 32m

5 Sichuan fir

**6 Veitch's
silver fir** 25m

bole

White, Noble and other Silver firs

CALIFORNIA WHITE FIR (1), *Abies concolor* in the eastern Rocky Mountains from ID to NM and AZ, is the eastern form of the much bigger, Pacific White fir. It is called 'concolor' because the leaves are the same green-blue with gray-blue stripes each side, unlike those of the similar foliaged Pacific and Grand firs. It grows with a regularly narrow conic crown with short level branches. There are fine 100ft trees in Santa Fe, NM and in Oak Creek Canyon, AZ and it is the only silver fir seen in Las Vegas, NV. It is also much the commonest western silver fir planted in the east, where it grows well. It is in the botanic gardens at Montreal, PQ and Ottawa, ON and in small gardens near Freeport, ME and quite often in PA, MD and OH. It is also frequent in MN in gardens around Minneapolis and in Lyndale Park, and in Ogden, Boone and Des Moines, IA. It is even planted north of the range of its western form in southern BC and in Everett and Tacoma, WA. Trees 80–90ft x 7ft are at Highland Park, Rochester, Vanderbilt Mansion and the Bayard Cutting Arboretum NY. At Winterthur Garden, DE the best of three was 70ft x 5ft 3in. A form with paler blue-gray leaves, **'Glauca'** is sometimes planted and is 80ft x 5ft at Vanderbilt Mansion, and a blue-white form, **'Violacea' (2)** is 40ft x 4ft 4in in the Bayard Cutting Arboretum.

Pacific white fir (3), var. *lowiana* was sent to Low's Nursery near London, England in 1851. It grows from around Diamond Lake in the Cascades of OR, through the Siskiyou Mountains and in the Coast Range to the Salmon Mountains in CA and all down the Sierra Nevada extending east of the summits into the heads of some valleys, as in Independence Creek where it is at 9000ft by the stream. It is a link between the White fir type and the Grand fir and has some variable features. The shoot is slender compared with the White fir and pale orange-brown and the buds much smaller, but the leaves can be as green above and set as flat as in the Grand fir or striped blue-gray above and curved up each side of the shoot, while in the southern cross-ranges they are short and nearly vertical. The bark can be corky fissured like that of the Douglas fir. It is a superb and shapely tree by the road at Union Creek, OR, 170ft tall and below the parking-lot at Glacier Point, Yosemite, CA to 175 ft x 20ft, while a curiously shaped tree stands on the beach of Lake Tahoe, at Sandy Cove, 160ft x 14ft 7in. One at Bluff Lake near Big Bear Lake in the San Bernardinos dates from a fire in 1563 and was 135ft x 19ft 7in in 1971. At Giant Forest Village in Sequoia National Park a stump 17ft round showed 375 rings and trees of 200–220ft are all around. In Yosemite, a tree in Tuolumne Grove is 197ft x 19ft 9in and one in Merced Grove is 246ft x 15ft 3in. Few are planted in the east where the White fir itself is thought to be superior. There are trees in the Royal Botanic Gardens, Hamilton, ON and in Lyndale Park, Minneapolis, MN.

NOBLE FIR (4), *Abies procera* stands out in the forest with its blue-gray foliage. It is apt to lose its shape and have a broken top because it lines the top shoots with big, heavy cones from fairly early in life. It is restricted to the Cascade Mountains in WA and OR and a few peaks in the Coast Range and a little into CA in the Siskiyou Mountains. Some immense trees have been found, like the 1972 Champion, 272ft x 28ft 4in in the Gifford Pinchot Nation Forest, WA, but elsewhere rather few are left. The leaves lie close at the base to the shoot and hide it from above, unlike the more spread but very similar foliage of the California red fir, in which the leaf is also so nearly round in section that it can be rolled between finger and thumb, whereas that of the Noble fir is altogether too flat for this. Wild trees vary in the brightness of the gray-blue towards blue-white and selections of these are the majority of those seen planted in the eastern gardens, where the tree is not a great success.

FORREST'S FIR (5), *Abies forrestii* and its high altitude form, **George's fir (6)**, were found by George Forrest in mountains in Yunnan, China in 1910 and 1923. The shoots are bright orange and the leaves brilliantly silvered beneath. They grow very fast in cool wet parts but are short-lived in warmer, drier areas and may be found in a few American collections with Asiatic trees.

MOMI FIR (7), *Abies firma* from Japan also prefers cool damp summers and makes a sturdy tree with straight branches raised at a low angle bearing very thick, hard leathery leaves, spined on young branches, rounded on old. There are trees of no great size at Prospect House, Princeton, NJ; the Tyler Arboretum, PA; the Secrest Arboretum, OH, the Morton Arboretum, IL and the University of Wisconsin Arboretum in Madison, WI. At Longwood one in a grove is 95ft x 8ft.

NIKKO FIR (8), *Abies homolepis*, from Japan also, is one of the most successful Asiatic conifers in North America. Its stout shoots are white or cream, divided into plates and its leaves, very blue-white striped beneath, are in two broad ranks separated by a narrow 'V'. Trees are growing well in most of the collections in ON, NY, MA, PA, MI and OH and there are two in Beacon Hill Park, Victoria, BC. Among the biggest are: Arnold Arboretum, MA, 78 years old, 75ft x 9ft 8in; Highland Park, NY, 67 years old, 70ft x 7ft 2in; Bailey Arboretum, 70ft x 7ft 7in; Winterthur Garden, DE, 75ft x 7ft and Secrest Arboretum, OH, 58 years old, 70ft x 5ft 4in and 45 years old, 68ft x 4ft. This species bears cones when quite young and, unusual in a silver fir, on the lowest branches, when somewhat older.

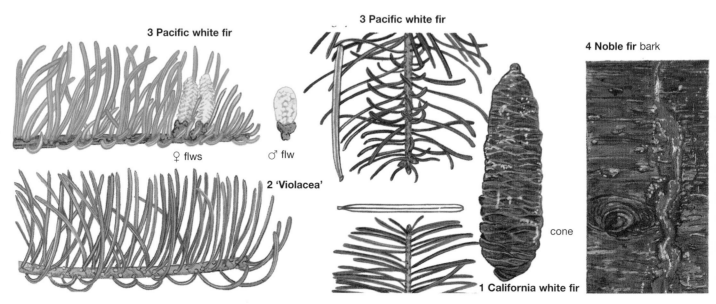

3 Pacific white fir

♀ flws   ♂ flw

2 'Violacea'

3 Pacific white fir

4 Noble fir bark

cone

1 California white fir

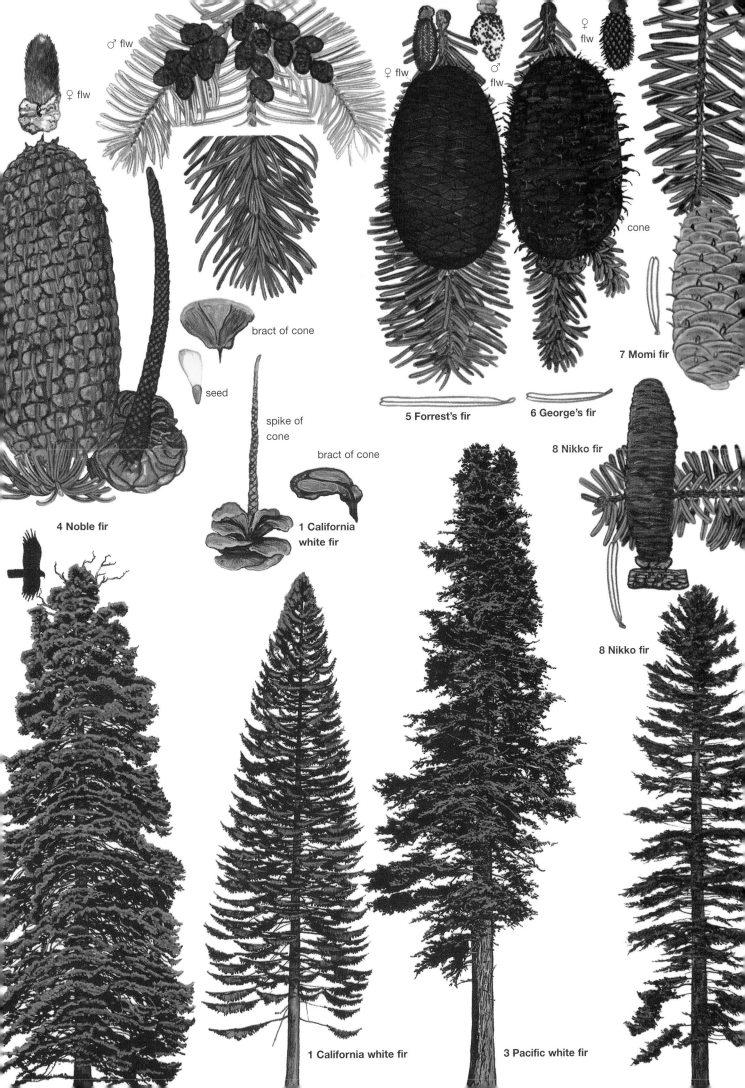

♂ flw

♀ flw

bract of cone

seed

spike of
cone

bract of cone

**1 California
white fir**

4 Noble fir

♀ flw

♂
flw

♀
flw

cone

7 Momi fir

5 Forrest's fir

6 George's fir

8 Nikko fir

8 Nikko fir

1 California white fir

3 Pacific white fir

Douglas firs

DOUGLAS FIR (1), *Pseudotsuga menziesii* was first noted by Archibald Menzies, who was with Vancouver's squadron in 1792, and introduced into cultivation by David Douglas who collected seeds in 1826 and sent them to London. By coincidence, Douglas lived near Perth, Scotland, so landowners in that district were naturally keen to grow his trees, and Perth grows the tree faster and better than almost anywhere else in the world. By another, even more outrageous coincidence, of all the vast area of Douglas fir almost throughout the Rockies System in the USA, the first seed was sent from near Portland, OR, the centre of a tiny area of stands yielding better trees in Europe than any other area whose seed has been tested. Douglas fir is one of the main timbers of the world, and is exceptionally strong and good for construction work. The vast stands in WA and OR carry more usable timber per acre than any other commercial stands except the Redwood, and created nearly all the wealth of those states for some 80 years, and are still the major source in OR. The tree grows from around Prince Rupert, BC, south along the coast to Monterey, CA with a scatter beyond towards San Simeon, and inland through southwest AB in mountains through MT and CO to NM and in CA to Sequoia National Park in the Sierra Nevada. In the USA the populations from the coast to the western crests of the Rockies are separable from those of the interior and the eastern crests, and are called **Coastal** or **Green Douglas fir** as opposed to the **Inland, Interior, Rocky Mountain** or **Blue Douglas fir (2)**, but in BC these types tend to merge and the interior BC form, sometimes separated as the Fraser River Douglas fir, is an intermediate one.

The **Coastal Douglas fir** forms some of the tallest and most magnificent woods in the world. In the valleys of Vancouver Island and in WA the world's tallest trees were growing until around 1900, several reliably recorded as over 350ft and the Mineral tree, WA as 385–395ft. The best left on the Island now are in a few little fragments with one tree 318ft (1984). The finest wood in the world today is usually agreed to be a grove of trees near Quinault Lake, WA, not as big individually as the Redwoods or Giant Sequoias but well-spaced, and each a superb specimen with a clean trunk 23–25ft round without a branch or blemish for 200ft, and with top heights 190–305ft. A few other fine trees are, north to south: milepost 38, Mount Baker NP, WA, 260ft x 14ft 6in; by the roadside at Longmire, Mount Rainier, NP, 250ft x 20ft 1in; Big Pine Wayside, OR, 255ft x 17ft; and Henry Cowell Redwood Park, CA, 270ft x 23ft 5in (1982). Planted trees within the range include three at the Capitol, Olympia, WA to 131ft x 11ft in 1981 and to the north of the range, trees in Jasper, AB and Revelstoke, BC. In the eastern states, the Rocky Mountain form is preferred but the Coastal is common on Long Island, NY. Otherwise it is found only in Montreal Botanic Garden, PQ, in the George Landis Arboretum, NY and in Manchester, NH apart from one isolated luxuriant tree in Tuxedo Road outside Atlanta, GA.

The **Rocky Mountain Douglas fir (3)**, var. *glauca* is the form found throughout the interior and eastern Rocky Mountains as a much smaller tree with usually black, rough bark and variably blueish foliage, but in Oak Creek Canyon, AZ it is quite fresh green. The leaves stand up more from the shoot and usually lack the strong, sweet, fruity fragrance of the Coastal form while the coppery coloured cones have long protruded bracts bent out level or curved downwards. The female flowers are usually bright crimson while those of the Coastal tend to be greenish pink, pure green, white, yellow or rose-pink to dull crimson. This tree occurs at 9500ft altitude in many parts, as is easily seen in the Togwatee Pass, WY, and to 8200ft in the Cameron Pass, CO/WY. At the highest altitudes it is normally seen, but the 1981 champion is 140ft x 24ft 7in at Mount Orange, broadly and shallowly ridged. A tree of this kind by the road near Jenny Lake, Teron National Park is 50ft x 12ft, a large girth for this tree as it is normally seen but the 1981 champion is 140ft x 24ft 7in at Mount Jefferson Trail Head, Candle Creek, OR. This form is widely planted in the eastern states in towns and gardens from Montreal, PQ to MD, inland to TN, MO, IA and MN and in downtown Tulsa, OK. There are good trees in Toronto, ON and around many cities in PA and OH and a few in MI.

BIG-CONE DOUGLAS FIR (4), *Pseudotsuga macrocarpa* is the only Douglas fir with hard and spine-tipped leaves and cones up to 7in long, although mostly around 5in. The crown is broadly conic with sparse, long nearly level branches from which the foliage droops. It is found only in south CA in the cross-ranges at 1500–7000ft from the Santa Inez Mountains above Santa Barbara to the San Bernardino Mountains and on a few ranges southward to the border and Baja California. At City Creek and Long Point the trees above San Bernardino have dead upper crowns due to smog blowing up from the Los Angeles area, but northward they are healthy and in Angeles National Forest a pair stand 3ft apart in front of the Combo Inn, the larger 115ft x 12ft. None has been noted planted anywhere. The Asiatic Douglas firs have soft leaves with indented tips.

JAPANESE DOUGLAS FIR, *Pseudotsuga japonica* may perhaps be found as a small tree in a few collections.

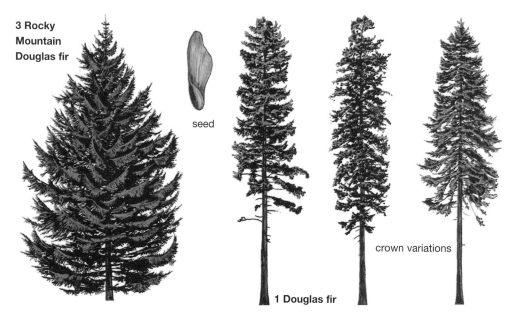

3 Rocky Mountain Douglas fir

seed

1 Douglas fir

crown variations

♂ flws

buds

leaf

4 Big-cone Douglas fir

1 Douglas fir

seed

cone variations

♀ flws

2 Blue Douglas fir

1 Douglas fir

♂ flw

cone

1 Douglas fir

4 Big-cone Douglas fir

True cedars

The early settlers had never seen a cedar tree but they had heard of the legendary fragrant, decay-resistant wood. They found many unfamiliar conifers in their new land with durable, hard, fragrant wood and the sale of this timber was made much easier by calling it some sort of cedar than it would have been under various obscure new names. This tradition was carried on during the expansion west over the next 200 years, so North America is awash with 'cedars', none of which is a true Cedar. There are White, Red, Port Orford, Alaska and Incense cedars as currently accepted names, and Canoe, Giant, Mountain, Oregon, Post, Rock, Sand, Stinking, Swamp and Yellow as alternative names. And all are members of the Cypress Family, variously in four genera. One accepted name, 'red cedar', is given to two different species in different genera which often causes confusion.

The true Cedars are four species in the genus *Cedrus* in the Family *Pinaceae* which is characterised by woody cones, a strictly Old World group confined to the Mediterranean area and the Western Himalayas. The three around the Mediterranean differ in minor details only, although specimens in cultivation can be very distinct, and many botanists treat them as one species with two varieties.

CEDAR OF LEBANON (1),

Cedrus libani grows in the small grove on Mount Lebanon, Syria, where it has been known from ancient times, and on the Taurus and Antitaurus Mountains in Turkey. It has been in cultivation in Europe since 1638 when seed was brought to England. It is rare in North America and grows in a few large gardens from MA to OH and in BC and WA where one in 16th Street, NE in Seattle was 13ft round when a little over 70 years old. In the Arnold Arboretum, MA two trees raised in 1906 from seed sent from Anatolia were 62ft x 6ft 3in and 60ft x 5ft 3in in 1975. At Highland Park, Rochester, NY one planted in 1953 had grown remarkably fast and was 62ft x 4ft 1in by 1976. Two at Planting Fields were over 70ft x 9ft 6in. One at Prospect House, Princeton, NJ was 46ft x 11ft 7in at 3ft in 1981 and a big one in the Tyler Arboretum, PA was 108ft x 14ft 6in at 3ft in 1976. The branches from the trunk, or more often from several trunks close together, spread far and level with the tips level or slightly drooped in old trees. The length of the leaves, also useful in separating cedars, is around 1in.

ATLAS CEDAR (2),

Cedrus atlantica from the Atlas Mountains in Algeria and Morocco is almost always seen in one of the very gray-blue forms selected from seedlings arising from a very blue tree, collected in 1845 by Lord Somers. The leaves are shorter than in the Lebanon tree in general; the bark much paler gray and the branches rise at about 45° with their tips at the same angle. It is common from MA and notably in RI in small gardens, along the Coastal Plain to Atlanta and Hogansville, GA but not further south while inland it is scarce in ON and OH but frequent in PA and from KY to Memphis, TN. There are trees in Planting Fields and the Bailey Arboretum on Long Island; one in Marquand Park, Princeton, NJ is 60ft x 9ft 5in and at Winterthur, DE it is 65ft x 8ft 2in. In the far west it is very common on Vancouver Island and frequent from Vancouver to Tacoma, WA. In CA it is at Mariposa and Bishop and infrequent in the Bay Area. One in the Strybing Arboretum only 18 years planted was 50ft x 4ft. Around Los Angeles and San Diego it is fairly frequent as a park and boulevard tree and most of these were raised from a tree in the Huntington Gardens, Pasadena. At Sacramento Capitol it is 88ft x 14ft 2in and at Olympia Capitol, WA, it is 85ft x 10ft 6in.

Weeping atlas cedar (3), 'Pendula' is a sparsely branched mound, very weeping and very slow. There is one in the Cutting Arboretum, NY and many more in the parks and gardens of Victoria and Vancouver, BC a few in Seattle and one at South Bend, WA.

DEODAR CEDAR (4),

Cedrus deodara has been reported as 250ft tall in the Punjab, about the middle of its range from Afghanistan along the Western Himalaya. It grows with a 'dropper' leader, arching over at the tip, a feature shared by only the Port Orford cedar and the Western hemlock, and usually maintains a single stem through the conic crown to the drooping tip. It has longer leaves than the other true cedars, to 1⅛in long, stout and deep green although in the hot, dry areas of CA they can be dusty gray. It is less hardy than the other two and grows no further north than the southern end of NY where there are trees in Tarrytown, Brooklyn Botanic Garden and Planting Fields. It is more frequent in MD, with shapely trees in Annapolis, in NJ, with a 60ft tree at Prospect House, Princeton, and in DC. It becomes really common from VA southwards, along the Gulf Coast into west TX and north in the Mississippi Valley through AR, TN, MO and KY and uncommon in OH. There is a tree in Madison, WI. In the west it is very common on Vancouver Island and round the city of Vancouver south to Tacoma, with one in Leschi Park, Seattle 11ft 4in round. There are a few in OR and inland in CA at Booneville and Bishop but it is common again, and large further south with trees of 108ft x 16ft and 100ft x 17ft in the Capitol Park at Sacramento, and a boulevard of trees as tall along Colorado Avenue, Los Angeles. It is common from there to San Diego, and in the Bay Area. There is a tree in Las Vegas, NV.

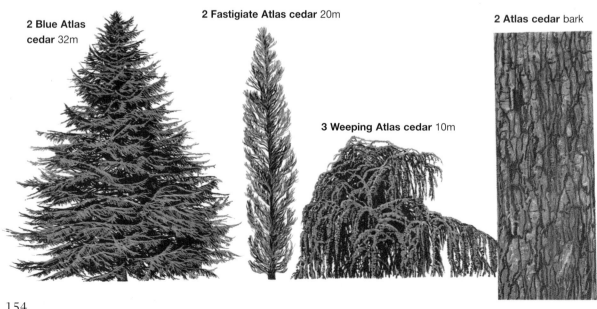

2 **Blue Atlas cedar** 32m

2 **Fastigiate Atlas cedar** 20m

3 **Weeping Atlas cedar** 10m

2 **Atlas cedar** bark

4 Deodar cedar ♂ flw

1 Cedar of Lebanon

2 Blue Atlas cedar

♂ flw

♂ flw

Cyprus cedar

bark

1 Cedar of Lebanon 40m

cone

bract from
cone

**4 Deodar
cedar**
35m

Tamarack and other Larches

The larches are conifers bearing woody cones ripening within the year, and are deciduous. Before falling off, the leaves turn luminous gold. The only other deciduous conifers are several in the more primitive Redwood Family, and they shed minor shoots as well. The larches' leaves are borne in the same way as in the true cedars. A new shoot has spirally arranged single leaves and lateral buds. Next year, the buds enlarge into short spurs bearing close whorls of 30–40 leaves. Larches are pioneer trees, seeding out on to open land, and so they have rapid early growth in full light and will not grow properly in shade. Fully grown trees must be well separated to retain live crowns in depth and plantations have to be thinned regularly. The timber is strong and durable when the whitish sapwood is removed, and large sizes are used in the construction of trawlers. The ten species of larch divide clearly into three with extensive lowland ranges, together ringing the north polar plains, and seven relict species surviving in small areas in mountains to the south. One lowland and two montane relict species are native to North America.

TAMARACK (1), *Larix laricina* grows from near the northern limit for trees from Labrador to AK, south to northeastern BC and round the Great Lakes to PA and MD. Many areas of very shapely small trees border the roads in northern NY, in VT, CT, ME and in ON with dense woods by Rt 401 from London to Toronto, also in WI and MN. Some are planted in IA around Fort Dodge and Ames. The tamarack bark has no ridges at any age but is finely flaking dull pink or pink-brown. The flowers are very small, slender and bright red.

WESTERN LARCH (2), *Larix occidentalis* is the biggest larch of all and has been recorded 220ft tall while the 1972 champion, in MT, was 177ft x 24ft 5in. It grows at 2–7000ft altitude from southeast BC into ID and MT and eastern WA and OR. Its leaves are bright grassy green on both sides and keeled beneath, and the bracts of the cone project as whiskers. In BC it tends to be broadly conic with rising branches but in the USA it has a long, narrow spire top and level branches. It is abundant by Rt 200 west of Missoula, MT to Cour d'Alene, ID and by Rt 3, BC around Greenwood. In eastern WA it grows in dry sandy woods. The bark soon becomes widely fissured into thick pink-brown scaly ridges.

SUBALPINE LARCH (3), *Larix lyallii* is a timberline tree at between 5000 and 8000ft each side of the southern end of the AB/BC border, on a few peaks in ID and MT and on the eastern flanks of the Cascades in WA, everywhere within the range of the Western larch but above it. In the fall it is the vivid gold seen from the air often separating the snowy tops from the dark green forest. It is like a short, stunted, rather weeping Western larch with dense, soft white hairs on its shoots and cone-scales.

EUROPEAN LARCH (4), *Larix decidua* from the Alps, with superior forms in the Tatra Mountains and on the Polish plains, varies considerably with the source of seed. In general, trees from the western Alps have fairly stout pink shoots and large cones 2in long while those from the Sudeten and Tatra Mountains have slender white shoots and small, 1in cones. In America they are mostly somewhere between. There are trees in the botanic gardens in PQ and ON and in parks, squares and some small gardens in ME, MA, CT and NY to DE and from PA to OH and in botanic gardens to WI.

JAPANESE LARCH (5), *Larix kaempferi* has dark orange to purple shoots, broader leaves with two gray bands beneath and a squat cone with down-curled scales. It is seen over the same range as the European but rather less frequently, although more in residential areas of Pittsburg, PA and Canton to Wooster in OH.

HYBRID LARCH (6), *Larix × eurolepis* came from cones of Japanese larch in Scotland pollinated by nearby European larch and is variably intermediate in most ways but has taller cones. It is grown in the Montreal Botanic Garden, PQ and the Dawes Arboretum, OH.

SIBERIAN LARCH (7), *Larix sibirica* is like the European but has softly hairy shoots and cone-scales. It is rare but there are trees at the Arnold Arboretum, MA; Ottawa Botanic Garden, ON to 60ft x 5ft; the George Landis Arboretum, NY, 50ft and the Secrest and Holden Arboreta, OH.

DAHURIAN LARCH (8), *Larix gmelinii* from Siberia east of the Yenisei River is a low tree with spreading branches bearing grassy foliage after January and small cones. It grows in the Ottawa Botanic Garden, ON, the Arnold Arboretum, MA and most of the OH botanic gardens.

GOLDEN LARCH (9), *Pseudolarix amabilis* from China has spurs which increase in size annually, larger broader leaves, bunched male flowers and cones like globe artichokes. It is a good park tree only from MA to PA and DE with fine trees in Central Park, New York; Fairmount Park, Philadelphia; by Carnegie Lake, Princeton, NJ with outliers in the Missouri Botanic Garden, St. Louis and Lyndale Park, Minneapolis, MN.

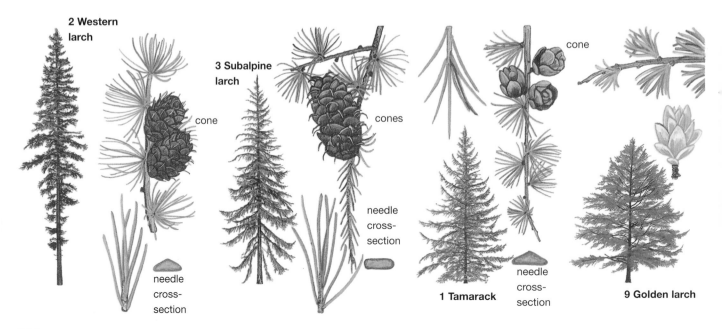

2 Western larch

3 Subalpine larch

cone

cones

cone

needle cross-section

needle cross-section

needle cross-section

1 Tamarack

9 Golden larch

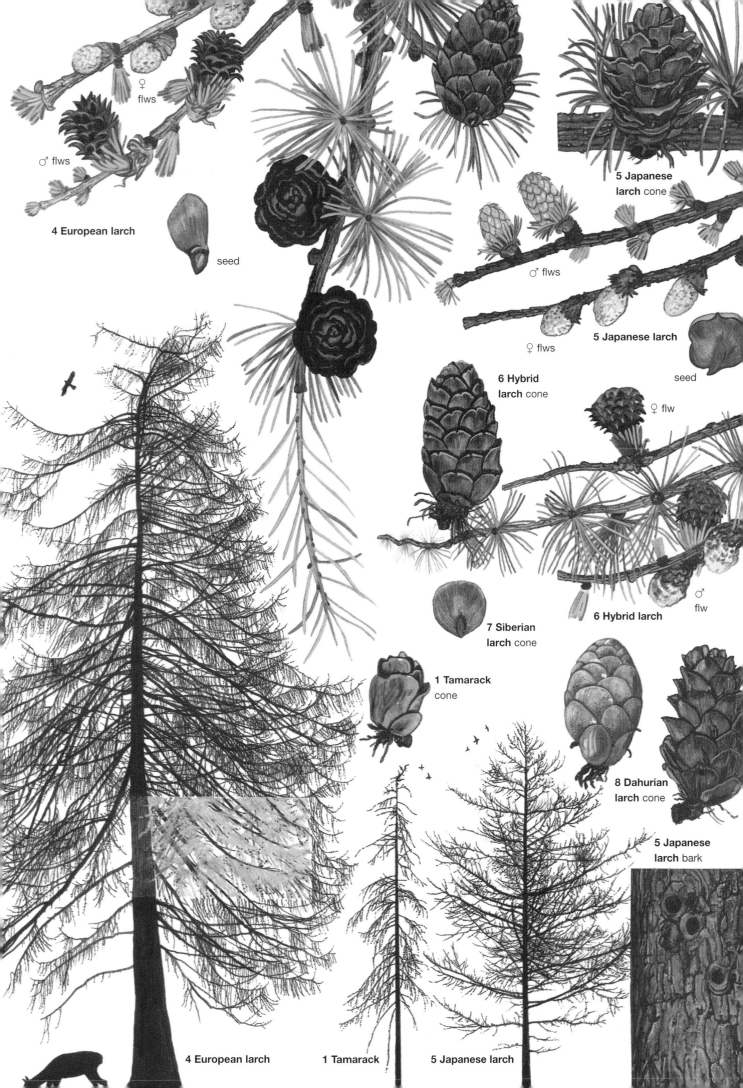

♀ flws

♂ flws

4 European larch

seed

5 Japanese larch cone

♂ flws

♀ flws

5 Japanese larch

seed

6 Hybrid larch cone

♀ flw

7 Siberian larch cone

1 Tamarack cone

6 Hybrid larch

♂ flw

8 Dahurian larch cone

5 Japanese larch bark

4 European larch

1 Tamarack

5 Japanese larch

White and Eurasian spruces

The Spruces or Spruce firs are about 35 species across the Northern Hemisphere in a pattern similar to that of the larches, with a few widely spread across the northern plains and the majority reduced to small areas in mountains to the south. They are characterised by scaling and flaking but never ridged bark; harsh foliage with stiff, often spine-tipped leaves, and shoots roughened by pegs left when the leaves fall. Also by hanging cones, woody or leathery, ripening in their first year and shed complete. They have big winter buds which contain all the tissues for the next year's shoots, like the silver firs, and expand them rapidly in spring, completing the extension by June leaving the rest of the growing season to fill the buds for the next year's growth. The female flowers of all spruces are erect and bright red, quite spectacular when bunched in large numbers as they can be on the Dragon and Likiang spruces, and some turn purple as they bend over to enlarge into cones. The male flowers are ovoid or globular, at various angles on upper shoots and strung around lower hanging shoots. Before shedding pollen they are covered by thin filmy tissue, red or yellow.

NORWAY SPRUCE (1), *Picea abies* from the European Alps, Scandinavia and Western Russia is the most widespread and common spruce in North America. It will have been brought by early settlers and in many parts each side of the US/Canada border it seems to have been used to rectify the disastrous wholesale clearance of the native woods which left the farmland grievously exposed, for it is as farm shelterbelt that it dominates so much countryside there. The two main forms of crown, 'brush' and 'comb', are often seen adjacent and mixed in these belts, the 'brush' with normal spruce, bunched shoots and the 'comb' with more sparse, upcurving branches from which the minor shoots hang in lines. In Winnipeg, MB the trees are injured by winter frosts and are poorly shaped and small. From Montreal, PQ it is shapely and common south to Norfolk, VA and on the plains to NC where it is also common in the valleys in the Allegheny Mountains. Here the trees are mainly of the 'comb' form and the foliage is very dark green contrasting with the very pale brown of the numerous long cones. It is common through MI, IN and IL to MO and south in the Mississippi Valley to Dyersburg, TN and infrequent into the hills of AR and OK, and becomes less frequent from WI and MN to IA. In the Arnold Arboretum, MA the trees are to 105ft tall and 11ft round and one in Marquand Park, Princeton, NJ was 92ft x 11ft 2in in 1981. In the west, there are 80ft trees by the Federal Building in Missoula, MT and the Capitol at Cheyenne, WY and beyond again near the Capitol in Carson City, NV, 105ft x 8ft. It is common

around Vancouver and in the Okanagan Valley, BC and in WA into OR less frequently. The **Golden spruce (2)**, **'Aurea'** has golden new shoots, almost green by the winter and is in a few eastern collections, as is the densely conical **'Pyramidata'**.

WHITE SPRUCE (3), *Picea glauca* is native in a broad band across the continent from Labrador and ME to AK south to MI, mid-SK and interior BC with an arm down into MT and an outlier in the Black Hills of SD. It is planted commonly southward in NY and OH and less frequently in PA, MD and DE. It has a remarkably slender crown in snowy, mountainous areas as by the Icefield Parkway in AB but in the east it ages with a domed top. Where much mixed with planted Blue spruce, as around Winnipeg, MB, its thin leading and top shoots contrast with the stout ones of that species. The shoot is clean white or pale pink and smoothly and faintly grooved. The bud is pale orange-brown. Crushed foliage emits a scent often described as mousey but to some it seems more fruity with flavours of blackcurrant or grapefruit.

SERBIAN SPRUCE (4), *Picea omorika* grows in a small area of valley in mountains in Yugoslavia by the River Drina and caused a botanical sensation when it was found, in 1876. It is a flat-needle spruce and all these hitherto known belong to the Pacific shores of America and Asia, and the eastern Himalaya, while all the western Asiatic, European and eastern American spruces have needles almost square in section. This spruce belongs to an older flora and survived the Ice Ages in its mountain retreat. It is very hardy and grows equally well on chalk and limestone and acid peats. It is seen, with its distinct spired crown, in parks and gardens from ON and MA through PA and OH to WI and MN, and in the west, in Victoria and Vancouver, BC. There is a line by the Smithsonian Institute in Washington, DC, and trees in Market Square, Lancaster, and along Beechwood Boulevard, Pittsburg in PA. It is frequent in roadside gardens in Manchester, NH, Albany and Graymoor, NY and in most botanic gardens from ON to MN.

SIBERIAN SPRUCE, *Picea obovata* is what the Norway spruce turns into in eastern Russia and Siberia with pale hairy shoots and brighter green leaves and smaller cones. It is a small, shapely tree.

SARGENT SPRUCE (5), *Picea brachytyla* is a tree of beautiful, bright, rather pendulous foliage from western China. It is grown at the Dawes Arboretum, OH.

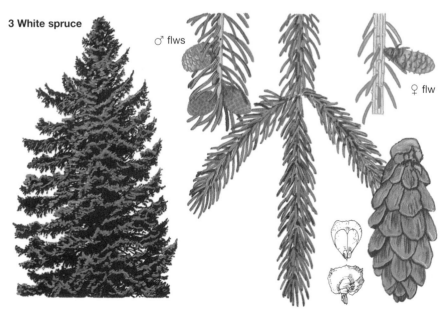

3 White spruce ♂ flws ♀ flw

1 Norway spruce 'Cupressina'

1 Norway spruce

♂ flws

♀ flws

immature cone

cone

twig
detail

♂ flw

♀ flw

under

4 Serbian spruce

♂ flw

5 Sargent spruce

♀ flw

mature
cone

old bark

seed

1 Norway spruce

young bark

cone

bark

cone
scale

1 Norway spruce

Northern
Swedish type

5 Sargent spruce

4 Serbian spruce

2 'Aurea'

Sitka, Blue and Asiatic spruces

SITKA SPRUCE (1), *Picea sitchensis* is the biggest spruce in the world and the fastest growing. In its native stands by the Pacific Coast it has been found 305ft tall and over 52ft round. It is also the spruce with the greatest north–south spread, from the Alaskan Kodiak Island and north to Anchorage, on islands and mainland coast inlets and hillsides through BC, WA and OR to river mouths in CA ending with a last wood on low cliff at Caspar near Fort Bragg some 1900 miles to the south. From Vancouver to Tacoma outside the National Parks, there are only small fieldside trees left, but the clifftops along most of the OR coast are thickly covered in a mixture of scattered old broken-topped trees above wind-sheared regrowth skirted by younger trees with 3ft leading shoots. The big trees are in the Olympic Rain Forest areas. By the road into the Hoh River, a superb tree with a noticeboard was 265ft x 37ft 3in in 1971 and one by the trail was 260ft x 27ft 10in. Surprisingly for a tree so adaptable, the Sitka seems rarely to be planted within or beyond its range. In the eastern states a small plot in the Secrest Arboretum, OH planted in 1969 had trees to 13ft tall with leading shoots 3ft long in 1976. The Sitka is one of the prickliest spruces, its stiff, hard needles being sharply spined. Old trees have broadly columnar crowns of long, gently arched branches sparsely set with short, hanging shoots.

ENGELMANN SPRUCE (2), *Picea engelmannii* also has a big north–south range, nearly as long but much broader and inland, from northern BC and AB on interior mountains to CO, NM and AZ and along the Cascades to the CA border. There are fine trees to 130ft by Sunday Pass and near Greenwood, BC. In WY there are very slender spires in Grand Tetons National Park and in the Togwatee Pass. On the Cameron Pass to CO it grows at from 9–10,000ft. It is planted in roadside gardens and in parks commonly in AB, MT and CO. Further east it is commonly planted in MN and WI, less commonly in NE and IA. The leaves are soft or rather stiff but not rigid, and are short-spined. Crushed, they have a scent of menthol or camphor. The distinctively orange-brown ripe cones have scales with toothed margins.

BLUE SPRUCE (3), *Picea pungens* is variably blue-gray to dark blue-green in the wild stands from 6–11000ft in ID, UT, WY and CO to NM. There are stands of very slender 100ft trees in the Grand Tetons National Park, WY and it has been recorded to 150ft tall and nearly 16ft round. The discoverer, Dr. Parry in 1865 sent seed to Sargent which yielded a particularly blue tree and this was propagated and sent to England in 1877 and to Holland. Nurseries in both countries and in the USA soon distributed several as 'Glauca' or 'Koster's' and these are now the commonest and most widely spread spruce in towns and gardens in North America. It is planted from Montreal, PQ to Winnipeg, MB and Regina, SK and Banff, AB through BC. Southward it is scarce on the eastern Coastal Plain, except for a few in GA and in the Allegheny Mountain towns to NC, but common in north TX and in the Prairie States. It is very prominent in New England gardens. The name 'pungens' means 'sharp' and the rigid, stout leaves are well spined and stand up from stout shoots which, in the blue forms can be orange or dark brown. An ice-blue-white selection, **'Hoopsii'** is now becoming common.

BREWER SPRUCE (4), *Picea breweriana* was discovered by Professor W.H. Brewer in 1863 and grows only in a few small groves at around 7000ft in the Siskiyou and Klamath Mountains on the OR/CA border. One accessible group in OR is at Camp Hill above Galice and one in CA is in Bear Basin above Gasquet. This is a flat-needle spruce like the Sitka and has a similar bark of raised, large circular plates but very different foliage. The finely hairy shoots have leaves sparsely set and slender, many curving gently, and hang in dark curtains from upcurved branches. The inner shoots on immature trees are 5–6ft long and are strung at intervals with 1½in globular male flowers. Trees 70 years planted in Britain are 60ft x 6ft and luxuriant, but the species does not find much of America congenial. A scrawny little one exists in Highland Park, Rochester, NY and there are tiny ones in Queen Elizabeth Park, Vancouver, BC and Point Defiance Park, Tacoma, WA.

MORINDA SPRUCE (5), *Picea smithiana* is nearly as weeping as the Brewer spruce but has almost rounded, long, stiff leaves dark green all round. It comes from the western Himalayas and is hardly seen at all in America but there is one at the Capitol in Sacramento, CA 56ft x 6ft 3in.

HONDO SPRUCE (6), *Picea jezoensis* from Japan is a flat-needle spruce, with blue-white bands on the underside of the stiff, spine-tipped leaves and is very rare, with one in Point Defiance Park.

LIKIANG SPRUCE (7), *Picea likiangensis*, a very variable tree from mountain ranges in western China, may be in a few collections. Its blue-gray foliage can be thickly set with scarlet and crimson flowers followed by long, 5in cones.

6 Hondo spruce

♀ flws

♀ flws

7 Likiang spruce

♂ flws

Koyama's spruce

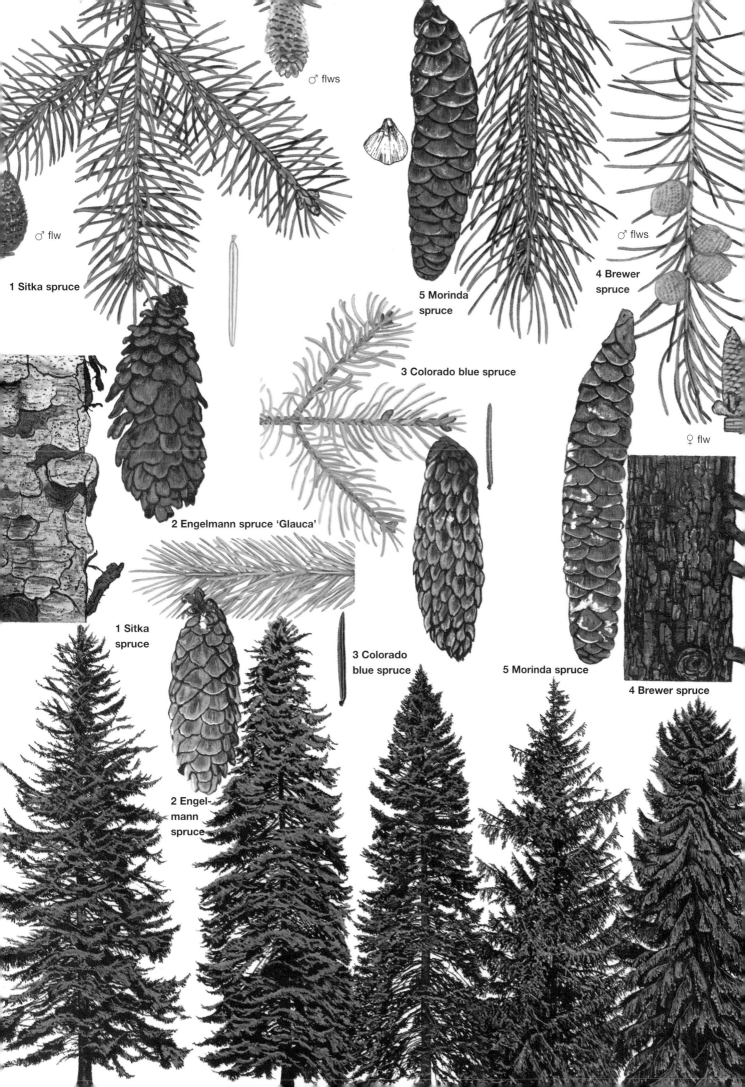

♂ flws

♂ flw

1 Sitka spruce

5 Morinda spruce

4 Brewer spruce

♂ flws

3 Colorado blue spruce

2 Engelmann spruce 'Glauca'

♀ flw

1 Sitka spruce

3 Colorado blue spruce

5 Morinda spruce

4 Brewer spruce

2 Engel-mann spruce

Red, Black and Asiatic spruces

RED SPRUCE (1), *Picea rubens* grows from Cape Breton Island, NS through NB and ME to southern PQ and ON and southward on mountain tops through NY, PA, VA and NC just into TN. It is the spruce which, with the Fraser fir, clothes many of the highest peaks of the Blue Ridge Mountains, NC, to 6000ft. By the Spruce Fir Trail in the Great Smoky Mountains in TN there are trees to 100ft x 10ft. It is planted to the west of its range in roadside gardens in OH, WI and IA. Typically the bright grassy green leaves stand nearly vertically slender, wiry and short, nearly round in section, and when crushed they give scents of apples or candlewax, but in parts of the north it has hybridised with the Black spruce so they are darker, bluer green and more spreading. The crimson male flowers curve upwards as they shed pollen and the 2in cones ripen pale orange-brown, often in bunches. The bark is a rich purple-brown or dark orange-brown, dark gray on older trees at high altitudes. It flakes finely until it fissures into small, concave plates. The crown is narrowly conic and dense with lower branches bending down then sweeping upwards to the tips, and has a good spire top.

BLACK SPRUCE (2), *Picea mariana* was named from Maryland when that term was a general one for a large area, and it is not native to the modern state. It is native from nearby northeastern PA across a vast area to Labrador and AK, through all Canada except BC where it is only in the northeastern part, also missing southern AB and SK. In its most southern extension in the Rocky Mountains by the Icefield Parkway, AB, it is in small groups on boggy flats among woods of White and Engelmann spruce and its crowns are even more slender and bluer. It has been planted rather infrequently south of its range in OH and DE. It has short hairs on its pink-brown shoot and very small, slender, ⅛in leaves spread all round it, with the scent of menthol cough-sweets when crushed. The crown is a dense mass of fine twigs and looks quite blue from a distance and, away from the areas where it is very slim, it ages with a bushy, domed top. Growth is always slow, so the leading shoot on immature trees is short. Male flowers are small, conic, numerous and crimson while females are crowded on the topmost few branches and are deep red. They are borne by young trees not yet 10ft tall and ripen into bunched, shiny red-brown cones less than 2in long.

ORIENTAL SPRUCE (3), *Picea orientalis*, is the only spruce with leaves even shorter than those of the Black spruce. They are ¼–⅓in long, deep glossy green on all four surfaces and bevelled to a round tip. They lie closely all round young shoots and are parted beneath as they age,

persisting for eight years or more. It comes from the Caucasus Mountains and northeastern Turkey and is, after the Norway spruce, the most successful and frequently planted exotic spruce in North America, although seemingly only in the northeastern parts, from ON to OH and rarely in the west. The bark is pale gray with dark freckles until it browns with age and cracks into regular small raised plates. The crown is a narrow spire. In the main crown the new shoots project as spikes. Male flowers are pointed and dark red, numerous on the underside of small shoots near their tips. Female flowers are confined to the top few branches until the tree is mature when they are on the stronger branches all over the crown. At the Arnold Arboretum, MA a specimen 72 years old was 66ft x 6ft 2in while at Highland Park, Rochester, NY, one 78 years old was 82ft x 6ft 4in. A fine tree in the Tyler Arboretum, PA was 98ft x 8ft 9in in 1976 and good ones are frequent in OH where Spring Grove Cemetery, Cincinnati has many 85ft tall and Mount Airy Arboretum many to 65 ft.

TIGERTAIL SPRUCE (4), *Picea polita* from Japan has stout, rigid, ferociously spined leaves which make a shoot very painful to grasp even quite lightly, which explains the common name, while 'polita' means 'polished' from the shining chestnut-brown big buds and white shoots. The tree is an unusual fresh yellowish green, for a spruce, and its level branches carry a dense mass of shoots which in older trees remain in the interior crown, bare and congested. It is infrequent in collections from MA and OH to NC. At Winterthur, DE one was 80ft x 5ft 10in and one planted in 1914 was 70ft x 6ft 10in in 1987. Two in the New York Botanic Garden are about 50ft tall.

DRAGON SPRUCE (5), *Picea asperata* from China is a little less hostile but also has rigid, spined but shorter, blue-gray lined leaves. Its bark shreds away in big, papery flakes. It is in collections from Montreal, PQ, to OH, DE, the Morton Arboretum, IL and the Boerner Botanic Garden, WI. The biggest is at Highland Park, 75ft x 6ft 4in when 69 years old.

ALCOCK SPRUCE (6), *Picea bicolor* from Japan is a square-needle spruce with the two interior faces broadly banded white and the outer two dark blue-green, hence the botanic name. It makes a very broadly conic tree with lower branches sweeping out and up with rather closer systems of stout white shoots. It is in some collections in NH and NY with one tree also in a roadside garden in Manchester, NH. The finest is a great tree in the Bayard Cutting Arboretum, NY, 75ft x 9ft.

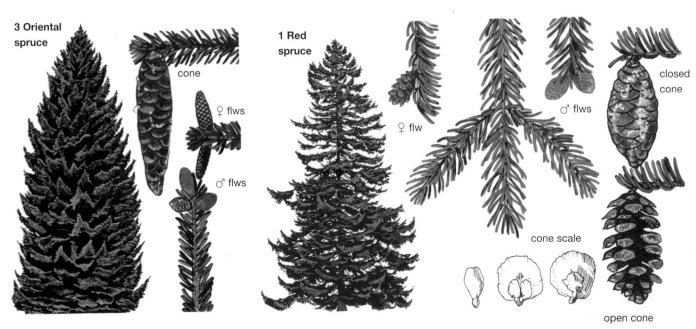

3 Oriental spruce
cone
♀ flws
♂ flws

1 Red spruce
♀ flw
♂ flws

♂ flws
closed cone
cone scale
open cone

♀ flws

♂ flws

5 Dragon spruce

immature
cone

cone

bark

end view
of shoot

cone scale

6 Alcock spruce
immature cone

cone
scale

6 Alcock spruce open cone

♂ flws

4 Tigertail spruce

♀ flws

6 Alcock spruce

immature
cone

4 Tigertail spruce

mature cone

2 Black spruce

♂ flws

♀ flws

cone

**2 Black
spruce**

**5 Dragon
spruce**

**6 Alcock
spruce**

**4 Tigertail
spruce**

2 Black spruce

Hemlocks

The Hemlocks are close relatives of the spruces named after the poisonous herb of that name because the crushed foliage of the Eastern hemlock was deemed to have the same scent. They have small, slender leaves, and, with one exception, very small, often droplet-like cones borne freely over densely foliaged crowns. There are four in North America, two in the east and two in the west.

WESTERN HEMLOCK (1), *Tsuga heterophylla* is the tallest and finest by far, and its range extends from the Kenai Peninsula in AK along the coastal slopes and islands to northern CA, inland to the Cascade Mountains in OR and in an interior belt from the Selkirk Mountains, BC, to MT and ID. It bears deep shade when young, better than any other conifer except the Redwood sprouting from living stumps, and in dense rain-forest seedlings grow mainly on the decaying logs where they are free from competing ground-plants with their roots straddling the log, in lines, as Sitka spruce will. The hemlock has a 'dropper' leading shoot, on which the new, sappy and vulnerable extension hangs 1–2ft below the woody, tough apex of the arch, which thus takes the knocks as it grows between overhead branches. So the hemlock weaves through the canopy and comes to dominate the forest. The western hemlock makes a very elegant, slender tall tree with slightly up-curved branches arching to dangle great quantities of hanging foliage and can grow 4ft in a year on a variety of damp soils.

EASTERN HEMLOCK (2), *Tsuga canadensis* has leaves tapering from their broadest part near the base, unlike the others, and a line of leaves along and closely above the shoot, twisted to show the silver-banded underside, which makes a unique pattern. On the northern plains it can be broad and strongly branched but in the mountain valleys towards the south, the big trees are mostly as slender and conic as the western species, and a distinctive pale yellowish green. The bark is soon heavily ridged and dark, sometimes nearly black The range is from NS and NB across southern PQ and ON, south of Lake Superior to WI and MN, and south to MD by the coast and through PA, OH, and the Allegheny Mountains to GA and AL. It is common in parks and gardens throughout this range but little beyond it.

CAROLINA HEMLOCK (3), *Tsuga caroliniana* is rare in the wild in deep valleys in the highest parts of VA, NC, TN and GA and was first found at Lynville Falls, NC in 1880. It is however not so rare in parks and gardens where its deep rich green foliage makes it attractive as a small tree of distinction. Close to, the leaves are well spaced and radiate from the shiny, hairy-grooved pale brown shoots, but they form a densely leafy crown. An early one planted in the Arnold Arboretum in 1886 was 50ft x 6ft when 90 years old and there are trees at Smith College also in MA, Highland Park, Bayard Cutting Arboretum NY, and Winterthur Garden, DE, with two 60ft tall. There are trees in most collections through OH, IL and MI, and in Lyndale Park, Minneapolis, MN.

MOUNTAIN HEMLOCK (4), *Tsuga mertensiana* is almost a snowline tree from the Kenai Peninsular, AK by the coast on mountain tops to the Olympic Mountains and along the Cascades and Sierra Nevada and in the Siskiyou Mountains, with an interior range from the Selkirk Mountains, BC to ID and western MT. It is often seen struggling against extreme exposure, as in the moonscape lavas of the Mackenzie Pass, OR, but in slight shelter, as around Crater Lake at the same altitudes, around 5,700ft it makes a shapely, conic tree to 110ft tall. It is an aberrant hemlock in its large, spruce-like cones and in having blue-gray leaves all round short spur-like shoots, mimicking the Blue Atlas cedar, but they are various shades to deep green also and they are the same color all round, which is unlike other hemlocks. The bark is orange-brown, thinly flaking and stripping vertically until it becomes hard and ridged with age.

JEFFREY'S HYBRID HEMLOCK (5), *Tsuga × jeffreyi* is of interest for its origin. It was known first as the only seedling arising from a batch of seed sent to England by John Jeffrey in 1851. The second appearance was of seedlings among a batch of rhododendrons, also in England. It was not found in the wild until 1969 in WA in a stand with both parents, the Western and Mountain hemlocks. It is much more like the Mountain hemlock in bark, crown and foliage.

NORTHERN JAPANESE HEMLOCK (6), *Tsuga diversifolia* from northern Honshu and Hokkaido has short, ½in, blunt, notched leaves very silvered beneath, on an orange shoot with tiny hairs in grooves. It is rare but small trees are in the George Landis Arboretum and at Highland Park, and Bailey Arboretum, NY.

SOUTHERN JAPANESE HEMLOCK (7), *Tsuga sieboldii* from southern Honshu and Shikoku has variably longer and less silvered leaves on a shiny cream or brown shoot without hairs. This is rare, too, with one in the Barnes Arboretum, Philadelphia, PA 31ft x 2ft 4in in 1971.

CHINESE HEMLOCK (8), *Tsuga chinensis* has yellow-green leaves with gray-green stripes beneath. It has a broad crown and blackish rough bark.

7 Southern Japanese hemlock

6 Northern Japanese hemlock

4 Mountain hemlock

2 Eastern hemlock

1 Western hemlock

7 Southern Japanese hemlock

bark

6 Northern Japanese hemlock

3 Carolina hemlock

5 Jeffrey's hybrid hemlock

under

8 Chinese hemlock

Weeping hemlock 'Sargentii'

4 Mountain hemlock

2 Eastern hemlock

1 Western hemlock

Weeping hemlock 'Sargentii'

Shore and other Two-needle pines

The Pines number about 110, of which 36 are native to North America. Pines are alone among the conifers in having their leaves or needles united at the base in bundles in a sheath. These are short shoots split into two, three or five so the needles of a two-needle pine are semicircular in cross-section and are thick and stiff, those in bundles of three are triangular and more slender and those in fives tend to be more slender still and often drooping, and are called Blue or White pines. White pines have easily worked timber and are distinguished in America as 'soft pines' while two- and three-needle pines are 'hard pines'. Seedlings have true leaves, flat, often silvery blue and saw-edged. These are grown for many years by pinyons and on sprouts on adult Canary and Stone pines.

SHORE PINE (1), *Pinus contorta* is the coastal form of the Lodgepole pine from Alaska to Mendocino, CA. It is usually a wind-blown bushy tree of small size but seedlings spreading on the shore at Long Beach, WA have splendid 3ft leaders. The Sierra Nevada form, var. *murrayana* from the Columbia River to the cross-ranges is a fine tree.

Lodgepole pine (2), var. *latifolia* has longer, broader and paler, yellowish leaves and ranges from central AK down the interior and eastern Rocky Mountains and the Black Hills in SD, to Mexico. This is the pine of the Yellowstone Park geyser-basins and gorge. The prickly cones stay on the tree with seed enclosed for decades until a fire comes through and the whole area is regenerated with trees all of the same age.

BISHOP PINE (3), *Pinus muricata* holds more formidably armed cones very tightly for more than 60 years. It grows in small coastal groves in CA with fine, blue-gray conic, long-spired trees in the northernmost and in Pigmy Forest, and good trees by the Noyo River mouth, Fort Bragg, but yellowish-green spreading upright bushy trees around San Louis Obispo, where it was discovered, and Lompoc.

VIRGINIA PINE, *Pinus virginiana*, more aptly named Scrub pine, is wild from Long Island by the coast to NC and inland in the mountains to AL and TN. It seeds on to road-banks and disturbed soil.

JACK PINE (4), *Pinus banksiana* holds its cones pointing outwards and they stay closed until gray, lichened and grown into the bark, and fire is needed to spread the tree. It ranges from NS to WI, MI and NH. The bark is in long orange-brown plates.

RED PINE (5), *Pinus resinosa* is rather isolated genetically from others and will not cross with any. It ranges from Cape Breton Island, NS with small patches in NF, broadly to PA, MI, MN and MB. It is 92ft x 6ft in the Tyler Arboretum, PA. The rather slender leaves snap cleanly when bent in a sharp curve.

SPRUCE PINE (6), *Pinus glabra* has bark, smooth pale gray, becoming brown-gray fissured into smooth ridges. It grows from SC to LA, noticeably by US 17 and 80 around Savannah and 441 to Milledgeville, GA and planted in gardens up the Mississippi Valley to IN.

STONE PINE (7), *Pinus pinea* holds up its huge umbrella crowns only in southern CA where there are fine trees in Capitol Square, Sacramento to 92ft x 11ft and 85ft x 14ft 6in and trees in Saratoga, Salinas, Wasco, Ventura and in the Huntington Gardens, Pasadena, where three planted in 1907 were to 95ft tall and 11ft 4in round when 71 years old.

ALEPPO PINE, *Pinus halepensis* from the Mediterranean has a grassy gray-green almost filmy crown of slender leaves and purple cones. It is grown in AZ in Phoenix and in CA from Lemon Cove and Fresno to Sacramento, where a remarkable tree in the Capitol Park is 108ft x 9ft, through Monterey to San Diego.

AUSTRIAN PINE (8), *Pinus nigra* var. *nigra* is a common farm-shelter tree from Montreal, PQ to NY, with groups in Central Park, to MO and TN and frequent in KS and OK. There are trees in Denver, CO, Salt Lake City, UT and Reno, NV and Rawlins, WY. It is common in BC.

The **Corsican pine**, var. *maritima* is a grayer, shapely, level branched version of it, with longer leaves letting through much more light. It is rare, with some on Mount Royal, Montreal, PQ; at Hyde Park Mansion, NY; a plot and a single tree 80ft x 5ft at the Secrest Arboretum, OH and trees in Forest Park, St. Louis, MO.

SCOTS PINE (9), *Pinus sylvestris* with short, twisted blue-gray leaves and dark red or pink bark is common in town and country from PQ to Norfolk, VA and from SK to AR, Omaha and Waterworks Park, Des Moines, IA. There are trees in Salt Lake City, UT and Washington Square, San Francisco, CA, a few through OR and WA to where it is common again in NC.

Japanese black pine

8 Austrian pine

9 Scots pine

7 Stone pine

bark

bark

bark

9 Scots pine

8 Austrian pine

(2)

(2)

2 Lodgepole pine

Japanese black pine

(2)

(2)

6 Spruce pine

3 Bishop pine

7 Stone pine

bark

(2)

4 Jack pine

(2)

5 Red pine

bark

1 Shore pine

(2)

(2)

(2)

bark

bark

(2)

bark

6 Spruce pine bark

1 Shore pine young tree

2 Lodgepole pine

6 Spruce pine

3 Bishop pine

4 Jack pine

5 Red pine

Ponderosa and other Pines

PONDEROSA PINE (1), *Pinus ponderosa* or Western yellow pine is, in its three forms, the dominant pine of the United States Rocky Mountains from the Canadian border to the Mexican border, both of which it crosses. Vast areas of the southwest, now semi-desert or thin scrub, were splended stands of this pine until cleared by logging, fire and over-grazing. Ponderosa grows from near sea-level in WA to 10,000ft in AZ, in rainfalls from 100in or more to 10in or less, and on any soil. The bark is gray-pink to pink-brown in long plates, shedding 2in, irregularly lobed flakes like jigsaw puzzle pieces, which pile up around its base. In some of the drier areas, as in the Santiam Pass, OR, the bark is bright orange-pink and in some others it is red-brown in shallow plates like crocodile skin. The crown retains its neat conic shape with a spire of closely upswept small side-branches above more level branching, in the best stands, to 150–180ft. The cone is 4–5in long, about half the size of that of the similar Jeffrey pine, and, like it, has a down-curved prickle on each scale.

The range in BC is south of the Fraser River, with good 100ft trees by the Sunday Pass to Penticton and it is common around Vancouver. The finest trees are in the OR Cascades, Siskiyou Mountains and Sierra Nevada, CA. The Merced Canyon, Yosemite, CA has superb 150ft trees along the flat and one by the entrance gate at El Portal is 185ft x 15ft. In the east, Ottawa Botanic Garden has a line of fine trees 80ft tall, Rochester University, NY has two to 90ft x 9ft and there are trees in the big gardens in OH, PA, IL and WI.

JEFFREY PINE (2), *Pinus jeffreyi*, closely related to the Ponderosa, replaces it at above 6000ft in CA and somewhat lower in the Siskiyou Mountains into OR. It is the tree of the white granite of Glacier Point, Yosemite; of the woods around the south shore of Lake Tahoe and of high in the San Bernardino Mountains where, at Bear Lake one probably 410 years old was 155ft x 16ft 6in in 1971. Planted in the east it has grown into splendid conic trees at Cornell University, Highland Park, NY, the Secrest Arboretum, OH and the Morton Arboretum, IL. It has longer needles than the Ponderosa, 8–10in long, paler, blue-gray, stouter and stiffer, the shoot bloomed white and longer and much broader cones.

COULTER PINE (3), *Pinus coulteri* has the most massive and fiercely hook-spined cone of any tree, weighing up to 5lb. The tree is broad with heavy low branches and stout blue-white shoots. The needles are stout, stiff and 10–12in long and the bark very rough dark purplish-gray in thick, scaly ridges. It is wild in the mountains at 3–6000ft from the Santa Lucia Mountains to the San Bernardino Mountains, CA and into Mexico.

DIGGER PINE (4), *Pinus sabiniana* is the pine of the drier foothills around the Central Valley of CA where it has such peculiarly thin foliage that the woodland is almost transparent. The slender, bloomed shoot is curved and bears thin whorls, widely separated, of needles 10–12in long. The stem divides low into several vertical trunks which divide again at narrow angles to make a tall dome often heavily clustered with the 10in, squat cones. In Paso Robles, one of two similar trees is 118ft x 10ft and at Sacramento Capitol one is 108ft x 10ft but the long stands beside Rt 49 and Rt 140 around Mariposa and El Portal are half these heights.

KNOBCONE PINE (5), *Pinus attenuata* is at once recognised by its bright, grass-green foliage and the upright branches tightly invested by cones weathering gray and pointing downwards. It is a foothill tree, often under open stands of Sugar pine, from south OR throughout northern CA but in the southern half restricted to a few areas.

SLASH PINE (6), *Pinus elliottii* has its needles in twos and threes 8–12in long with a lemon scent when crushed. It makes a broad columnar dark tree with upper branches rising to a big dome and lower tending to droop, and all are sinuous. It is native near the coast from SC to LA and replaces loblolly and longleaf pines in south FL. In Duncan Park, Natchez, MS it is 100ft x 10ft. It is planted quite commonly north and west into OK and AR.

SHORTLEAF PINE (7), *Pinus echinata* also has its leaves mixed two or three per bundle but they are only 2–3in long. It has pink-gray or dark orange-gray, scaly, often shaggy bark and an open, broad columnar crown showing abundant adhering old cones. The branches bear many short, grassy sprouts, as in pitch and pond pines. It is native from NY to IL south to east TX and is the only roadside pine seen north of Little Rock in AR and in the Ozark area. It grows at 3000ft along the Skyline Drive, VA and extensively on the Coastal Plain. A big one in Park Drive, Dangerfield, TX is 85ft x 11ft.

TABLE MOUNTAIN PINE (8), *Pinus pungens* is also seen along the Skyline Drive and is more typical of the high rocky bluffs where its widespreading, level middle branches carrying old cones and its flat dome of upcurved ends of upper branches are common. It is a tree of the Alleghenies from PA to GA and there are two small outliers in NJ and MD. Its needles are in pairs, twisted, stiff and 2–3in long. The stalkless 2–3in cone has a broad-based, flat, hooked spine on each scale.

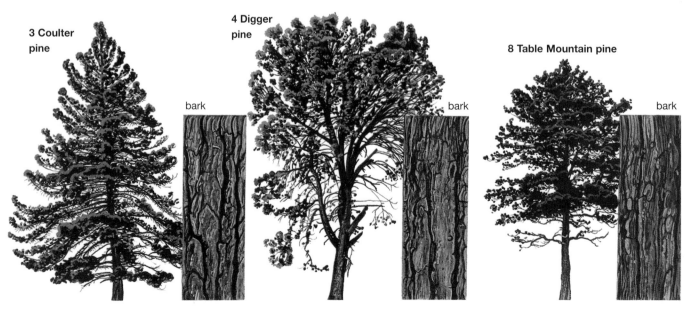

3 Coulter pine

4 Digger pine

bark

8 Table Mountain pine

bark

bark

8 Table
Mountain
pine

(2)

(3)

4 Digger
pine

1 Ponderosa pine

(3)

2 Jeffrey
pine

(3)

3 Coulter
pine

(3)

scale

5 Knobcone
pine

(3)

7 Shortleaf pine

(3)

(2)

6 Slash pine

(2)

bark

cone

cone

cone

1 Ponderosa
pine bark

2 Jeffrey
pine bark

5 Knobcone
pine bark

6 Slash
pine

7 Shortleaf
pine

Monterey and other Pines

MONTEREY PINE (1), *Pinus radiata* is one of the conifers that was migrating northwards again after the Ice Ages, close to the Californian coast, and was trapped in little pockets of land when the coast eroded into islands and bays preventing further progress. The Monterey and Cowen cypresses were caught on the Monterey peninsular, the Bishop pine reached Big Lagoon; the Torrey pine stuck at La Jolla. The Monterey pine has one outlier north near Santa Cruz and Pescadera and another south near Cambria, but the main area is a 6000 acre stand near Carmel with the Seventeen Mile Drive round it. Here the trees are 60–80ft tall and die young, infested by dwarf mistletoe. The tree does not like its native areas. It is not planted north beyond Gold Beach, OR, although common near the coast to the south around Fort Bragg, Fortuna and Eureka, CA, inland to Cloverdale and again well to the south of its native areas, where neatly conic young trees are common from Los Angeles to San Diego. In the Central Valley it is common in shelterbelts from Hollister to Merced and inland at Fresno. This is a 3-needle pine with soft, slender needles, bright green at close quarters but nearly black on a distant tree.

PITCH PINE (2), *Pinus rigida* is also a 3-needle pine but with the needles thick, stiff and only 4in long in the main crown. But it grows great numbers of short sprouts and these have needles 5in long on white shoots. The trunk and main branches can be densely covered in this hanging foliage. It is common in the mountains from NY to GA and local in small numbers into the extreme south of PQ and ON. There are large stands in ME beside Rt 26 and US 1 from Portland ME through RI to CT. A specimen on Long Island, NY, in the Cutting Arboretum is 72ft x 8ft.

POND PINE (3), *Pinus serotina* is like the pitch pine but has dark gray, roughly cracked bark, needles 6–10in long and even more sprouts on the short, sinuous trunk. It replaces pitch pine on the Coastal Plain from DE to central FL, locally in swampy woods, and can be seen around Middleton Gardens, SC and near Ridgeland, US 17.

LONGLEAF PINE (4), *Pinus palustris* is another 3-needle pine and has slender, 10–16in needles, bright green for the first year, arching out and drooping from stout orange-brown shoots, and a cone 8–10in long, leaving its base on the tree. On the Coastal Plain from VA to east TX patches of sturdy seedlings like green fountains are common by roadsides and spread along new embankments. In summer, older trees bear a bright green cone near the rip of every shoot. A few grow in Annapolis, MD.

LOBLOLLY PINE (5), *Pinus taeda* is the common, tall, roadside plantation pine from Williamsburg, VA on the plains to east TX and into the Ozarks of AR, and its native range extends into NJ and south FL. It has a slender red-brown or pinkish shoot and the needles, in threes, are slender and 6–7in long. The cone, 4–5in long, has a very short stalk and sharp, spreading spines.

MEXICAN PINYON (6), *Pinus cembroides* is one of the four species of Pinyon pines: bushy little trees bearing large cones of a few scales and big, edible seeds. This has its needles in threes and is found only near the Mexican border.

PINYON (7), *Pinus edulis* has hard, thick, curved 2in needles mostly in pairs. Its shoots become pinkish-white when about 5 years old and retain leaves for 7 years. This is the little pine on the rocks at the rim of the Grand Canyon, AZ and abundant on dry hills in AZ and NM, north to CO and UT. It is planted in tubs in the streets of Denver, CO.

PARRY PINYON (8), *Pinus quadrifolia* has four needles in a bundle and is rare, locally in the mountains of south CA.

SINGLE-LEAF PINYON (9), *Pinus monophylla* has its needles fused into a single, rigid, sharp spine. It ranges north to the Wasatch Mountains UT and across the interior ranges in NV to the Sierra Nevada, Mojave Desert, CA to Mexico. It is by the Tioga Pass at one point at 9000ft and prominent beside US 395 around Mono Lake.

LIMBER PINE (10), *Pinus flexilis* is a 5-needle pine whose small shoots can be bent, looped and knotted without breaking. Its broad dome of vertical spiky stems is commonly seen in the higher parts of WY, as in Grand Teton and Yellowstone National Parks, with a fine spreading tree at Mammoth Springs, and in CO on high passes. It extends from the AB/BC border mountains to NM and west to south and east CA, where in gulches at 10–12000ft on the eastern flanks of the Sierra Nevada it is a tall, slender tree with white bark.

TORREY PINE (11), *Pinus torreyana* is the rarest pine in the world with a single native stand of 3000 trees in 1600 acres 3 miles north of La Jolla, CA. By the old US 101 are some trees of reasonable shape but in the more exposed parts it is only 15ft high. Yet in cultivation it makes a huge and handsome specimen. The cones are 6 x 6in and weigh 1lb or more.

2 Pitch pine

7 Pinyon

10 Limber pine

bark

bark

bark

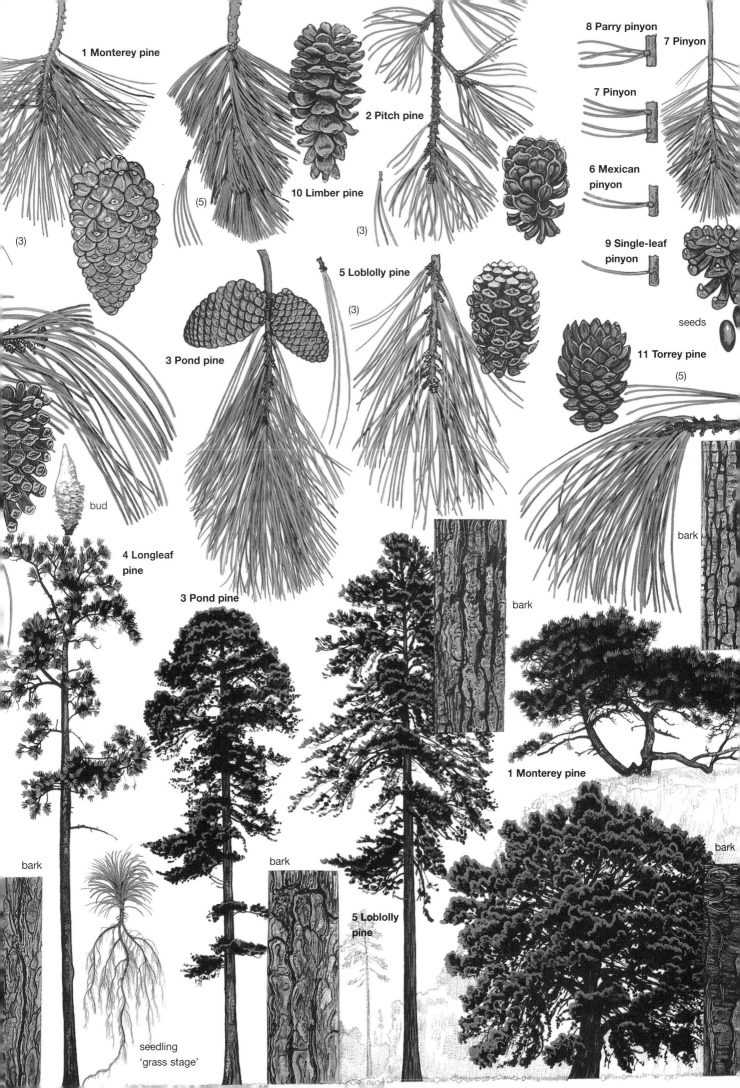

1 Monterey pine

2 Pitch pine

10 Limber pine

(5)

(3)

(3)

8 Parry pinyon

7 Pinyon

7 Pinyon

6 Mexican pinyon

9 Single-leaf pinyon

seeds

3 Pond pine

5 Loblolly pine

(3)

11 Torrey pine

(5)

bud

4 Longleaf pine

3 Pond pine

bark

bark

1 Monterey pine

bark

bark

bark

bark

5 Loblolly pine

seedling 'grass stage'

Sugar and other Five-needle pines

SUGAR PINE (1), *Pinus lambertiana*, is the largest of all the world's pines and grows the largest cones, 15–24in long, 2in across when green and 4in when woody and open. The bark is usually orange-pink finely fissured into small regular, smoothly rounded scales but in OR it is often purplish red-brown and coarsely ridged. It is reputed to have been known 300ft tall but today few are known over 220ft. In large areas of the Siskiyou and Klamath Mountains in OR and CA beautiful Sugar pines 200ft x 15ft line the forest roads, standing above Knobcone pine and manzanita, widely spaced, with long branches projecting level at 150ft and above, each ended by a drooping cone. The range is from Sawyer's Cave in the Cascades in mid-OR where a group is by Rt 126, south at 2–10,000ft along the Sierra Nevada to the cross-ranges and through the Siskiyous to the Coast Ranges to Sonoma County and again in the Santa Lucia Mountains. In the Tuolumne Grove, Yosemite, a tree 5 miles down the loop is 235ft x 22ft. At Giant Sugar Pine Wayside, OR, one is 220ft x 18ft. One planted in the Arnold Arboretum, MA in 1884 was 62ft x 7ft 7in when 90 years old.

WESTERN WHITE PINE (2), *Pinus monticola* grows in the Eastern Rocky Mountains from AB and BC to ID and MT and on the western coast and hills from BC and WA south in mountains to the Sierra Nevada, CA. Young trees are slender, and upswept and old trees are also slender with short level branches, often conic tops and splendidly clean, cylindrical trunks clad in smooth regular rounded scales of shiny brown, black or red-brown. Superb boles stand by the roads near Cameron Lake, Vancouver Island, BC and in Yosemite NP, CA. One at Giant Sugar Pine Wayside, OR is 180ft x 10ft and good trees line Rogers Pass BC and the road above Longmire Rainier NP, WA.

EASTERN WHITE PINE (3), *Pinus strobus* is the only 5-needle pine east of the Rocky Mountains and was the biggest tree there and the most important timber-tree in all America in the last century. From NF, to MN and IA it is in large pure stands and south in the Allegheny Mountains to TN and GA it becomes more scattered among the hardwood and hemlock forests. At Vanderbilt Mansion NY it is 112ft x 12ft 4in; and in Cade's Cove, TN one is 133ft x 12ft. Surprisingly, this tree is frequently planted in the west where there are so many better native pines in BC and WA in small gardens. It is planted in the east around Atlanta, GA and sometimes in NE and AR while in NC it is often clipped into a hedge. **'Fastigiata' (4)** is grown in many arboreta from ON to IL and is 50ft x 5ft at Planting Fields, NY.

WHITEBARK PINE (5), *Pinus albicaulis* is a high altitude pine of the Rockies from to WY on eastern crests and BC to NV and central CA on the western crests, reaching 12,000ft in the Sierra Nevada. It is very like the Limber pine except for the squat cone and replaces it from BC to north CA but the two overlap in the eastern crests and in the central Sierra Nevada. By the Tioga Pass there, the Whitebark at 10,000ft breaks into many vertical, pink-white barked stems to 50ft from near the base and some have branches along the ground.

BRISTLECONE PINE (6), *Pinus aristata* is found, in the typical form with leaves heavily white-speckled with resin, high in the dry mountains of CO and NM. It is a 'foxtail pine' in which the 1½in leaves, in fives, persist for 12 years, pressed rather near the shoot and making it look like a rope. It is planted in botanic gardens in BC and WA, also in WI in the Boerner Botanic Garden, in the George Landis Arboretum, NY and the Secrest Arboretum, OH. There are plants in Denver and in Flagstaff, AZ. The **Intermountain bristlecone pine**, var. *longaeva*, differing in the lack of white spots and in having shorter spines on the cone and a sweet resin scent instead of that of turpentine, is on the White and Inyo Mountains in CA and on high ranges in NV and UT. It is among these that the oldest trees in the world, to 5000 years old, are found.

FOXTAIL PINE (7), *Pinus balfouriana* is similar except for dark orange-red male flowers and purple conic cones without awns but with minute incurved spines. It is found in Onion Valley south of Mount Whitney in the Sierra Nevada, a tall, slender tree, conic topped and upswept, to 100ft tall, and in the Coast Range to the north.

AROLLA PINE (8), *Pinus cembra* from the European Alps and Carpathian Mountains is a similar 5-needle pine with dense brown hairs on the shoot and densely held foliage. The cone, dark blue in summer, is shed with the seed intact. It is common only in Newport, RI and is in many collections from ON to DE and MI.

BHUTAN PINE (9), *Pinus wallichiana* from the western Himalaya, has a stout pale gray-green shoot bloomed blue-gray and needles 6–8in long, lax and bluish-gray. An open crowned tree with level and drooping branches in whorls with foliage and numerous cones near the tips, it is in park and gardens from ON and MA to MN and MD, in the east, and in Vancouver, Victoria, BC and Seattle, WA. There are trees to 90ft x 8ft in Spring Grove Cemetery, Cincinnati, OH.

6 Bristlecone pine

(5)

5 Whitebark pine

(5)

8 Arolla pine

stunted form

9 Bhutan pine

(5)

8 Arolla pine

(5)

1 Sugar pine

2 Western white pine

(5)

7 Foxtail pine

(5)

closed cone

3 Eastern white pine

(5)

bark

bark

bark

4 Eastern white pine 'Fastigiata'

1 Sugar pine

2 Western white pine

3 Eastern white pine

7 Foxtail pine stunted form

Yuccas and Palms

The non-coniferous plants are divided into two groups, the Dicotyledons and the Monocotyledons. The first leaves from the seed are the cotyledons and in Dicotyledons these are often modified as storage tissue and are always an opposite pair. In Monocotyledons the single seedleaf arises as a slender, vertical grasslike leaf encircling a stem at the base. New leaves grow up from within this stem and usually continue linear in shape with parallel main veins. The stem does not add a layer of new wood annually as in other plants and any 'secondary thickening' comes from internal growth around each bundle of vessels leading to a leaf. Branching is not possible in the true palms and can occur in the Agaves only by a division at the base of a flowerhead. In both Agaves and palms the leaves are evergreen and large and the flowering parts are in threes. The Yuccas, in the Agave Family, are mostly large, multiple crowns sitting on the ground eventually rising on stout short stems in a close group. They are confined to hot, sandy or rocky places.

JOSHUA TREE (1), *Yucca brevifolia* is a true tree which can be 35ft tall. It begins to flower when about 10ft tall so its short, upturned branches start at this height. The big, ovoid flowerbud unfolds a stout, finely hairy spike 10in long. Joshua trees are the mark of the Mojave Desert and grow from southwest UT round this desert in CA and AZ. They are by the I 15, US 395 and Rt 247. The 'Champion' is 35ft x 16ft at 2ft.

CALIFORNIA WASHINGTONIA (2), *Washingtonia filifera* is native from around Palm Springs to the Mexican border but has been planted north to Cloverdale, Sonora County, commonly in the Bay Area and Sacramento and to Fresno in Central Valley, with one or two in Las Vegas, NV. It is also occasional from Savannah, GA and Gulfpoint, MS to LA. A cluster of dead fan-leaves held tightly to the stem below the crown is typical of Washingtonias. The leaf is 6ft long on a spine-edged 5ft stem and is cut deeply into 40–70 slender lobes. Each year about four panicles 10ft long bear yellow flowers and persist dead on the tree.

MEXICAN WASHINGTONIA (3), *Washingtonia robusta* is the slender version, to 90ft tall, common around Los Angeles and occasional in the Bay Area and the Central Valley, CA with a curved or leaning stem and resembling a feather-duster.

FLORIDA THATCHPALM (4), *Thrinax radiata* is a fanpalm native to Dade and Monroe Counties, FL, and the Keys, with a pale gray, smooth trunk to 25ft long and leaves 3ft across divided into 60 or more lobes.

FLORIDA SILVER PALM (5), *Coccothrinax argentata* is named from the bright silvery white undersurface of the 2ft leaf of folded lobes divided at the tip. It is native from Palm Beach county to the Keys, FL.

CABBAGE PALMETTO (6), *Sabal palmetto* is native by the coast from Cape Hatteras, NC to south FL but has been widely planted and is common in streets and parks near the coast into TX north to Livingston and inland in NC to Florence, in GA to Statesboro, in AL to Brewton, and in LA nearly to Bunkie. It is common in Phoenix and Florence and by I 10 to Tucson, AZ, and from San Diego, El Centro and Alpine to San Bernardino, CA and is grown in Las Vegas, NV. Left to itself, the trunk is covered in interlacing leaf-bases with 1ft stubs but in streets this is often cleaned down to the dark gray smooth bark. The 6ft orange flower panicles open in June.

DATE PALM (7), *Phoenix dactylifera* from North Africa and south-west Asia is a plumeleaf palm like the Canary palm but more squat, rougher and with dull dusty dark gray-green leaves. Male and female flowers are on separate trees. It is occasional from Charleston, SC to FL and by the Gulf Coast to LA, in the Bay Area, CA, in Salinas and the Central Valley to Fresno and around Los Angeles. It is common and in avenues 40ft tall in Phoenix, AZ which takes its name from the tree.

BUTIA PALM (8), *Butia capitata* is a squat, pinnate palm with 10ft leaves arching elegantly from its crown. They have spined edges to their stalks so are often removed from street trees to reveal gray smooth bark. It is frequent from the promenade at Charleston, SC to New Orleans and Natchez, LA, inland in GA to Twin City and Adrian. It is also frequent in Phoenix, AZ and is grown in the Huntington Gardens, Pasadena, CA.

QUEEN PALM (9), *Arecastrum romanzoffianum*, from South America is an elegant pinnate palm bearing only about 10 leaves at a time, arching loosely out, 15ft long from a brown, smooth, vase-shaped sheath. Long-conic flower-heads droop from the base of the crown and the bark is rings of pale and dark gray. It is the palm of the city square in San Diego and is infrequent around Los Angeles. It is common in Miami, FL.

FLORIDA ROYAL PALM (10), *Roystonea elata* is very like the Queen palm but at once recognised by the big, smooth, bright green flask-shaped sheath. It is native to the far south of FL, but is commonly seen only in and around Miami.

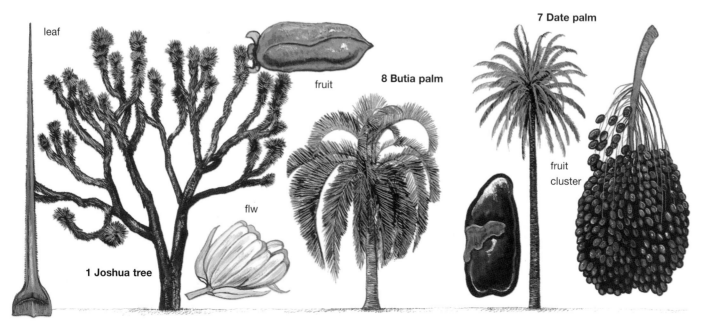

leaf

7 Date palm

fruit

8 Butia palm

fruit cluster

flw

1 Joshua tree

9 Queen palm

fruit

fruit

5 Florida silver palm

6 Cabbage palmetto

leaf

10 Florida royal palm

fruit

2 California washingtonia

4 Florida thatchpalm

leaf

fruit

leaf

3 Mexican washingtonia

fruit

Palms

CABBAGE TREE (1), *Cordyline australis* from New Zealand is in the same family as the Joshua tree and is not a palm. Like the Joshua tree it can branch only where it bears a flower so that young trees are single crowns on a pole. The leaves are up to 3ft long and exceedingly strong, being related to Sisal. The flowerhead is 4ft long. Although there are Cabbage trees in Beacon Hill Park, Victoria, BC there are few or none southward until Orick, CA and it is not common until Monterey. Away from the coast, it grows in Wasco, Simi Valley and Hollister.

CHUSAN PALM (2), *Trachycarpus fortunei* from China is a true fan-palm and the hardiest of them all. Its leaves are 2ft 6in long and 4ft across with a row of spines each side of the stout 3ft stalk. Old leaves may turn bright yellow before being shed. Mature trees usually carry several flowerheads each season. This is grown from Orick, CA south along the coast and inland at Mariposa, Hollister and Paso Robles but is far from common.

CANARY PALM (3), *Phoenix canariensis* is the most majestic and imposing of all the palms outside the Tropics. It makes the related Date palm look stunted, dusty and spiky by comparison. The leaves are 15–20ft long, 6ft across at the base and tapered evenly to the tip, and are made up of about 200 leaflets. Flower panicles emerge continually and are 3–5ft long, remaining dead on the tree for a long time. In the east, Canary palms begin near Charleston, SC and are uncommon south to mid-FL around Orlando and Lakeland and to Tallahassee. They become common only by the Gulf Coast at Biloxi, MS in parks and streets to New Orleans and Baton Rouge, LA. In the west they are grown by the coast from Fort Bragg, CA to San Diego, commonly in the Bay Area and around Los Angeles. Inland there are some in Central Valley from Fresno to Merced and at Hollister while some small trees are in Mariposa.

fruit

1 Cabbage tree

2 Chusan palm

3 Canary palm

Practical Reference Section

A concise guide to the practicalities of the
selection and cultivation of trees.

Contents

Suitable Trees for the Garden

Given here is a list of particularly good trees to plant for the garden, with an indication of the type of climate they need. Where no climatic needs are given, the tree is tolerant of considerable heat, cold and drought. If planted in an arid zone, it will only thrive under irrigation.

Key

F	Few and light frosts	R	Rainy; no long dry summer
FF	No frosts	T	Temperate, general
H	Hot summers	TC	Temperate, cool
		TW	Temperate, warm

Common Name		Climate	Good Features
Alder	Italian	TR	Robust grower, fine foliage and early catkins
Apple	'Charlottae'	T	Flowers and fruit
	'Dorothea'	T	Flowers and fruit
	Hupeh crab	T	Flowers and fruit, strong growth
	Pillar	T	Neat upright shape; fall color
Ash	Caucasian	T	Fine foliage; fall color; robust
	Claret		
Basswood	American	TR	Fine foliage; good shape; good in cities
Beech	American	TR	Foliage, bark, fall color
	'Dawyck'	TR	Shape; fall color
Birch	Swedish	T	Weeping, deeply cut foliage; bark
Buckeye	Yellow	TR	Foliage; fall color
Catalpa	Hybrid	T	Vigor; big foliage and flowerheads
Cherry	Sato	TC	Flowers, fall color
Crape myrtle		FH	Flowers, bark
Chestnut	Japanese Horse	TR	Foliage, flowers, fall color
	Indian	TR	Foliage, late flowers,
Cypress	Arizona Smooth	T	Shape, color
	Cripps's Golden	TR	Shape, color
	Leyland	TR	Extreme vigor
Dogwood	Flowering	T	Flowers, fruit, fall color, bark
Dovetree		TR	Flowers
Elm	Chinese		Foliage, bark, resistance to disease
Fir	Bristlecone	TR	Foliage, shape, cone
	Californian silver	TR	Vigor, foliage, shape
	Caucasian	TR	Foliage, shape
	Douglas	TR	Foliage, vigor
	Nikko	TR	Foliage, shape, good near cities
	Noble	TR	Blue-grey foliage, cone
	White	TR	Blue-grey foliage, esp. 'Violacea'
Ginkgo			Foliage, fall color, shape, interest
Goldenrain tree	Formosan	FH	Flowers, fruit, foliage
Hazel	Turkish	T	Early catkins, vigor, shape; good in cities
Hemlock	Carolina	TR	Foliage
	Western	TR	Vigor, shape
Honeylocust	'Sunburst'		Color, tolerance
Hornbeam	Pyramidal	TR	Shape, fall color
Katsura		TR	Foliage, fall color, shape
Keaki		T	Foliage, fall color

Common Name		Climate	Good Features
Larch	European	R	Early foliage, fall color, vigor
Linden	Silver	TR	Robust growth cities, foliage, scent
	Silver pendent	TR	Robust growth cities, foliage, scent
Madrone		TR	Bark, foliage, flowers, fruit
Maple	Amur		Tolerance cold and heat, foliage
	Oregon	TR	Foliage, flowers, fall color
	Paperbark	TR	Bark, fall color
	Snakebarks	TR	(Several species.) Bark, foliage, fall color
	Trident	T	Foliage, fall color
Oak	Black	TR	Foliage, fall color
	Chinkapin	HR	Foliage
	Cypress	TR	Shape
	Pin	R	Vigor, foliage, fall color
	Scarlet	R	Foliage, fall color
	Shingle	R	Foliage
Parasol tree		HR	Foliage
Pear	Bradford		Shape, fall color
	Chanticleer		Shape, fall color
Pine	Bhutan	TR	Foliage, vigor, cones
	Bishop		Resistance to sea wind
	Canary	H	Shape, foliage
	Japanese black		Resistance to sea wind
	Jeffrey	TR	Shape, tolerance, cones
	Slash	HF	Foliage, vigor
	Torrey	HF	Foliage, vigor
Poplar	Bolle's		Shape, foliage
	Lombardy		Shape, fall color
Redwood	Dawn	R	Foliage, shape, vigor
Spruce	Brewer	TR	Shape
	Colorado blue	R	Color
	Oriental	TR	Shape
	Serbian	TR	Narrow spire shape
	Sitka	TR	Vigor, color, resists sea winds
Sweetgum			Foliage, fall color
Tupelo		TR	Foliage, fall color
Thorn	Plumleaf	T	Foliage, fall color, toughness
	Scarlet	T	Foliage, fruit
	Washington		Foliage, fruit
Walnut	Black	TR	Foliage, fall color, shape
	Japanese	TR	Foliage, cold-resistance
Wingnut	Caucasian	TR	Foliage, vigor, fall color
	Hybrid	TR	Foliage, vigor, fruit

Planting a Tree

Preparing the Hole

Nearly all trees make more reliable, sturdy growth in their first few years if they are transplanted than when seed is sown and the plants left undisturbed. Nonetheless, it is a wholly unnatural break in its growth pattern for a tree to be planted – one to which it cannot have evolved a response – and the operation should be planned to cause the least possible disruption to growth. The crucial point is to make the move as early in the tree's life as possible, to allow it the formative first five or six years in its final position. The bigger and older a tree is when planted, the more its growth is retarded, the longer it takes to make the big root-system it needs for growth and stability. A tree three metres tall is easily crippled for life by being moved, and no tree so big should even be considered for purchase unless it has a big root-system prepared over several years in the nursery.

The best size for planting is 1–1½ ft, from open ground or a large container, where the roots have never been cramped. Such a plant, with all its roots, planted firmly, is stable from the start, must not be staked and will grow away rapidly to build a stout bole and shapely crown. A tall plant has already made its lower crown in response to conditions in the nursery lines, and so it will be drawn up with a slender, weak stem and often made worse by being tied to a stake. For a healthy plant, this vital part must be grown in the place where the tree is to spend its life, and in response to its surroundings there. The foliage of a tree feeds the roots and the roots feed the foliage. A tree planted out is usually in less shelter than it was in the nursery and its foliage is under more stress from drying wind. So it needs a vigorous root-system. With the usual tiny cramped, incomplete one of a tall plant, it can scarcely leaf out at all, much less make new shoots. So there is little leaf to feed the roots during their vital time for expansion into new soil. Thus, little growth can be made on roots, and little again on the shoots and the tree is locked in this stage of minimum growth and dire struggle to survive, for many years.

A small plant with almost natural rooting evades this trap. Roots must be spread to reach the new soil, not left in a ball. Pot-bound roots must be at least partially unravelled even if some break and need to be cut back. The size of hole needed can then be seen – big enough to take the spread roots with a small margin extra. The bottom of the hole is dug out to allow 6 in of good soil or leaf-mould beneath the tree, and the base well broken up if it is a heavy soil. A mixture of the surrounding soil, compost and sand is put round the spread roots, and gently firmed.

In poor, sandy soils, a little superphosphate fertilizer spread over the bottom before placing the tree in the hole aids rapid root-growth; while some slow-release nitrogenous fertilizers like bonemeal added to the backfill improve early shoot-growth.

The level of the surface on the stem before planting can be seen, and filling brings the new soil to the same place; then after heavy firming it is made good to that level again. In light soils the new tree and 3 ft radius around is left 4 in below the surrounding level to help keep the frequent waterings needed from flowing out of reach.

Preparing the Hole

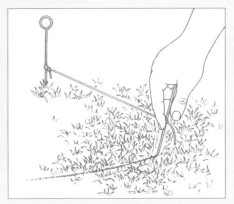

1. *A circular area of cleared ground is most suitable, and easily marked for the new tree. Swing a marker 3 ft from a pin.*

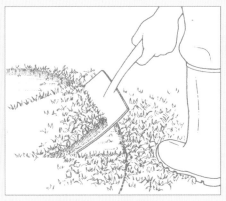

2. *Remove a thin top layer and put it aside. Most of the good topsoil stays to be dug out and mixed to make the backfill.*

3. *Break up the bottom of the hole well, if it is compacted, to give good drainage. If it is good loam, it can be dug over.*

4. *Break up the turf taken from the top and put it at the bottom of the hole, where it will break down into good rooting-soil.*

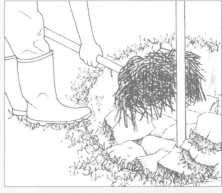

5. *Spread a layer of well-rotted manure, leaf-mould or compost over the turves to conserve moisture and allow easy rooting.*

6. *Firm in the bottom layers before the tree roots are put in place, to ensure there are no pockets of air in the lower layers.*

Planting a Tree

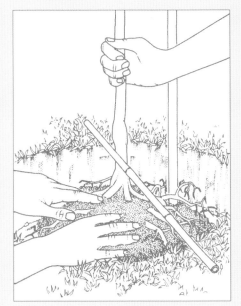

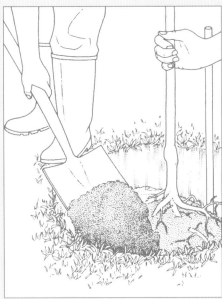

1. Hold the tree roughly in position and shake it up and down a little as the soil is spread around and among the roots.

2. Using a cane to mark the soil level, hold the tree for final filling to the old level and firming.

3. Tread the top firm: then lightly fork the surface to break it up slightly and to allow in water and air.

Staking and Tying

Standard and other large trees need a stake, not to hold the stem up but just to hold it still until the new roots have grown out. After that it is bad for the tree, which needs to sway to grow its proper, stout stem. A short stake, strong and firmly set 1 ft away holds a tie on the bole 1 ft from the ground and is removed after the second growing season and winter gales.

A large tree from a container is best held by a triangle of three short stakes, because driving one into the root-ball would very likely damage important roots. (One stake each side is adequate for trees of moderate size.)

Stakes should not be longer than is needed to hold the ties at 1 ft. Projecting into the crown they can damage branches, and serve no purpose unless sometimes, in public places, lessening vandal damage. The heaviest standards with big tops may need their support at one third of the height of their stem, and 1 ft is better for normal trees.

Stakes should be long enough to allow 1½–2 ft in the ground, and be knot-free and straight-grained for strength. They must be free from disease, preferably tanalized or otherwise treated with preservative unless they are Western red cedar.

Ties must have some elasticity to allow unhindered expansion of the stem even in the two seasons at most that they are needed. They must have spacers to prevent the stake rubbing the tree and be fixed on the stake to prevent slipping down in rough weather.

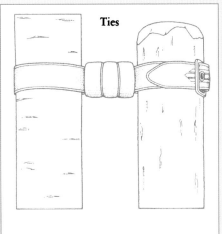

Ties

Solid plastic tie with buckle and spacer

Fabric tie arranged with knot as spacer.

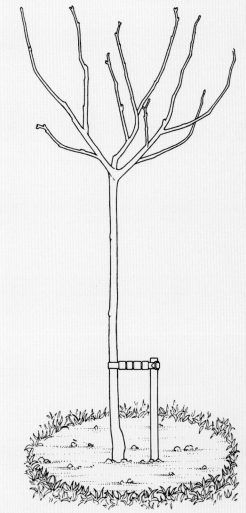

181

Pruning and Shaping

Trees normally assume their best shape in their own way. Only those grown for their fruit need annual pruning to increase the size, number or accessibility of the fruit. In the case of all other trees, the term 'pruning' has a very different meaning, covering two separate operations.

The first of these is to aid the natural process of shedding the first, lowest branches in order to give a clean, smooth bole. In woodland these are soon shaded out and shed, but on single trees the strongest branches extend into the light and keep growing at their tips while their inner shoots and smaller branches become bare. Left alone, these make a tangle of dead wood hiding the bole and soon full of nettles and rubbish, while big low branches disfigure the tree. Even where a lawn-tree is intended to be feathered to the ground, the early removal of the branch-tangle on the bottom 5 ft allows the next layer to droop around a clean bole. Other trees can have 6 ft of clean stem by the time they are 20 ft tall.

The second operation – shaping – is required only to rectify a fault in growth. A forking leading shoot can be singled as soon as it is seen. A forked, two-stem tree is ugly and vulnerable to storms. Misplaced or over-vigorously protruding branches should be removed when necessary.

Where to Cut

Cleaning a stem of side-branches early in its life removes dead and living wood only a few inches in diameter. It can be done at any time of year and the small scars will close within one or two years, leaving a smooth stem. Cleaning older stems and taking branches from the crown leave big scars. Branches usually swell out at their origin to a conic protrusion. This causes conflict between the two desired aims — a minimum size of scar and a cut flush with the major branch or stem to leave it smooth. Controversy raged for 400 years and decay followed pruning whether the cut was flush, left a marked stub, or if a rough unreasoned compromise were made. Dr A. Shigo of New Hampshire has shown exactly where the cuts should be and why.

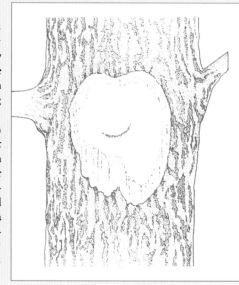

The Wrong Way

Cutting flush with the stem does leave a smooth surface, but usually a branch has a conical base so the nearer the stem, the bigger the scar. Worse, however, such a cut removes the collar of tissues whose function is to grow new tissue to heal the scar. Healing will thus be slow and have a greater area to cover. Wound-dressings are not the answer. Few of them inhibit decay at all and many make a skin which soon cracks and allows water to lodge against the scar. Unless re-painted regularly, dressings thus encourage decay. The correct cut leaves the collar intact to grow protective barriers and to close the scar. Left open to sun and air the wound heals most rapidly.

The Shigo Method

In beech alone there was an old method of pruning small branches leaving a 2 inch stub. Coral-spot fungus was sure to infect this but by the time it reached the main stem, the tree had sealed off the scar and the stub would fall off with the fungus to leave a healed scar. Were the cut flush with the bole the fungus could have entered the stem and decayed a large, deep scar.

Dr Shigo has shown that *all* trees isolate areas of decay with barriers of resistant cells; that the junctions of branches have the tissues for growing the barriers already disposed in a pattern to prepare for natural shedding, and he has described how these show on the tree. A 'branch bark ridge' on the upper side and a 'branch collar' on the underside mark the outer rim of tissues that will grow the barrier, which is conical, pointing inwards.

The natural death of a branch causes the collar to enlarge. When the branch is decayed and breaks off it will tend to take with it the conical insertion. However, if this remains and rots, it is isolated from the main stem, and the exterior is sealed in by active growth from the enlarged collar. The cut must be close to but clear of the collar.

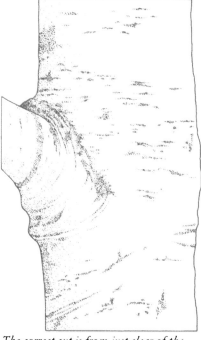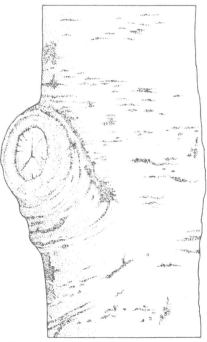

The correct cut is from just clear of the 'branch bark ridge' above to just clear of the collar beneath. The collar may not show and then the angle of the cut is shown by the angle that the branch bark ridge makes away from the branch. The cut is at the same angle from the vertical, in the opposite direction. With a branch arising almost vertically this makes a cut very close to the stem, but it is not flush, for it leaves the vital collar. Heavy branches must be cut off first to 6 in stubs before the final cut.

Singling a Fork

A symmetrical fork in new growth on a very young tree may be left until new growth begins next season but no longer.

Unequal forks may call for a choice between a weak shoot and a strong one that is more offset.

Cutting

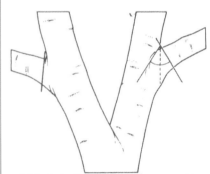

All but the lightest branches are cut to a stub before pruning, to prevent tearing. First a shallow undercut, then the full cut a few cm outside it.

Singling Sprouts

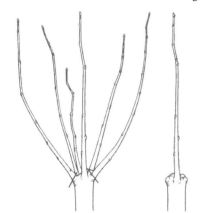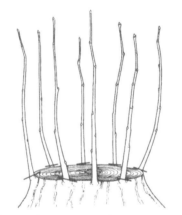

A eucalypt or similarly strong growing tree may regrow after a hard frost as many shoots from ground level. Choose one strong, straight shoot and cut the others.

A sprouting stump can be re-grown as a tree cutting out all but the single strongest and most shapely new shoot. Having a big root-system it will grow fast.

Cleaning the Bole

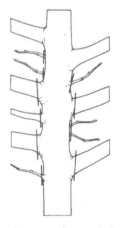

A neglected tree may have its bole spoiled by low branches which should have been removed with secateurs when still small. Now it will need a saw.

Crown Thinning

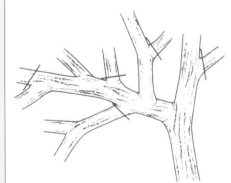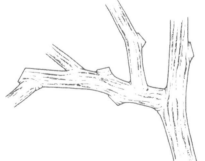

Some broadleaf trees have crowns which can become congested. They may take too much light and be untidy. Savage cutting makes them worse, and ugly.

Thinning the crown by intelligent removal of excess leafage on complete branch systems, always cutting back to a main branch, cures the trouble.

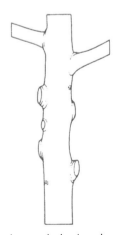

A bole can be rescued when branches are 4–6 in across. Beyond that it would leave too much scar. A clean bole for 5 ft is a minimum aim.

Improving Growth of Young Trees

Trees are sociable plants and in nature they normally arise and grow in groups of varying densities, either of their own species only or amongst others. Even the pioneer species — the first to colonize bare ground — usually spring up in numbers together.

The new, bare sites are very largely those cleared by fire (due to lightning before the arrival of man and often afterwards also) but greatly increased by deliberate burning to clear the land for grazing and crops.

In western North America most of the coniferous forests have large areas of uniform age which can be dated back to a fire and most of the trees have a life-cycle adapted to the average period between fires, which itself is fixed by the time needed for enough combustible material to accumulate. Other new sites arise on a smaller scale from landslides, rivers changing course and swamps drying out. Pioneer species have light seeds, often with fluff or wings and are carried by the wind much further than heavier fruits which rely on birds or mammals, which mostly frequent developed woodland. The trees bearing the heavier fruits therefore come in

only after the pioneers have created a form of woodland. Hence the successor species also are adapted to growing up among trees — at first those of a different species from themselves.

The aspen, poplars and willows have fluff on their seeds and are the long-distance pioneers. The birches with minute winged seeds can travel a fair distance, and pines, with their heavy winged seeds, are short-distance pioneers unless a crossbill should carry a cone and drop some seed further away.

The first trees on new land grow in conditions very different from those found in woodlands. There will be an open sky and either newly formed soil or newly burned surfaces. If new, the soil will usually be short of the nutrients needed for growth, particularly in nitrogen, and lacking entirely in humus. If burned it will also lack nitrogen but be high in potash, and the top at least will lack humus. So pioneer species need to adapt to poor, often open, sandy soils and have low demand for nutrients. But the overwhelming factor on new sites is the

wind. Such sites are always more exposed than those in wooded areas and usually to a very high degree. This causes the soil, at best open and poor in humus, to dry out rapidly and often, so pioneer trees must be able to withstand drought. They can do so by deep and wide rooting early in life and by having small or thick-skinned leaves.

The most profound effect is however, from the wind on the foliage. Here again, small, tough leaves or dense hairs on shoots and leaves lessen the damaging drying effect. Big, thin leaves can be grown only by trees whose entire life is spent in the shelter of old woods. The pioneer trees, in full light, have no need of dense foliage to catch enough of it for their needs. Their leaves work only in nearly full light, and are shed when they become shaded by others and the crowns remain light and open. This allows the wind to filter through where a dense crown would be damaged by strong gusts. It also allows strong growth of the early arrivals among the ground herbs, and, later, the growth of the more shade-bearing trees that will take over when the pioneers have created shelter and

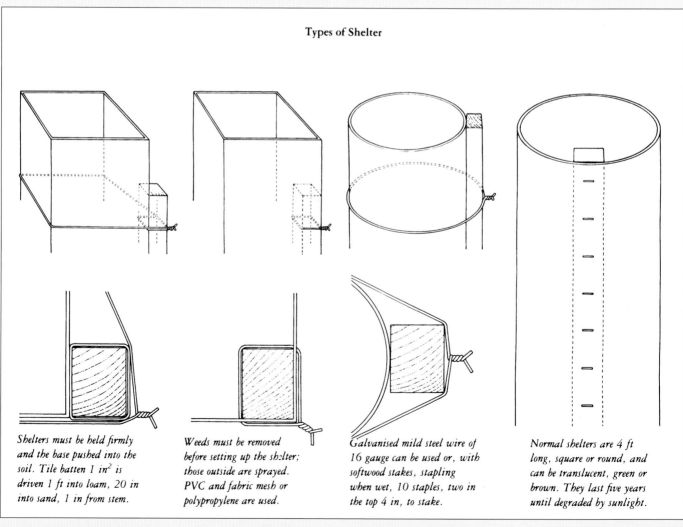

Types of Shelter

Shelters must be held firmly and the base pushed into the soil. Tile batten 1 in² is driven 1 ft into loam, 20 in into sand, 1 in from stem.

Weeds must be removed before setting up the shelter; those outside are sprayed. PVC and fabric mesh or polypropylene are used.

Galvanised mild steel wire of 16 gauge can be used or, with softwood stakes, stapling when wet, 10 staples, two in the top 4 in, to stake.

Normal shelters are 4 ft long, square or round, and can be translucent, green or brown. They last five years until degraded by sunlight.

their leaf-fall has built up a much improved soil.

The pioneers make rapid early growth, flower and fruit within a few years of germinating from seed and tend to be short-lived. These qualities are further adaptations to their life-style. They do need, however, to modify the severity of their surroundings in order to grow well, or, in the more extreme sites, to grow at all. This can be done only by growing in large numbers together from the start, which is the normal result of seeding on to bare ground. Each tree then benefits from the shelter of the others and this common shelter increases as the trees grow and improves greatly the microclimate within the stand. Even the trees on the periphery benefit, since the trees behind retard the wind that sweeps through them. Height growth increases with distance from the edge, giving a wedge-shaped profile.

The pioneer stands are usually fairly open, but there are exceptions such as the aspen tracts following heath fires and the lodgepole pine stands in the interior Rocky Mountains, which arise and largely remain in very dense groups, despite a high rate of suppression and death.

Successor species are adapted to starting life in the sheltered, relatively humid conditions of woodlands, in a developed, humus-rich, reasonably fertile soil. Many need open sky above them after varying periods and achieve this end either by outgrowing the species around them or by biding their time until the canopies above them fail and fall with age. The conclusion to be drawn from all these factors is that a tree of any kind, either planted singly, or widely spaced on an open site as in most amenity plantings in parks or around buildings, faces conditions from which its natural manner of growth largely shields it. To make matters worse, it is usually planted out when it is far too big, and has spent too many years in the very different conditions of the nursery. The worst aspect for the tree is the sudden subjection to exposure.

Tuley Tubes

Graham Tuley of Great Britain experimented with translucent plastic 'tree-shelters' of different materials, widths and heights. A narrow shelter gives a 'greenhouse effect', retaining within the heat it receives from radiated light — an effect that is very apparent if you put your hand into one on a cool day. In the calm, damp warmth, the side shoots grow big leaves which promote good growth in the stem and leading shoot. They are short and congested but are due for removal when the stem is cleaned-up. The shelter at the same time protects the tree from damage by animals. Growth in many broad-leaf trees is given a rapid early start, most spectacularly in oaks but all that have been tried have shown the benefits. Among conifers, only Japanese larch responds strongly. Some trees, notably the oaks, cannot hold up the big crown. They must be secured to the stake that held the shelter when the plastic has degraded away after the expected five years.

Materials and methods are still being developed but over 500,000 Tuley tubes were used during 1983 in Great Britain.

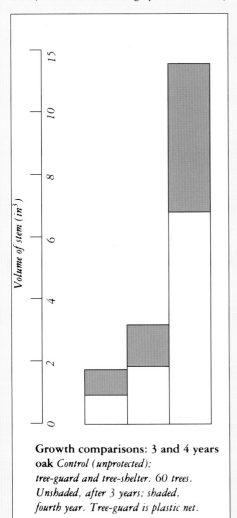

Growth comparisons: 3 and 4 years
oak *Control (unprotected);*
tree-guard and tree-shelter. 60 trees.
Unshaded, after 3 years; shaded,
fourth year. Tree-guard is plastic net.

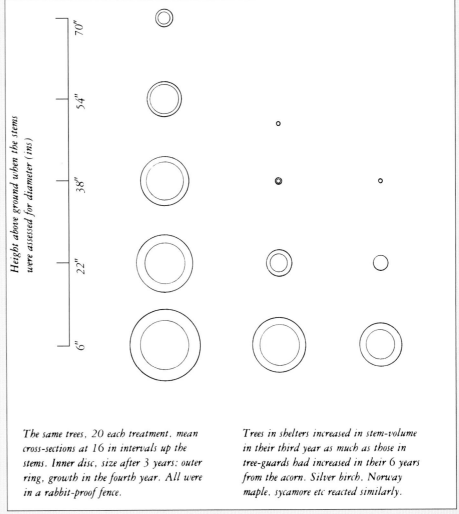

The same trees, 20 each treatment, mean cross-sections at 16 in intervals up the stems. Inner disc, size after 3 years; outer ring, growth in the fourth year. All were in a rabbit-proof fence.

Trees in shelters increased in stem-volume in their third year as much as those in tree-guards had increased in their 6 years from the acorn. Silver birch, Norway maple, sycamore etc reacted similarly.

Measuring Height

The height of a tree less than about 20 ft tall can be measured accurately with a rod. A tall tree can be measured easily and reasonably closely by several homemade methods, and more accurately and reliably by an instrument. Exact measurement of its height is, however, normally impracticable. Even climbing the tree can rarely solve the problem. The path for the tape down the bole cannot be quite direct, the precise tip often cannot be seen by the climber or judged closely to be level with his rod, and the tree may lean.

Height is reckoned from the highest point of the crown and this may, in an old, many-headed conifer, and in a broad, domed broadleaf tree, be many feet from the central axis. Its position has to be decided from a distance and the point directly beneath it estimated from under the crown. The bottom of a tree is the highest point to which the soil reaches up the bole. This prevents the extended bole and roots on the downhill side of a steep slope from counting in the height.

Having observed the points between which the measurement is to be made, the next thing to decide is the point from which to make it. Accuracy is best at a distance from the tree which is equal to its height and from the same level as its base. In fact even quite a marked slope makes little difference because measurement is made down to the base as well as up to the top, but an uphill shot from much below the tree is best avoided. So a rough estimate of the height of the tree — 60, 90 or 120 ft — is made and a position found at about the equivalent distance (with an instrument an exact distance is required) as nearly level with the base as possible, from which the top and the bottom can be seen. A tree with an obvious lean is sighted at a right-angle to the direction of lean if possible. If it cannot be, then, as is worth doing for all very tall trees, two shots from opposite directions given a mean which is the height.

Interestingly, unpractised estimates by eye usually much underestimate trees of 20–40 ft, and grossly overestimate trees of 80–100 ft in height.

Method 1
The top of a tree, its base and your eye form a triangle with a right-angle between the stem of the tree and the ground. Hence, when the whole tree makes an angle of 45° from your eye, the two sides formed by the tree and your distance from it are equal. You are the same distance from the base as the tip is, and were the tree to fall, its tip would land at your feet. This distance can be measured precisely along the ground. To find the point at which the angle is 45°, a miniature of the real triangle is made. Break a stick so that its length is exactly equal to the length of your fully stretched arm. Hold it vertically at arm's length. Move to where the top and bottom of the stick align with those of the tree. You are then at the desired point.

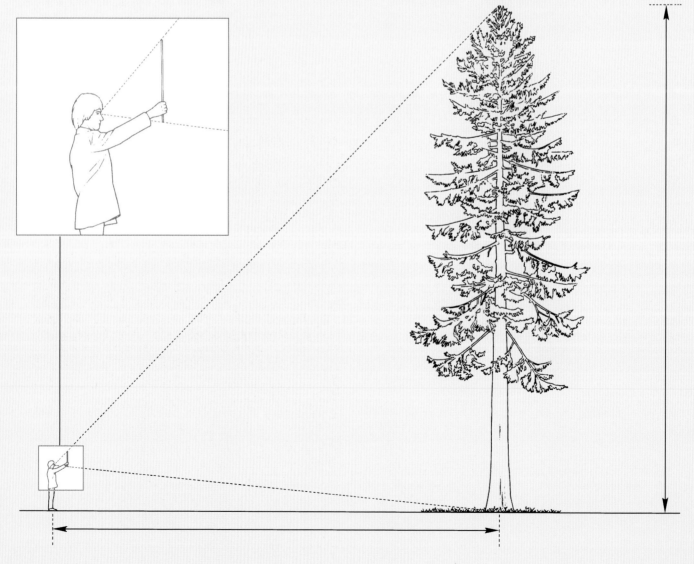

Method 2

Unlike Method 1, this requires two people. A small nick is cut into a ruler, or a rod similarly marked, at the one-inch mark or at 3 in on a 3 ft rod. Hold the ruler at full stretch (which is a constant and the easiest distance) and move to where the tree top and base line up with those of the ruler. Now ask your assistant to move a white marker (a notebook page folded into a broad triangle will do) to bring it exactly into the notch. The height at which this occurs is one twelfth of the full height of the tree.

Method 3

The sun is not always out and tree shadows are not very often thrown on to open ground, but for lawn specimens the shadow method can be useful. The height of the sun at any hour and day can be determined by reference to a Nautical Almanack but this process can be short-circuited by a simple device. The length of the tree-shadow is compared with that of the shadow of a 5 ft rod taken at the same time and the height arrived at by simple proportion.

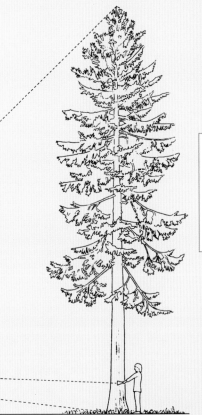

Using a Hypsometer

A hypsometer is an instrument for measuring height. A free-hanging needle reads directly on several scales or else a bob rotates a cylinder with scales against a marker. Most have scales for distances from the tree, marked 15, 20, 30 and 40 and these can be feet, yards or metres, whichever is used for the baseline. Hypsometers are expensive. Workable ones can be devised.

Estimating Age

The height and spread of a tree increase with age until senility begins and then they decrease again. Both fail as indicators of age beyond the early years. Diameter and bole circumference must increase every year of life, a ring of new wood being added annually. The circumference, measured at 5 ft is a guide to the age.

For big-growing trees (not those like apples and holly) the broad rule 'one inch a year' (roughly 2.5 cm) increase in circumference applies regardless of species, region or altitude of site, over a wide span of ages. The reason is that most trees add well over one inch a year in youth and gradually decline first to one inch and then to less. Once they are past one inch a year their mean annual increase becomes nearer to that rate every year and in an old tree it is on or close to it over a very long period. Wood added depends on the amount of foliage, so a tree crowded in a wood or having lost branches adds less each year and may fit 'one inch in two years'. A fully crowned oak 20 feet round will usually be about 250 years old.

There are, however, both hares and tortoises among trees. Fast growth, that is three to four inches, is made each year by the best eucalypts, willows, giant sequoias, coast redwoods, dawn redwoods, some grand firs and poplars.

A few trees grow more than one inch a year for less than 100 years and then become very slow. Examples are Scots pine, Norway spruce, Planeleaf maple, and European linden. Approximate age for these is 100 years plus 2 years for every inch of circumference above 100 inches.

Gilbert White recorded the Selborne Yew to be 23 ft round at three ft up in 1789. In 1984 it was 25 ft 7 in (7.8 m) at the same point. A uniform decline from $\frac{1}{2}$ in/yr in youth gives the age as about 1200 years in White's day. 1400 years today.

Range Maps

The historic, natural ranges of native species are shown by SOLID shading. The main areas of extension of ranges by planting are shown in cross-shading. Exotic species have, therefore, entirely cross-shaded range-maps. Natural ranges have been much fragmented by clearance. Some trees were always confined to river-bottomland or to scattered hillsides. Large-scale maps can show these in detail; as the scale is decreased, the number of small areas which have to be combined in larger blocks increases, and on the very small scale here, most of the larger blocks must be combined and only very large or widely spaced outliers can be shown. In exotic species, main areas of planting and naturalised seeding have been plotted from observation. While areas within which the trees are scattered in gardens can be broadly marked, isolated plantings in botanic gardens remote from other plantings, like some in Denver, CO but seen elsewhere no nearer than MO or CA, cannot be marked.

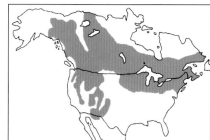

Quaking aspen   Prominent in the Rocky Mountains, as dense roadside thickets of clean white stems, especially in CO and WY. Less striking bark and growth over much of the extensive eastern range, but equally spectacular bright gold foliage in the fall.

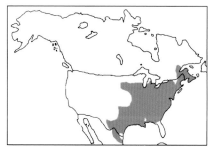

Black willow   Named from the bark which is a useful feature in winter and in summer. Rarely planted but common within the natural range in or beside swampy river bottomlands and the tallest willow there, usually with three or four stems.

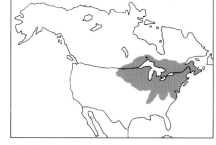

Bigtooth aspen   The leaf may be 6in x 5in and is firm and solid. It is a fresh bright green and makes this a handsome tree, although a short-lived one achieving no great size. The bark is very smooth, gray-green.

Mackenzie willow   Usually seen as bushy, roadside low trees or many-stemmed bushes. Grown in some small gardens in Canada and cut back regularly partly for the bright orange bark of long young shoots.

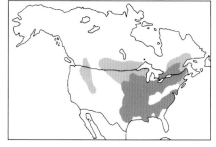

Eastern cottonwood   As a young tree, slender, conic with small branches in whorls; very open. Broadly domed, dense and leafy with age, and reaching a great size. Quite bare of foliage when the catkins open in March at branch-tips.

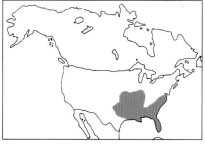

Coastal Plain willow   A low, rounded, bushy little tree on the margins of swampy bottomlands, in front of the tall Black willows. Distinctively yellow-green in leaf, it has a dark gray, scaly and ridged bark. The leaf is to 4in long.

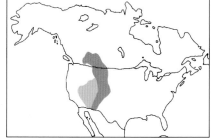

Plains cottonwood   Much planted in the Prairie States for shade. The leaf is drawn out to a long, entire tip and big branches bend down then sweep up with dense brushes of foliage, brilliant gold in the fall.

Black cottonwood   A tall and often untidy, upright-branched tree, vulnerable to wind-damage near the top. The heavy leaves are dark above but show their white-painted undersides. The buds are large, very resinous, and fragrant when opening.

 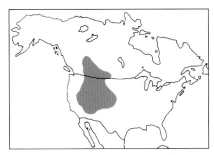

Water birch   Over a large area of the Interiormid-Rocky Mountains, this is common beside rocky watercourses. Slender shoots rise from clusters of up to half a dozen stems which have variably orange or brown bark.

 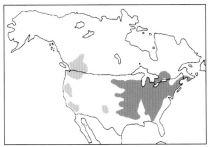

Black walnut   A fine tree with large, bright green foliage. The crown of old trees is gaunt with a few large level, twisting branches high on a long, clear stem, all with a nearly black bark with deep, complex ridging.

 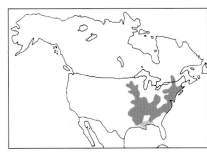

River birch   The only birch with lobed leaves or with silvered undersides, this is commonly beside watercourses in the east, but is not confined to them. It may be a many-stemmed shrub but is often a single-boled tree of good size.

 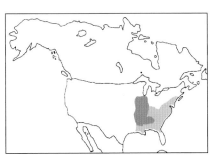

Pecan   A fine tree not unlike the Black walnut, but the bark is scaly gray and becomes whiter with age. Hardy little beyond Washington DC it has been planted extensively south of there, far beyond its assumed natural range.

 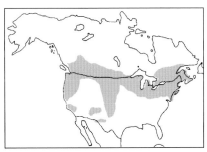

European white birch   has been planted widely in North America. It differs from all native birches in the slender, pendulous outer shoots and in the diamond-shaped black patches on the bark. The warted shoots bear coarsely toothed rather small leaves.

 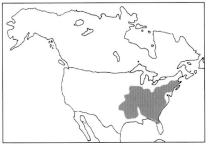

Mockernut hickory   A hickory with smoother bark than most and heavy dark foliage which hangs in the summer. The shoot has a covering of dense, fine, but hard hairs, prominent also on the swollen base of the leafstalk.

 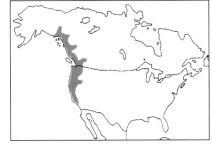

Red alder   Confined to the damp woods of the lower hills of the Pacific Slopes, this has the largest leaves and fruit of any native alder. The leaf margins are minutely rolled down. The bark is clearest white mid-range, in Oregon.

 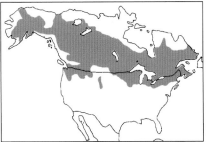

Paper birch   A highly variable tree across its great range. It has a warty shoot, hairy leafstalk and few veins for the large size of birch leaf. The bark is usually very white but in parts of the range it is orange or tends to dark purple.

 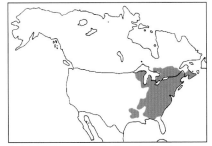

American beech   In eastern woods in winter, the pale silvery bark and persisting bleached cream leaves give a ghostly aspect to these trees. Many have brushes of thin sprouts around the base. Beech plantings outside this range, and often within it, tend to be of European beech.

189

 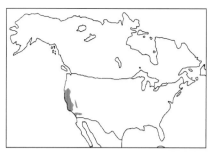

Tanoak The only representative of this large group of oaks outside China, grows only in the far west, in the Coast Range, and the Sierra Nevada. The leaves last for four years, unfolding with brown woolly hairs beneath, soon blue-white.

 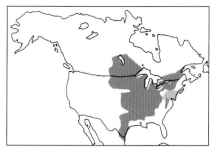

Bur oak This can grow the biggest acorn of any American oak, to two inches long in a cup two inches across, with large protruding scales. In the Middle West it ranges far to the north of other oaks.

 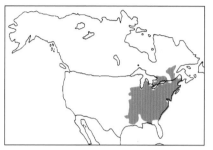

White oak Some fine old specimens have hugely spreading, level, low branches although in woods the crown is mainly upright. Patches of shallow, finely plated bark often come away leaving paler areas. The upper leaves are cut deeply into elegantly curved lobes.

 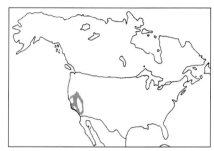

Valley oak This covers miles of low, dry hill-country with few other trees near the coast and in the Sierra foothills in southern CA. It has wide spreading, twisting big branches and a broadly domed crown.

 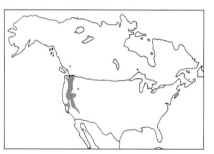

Oregon white oak A broad-crowned tree with stout low branches, this has dense fine hairs on the shoot and the leaf underside, and a dark gray bark. In the fall the leaves are a muddy dark brown.

 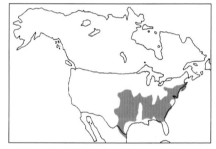

Blackjack oak Plainly a Red oak from the whisker-tipped lobes and the acorn taking two years to ripen, this has quite a different leaf from the others. Its very broad, shallow and rounded lobes are distinct.

 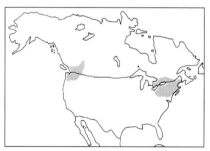

English oak Not thriving in the long, hot summers south of NY, this is now frequent only in southern New England. An important feature found in no American oak is the little ear-like lobes each side of the very short leafstalk.

 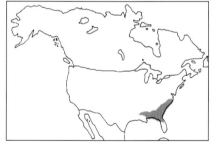

Turkey oak A small, shrubby tree of the low sandy tracts and hills not far from the coast, this has slender curved lobes on its leaf like the Southern red oak. It is an abundant roadside tree over much of its range.

Overcup oak Named from the acorn being almost enfolded by the cup and scarcely visible. The leaf is about ten inches long, irregularly lobed to a long wedge-shaped base. it makes a fine tree in city parks near the Gulf Coast.

 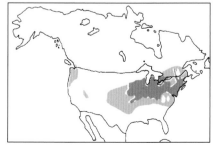

Pin oak The shapely growth of this tree, with a clean stem and regular, slender branching makes it popular for city streets. The leaf underside has large tufts of pale brown hairs in the main vein-angles.

 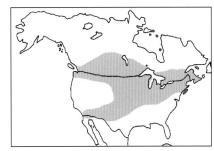

Emory oak   This is a small tree of dry rocky and sandy sides of gulches and canyons around AZ. Its evergreen little two-inch leaf is hard, firm, dark green above and bright gray-green beneath with pale brown hairs.

Siberian elm   Native to the same regions as the elm disease, this has a natural resistance to it and is abundantly planted for shade throughout the prairie regions, and frequently in many other parts. It has widely arched branching.

 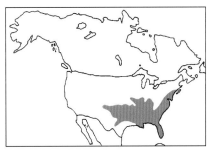

Live oak   This is the tree whose arching branches spread widely, draped with Spanish moss to shade the approaches to the old plantation houses in SC. The hard, dark, evergreen leaves vary greatly in shape.

Hackberry   Hackberries have leaves with bases prominently three-nerved and margins entire or toothed or both. This one has the largest leaf which is toothed on the outer half, sometimes on one side only. Dark lumps and ridges protrude from the bark.

Coast live oak   An evergreen oak with hard, shortly spine-lobed leaves, smooth green beneath except for fine tufts of hairs in the main-vein angles. It grows only in the Coast Range hills and can be hugely spreading from several stems.

Sugarberry   This is in effect the hackberry of the southeast, with smaller leaves often not toothed at all. It is hardy when planted north to NY. It is quite a big street-tree in many southeastern cities.

American elm   Much the largest and most planted native elm, this is, despite losses from disease, still common in Main Street. Typically a broad dome is held high on radiating big branches. In early spring the flowers are brownish red.

Osage orange   A spined tree much planted long ago as hedges as far from its native Texas as PA and DE where there are the biggest old trees in parks and gardens. The female tree bears hard, heavy 4-inch globular fruit.

 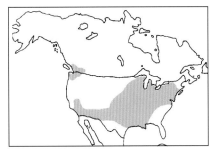

Cedar elm   In the southwestern interior States, this is commonly a small roadside tree with upright shoots, remarkable for the leaves being so stiffly held that they do not move as the shoot is blown around. Fall colors are gray.

White mulberry   A Chinese tree planted very widely but fragile so it becomes a large bush of stems from a broken hulk of bole. The fruit turn pink then ripen red, not purple or dark blackish red as in other mulberries.

 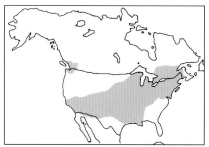

Tea's Weeping mulberry A mushroom of a tree, planted commonly where the White mulberry is but also a good way north of that as it is hardier. A form 'Acerifolia', with larger, glossy leaves is common in the southwestern USA.

California-laurel The leaves of this evergreen tree from the west coast emit a powerful spicy scent which can easily cause a sharp headache. It is usually seen as a number of stems rising from a base but can be on a single trunk and 150 feet tall.

 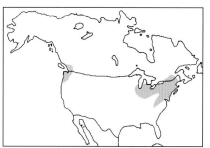

Katsura tree A delicate-looking tree with slender shoots bearing round leaves in opposite pairs, this is hardy north to ON and grows very fast. It is often bushy from the base but 80 feet tall. Its leaves unfold red.

 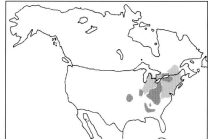

Cucumbertree This magnolia is the only one with a rich brown, narrowly ridged bark. It ranges further north and reaches greater sizes than any other, often with a good, straight trunk. The underleaf is covered in soft, fine hairs.

Yellow poplar A tree in the Magnolia Family with similar flowers but very different, broadly lobe-ended leaves. The dark brown shallowly ridged bark is often on splendid columns of trunk for 60 feet without a branch.

 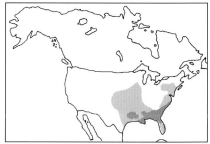

Southern magnolia Planted well to the north of its natural range, 40–50ft tall in Pennsylvania gardens and in town streets in Arkansas, this is often twice as big in the Gulf Coast area. The open flower is strongly fragrant.

 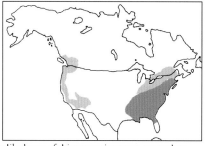

Sweetgum The handsome starlike leaves of this tree emit a sweet scent when torn and turn gold, orange and scarlet, often mottled, in the fall. An eastern tree, it is much planted in the west.

 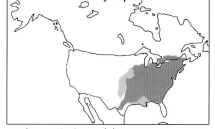

Sycamore This is often seen standing out in the woods by eastern streams with its tall crown of branches with white bark mottled blue and orange. The fruit is a single ball 1½ inches across on a 5-inch stem.

Sassafras The leaves of this tree may have a lobe on one side, on both or none at all. Crushed, they give a vanilla and orange scent. In the fall they turn fiery red. The bark is very dark and ridged.

California sycamore A smaller and less striking tree than the eastern Sycamore with five 1-inch fruit on each stalk. The leaf is hairy beneath and deeply cut into five lobes, either entire or with peg-like teeth.

192

 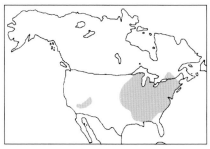

Bradford pear   A seedling selected in Maryland from a Chinese species, this shapely tree is widely planted in streets and precincts. The white flowers begin to open in March before the leaves, from red-tipped buds.

 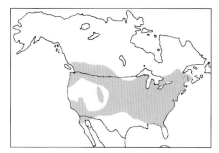

Tree of Heaven   A very vigorous, strongly suckering tree from North China, this spreads also by its copious seeding and has invaded inner suburbs of many cities in the warmer parts. Its big, many-leaflet leaves unfold late and red.

 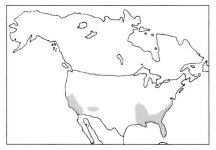

Loquat   The big, dark wrinkled leaves of this Japanese fruit-tree are evergreen and seen on low, wide-branched trees only south from Charleston SC in an arc round to the Bay Area, CA.

 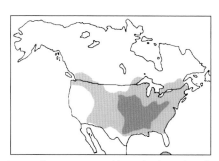

Honeylocust   From its already extensive eastern range this tree has been planted west and north in almost all city centres as it can survive well where few other trees can, in sidewalks among skyscrapers. It has brief pale gold fall coloring.

 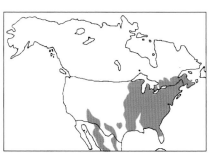

Black cherry   This tree is small in the lowlands but tall, to over 100 feet in high valleys in the Great Smoky Mountains. It ranges widely across America with one form or another from Nova Scotia to Guatemala.

 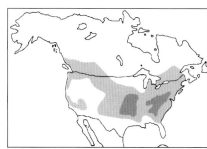

Black locust   From a small eastern and central range, this has been planted far and wide and spreads by spiny suckers and by seeds. It is late to unfold its leaves and early to shed them.

 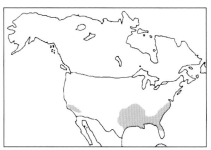

Chinaberry   Domed bushes of this Chinese tree are common in the deep south each side of the door or gate of little houses. There are a few tall trees in city squares. The doubly compound leaves tend to hang, dark green.

 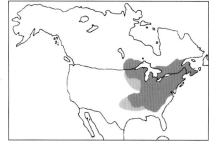

Sugar maple   The fall colors of this tree are unexcelled in the fiery orange-scarlet, mixed, then more uniform brilliant red. The crown is usually tall-ovoid. The lobes of many leaves narrow towards their bases. The fruit are shed by midsummer.

 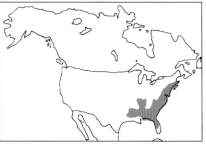

American holly   A dark, evergreen, sturdy and usually shapely tree, this is valued in PA and DE where summers are too hot for European holly to be grown. The female trees bear rather small red berries through the winter until spring.

 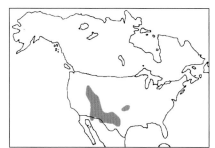

Canyon maple   This is one of several species which are divergent forms of the Sugar maple, and grows much further south and west than any other. Its small leaves turn orange in the fall.

 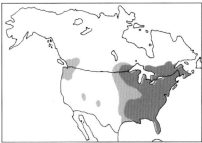

Red maple In early spring the trees stand out in woods, parks and gardens with all the shoots wreathed in flowers ranging from bright red to somewhat brownish red, from which its name is derived.

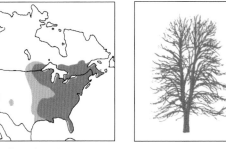

European horse-chestnut This large-growing, coarse buckeye has been much planted in streets. The flowers are on 1ft panicles and open with chrome yellow blotches which turn crimson when the flower has been pollinated. The fruit husk is well-spined.

 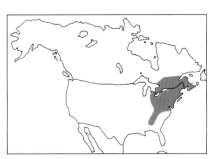

Norway maple Often planted among Sugar maples, this has pale brown bark finely ridged; the teeth on the leaf finely whiskered and bunches of bright yellow flowers opening before the leaves. It turns yellow and orange in the fall.

California buckeye A low tree of the foothills, this has small leaves with well-stalked leaflets. In summer they turn brown and nearly black then fall early. The smooth pear-shaped fruit project on curved stalks.

 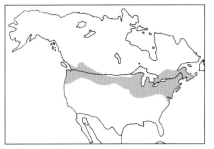

Striped maple The only snakebark maple not confined to eastern Asia. The large, broad leaves, very shallowly 3-lobed are rich green until turning pale yellow and falling early. The flowers are on slender, paired catkin-like racemes.

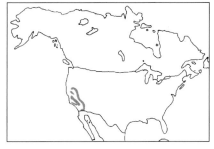

American basswood Distinct from other lindens by the shiny rich green leaves with prominent systems of parallel veins, this makes a shapely tree in city streets. It is a frequent victim of attack by sapsuckers.

 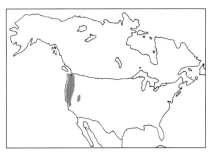

Vine maple In far western woods this starts as a bush then rests wandering slender branches in the crowns of surrounding trees. Its fall colors are bright orange and scarlet.

 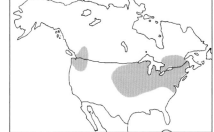

Littleleaf linden An attractive North European species which has been found to be well adapted to cities as far south as DC. The flowers are small and bright yellow in spreading sprays, not hanging as in most other lindens.

 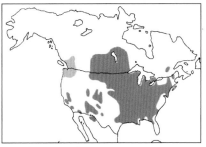

Boxelder This is unique among maples in its leaf, in some forms having five leaflets, and in ranging from coast to coast and from Winnipeg to Mexico. The leaves of eastern forms is largest and glossy bright green.

Black tupelo In the craggy bark and elliptic leaf, like the Sourwood, but the leaf margin is smooth. Fall colors progress from pale yellow to mottled yellow, orange and red until fully bright red.

 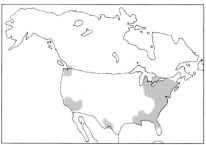

Golden rain-tree The flowers are bright yellow but small and sparsely set on a 15-in very open panicle so they are less prominent than the pink, bladder-like fruit. From SC south, the Formosan species bears big bunches of fruit and flowers.

 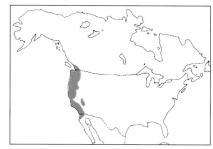

Pacific madrone A tall evergreen with dark orange-red branches and big smooth patches of pink on the trunk, from Vancouver Island along the western slopes to the Mexican border. In late spring or early summer erect plumes of white flowers open.

 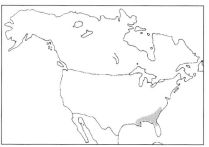

Silver dollar tree Also known as Redbox eucalyptus, this is the only gum grown in the east outside Florida. It is often a clump of stems, but in southern CA and AZ it is a single-stemmed tree.

 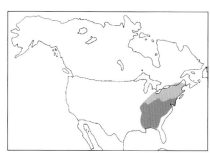

Sourwood The little urn-shaped white flowers in long, curved sprays mature into capsules of similar size and color as the leaves turn bright red in the fall. The slender elliptic leaves are finely toothed.

 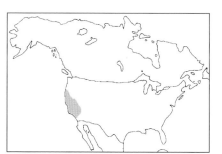

Bluegum eucalyptus A rampant, fast-growing tree which flowers and fruits all the year in CA, spreading seedlings which grow 6ft a year. It is the only common gum with a solitary, large fruit, bloomed bright blue-white.

Common persimmon The 1½-in fruit are much smaller than the Chinese persimmons in the shops but, after frosting, they are prized as food. In late summer they hang, pale orange among leaves turning blackish. The dark brown bark is in small plates.

 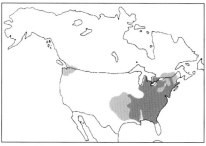

Flowering dogwood A small tree seldom more than 3½ft in girth, but prominent in winter with checkered red-brown bark and with shoots tipped by flower-buds. Spectacular in flower, also in the fall with dark red foliage and bright red berries.

 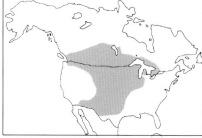

Russian olive This is no relation of the olive fruit and is in a different family. A tough, large shrub from western Asia it is silvery gray and much planted for shelter in the prairie regions.

Pacific dogwood A taller tree than the Flowering dogwood, with smooth bark and six un-notched bracts surrounding the flowerheads instead of four with notched tips. It opens a second set of flowers during the fall among the red leaves.

 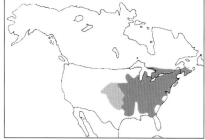

White ash This is the biggest ash outside Mexico and the most distinct in fall colors. From yellow, the leaves turn orange and then purplish. Male and female flowers are on different trees. The underleaf is variably whitish green.

 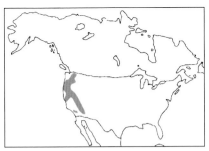

Oregon ash The only ash of the Pacific slopes this just fails to extend into Canada, but has been planted there, occasionally. The shoot and underleaf are covered in dense, soft, pale hairs. The sexes are on separate trees.

Peppertree A native of Peru, this has taken over huge areas of Mexico and is a common street tree in southwest CA. The long, pinnate leaves hang in plumes and the dark red fruit hang in long bunches among them in summer.

 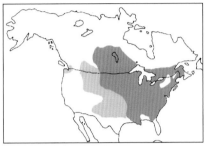

Green ash This includes the form often separated as Red ash and is highly variable in the presence of dense, soft hairs. The Green form has stout shoots, quite smooth and shining bright green. Fall colors are bright yellow.

 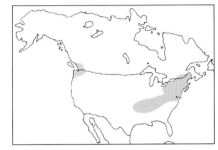

Royal paulownia A tree of very rapid, often fragile growth, reaching a good size but of no great age. The heads of brown hairy flower buds tip each shoot through the winter and open in late spring if not damaged by frost.

 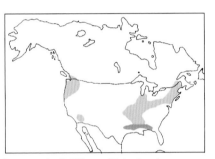

Southern catalpa Native only to near the Gulf Coast, this has long been planted northward to provide durable fencepost timber and is now a park, garden and street tree in many parts from ON to WA. The 15-in long capsules resemble bean-pods.

Ginkgo Once worldwide, this relic, unrelated to any modern plant, survived in China. The first two in America, planted in 1784 at Woodlands Cemetery, Philadelphia were destroyed by lightning in 1985. It is now in almost every city.

 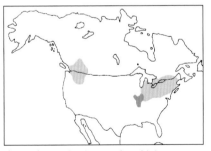

Northern catalpa Now as widespread as the Southern catalpa, this is distinguished by the ridged bark, taller, more upright crown and longer, narrower leaf-tips. The foliage is yellower green and the fall color bright yellow.

 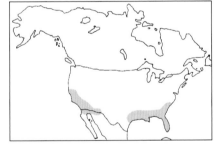

Yew podocarp A Japanese tree planted commonly against buildings or trimmed in shrubberies in the far south, from SC and in CA. The fruit-stalk is succulent, blue-gray and, apparently, edible. The leaf is leathery and 3–5in long.

 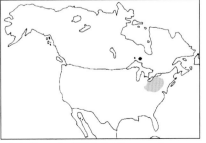

Hybrid catalpa Tea's Nursery in Indiana raised this hybrid between the Southern and the Chinese yellow catalpa. It has a bigger, more open flowerhead and bigger, more positively lobed leaves and gray-brown ridged bark.

 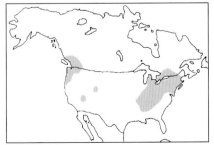

English yew A very slow-growing tree with exceedingly strong timber, which can live, in England, for some 3000 years and has not yet reached great size in America. It is unequalled for clipping into various shapes.

 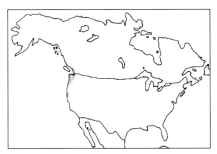

Monkey-puzzle A primitive tree from the Andes on the Chile-Argentine border and seen frequently only in the Puget Sound area. Male trees bear large catkins at branch-tips and females grow big globular cones taking three years to ripen.

 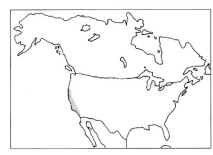

Monterey cypress In the tiny native stand at Point Lobos, the old trees are squat and wide-spreading. Young trees there and planted nearby are bizarre shapes with wandering rope-like branches. Further north, older trees are columnar and spire-topped.

 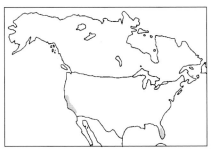

Bunya-bunya pine Coming from Queensland, Australia, this tree can survive only a slight frost and needs a hot summer. Bunya-bunya and the Monkey-puzzle cannot be grown in the same places. Hanging, yellowish green shoots and deeply wrinkled bark are signs of bunya-bunya.

 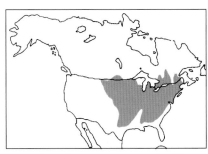

Eastern redcedar This juniper spreads rapidly on to unused ground and shows great variety in color of foliage from very dark green to pale blue-green. Fruit, usually on separate trees from male flowers, add to the blue-white appearance.

Norfolk Island pine The peculiar crown typifies subtropical towns everywhere. Young trees, often grown further north under glass, have bright green spreading leaves incurved at the tip. On older trees they are dull yellow-green pressed to the shoot.

 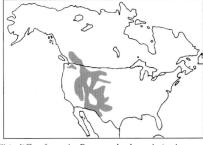

Rocky Mountain juniper This differs from the Easter redcedar only in the male flower having more stamens and the fruit taking two years to ripen. Luckily the natural ranges are well separated, but plantings between and into these are a problem.

 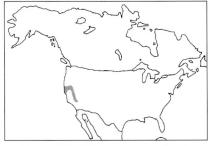

California torreya This native of the humid low hill-country has hard, rather stiff, spine-tipped 3-in leaves. Male flowers, on separate trees, are globules beneath each leaf. The plum-like fruit are green turning purple, with a single seed.

 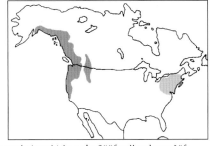

Western redcedar A cypress relative which can be 200ft tall and over 30ft round the trunk. The foliage readily emits a scent of apples or acetone. Planted a little in the east it makes a neat, conic bright green tree.

 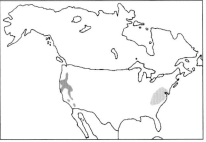

Incense cedar A cypress related to the Western redcedar, this is open-crowned with level branches in its native stands but in gardens in PA, DE and around it is slender with upswept branches, and quite dense.

 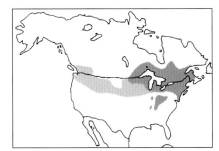

Northern white-cedar This is a much smaller, shorter-lived tree of wet east coast woods. The leaves are matt yellow-green beneath and have the scent of apple-peel. The pale brown bark comes away in thin, often spiralled strips.

197

 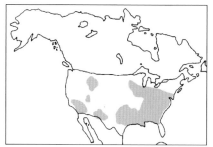

Oriental arborvitae   Equally at home in humid or near-desert heat, this is an upright dense ovoid each side of many a front path. The foliage is bright green each side and numerous gray-blue cones have curved beaks.

Baldcypress   This deciduous redwood sheds the slender shoots with the little leaves they bear, and leafs out bright fresh green late in the spring. It has been widely planted outside its native east coast and Mississippi bottomlands.

 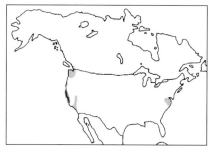

Redwood   Many groves of this tree are mainly 340−350ft tall, the tallest forest stands in the world. Highway 101 has 49 miles unbroken in Avenue of The Giants. In old stands the bark is often pale gray.

Noble fir   This silver fir stands out in the forests of the Cascades and some high Coast Range mountains because of its variably blue-gray foliage. A blue selection, *glauca* is grown but rarely thrives in many eastern gardens.

 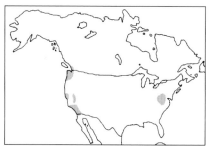

Giant sequoia   Also known as "Sierra redwood" to distinguish it from the "Coast redwood" this tree may live 4000 years. "General Sherman" has the biggest timber volume of any tree known. Growth from MA to DC is low and branchy.

 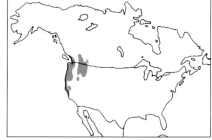

Grand fir   Large pure stands grow on the eastern flanks of the Cascades but the trees are not as big as in the scattered remnants nearer the coast, where trees to 250ft or more are occasional.

Japanese redcedar   A sequoia relative with more spreading, curved leaves, this is brighter, more yellow-green, partly from poor health near the east coast. The little globular, much-spined cones are borne in large numbers from an early age.

Balsam fir   The common silver fir of the northeastern hills and bogs across to Alberta, spreading widely out of woods on to roadside banks and fields. The leaves have two broad silvery bands beneath and a silvery splash above near the tip.

 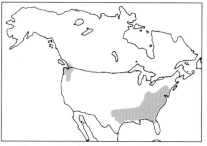

Chinese fir   This resembles a monkey-puzzle but it is a redwood and is much brighter green with two broad silvery bands beneath narrower, more flexible leaves. In roadside gardens in southeastern states it is commonly a group of 3−4 stems.

Fraser fir   A close relative of Balsam fir, extending the range into the high Alleghenies of VA, NC and TN. It differs in its protruding cone-scales and more white on the upper leaf. Young trees are slender with long leading shoots.

198

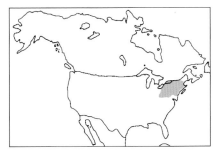

Subalpine fir This grows extraordinarily slender snow-shedding spires at 5–7000ft in BC and the Cascades and at 10,000ft by southern passes. In the Olympic Mountains, very broad skirts spread from the base and remain under the snow.

Golden larch This tree from south coastal China is named from its fine fall color, which matures into bright orange. The cones have thick, pale green scales and break up on the tree. The straight stem bears level branches.

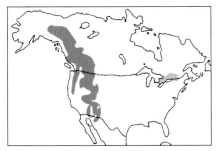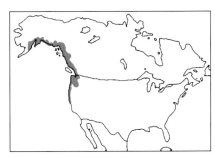

Douglas fir Related more to spruces and hemlocks than to silver firs, this has slender, pointed buds and soft, fruity scented foliage. Three-pronged bracts protrude from the cone. Trees over 250ft tall are in many groves.

Sitka spruce From Kodiak Island to Mendocino, CA this tree is almost everywhere within sight of tidal water. Vast trees once grew in BC and WA but only a few remain, by the Hoh River, WA. Windswept stands crown the cliffs of OR.

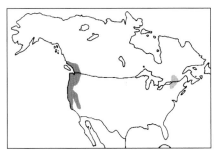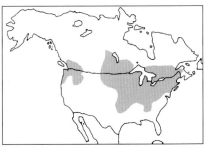

Rocky Mountain Douglas fir The central and eastern Rockies form, has blackish bark, often bluer foliage and the three-pronged bract on the cone extends further, curved downwards. It is commonly planted in the east, notably on Long Island, NY.

Norway spruce This European tree is among the commonest trees seen from PA to New England and ON. Two forms occur at random, the "comb" with shoots hanging in rows from level branches and the "brush" with normal, dense crowns.

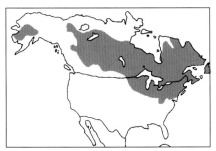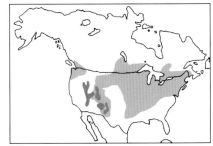

Tamarack A tree of the muskeg across the north and the northeastern hills, this opens tiny bright, deep red flowers before its leaves unfold. They ripen into very small, few-scaled cones. The bark is unridged, smooth but scaly purplish brown.

Blue spruce Native only to the high ranges of WY and CO, this is among the commonest town and garden trees from Winnipeg to TX and ME and around Puget Sound, in many selected bright blue-white foliaged forms.

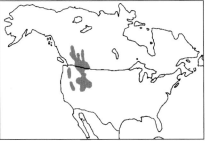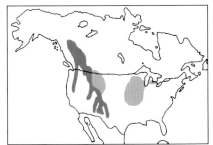

Western larch The biggest of the world's ten larches, this can be 200ft tall, but it adapts poorly to being grown out of range and plantation larches in the east are of European or Japanese larch.

Engelmann spruce Resembles Blue spruce but has soft, menthol-scented darker foliage, more slender shoots and orange-brown flaking bark. The cones are cylindric, 2in long, curved and purplish brown. Those of Blue spruce are broad with hard, crinkled white scales.

199

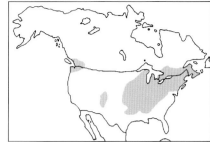

Western hemlock   The finest of all hemlocks; an elegant tree to over 230ft with pendulous fine foliage. The leaves are of mixed sizes on the hairy shoot and have two broad silvery bands beneath. It seems unable to grow in the east.

Austrian pine   An exceedingly resilient tree little affected by sea winds, industrial pollution or the poorest soils, this is widely planted for shelter. It has a poorly shaped, blackish crown of thick, paired needles, curved and in whorls.

 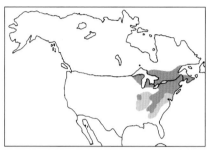

 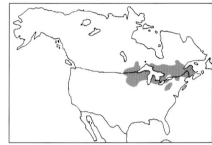

Eastern hemlock   The common hemlock of the northeast and abundant throughout its range and planted a little beyond. Around PA and DC now badly infested with an aphid, garden trees are having to be sprayed to survive.

Red pine   A two-needle pine with long, cleanly snapping needles in whorls and resembling Ponderosa pine from a distance. The bark of upper branches sheds gray scales to show dark red.

 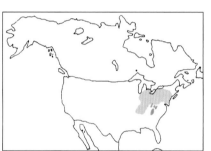

Carolina hemlock   In the wild, tucked away in a few deep valleys, this is planted in some gardens for its more luxuriant, healthy, dark shining foliage. The cone is orange-brown when ripe and 1in long.

Spruce pine   This southeastern tree is remarkable for its largely smooth gray bark unlike any other pine. It has a narrowly columnar crown with small, level, then upswept branches and the shoots have dense foliage like a Foxtail pine.

 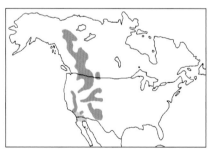

Lodgepole pine   The pine of the Yellowstone NP geyser areas and the interior Rockies generally. The paired needles are leathery and flattened and the cone has small, sharp spines. The cones are held closed on the tree awaiting a fire.

Singleleaf pinyon   This curious little tree makes upswept conic bushes of pale gray-green slightly blued by high passes or on plateaux in the southwest. Each needle is solitary and has a round cross-section and is spine-tipped.

Shore pine   The form of Lodgepole from the sea to the Coast Ranges, with more densely held, thinner needles and bark broken into square blocks. Young trees grow 3ft shoots until the ocean winds affect them.

Pinyon   The pine of the Grand Canyon of AZ and of large areas of mountains in that region and southwards. The large, edible seeds are borne in broad, flattened cones with few, thick scales.

Pond pine   This is a form of Pitch pine replacing that tree in swampy woods near the east coast. It has even more grassy sprouts on the trunk and dark gray, coarsely cracked bark.

 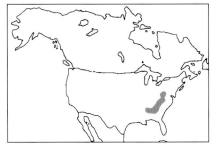

Table Mountain pine   A two-needle pine of the high Alleghenies with a sparse crown of level branches and the interior with numerous retained ovoid cones. The lower cone-scales project stout, curved sharply spined ends.

 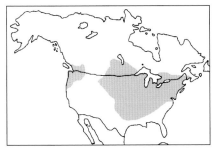

Scots pine   The correct name for the "Scotch pine" that is so widely planted. The needles are in pairs, broad, twisted and dark blue-gray and the branches and upper bole have scaling orange-red or dark red bark.

 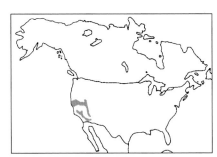

Knobcone pine   The cones have protruding spined scales like the Table Mountain pine but the cone is long-conic and held in long, dense clusters close around the upper stem and main branches. The crown is upswept with bright grassy-green foliage.

Aleppo pine   Native to the hot, usually dry rocks of the Eastern Mediterranean, this is planted only where conditions are similar. The slender, pale green needles form an open, light crown bearing pointed cones which ripen purple-red.

 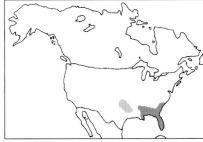

Slash pine   This southern tree has its needles in twos and threes, 10−12in long, stout and lemon-scented when broken. The shoot is stout, ridged and bloomed violet on pale red-brown. The dull purplish gray bark is coarsely short-ridged.

 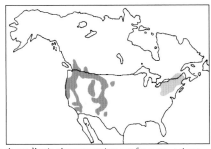

Ponderosa pine   With 10-inch needles in threes spraying out from stout shoots, a fine straight trunk of brown to bright orange flaking bark and a neat conic crown to a great height, this is one of the great trees of the world.

Coulter pine   A three-needle pine related to Jeffrey pine and with similar stout, blue-white shoots. It has bigger orange-red buds and longer stouter needles and the cone is massive, to 5lbs weight, with shiny brown large, incurved, hooked spines.

 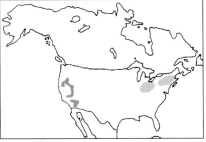

Jeffrey pine   Similar to Ponderosa pine but with blue-white shoot, blue-gray needles and a big, broad cone, and restricted to the higher ranges in the southern Rockies. Young trees planted in some northeastern gardens are very handsome.

 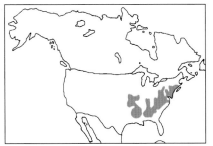

Shortleaf pine   This, like the Pitch and Pond pines has sprouts on its trunk but it has a much more open crown with drooped branches showing interior masses of retained 2in ovoid cones. The needles are in twos and threes.

201

 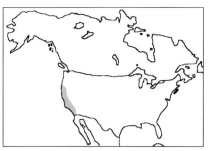

 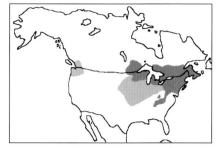

Monterey pine   A three-needle pine with heavy ovoid cones. In the small native area it is attacked by a mistletoe and dies young. Narrow young trees are seen planted by the coast to the north and south.

Eastern white pine   The common 5-needle pine of the northeast. Needles are rarely held for more than two years so it has an open, airy crown. Known before logging to over 220ft, few are now over 130ft.

 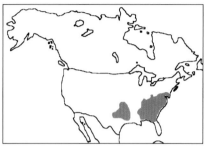

 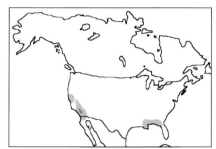

Loblolly pine   This is the major timber-tree in the southeast and stands with long clear stems are common from SC to TX. The cone is long-conic, 5in with short spines on the scales. The slender 6in needles are in threes.

California washingtonia   A stout-stemmed palm, this is unlike the slender-stemmed Mexican washingtonia which is like a feather-duster all round Los Angeles. Both species hold a mat of dead leaves pressed to the upper stem.

 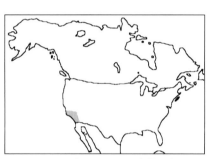

 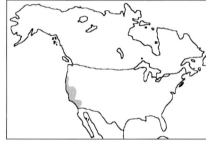

Torrey pine   This has the smallest native area of any pine, a low hill to the sea at La Jolla. Grown in a few gardens it makes a very sturdy, handsome tree with long, dark needles held closely in bundles of five. One is 135ft tall by the Capitol in Sacramento.

Cabbage-tree   This is not a palm but a relative of the Joshua-tree. It has pale gray, rough, corky bark and can grow a branch only by each flowerhead. Until it flowers it is an unbranched pole.

 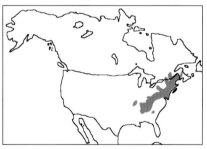

Pitch pine   A broadly domed tree with few large branches which are, like the trunk, nearly covered in masses of hanging, slender, bright green sprouts. The bark is brown, deeply fissured into big ridges.

Canary palm   The noblest of the palms with arching 20ft bright green leaves and a continuous supply of 5ft orange stemmed flowerheads. It makes the Date-palm look dumpy, dowdy and spiky. Palms cannot branch at all, and their timber has no annual rings.

Sugar pine   The tallest pine in the world, with Ponderosa, and many trees over 220ft survive in the Siskiyou and Yosemite areas. Long level branches stretch out from 150ft up the stem and are tipped by hanging cones to 2ft long.

Cabbage palmetto   Prettily interlaced leaf-bases on the stem are often cleaned off or wear off in streets. The leaf is about 10ft across, round and cut deeply into slender lobes, on a 6ft stalk rounded slightly above and deeply keeled.

Index

Trees are listed mainly under their popular name, in roman, with their generic name in italics. Names of cultivars appears in inverted commas.